Wine, A Way of Life

Also by Steven Spurrier

The *Académie du Vin* Wine Course (1983)
French Country Wines (1984)
French Fine Wines (1984)
The *Académie du Vin* Guide to French Wines (1985)
How to Buy Fine Wines (1986)
The *Académie du Vin* Wine Cellar Book (1986)
Clarke and Spurrier's Fine Wine Guide (1988)

Wine, A Way of Life

Steven Spurrier

ADELPHI

First published in 2018 by Adelphi Publishers

Text Copyright © Steven Spurrier, 2018
This edition © Adelphi Publishers, 2018

Photographs ©: p.12 Nicholas Spurrier;
p.143 Bella Spurrier from George Taber, *The Judgement of Paris*;
p.243 Sarah Kemp; p.275 Eduardo Chadwick from
The Berlin Tasting 2004-2014; p.336, Ian Harris.
All other photographs © Steven Spurrier.

ISBN 978-0-95623-878-8

A CIP catalogue reference for this book is available from the British Library

Typography and typesetting by Peter B. Willberg
Typeset in Monotype Fournier

Printed and bound by CPI, Moravia

To Bella, and to Wine

Contents

Foreword

At the end of the Christmas Eve 1954 dinner at Marston Hall, my family home in Derbyshire, probably at thirteen years old, my first in long trousers, my grandfather said that he thought I was old enough to taste Port, offered me a glass and moved the decanter in my direction. The wine was quite extraordinary: 'Gosh, Grandpa, what's this?' 'Cockburn's 1908, my boy.' From that moment I began, bit by bit, to search out wine regions from my history and geography lessons. In my teens, my parents took my elder brother and me with them on trips to France and Italy, and introduced us to the 'conviviality' of wine. Later I joined the London School of Economics Wine Society, and there was never any doubt in my mind that I would make wine my career.

Fast forward to 2010, when the Symington family, having recently added the historic House of Cockburn to their portfolio of Port estates that included Dow, Graham and Warre, held a tasting at the famous Factory House in Oporto to show Cockburn's vintages from 1977 down to 1874. The 1908 was there and after various Symingtons had recounted the history of that year and of this vintage over its lifetime, Paul Symington asked if there were any comments from the sixty or so of us present. I put my hand up and said that the first and only time I had tasted this wine was on Christmas Eve 1954 and it had placed me on the path to a life in wine. (The 1908 was reckoned to be the finest of all the vintages that day.) A couple of years later, attending another Cockburn's tasting where the 1908 was shown, Paul Symington (not knowing I was in the room) said, 'this is the vintage that inspired Steven Spurrier to go into the wine trade.'

It has, as will be shown, made for a bumpy ride. I could be the poster boy for the old adage 'To make a small fortune in the wine trade, start with a large one', but it has been worth it. At the end of George Taber's book on The Judgement of Paris, I am quoted as saying that 'I am still totally, 100% in love with wine, the places where it is produced and the people who produce it, for wine has given me more than I could ever have imagined.' This remains the case.

1. Early Days and School Days

I was born shortly after midnight on 5 October 1941 in Cambridge. I should have been born a day or so later at the Royal Infirmary in Derby, near to our family home at Marston-on-Dove, but my mother was visiting friends in Cambridge, and when the car to drive her to Derby appeared on time after lunch on the 4th, she said that plans had been made for that evening and arranged that he return the following morning. A game of poker, with my mother playing for matchsticks rather than for money, duly happened, but then so did I.

I was also supposed to be a girl named Sarah. Family circumstances were secure and comfortable, though plainly there was little actual money around during the Second World War and as Britain recovered in the 1950s. On my father's side a great uncle had founded an engineering enterprise in Leyland, Lancashire that turned into Leyland Motors, which built most of the buses and trucks for Britain and the Empire. On my mother's side, the Strutt family had formed a partnership in the early days of the 19th century's Industrial Revolution with Joseph Arkwright, creator of the weaving machine known as The Spinning Jenny and were based in the little town of Belper, Derbyshire, where they prospered and built hospitals, schools and parks which were donated to the town.

While this was all in the past, ownership of the various companies having long since passed out of family hands, the family remained in their house at Marston-on-Dove, where my grandfather, a hunting/shooting/fishing country squire funded this by running a small — to become much larger post-war — sand and gravel business, while being a hands-on and canny manager of the properties and land which made up the estate.

My first memories are of a detached white-plastered and timbered cottage with a front and much larger back garden in the little village of Aston Clinton, near Aylesbury in Buckinghamshire. My parents had moved there early in the Second World War as London was not a place for my mother to bring up two small children while her husband was away with the Derbyshire Yeomanry as part of Britain's 8th Army under General Montgomery — first in Africa, later moving from south to north to push

Nicky's christening at Marston in October 1939.
Seated in front: Pamela Spurrier. Standing left to right: Jack Spurrier,
Bernard Neame, John Spurrier, Margery Spurrier, Agnes Neame.

the Germans out of Italy. My father was a Captain, part of a tank regiment that followed behind Montgomery as he swept General Rommel out of North Africa. I don't believe he ever fired a shot in anger, for he told me that the gun barrel of his tank would have been better for carrying much needed tins of food than the use it was designed for. Indeed, his only war accolade, a mention in dispatches, had been for crossing a field in southern Italy to get peaches for the crew, unaware that the retreating army had mined it. For me in those days he was a person of mysterious glamour.

My mother Pamela had spent her early years in India where her father Bernard Neame was a dashing cavalry officer with the Queen's Own 4th Hussars. Winston Churchill had been an officer in this august regiment and in the hall of The Bangalore Club there is a framed copy of his unpaid bar bills. My maternal grandfather came from a proud family known as the 'Neames of Kent' and money had been made through the brewery business Shepherd Neame, which still flourishes to this day. His father, thinking to diversify substantial funds from his share of the company, had in 1913 purchased hundreds of thousands of acres of forest land in Russia, and was organising ships to transport timber around the world when the war broke out in 1914; after the Russian Revolution the State took it all

Steven and Tadpole at Brills, 1945

back in 1919. The 'Russian Millions' were often referred to in a wistful manner and the share certificates were framed as a memory.

Life at Brills, as our cottage was called, was serene. There was just Nicky, my elder brother by two years, my mother and Nanny. My mother was always there, so was in no way mysterious, but she certainly was glamorous. In Derbyshire society, she was known as 'The Silver Whippet', being tall, fair, slim and always beautifully turned out. When I mentioned that I was planning to go into the wine trade, she quite approved and said that she had once worked briefly for someone named Tommy Layton in what was London's first true wine bar in Museum Street, opposite the British Museum. Tommy Layton was a complete wine man, incredibly creative and author of the first 'wine primers', at a time when most wine books looked back into the past with titles like *The Wayward Tendrils of the Vine*. He was also Michael Broadbent's first employer and subsequent mentor, just as Michael became my mentor through his book *Wine Tasting*. In September 1971, I was at Château Pontet-Canet in Pauillac for the Ban des Vendanges Dinner, to be 'intronised' into the Commanderie du Bontemps de Médoc and found myself waiting in line beside Tommy Layton, who I had never met. I introduced myself, said I had read all his books and added that perhaps one of the reasons for my being in the wine trade was the fact that my mother had worked for him in Museum Street. He asked her name, reflected for a moment, and replied: 'Pammy Neame, of course I remember her, very pretty, had to go, too many rich boyfriends!'

Both my parents were only children, rare in those days when families were large, so I had no cousins, or none I met until well into my twenties. My father's parents were very different, Jack Spurrier was a Derbyshire squire and his wife Margery was the beautiful daughter of wealthy silk merchants from near Manchester. They had little in common, my grandmother finding Derbyshire very dull, spending time in London and travelling abroad whenever she felt like it, so perhaps one child was enough. My mother's parents were quite similar in background but totally different in character. Bernard Neame, despite his advice to me (sadly wasted) to 'always keep a straight bat', didn't pay much attention to Agnes Strutt who worshipped him, but he was adored by my mother, whom he treated as though she were a boy, giving her freedom in everything. No more children there, either.

By contrast, my parents' marriage was a love match. Apparently their first meeting had been on a train from London to Derby. With his easy charm, my father began chatting to the pretty girl on the seat opposite, but she made it plain that the book she was reading interested her more than he did. He lit a cigarette, offered her one, she declined and requested that he open the window. The rest of the journey took place in silence. The following evening was the Meynell Hunt Ball, a white tie and tails affair and the reason for the journey from London. A mutual friend said, 'you two must meet,' to which they both replied, 'we already have,' and from that evening stemmed a correspondence, a courtship, and in 1938 a marriage, my father being twenty-five, my mother twenty-three. After her death I inherited all my mother's effects and found that she had kept every single letter my father had written to her, from that first meeting at the dance. John and Pamela Spurrier were very social animals, but they never really needed anyone else.

In the autumn of 1946 we returned to Derbyshire. Before the war my father had been in publishing with Hutchinson and my mother had been a 'cub' reporter on the *Daily Mirror* covering food and fashion. Neither position was open to them in the devastated post-war economy and when

Grandpa Spurrier offered the position of transport director in his company Hilton Gravel to my father, there was little choice, nor inclination, to refuse. The company rented a large house with extensive flower and kitchen gardens, a park and installed the family there. This was Holbrook Hall in a village of the same name six miles north of Derby, three miles south of Belper, the past stomping ground of the Strutts who had brought prosperity to the town during the 1800s. One of the unknown later advantages of moving so near to my mother's forbears was that George Brown, the notoriously drunk Labour Member of Parliament who was to become Minister of Transport in the early 1950s, was MP for Belper and, on his rare visits to the constituency, a drinking buddy with my father. When the M1, Britain's first motorway, had its extension planned from Rugby to Derby, two bids were submitted to supply the gravel, one from Hilton Gravel, the other from our rival Helmington Gravel in nearby Nottinghamshire. Access to petrol was still hard to come by and without petrol the trucks couldn't deliver the gravel. Thanks to George Brown, Hilton Gravel got the petrol and the contract.

In the summer of 1949 I was told by my parents that I could no longer hang out with the gang of village boys at the bottom of our back drive, and I would be joining Nicky at his prep school, where I was to stay for the next five years. The school was Summerfields, St Leonards, near Hastings in Sussex. Years later it occurred to me that my father had chosen Summerfields as the farthest location in the country from Derbyshire, so as not to disturb his idyllic life with my mother by coming down to take me out, but it was a brilliant choice and whilst the saying that your schooldays are 'the best years of your life' is plainly rubbish, I cannot remember an unhappy moment. Those five years were crammed with learning on all levels, playing sports, making friends and generally having fun before the next step of growing up began at Rugby School.

There were about 100 boys in the school and having an elder brother meant that I knew 'the drill' – what to expect and how to behave, which was an advantage – but I didn't need to rely on him for anything else, as everything was so exciting and new and anyway seniors and juniors lived in different worlds. Summerfields was basically a prep school for Eton, over 90% of the boys already having been put down at birth for the school by their parents. However, my father had gone to Rugby so that was where Nicky and I were destined to spend the five years between thirteen and eighteen, but that seemed a vision of the future too far away to imagine. For an 8-year-old boy Summerfields had simply everything. Here I learnt to swim, to play tennis, squash and golf (it had a small course of its own). The terrace on which we did our morning exercises – the school motto was '*Mens Sana Corpore Sano*', A Healthy Mind in a Healthy Body – ran the length of the house, the formal gardens were impressive, the grounds seemingly endless, the woods mysterious and the sea-side weather was better than in Derbyshire. The teaching was of the best, but no one was left behind, the library was vast, with every sort of book an inquisitive boy would want to read and there was a flourishing artistic side with play-acting encouraged.

I made and have kept many friends from Summerfields and would have far preferred to have been swept along with them into Eton, but perhaps it was just as well that Rugby brought me down to earth. Summerfields was an adventure from start to finish and I did well, winning a few prizes and while the teaching and learning at Rugby stepped up a gear or two, it was not the same and in the end was stultifyingly boring.

So, in September 1954 I arrived at Rugby at the age of twelve years and eleven months for, being born in October, I would always be the youngest in the year group. Nicky and I were both in the same House of around seventy boys, of which there were ten making the total school numbers, all boys of course, up to around seven hundred. We were in Cotton House, where my father had been. The Houses played each other at games – cricket in the summer, rugby and hockey in the winter terms – and it was mostly up to the House Master, who could rule your life, how ambitious he wished to be for sporting prowess.

I had had very little contact with Nicky at Summerfields, but of course he was always around at home and seemed much the same to me, except he was progressively putting on weight. We had a tennis court but he seldom played and I played mostly with my father. By the time I arrived at Rugby it was plain that while he was exceptionally clever, he was anti-sport. Our housemaster Dick Stott didn't mind, since he acknowledged the brain-power, but everything changed in the third year when he retired and was replaced by Donald Bulmer, and Walter Hamilton became the new Headmaster.

By this time, Nicky was in his last year, already in the 6th form and a recognised scholar, but one who was determined to play no sport, partially through disinclination bordering on bloody-mindedness but also because he had become too fat. Mr Bulmer could not deny his scholarly success, but refused to make him a 'sixth' as the House prefects were known. As a scholar, he had a study of his own, but was progressively shunned by his peers, so remained holed up there, working, playing jazz records and eating. Bulmer was determined to show him up as a poor example who was letting the House down and did so very effectively. Having hardly seen anything of him at Summerfields, I became Nicky's only supporter and seeing his visible deterioration affected me deeply for the coming year.

At this point I have to address the fact that we both stammered very badly. Whether this is known as 'stammering' or 'stuttering' the actual infliction is recognised as a 'speech impediment'. For Nicky, more than for me, this was putting it mildly. Apparently both our parents had stammered when they were young but had got over it. Now in our 70s, and for many years, there is hardly any hint of a stammer left in either of us, but it was extremely restricting and damaging while growing up and Mr Bulmer pushed Nicky to the limit, rendering him virtually speechless in public.

Seeing the effects on Nicky of his obesity and the openness to taunts that this allowed, the following year I decided to stop eating. This idea took shape after a usually over-fed Christmas and I gradually cut down on everything during the Spring term, having to keep up some calorific intake as there was no heating in Cotton House, the dormitory windows were often iced up in the mornings, but in the summer term I was able to get by on virtually nothing. This was popular at lunchtimes, the only hot meal of the day, as I shared my plate with hungry friends, and especially popular on Fridays when we had fish and chips. I kept up summer sports, bowling for the House cricket team and swimming, but it became plain that I was getting thinner and thinner, which was the aim. The matron realised this and sent me to the Sanitorium to be weighed once a week. At first I put weights in my pockets to add to the ounces, but this was discovered and I was asked to strip. Towards the end of term I began to realise that it would all end badly – I had stopped growing and would never reach Nicky's six foot – and came to my senses. While this was bad for my health, it was good for my work as my mind was clear and concentrated. At the end of the summer term I sat 'mock' History exams, alongside a friend in the same class under the inspiring Mr Hele (every schoolboy has to have one inspiring teacher and Mr Hele was this, in spades) who was aiming for a scholarship to Oxford, coming out ahead when the papers were marked. This was oddly useful for my decision the following year not to take up a place at Cambridge! Once at home, I slowly got back to normal and our parents took Nicky and me to Italy with them. Now when I am asked how I stay so 'trim' I have a single and simple answer: vanity. Back in 1958 it was not so simple.

While I was quite happy at Rugby with many friends, my final year pretty much settled into a fight with boredom and Mr Bulmer. My 'mock' exams in History had established that a university entrance would be no problem and my other 'A Level' subject was German which was going fine. In circumstances where there were not many lessons to attend, students had 'out periods', time during the day when other studies could be followed. I took up Spanish, which proved a godsend a year or two later when I became passionate about bullfighting and spent three seasons following the bulls to every great bullring in Spain. I also began work on a thesis on late 19th century art in France. This was suggested by Mr Hele who had sensed my interest in art, especially the Impressionists and a bit later, since as a 'sixth' or prefect, I was allowed a room of my own (I was also allowed an umbrella, non-prefects just had to get wet) and my study was covered with reproductions of their paintings.

Under Walter Hamilton's leadership Rugby, which had seemed at the start to be a well-intentioned seat of learning, became a regimented camp where work came first, sports as long as you were good at them came second and rules were meant to be obeyed. After my first taste of Cockburn's 1908 at Marston I had read about wine and the places it came from and looked forward to my parents' once a term visit when we would lunch either at the Grand Hotel or the more casual Three Horseshoes and I would be allowed a glass of wine. This was too self-indulgent for Mr Hamilton, who banned it and had spies in these places to make sure it remained banned or was punished. My parents side-stepped this by coming down with marvellous picnics with wine to match, driving outside the town into spy-free countryside. Not only was this fun, but it reminded me of the countless picnics at the point-to-point race meetings that Nicky and I went to with Grandpa Spurrier, who bred some fine horses that often led the field while we watched through field glasses and the chauffeur made sure we didn't have more than one glass of sloe gin.

Having time on my hands in my last year and what was becoming a strong interest in looking at art, I proposed to Mr Bulmer that on one or two Saturdays a term, if the boys were interested and weren't required to play for their House in some match or other, we could go and visit some of the historic country houses that were not too far away. This began on a small base and then burgeoned into becoming the Rugby Architectural Society, the high point being in the middle of my last term when I took three dozen boys, mostly from Cotton House, to visit the great colleges of Oxford, the tour being organised by Nicky, who was then at Christ Church. A lunch took place on the banks of the River Cherwell, and Nicky, at my request, had brought along quite a bit of wine. I overdid it, was embarrassingly sick in the bus on the way back, and the Rugby Architectural Society had seen its last outing. This was a marvellous excuse for Mr Bulmer, who was affronted by my taking, Pied Piper-like, half his House out on a jaunt over which he had no control.

I was also getting quite interested in Jazz, not quite as 'original' as the New Orleans style of King Oliver that Nicky liked, but certainly Louis Armstrong, Jelly Roll Morton, the blues of Bessie Smith and early white Dixieland. I collected records and, knowing there was a Classical Music Society that met in the School Theatre and Concert Hall to listen to their music, I started the Jazz Society. This became quite popular, but wasn't allowed to last very long, either. One further burst for independence, or just for being different, was to bend the school dress code, which was a jacket (generally tweed, not a blazer), grey flannel trousers, white shirt and tie, black until you were a 'sixth', blue once you were. A few coloured pocket handkerchiefs borrowed from my father were banned in favour of just white or none; my attempt to introduce the 'Windsor knot' a wider tie knot favoured by the Duke of Windsor, and the even wider 'double Windsor', suffered a similar fate.

One self-inflicted incident happened in the middle of my last term that might have ended very badly: word got around that if one smelled 'Dab it Off', a bottled remover of spots or stains from clothes, one got a 'high'. Since this was something I had never experienced, I bought a bottle with its gauze 'dabbing off' cap and settled in one evening in my study, soaking a handkerchief in the liquid and holding it to my nose. After several intensive sniffs my head began to buzz and to see what happened next I continued sniffing, only to find myself an hour or so later face down on my desk in my own vomit. In this position there was little risk I would have choked on it and died, but an unexplained suicide would have been bad news all round, especially for me. Lengthy cleaning up ensued nothing came of it, but at only one point in my future life did I attempt 'mind-altering' substances, which certainly singled me out in the swinging sixties and beyond. This occasion was in Paris at a party given by a charming photographer, where around the table a hash-filled joint or two were passed. I refused and was told it was just fun, so took a couple of pulls – I had never smoked, being uninterested and coughing every time I tried to inhale – and the effect was so dramatically negative that I left, leaving my wife behind but taking my trusty dog Digby, a fine Berger Briard that we had acquired when in Provence a few years earlier. Digby and I adored each other – I dedicated my second book *French Country Wines* to 'In memory of Digby, a French country dog' – and he used to walk at my heels across Paris without ever a lead. That night, despite constant calling on the way back the barge on the Seine where we lived at that time, he lagged behind. I went to bed and the next day he was there on the deck but didn't come near me for another day, such were the negative vibes he felt.

As a respected 'sixth', friendly with my peers, I was pretty much left alone, but such was the combative severity of the Bulmer regime that some of my fellow prefects began to remark that I was not ruling my dormitory sufficiently strongly. 'Spurrier (first names were discouraged as being too friendly), I hear that your boys are talking after lights out.' 'Does it matter?' I replied. 'Yes it does, they are not allowed to and we've found some talking in our own dorms, and given them a good beating and they don't do it again, you are letting the House down by being so lax.' This posed me a problem, as I had no intention of 'beating' – three hard strokes with the sole of a leather slipper on a pyjama-ed bottom, with the slipper heel if they felt like it – anybody, so after some thought I discovered a way to get up into the rafters above the dormitory where I was in charge of a dozen or so boys. Having given them fifteen minutes to make sure I was out of the way after the compulsory 'Good night and no talking now,' I was up above them and while some were quiet, others were reading by torch light (not allowed) and a few were quietly chatting. I shouted down, 'RIGHT, ALL OF YOU ARE TALKING AND READING, DOWNSTAIRS IN FIVE MINUTES.' This gave me time to get to the Sixth's Room, where generally we lounged about during the day, but which was reserved for such things, with the slipper in my hand. I lined them up, the innocent boys stating their case, being told to shut up as 'my fellow sixths have told me this has been going on far too long and you are all to blame.' A couple of my peers were astounded by this happening and hung around outside the door. The boys were required to remove their dressing gowns and bend over to touch their toes to receive punishment. I called them in one by one, saying loudly 'dressing gown off, bend over' and then brought the sole of the slipper down three times with a loud thwack on the adjoining table. 'Now go to bed and I hope you have learnt your lesson.' After that night I never paid the slightest attention to them, nor did my peers complain about my being 'lax'. Word got around the school that 'Spurrier had beaten a whole dormitory', which was very amusing and upped my rating in Mr Bulmer's eyes, not that I cared.

The 1959 summer term came to an end and I sent my trunk and few possessions I wanted to keep back home and took the train to London, never to set foot in Rugby again. That evening, staying at a friend's house in Chelsea, we had to convince his conservative father that we could go to The 100 Club, a jazz dive in Oxford Street, since the lead band was headed by Humphrey Lyttleton, the leading light of British Jazz then and for more than 40 years). The next day we all attended the Rugby v Marlborough cricket match at Lords. Mr Bulmer was there: 'Well, Spurrier, happy to have left?' 'Yes, Mr Bulmer.' (No more 'sir' now) 'Would you like to do a favour for your old House?' 'How could I do this?' 'Your family is in the gravel business I believe and you remember the large front drive, which could need a lot of freshening up.' 'Of course, I will arrange this before the start of next term and have the company call you.' I could have ignored this, but it was an opportunity not to be missed. During the holidays I arranged with my father that if the company had a truck delivering nearby, I would pay for a bumper load of gravel for Mr Bulmer, so in early September this was arranged, Mr Bulmer was advised to remove all vehicles from the drive and the truck duly appeared at the entrance, checked the address and was given permission to deposit its load, backed slowly up, on my instructions, close to the front door and up-ended the load, the pile blocking the door and rising well above the front windows. Apparently even Rugby Council couldn't dig Mr Bulmer out for access before start of the winter term.

2. Off to London

During the 'half holiday' of the summer term I had told my father that I would not be taking up my place at Cambridge, but would prefer to go to London. The fact was that I couldn't take any more of the 'cap and gown' atmosphere of expensive private education, saluting the masters when you passed them in the street and respecting the hierarchy of previous centuries. Although I went back to Derbyshire most weekends, mentally when I left Rugby I left home as well. My father was appalled, but he was on weak ground, since he hadn't lasted a full year at Christ Church, Oxford and to make him feel better his mother had given him a 21st birthday party in September 1934 at the Palace Hotel in St Moritz.

Having grudgingly accepted the idea of London, my parents insisted I go to university, my father selecting the London School of Economics, probably to teach me a lesson as mathematics was not my strong point. Indeed, I failed my first year exams but was allowed to take them again, since I was almost alone in paying fees to attend, the vast majority from state schools or abroad being on a student grant. From the start I could not have been happier, treating it like a 9 to 5 job, fraternising with my classmates, but playing no part in university life as Nicky was in London (he hadn't lasted more than a year at Christ Church either) and there was everything to explore in the early 1960s, from cinemas to coffee bars, restaurants and pubs for the first time on my own, art galleries and museums. I lived in a spacious first floor bedroom with its own washbasin (only one bathroom a floor in those days) and a gas fire one fed with penny pieces, at 19 The Little Boltons in South Kensington. The house had seven or eight lodgers, some who had been there for years, and I paid £5 a week, cooked breakfast included, dinner a little extra if required.

A contemporary at Rugby, David Zambra, almost my twin as he was born on 3 October and indeed our lives would be intertwined due to wine for many years and we remain the closest of friends, had been lodging in similar circumstances in an equally spacious house in the less salubrious Devonshire Terrace in Bayswater, but more glamourous since it was owned by a French baroness, Jeanne de Lagatinerie. We met up there from time to time in his room, for the baroness (she was never referred to in any other way) only allowed lodgers into the drawing room briefly before dinner, the dinners being simple but formal with wine served 'en carafe' which went on the weekly tab, and when he told me he was leaving I took over his room the following spring. This was on the top floor, lit by a dormer window, smaller and more intimate than before, but quite enough room for a young student and the usual penny in the slot gas fire. The fellow lodgers were all young from similar backgrounds and I took to it like a duck to water. At that time nearby Notting Hill was both run down and louche, having known better times with far, far better times to come from the area's 'gentrification' from the next decade, but it was already proud of its broad ethnic mix and it was edgy but never dangerous. At this time I discovered the antique markets of the Portobello Road on Saturdays and after lunch at the local Italian (lots of rough Chianti) or Spanish (lots of Spanish Burgundy as the red was known then) I lost myself amongst the long street of stalls, picking up something for nothing here and there. When I told my mother how fascinating this all was, she said that her Uncle Alec's younger son Michael had a stall there and we soon met up.

Michael had a day job with a big brewing company, visiting their country pubs to check them out and collecting bric-à-brac from the antique shops that were then in every little town. He was charming, had a slight stammer so we embarrassed each other and then laughed about it, and he very quickly inoculated me with the collector's gene. Michael and his ebullient American wife Cordelia, stayed in close touch over the years. Over my life I have spent much, much more on art than on wine, it was my second idea for a profession, and I have surrounded myself with the stuff wherever I have lived and only regret what I've had to sell. Buying art is just like buying wine: you find it/taste it, want it, check if you can afford it (not thinking you might have too much of it already, or can't afford it) and buy it. Having it is the aim, looking at it for art, thinking about it and then drinking it for wine and then, inevitably, leaving it for the next generation. Apparently the great André Simon died with just one bottle of Champagne in his cellar. This will not be the case for me.

While at the baroness's I also discovered wine at Peter Dominic, a treasure trove rambling basement shop in Orange Street, off the Haymarket in Piccadilly. There were the very smart shops in Saint James's Street —

Berry Brothers and Rudd, Justerini and Brooks and Christopher's (my subsequent employers) – but they were too grand to go into, while this was more like the stalls in the Portobello Road, open for endless browsing and always a bargain to catch the eye. Their wine list was called The Wine Mine and indeed it was, an idea to be copied later by Oddbins and Majestic Wine with great success, but this was 1960. They even held the first ever wine fair in London, in Seymour Hall off the Marylebone Road, a stone's throw from where *Decanter* would launch its first Fine Wine Encounter thirty-five years later at the Landmark Hotel.

Meanwhile life went on at the LSE. I was beginning to find my way around all parts of London, gave a well-attended 19th birthday party in my top floor room, wines from Peter Dominic of course, but girls were still a closed book. That autumn a charming French girl named Marie-Claire had arrived at the baroness's, moving into the other top room across the landing from mine and we shared the bathroom with mutual respect. None of the others seemed to pay much attention to her, so I asked her out to the occasional party in my school boy French, 'Il y a un parti ce week-end,' and before she left before Christmas to go home, bought some nice wines from Peter Dominic for her last dinner and a good time was had by all. Later that evening, seated at my desk and checking through stuff for the next day's lectures at the LSE, I heard a knock on my door: 'Come in,' and it was Marie-Claire in her nightdress, pausing in the doorway: 'I just wanted to thank you properly for tonight.' 'My pleasure, Marie-Claire, see you tomorrow at breakfast.' I had a lot to learn.

By early spring 1961 I had moved again, to a six room flat on two floors in Stanhope Gardens in South Kensington. 'Your problem, Dad,' my daughter Kate told me recently 'is that you are bored with the present.' This is absolutely true and while many of the changes in my commercial life have been 'out of the frying pan into the fire' I have always been lucky with where I've lived. Amongst the lodgers at the baroness's were two contempories – James Sholto Douglas and Adrian Cooper-Key, so we needed just one more boy to make up a foursome and this turned out to be Nicholas Gormanston, who had been to the Roman Catholic school Downside. Adrian (known as Ade) and I would set up together later that year (another move), but it was Nicholas who introduced more new friends and we all began to join the social swirl. There was the occasional ball, needing a 'white tie' in those days, but mostly cocktail parties, and especially 'bottle parties' where someone's flat was the base and everyone bought bottles and food. One day two young Mormons from the Church of the Latter Day Saints in Salt Lake City (USA) knocked on our door and tried to convince us to join their faith. We didn't, but they left a leaflet to show they were building a church in Exhibition Road nearby. Late one night, after a particularly heavy party nearby, Nicholas and I left to stagger back home and found ourselves passing the scaffolding-clad soon to be Mormon church, just up to its first floor. Remembering the young Mormons' preposterous proposition, I suggest to him that we knock it down and we climbed the scaffolding to begin to dislodge several large bricks to our huge amusement. Soon after the police arrived and we ended up in Chelsea gaol. The following morning we were paraded at the Earl's Court law court on the charges of 'being, whilst drunk, guilty of disorderly conduct' and were fined 10 shillings. Passing the box which housed a red-faced and robust policeman to pay up, Nicholas – a beautifully effete young man who much resembled Lord Alfred Douglas from the Oscar Wilde days – said politely that he hoped our money was going towards the Policeman's Ball. A gruff 'Why?' was asked. 'Because policemen's balls are so much smaller than firemen's balls.' We got out fast. This got into the newspapers, even as far as the *Derby Evening Telegraph*, which did not go down well.

I have only been to gaol one more time, the following summer in Pamplona (Spain) in the first of three years at the Feria San Fermin's bullfighting fiesta in early July that began for me a month of criss-crossing Spain to 'follow the bulls' in Madrid, Valencia, Malaga and finally up north to Bilbao. With a group of friends mostly from Cambridge, we stayed up until the early hours in the bars around the Plaza Mayor then crashed out on a park bench to get some sleep before the traditional running with the bulls at 7am, then freshened up at the public swimming pool in the camping ground before the evening bullfights. One night, over a final drink in a café on the north west corner of the square, I offered my friends a bet that I could walk round to the fashionable Hotel La Perla in the south west corner, where the top matadors and Ernest Hemingway used to stay, without touching the ground. Of course they took the bet and, just wearing espadrilles, I hopped onto the roof of the first of the cars which were parked jampacked around the square and did indeed make it to La Perla as planned, but then to celebrate did a small 'zapateado' dance on the roof of the final car, which unfortunately had a chauffeur inside. The hotel called the police and I spent a comfortable night in a cell, speaking enough Spanish to tell the gaolers how much I loved bullfighting and they, modestly bribed, gave me lunch and released me in time for the evening performance with Paco Camino, Jaime Ostos and El Viti.

Summer 1961 was good fun with people coming and going in the Stanhope Gardens flat but I was getting behind on my studies at the LSE and suggested to Ade that we find somewhere together and by September we were happily ensconced on the top floor at 10 Eaton Terrace, bang in the middle of Belgravia, just up the road from the very good and fashionable Antelope pub. Our sitting room had room for a table and chairs and here I learned to cook.

Ade and I had friends round to supper and I even learnt to bake bread, but actually we were going out even more. Ade was tall and glamourous, yet shyly unaware of this and we were quite popular. My brother Nicky was in the more senior league, totally slimmed down, tall and fair and liked to pass himself off as a German count – Claus von und zu Zwischen, which translated to as Claus from, towards and together – which some girls fell for.

The contrast between this night life and my daily appearances at the LSE could not have been more marked nor more enjoyable. My only and selfish contribution to communal university life was to join the Wine Society. The LSE was notoriously Left Wing and very concerned with questions of race and human rights and I had stayed away from all these debates, but was finally strong-armed into taking part in one on Apartheid in South Africa. By this time I was studying for my finals, on a carefully chosen subject The History of Economic Thought 1760-1820. There were four papers on this and one on The History of American Economic Thought 1860-1920. The LSE rules allowed you to fail one paper and still get a degree and having attended one class on the latter subject, I decided not to continue, taking the risk that my marks in the other four would suffice. This gave me more free time to visit art galleries or my friends in Cambridge and luckily the gamble paid off and I emerged in summer 1963 with a Second B.Sc (Econ).

Around the time of the 1962 summer holidays, Ade told me that his parents wanted him to set up on his own and had found a lovely ground floor flat a couple of streets away in Chesham Place. While Ade's mother could not have been nicer to me and we remained friends right up to her death, his father was an upright Conservative MP and being already worried that the wealth of his wife's family would discourage Ade from getting a proper job, and he was concerned that I was leading him astray. I have to admit that we were both drinking a lot, Ade probably out of boredom, me because I quite liked to get drunk and booze was always to hand. My father, who was himself not immune to drink, always put NSI – Normal Social Intake - in the box on medical insurance papers to describe his consumption of alcohol. In the 60s I would have had to enter ASI – Abnormal Social Intake. When I told my father I planned to go into the wine trade his reply was 'you're quite mad, at the rate you're going, you'll be dead in ten years'. In fact, it was the wine trade that saved me for although I never minded losing control socially, relying on charm to smooth over the consequences, I soon realised that to make a life in wine I could not do this professionally. The conversion was not overnight and I remember touring the south of France in summer 1967 in my Mercedes convertible, with lots of money, having a great time and the girl of the moment asking me 'Sweetie, do you have to get drunk *every* night?' She had a point.

Knowing Ade was moving out, I began to look around for another flatmate, but then Nicky, who was living in a top floor flat in Cliveden Place just nearby, said he was moving, so in September I took over his 'two rooms, k&b (kitchen and bathroom)' as space like that was known in estate agent's jargon, and experienced total independence for the first time in my life at almost twenty-one, in the centre of the universe with lots of friends, starting my final year at the LSE before facing the real world.

My parents had long planned a 21st birthday party in Derbyshire, a dinner-dance on the actual day 5 October 1962. I had planned a breakfast party at my flat in London that day, not with Champagne as I couldn't afford it, but with a lethal 'Champagne cocktail' based on Merrydown Cider which was well over Champagne's 12 degrees of alcohol. This had been preceeded by a dance but I had prepared it all beforehand and the few hours sleep left me refreshed enough to welcome 50 or so friends who turned up on time at 8am. (Who on earth would go to a drinks party, even a birthday party at 8am these days?). Some food was served, but the Merrydown took hold and several people didn't make it to work and by the time almost everyone had left I was in such bad shape that, planning to take the train from St Pancras to Derby, I wouldn't even have made it to the Sloane Street Underground Station. Ade agreed to drive me, called my parents who of course were happy to see him and off we set, but I was still pretty much out of it when we arrived. Hot coffee and a cold shower helped a bit and while I made it through the dinner, I retired much the worse for wear before the dancing had got to its peak and the candle-lit birthday cake was to be passed around. Grandpa Spurrier summed it all up while I was trying to make some sense of the evening: 'My boy, you are what we in these parts call 'smock-raddled.'' Over my parents' lifetimes I know that I surprised them often, both positively and negatively, but this was one of the rare times I knew I had let them down. Smock-raddled, totally and utterly.

Apart from that, life went on well. My maternal grandmother had given me membership of the Wine Society and a 12 bottle wine rack for my birthday, presents which were to positively influence my life, the wine rack staying in the kitchen while my cupboards filled up with wine and my walls with prints and the flat with odds and ends bought on visits to the Portobello Road and with cousin Michael on his buying trips. It was a wonderful time. I had passed my driving test and, through Hilton Gravel, had acquired a Ford van, known as a Utility Vehicle as it only had side windows on the driver and passenger sides, inside which the local garage had set up bunk beds in the back as I planned to take it on holiday and wasn't going to waste money on hotels. I arrived in Pamplona for the start of the Feria on 7 July, the continued my usual bull-fighting tour – by this time I was reading *La Rueda*, the 'aficionado's' magazine and spoke better Spanish – through Madrid and Valencia where I met up with friends, some of us continuing on to Malaga and after that festival joined Ade in Marbella, where he was staying at the recently opened Marbella Club for our plan to drive into Morocco, down to Marrakech. This was an extraordinary trip – I was interested in architecture and history, Ade was interested in being in places where he could practice his new passion for drawing – and while we slummed it a bit in Marrakech, we stayed in style at Le Palais Jamai in Fez and after a wonderful eight days I dropped him back in Marbella saying that we would see each other in London in a couple of weeks. I drove back via Seville and San Sebastian, where my battered Ford had to be totally overhauled, up through France to the coast, arriving back in mid-September to meet a distraught Nicky who told me that Ade had been killed in a car accident. A hopeless driver himself due to poor eyesight, he had been in the passenger seat of a car which had veered too close to the hilly mountain wall, a jutting rock taking out the passenger seat and Ade with it. His body had been repatriated to England and the funeral was in two days' time. I met his mother Lorna the following day and she asked if I had taken any photos of him during our trip together. I hadn't. The funeral for me was a blur. What a terrible waste.

Now that the LSE was over, I needed some kind of a job before deciding on my next step and was taken on by an American company that published encyclopedias which was conveniently situated in Bowater House in Knightsbridge, a ten minute walk from my flat. This kept me going until Christmas, after which I was determined to find an entry into the wine trade. No employment agencies offered that sort of thing and I voiced my frustration over dinner with Nicky at our local restaurant Charco's which, for some reason, had very good value lobster. A strikingly suave and handsome young man on the next table lent over and said, 'If you are looking to go into the wine trade, here's my card, call me tomorrow.' This was Malcolm Gage and he worked for Christopher's and Co. in Jermyn Street, one of the 'big three' alongside Berry Brothers and Rudd and Justerini and Brooks, both a stone's throw away in grander Saint James's Street, none of whom I would have dared to approach. I made the call and was told that an appointment had been made for me to meet Peter Noble, the Managing Director, at 10am the following morning. I duly presented myself, was told to sit down and asked just one question: 'Where were you at school?' 'Rugby, sir.' 'Oh dear, we normally only employ Etonians, but since you would have been a fag (a junior polishing the shoes of seniors and running errands, a sort of indentured slave) at Rugby, you will know what a trainees' position with a company like Christopher's will be like. You can start on Monday.' And so, in early February 1964, I began my life in the wine trade and a year of hard learning under the rod of Mr Taylor and his son Malcolm in Christopher's cellars in Soho's Hollen Street. For some unknown reason the Taylors, father and son, referred to the Jermyn Street premises as PM.

3. Learning the Trade

The London Wine Trade in 1964 was very old fashioned and structured into a two-tier system, which pretty much exists to this day. There were Importers, known as Shippers, who sold to the Merchants, who sold both wholesale to Universities and Clubs and retail to the public. There were also regional wholesalers who bought from Shippers and sold to local Merchants. There were some smart restaurants mostly in the West End and mostly French with extensive lists and a growing number of Italian Trattorias, beginning in Soho and spreading out to fashionable Knightsbridge, Kensington and Chelsea who had their own Italian suppliers. The Shippers and Merchants having hardly discovered Enotria, the ubiquitous wicker flask Chianti bottles to be found on checkered table cloths with guttering candles. Then there were the pubs, almost entirely in the hands of the brewers, who sold beer, spirits, aperitifs, but not wine. Most London pubs of any size had a licence to sell off-premises, so one went to the Off Licence around the corner for all sorts of alcoholic drinks, as there were very few retail wine shops until licensing laws were relaxed in the 1960s, leading to the 'democratisation' of wine drinking in the following decade with competition for customers leading to wider and better-priced offers. Just as London in the 1960s witnessed the creation and appreciation of new styles of music and the arts, it was the same, but slower, for wine and food.

Christopher's, who stated that their historical documents had been destroyed in the 1666 Great Fire of London, thus laid claim to being the oldest wine merchant in London, established thirty years before what became Berry Brothers and Rudd was founded as a coffee shop at No 3 Saint James's Street. It was not interested in wine democracy, neither were their Saint James's street neighbours. While they had shop windows on the street, Christopher's at 94 Jermyn Street was between Paxton & Whitfield the famous cheese merchant and Floris known for its upmarket toiletries, both still strongly present today while Christopher's is long gone. If bottles were displayed they were ancient and dusty and carried no price tag. Clients entered to be received by an elegantly dressed young man at a polished mahogany desk and asked to sit in a comfortable chair to discuss their needs. In those days wine was a male prerogative – my mother shopped for groceries in Derby, always parking her car in the yard of the local brewer and liquor wholesaler, occasionally picking up a few bottles of what my father called 'the red infuriator', but their proper wines came from the elegant Dolamore's in London's Baker Street – and gentlemen had their own wine merchant alongside their own tailor, shirtmaker, and barber. Money seldom changed hands, everything was purchased 'on account'. Wine was a gentleman's profession, at least those front of house staff were supposed to be gentlemen. It used to be said that if there were four sons, the eldest inherited the estate, the second went into the Army, the third into the Church, the fourth was forced to earn his keep in some sort of commerce, the wine trade being very suitable. Seven years later when I gained possession of a small wine shop called Les Caves de la Madeleine in the centre of Paris, the social status of a 'caviste' as we were called was about that of a 'pompiste' of petrol pump attendant, clients coming in with empty bottles asking for them to be filled up. This didn't fit my ideas and I immediately abandoned the sale of wine 'in bulk', the previous owner's supplier of the stuff telling me that if I did so I would 'lose half the clientele', which was precisely the half I wished to lose.

It was due to the discretion of Christopher's shop window that my mother, on a shopping visit to Jermyn Street noticed above Christopher's door the words 'Colonel Olaf Wyck, licensed to sell wines and spirits'. Every such shop, every pub, had to have a licensee and Colonel Wyck as a young Lieutenant in the 4th Hussars had served under Grandpa Neame in India and had been impressed by my mother's irrepressible behaviour so, knowing he would remember her, she walked in and asked to see him. Once re-acquainted he asked what he could do for her and she replied 'my son wants to go into the wine trade and I think you should employ him.' 'Of course' he replied, retired to his office for a minute or two, returning to say 'it appears we already have'. Having been taken on by Peter Noble the day before, despite this family connection, I only set foot in PM, as the head office was called, once again, after an eight month tour of the wine regions of Europe working for their suppliers in 1965, to be told that my services would no longer be required.

Hollen Street was a true working cellar, bottling claret from Bordeaux's greatest châteaux – two barrels of the 1962 Cheval Blanc, the last vintage shipped in bulk from this Saint-Emilion Premier Grand Cru Classé A, passed through my hands – butts of Sherry, 'pipes' of Port, bottles lying quietly in large bins until ready for sale as *en primeur* or 'futures' sales were unheard of. A vast amount of wine and spirits was boxed up to be dispatched all over London and the country, some to the Royal Palaces, as Christopher's held a Royal Warrant. Most of the time there were three 'trainees', a permanent staff of four who were old hands, and the two Taylors. Mr Taylor Senior was a tough old-school manager, along the lines of a seasoned Sergeant-Major dealing with junior officer-quality recruits, who deserved our respect and in return respected us, while his son Malcolm was brashly authoritative with no concern that we were just beginning our careers in wine and wanted to learn as much as possible. It really was like being back at Rugby, except that I was paid £10 a week – a fair wage – and got 'luncheon vouchers' which I used to save up for a once-a-month splurge on Soho's Italian restaurants.

During the autumn of 1963 I moved again, this time to a top floor flat in South Kensington's Courtfield Gardens, taking on a leasehold after monthly rentals in my previous flats. My new flat had a large sitting room with fine views over the gardens, a sizeable bedroom, the usual k&b but a smaller third room that became my first ever dining room. The move from Cliveden Place was a bit of a break, it had been my first experience of independence and being, along with Ade, just about the only person in our circle who had a place of their own and who liked to have people round, it became quite a social gathering place. On occasions friends asked if they could borrow it while I was away for romantic interludes, one of whom was Willy Feilding, a school friend of Nicholas Gormanston, who had already become known as a painter of murals in the Whistler mode. Willy and his beautiful girlfriend Clare were often there and to thank me he suggested painting a mural on part of my sitting room wall under which I had suitably placed a Victorian chaise-longue. I gave him carte blanche and what transpired had a Grecian theme, with a discretely naked Clare on a Mediterranean shore leaning against a pillar, her feet being caressed by soft wavelets. It was quite lovely and much admired but then Clare left him and Willy used to call often late at night to say he was coming round for a drink. Once there, he made a 'roux' from tomato ketchup, Worcestershire sauce and flour and with his delicate fingers painted spiders and scorpions crawling all over Clare's naked body. Of course I washed these off the following morning, returning the mural to its pristine glory. Some months after moving out I was passing the front door and saw a young lady with her key in the lock. I asked if by any chance she lived on the top floor, which she did and said how nice it was. 'Do you like the mural?' I asked. 'That revolting thing,' she replied, 'we painted it over right after moving in.' An original Feilding gone for good. Luckily I have a couple of his watercolours in Dorset.

Very soon after I had moved to Courtfield Gardens, my brother Nicky was married in one of the Kensington churches, having himself moved nearby to Gloucester Road. His fiancée Virginia was a local Derbyshire girl whose family lived only a few miles from our family home at Marston and while her family and ours were social equals, they were different in every other way. Both sets of parents were vigorously against the match, mine describing them as 'deadly dull', they describing ours simply as 'fast' and damning Nicky as 'a pagan' for he was not a regular church-goer. In those days parental consent was required for girls under 21 years of age; Virginia turned 21 on December 21st 1963 and the wedding took place two days later. It was also customary that the bride's parents fund the whole cost of the wedding, Virginia's family refusing to, but turning up in force all the same. I knew of all this background and when it came to the choice of a 'best man', Nicky turned to me, wanting to have someone there who he knew was on his and Virginia's side. He was, as at Rugby and remains so, something of a 'loner' and the pre-wedding 'stag party' was just the two of us over dinner at Le Français, a genuinely good French restaurant in the Fulham Road, ending the evening next door at Apron Strings, a gaming club for members only, where Nicky was a regular (and regularly losing) member, playing chemin de fer or blackjack. Such clubs and the much flashier ones in the West End, offered free drinks to members as being a gaming club the licencing rules disapproved of them selling booze, so they had to give it away. For an hour or so Nicky played cards and I drank Champagne, chatting to the owners Joe and Pauline and a few of their regulars. Nicky dropped me off on his way home and, perhaps because it was raining but more likely due to the Champagne, I slipped on the front door steps and fell flat on my face. Since it was too late to worry, I went to sleep and woke up to find my right eye had become a complete 'shiner' as black eyes were called. There is a photograph which shows us walking to the church, Nicky most elegant in Grandpa Neame's

Walking to Nicky's wedding, December 1963

morning coat, with no sign of this at all. The professional photographer had airbrushed it out and did so in the formal group photo, but on the day it was loud and clear, confirming the opinion of Virginia's parents that the Spurrier boys were 'mad, bad and dangerous to know' as Caroline Lamb described Lord Byron. The marriage was a happy one, ending only on Virginia's early death about thirty years later.

As Peter Noble had suggested, being a trainee at Christopher's was like being back at Rugby, especially the rigid rules. One of these was that the trainees were to be seen and not heard and talking amongst ourselves whilst doing something mind-numbingly dull like making up the 12 bottle cardboard cartons was considered 'chatting' and so a distraction from the job in hand. We were there to learn and while I had read many books on wine, starting with Tommy Layton's *Wine Primers*, moving onto such exotica as Ian Maxwell Campbell's *The Wayward Tendrils of the Vine* and Maurice Healy's splendid *Stay Me with Flagons* and whatever the Wine and Food Society could come up with, I was looking for information and found it in marvellous books by Alexis Lichine, Russian by birth, a naturalised American who had been on General Eisenhower's staff towards the end of the war and had spent time freeing Bordeaux from the German occupation. His first book, *The Wines of Bordeaux*, covered the region with history, geography, people and places, facts and figures and was a mine of information which had to be committed to memory. My co-trainee who had arrived a little before me was James Radcliffe, still in the wine trade and still a great friend. We began to test each other on the rankings of the Bordeaux châteaux from the famous 1855 Classification: 'Château Ducru-Beaucaillou?' 'Second Growth Saint-Julien' 'Château Palmer?' 'Third growth Margaux' and so on only to be firmly reprimanded by Greg, the sub cellar manager and told to stop talking. At the tea break I knocked on the office door and suggested to Malcolm Taylor that since we were supposedly there to learn the wine trade, surely testing our knowledge in this way should be allowed. It was not.

By the mid-1960s Alexis Lichine had personally purchased Château Prieuré-Lichine (4th Growth Margaux) and set up a consortium to take over the much larger Château Lascombes (2nd Growth Margaux) as well as creating his own *négociant* business in Bordeaux and also in Burgundy, where he was the first *négociant* to encourage growers to bottle unblended produce from their own vineyards. In Burgundy, as in every wine region in Europe until perhaps the 1970s, the *négociants* or merchants controlled the market as not only did they have bottling facilities for quantities big and small, they had sales people at home and importers abroad and had clients which the actual producers had absolutely no access to. The *vignerons* were farmers, selling their grapes to the merchants or, if they had cellars to make the wine, selling it off in bulk after the harvest. The merchants decided the price which the growers had to accept. In the mid-1930s a small group of top estates such as Marquis d'Angerville in Volnay, Henri Gouges in Nuits-Saint-Georges, comte Georges de Vogüé in Chambolle-Musigny and Armand Rousseau in Gevrey-Chambertin began 'domaine bottling', still selling some wine in bulk while they built up sales, but even in the 1960s they were a rarity. Alexis Lichine did not follow the other merchants' practice of buying up barrels of say a Meursault or a Volnay from various growers and making a blend to sell a Meursault or a Volnay under their own name. Alexis Lichine encouraged growers to invest in their own cellars, practice domaine bottling and he would sell these unblended Meursaults or Volnays with both his and their name on the bottle.

Alexis Lichine also opened Château Pieuré-Lichine to sell direct to the public, something totally and utterly new in Bordeaux, especially in the

Médoc – there is an expression in French 'snob comme le Médoc' – but more and more commonplace today. Not many of the Classed Growth châteaux were lived in, the owners preferring Bordeaux or Paris, and if they were, their doors were firmly closed to commerce, the wines being sold to the *négociant*/merchants known collectively as La Place de Bordeaux. The owners knew each other, knew the brokers and merchants who they entertained for lunches and dinners to which the occasional importer, wine writer, even a lowly trainee might be invited, but never the public. Lichine was derided by his neighbours for conspicuous vulgarity for openly encouraging visits and tastings to offer 'the château experience' which usually ended in sales of his wine and of his books – he was the best promoter of himself and his brand in the most elegant way – and created an increasing mailing list. All this decade before the Napa Valley realised the full value of sales from the cellar door, although the great Robert Mondavi had pioneered this with his ground-breaking Napa Winery in the mid-1950s, as he was later to pioneer a joint venture with Mouton-Rothschild's baron Philippe called Opus One whose first vintage was 1979 and other joint ventures with Marchese Lodovico Antinori in Tuscany and with Eduardo Chadwick in Chile. The world of wine owes a great debt to visionaries like Lichine and Mondavi.

First from his books, then meeting Alexis Lichine in 1964 and later having got to know him well from the early 1970s, started a friendship that lasted until his death in 1989 and continues with his son, Sacha. Sacha sold Prieuré-Lichine after his father's death and finally, after many ups and downs, purchased a beautiful château in Provence and began to produce, a few thousand bottles at first, now over two million, with the help of Patrick Léon who had recently retired after years as head winemaker at Mouton-Rothschild, France's most expensive Rosé de Provence under the name of Château d'Esclans. He always sends me the new vintage to taste and, sending him my notes recently congratulating him on the quality and his stunning success, saying that Alexis would have been proud of him. His reply was brief: 'Papa always appreciated success'.

I have had two mentors, more like heroes really, in my wine life: Alexis Lichine and Michael Broadbent, and was immensely flattered that they both offered to write introductions to the books that I was to write in the 1980s. But it is not often one gets to meet one's heroes and certainly not in the following circumstances: one of my contemporaries and friends from

Summerfields, Michael Russell, was a cousin of the Duke of Bedford, who was one of the first to put their houses and parks to work by, like Alexis Lichine, opening them to the public. He created a safari park and when pop music was beginning to take on, opened the Woburn Abbey park for a weekend Music Fair, allowing the public to bring tents and camp out. Michael asked his cousin how it all went to be told laconically 'Forty acres fucked flat'. He didn't hold another one. Michael and I got on well and one day he told me that he had been invited to lunch at Woburn and if he had a friend who interested in wine, he should bring him. So one fine Saturday in May Michael and I set off and on arrival were told that the other two guests would be a little late and that after a drink we should start without them. The Duchess was French, with much more vivacity and charm than I was to encounter later from her peers on their home ground. After a glass or two of Champagne, lunch was announced and the doors to the famous Canaletto Room flung open and I walked in to see sixteen paintings by this Venetian artist from the years he had worked in England. If I had failed to find a start in wine, I would have applied to join Christie's Auctioneers as a trainee, so nothing could have impressed me more. Lunch began with an empty place on the right of our hosts, very shortly later the arrival of the guests was announced and in came Alexis Lichine with Arlene Dahl, one of the most beautiful Hollywood actresses ever, who had flown into London from New York for the start of their honeymoon. It doesn't get much better than that when you are just twenty-three years old.

Life at Christopher's continued well, despite the strictness, for I was learning all the time, and early that Spring two things happened that were to have a very deep effect on my life: meeting Bella Lawson, who was to become my wife, and receiving a cheque for my shares in Hilton Gravel Ltd, the company which Grandpa Spurrier had founded in 1922 to support his country pursuits, which had been sold at a high price to Blue Circle Cement. First, meeting Bella: I was looking forward to a summer of parties in London and more parties over weekends in country houses. One of the meeting places was at the Queensway Ice Skating Rink in Bayswater on Mondays. I usually went with a few male friends and on that particular night was with Ian Carr, a committed party-goer now sadly deceased. The plan was always to get the skates on first, which suited me as it made me taller, and then go into the bar for a drink. Around girls I was still shy, so my deal with Ian that he would get the girls and I would get the drinks. He pointed out a threesome near the bar and over we went. 'Hello, I'm Ian, this is my friend Steven who'd like to offer you a drink.' Two of them ordered something harmless like cider and I turned to the third who asked for a gin and orange. Now, in the early part of the war, before we moved to Brills, my mother had been a cub reporter for the *Daily Mirror* mostly on food and fashion and had told me that the Soho 'ladies' always drank gin and orange, orange for their health and gin to keep their spirits up, so I said she couldn't have what she wanted as 'it was what the 'tarts' drank', to which the seventeen-year-old Bella replied, 'In that case make it a double'. It appeared that Bella hadn't had a clue what to ask for and that gin and orange just came into her head without her knowing what it was, but having just left a sheltered upbringing to come to London, she wasn't going to be told what not to do on her first evening out. We got on right from the start and still do to this day, which is why this book is dedicated 'To Bella and to Wine'.

The other event actually created more problems than it might have solved, had there been problems to solve. Hilton Gravel had become successful with half a dozen large working pits as they were known and had expanded into Ready Mixed Cement and tennis courts. Grandpa Spurrier was a canny businessman not afraid to fly a little close to the wind if it brought financial advantage. In the early 1960s the company had built new offices in Hilton, a substantial village near to the hamlet of Marston-on-Dove where he lived. The building had a central core with two wings and his office was at the end of the right hand wing with a door from the outside where he parked his car and another door leading into the rest of the building. Grandpa always wore a hat when at his desk and I asked why. 'My boy, one never knows how quickly one might have to leave the office and a gentleman never goes outside without a hat.' Presumably if the tax inspectors came calling, he would be out and driving away in an instant.

My father had joined the company after the war as there was no work in publishing. London was bombed out and the offer of a large house was too good at that time to refuse. He told Nicky and me over Christmas in 1963 that a sale was on the cards. Over Easter 1964 he said it was to be concluded and we would soon receive a cheque in the post. No other information was given and none asked for and in April I did indeed receive a cheque for £250,000, the equivalent today of almost £5 million. I paid this into the Soho branch of Lloyds Bank along with my £10 weekly wage from

Christopher's and when the lady cashier looked surprised and asked if I wished to see the Manager, I just said 'No, thanks'. At that time I was on a monthly allowance of £60 so with my trainee's pay I had £100 a month to spend. I was already having my suits and shirts made and thought of commissioning a pair of bespoke shoes from Maxwell in Dover Street, since they were also makers of riding spurs on the Royal Warrant and had 'Spurriers to the Queen' on their window under their logo, but this was an unrealised extravagance. I had a busy social life, the London parties, dinners in my new dining room with wines from The Wine Society as I had moved upscale from the cheerful Peter Dominic's, restaurants and occasionally night clubs, but life was so cheap in those days. £5 could get a dinner for two at either the fashionable and very good Alvaro's – the great Alvaro died just one year before the 40th anniversary of his final *trattoria* La Famiglia in Chelsea's World's End, still my favourite London restaurant which I took over for Bella's 60th birthday in August 2006 – or David Hicks' restaurant nearby and still have change for a taxi after a couple of glasses of Champagne and a dance at Annabel's. Saturday forays to the Portobello Road always ended up with something to add to the flat. I was living a busy and interesting life in London and was very happy with it. The Hilton Gravel cheque represented over 200 times my yearly income and I simply had no clue what it really meant.

Many years later Nicky said that he thought that our father's total lack of advice, which he didn't need but I certainly did, was due to his great frustration of having spent the best two decades of his life working in a boring job for an autocratic father due to post-war lack of funds and opportunities, and since we now had masses of both, he wanted to see what we would make of the freedom he never had. I have never been good at taking advice, while very good at giving it to others, but I think some sort of direction would have helped, for within 25 years all the money had gone – 'lost, stolen or strayed' – and I was in debt. Having to start again from scratch approaching fifty years of age proved to be beneficial, but it didn't seem so at the time. I can certainly understand my father's attitude as he was as creative as he was charming and, while living well in Derbyshire, he was not always happy. My mother told me that, in hindsight, they should never have accepted Grandpa Spurrier's offer, should have moved back to London, made do with whatever, sent us to Westminster instead of Rugby, visiting Derbyshire regularly as they knew they would end up at Marston by inheritance, and it would have all worked out. I would have loved Westminster and growing up in London, but as it was I was growing up fast and it was to get a little faster.

My social was as busy as ever and my ASI (abnormal social intake) as high as ever, which didn't bother me as I thought it was fun and was very fit so didn't get hangovers, but it began to annoy a few friends. One of these was Arabella von Hoffmannstahl, whose grandfather Hugo von Hoffmannstahl had written many of Richard Strauss's libretti. They lived in a marvellous house on the corner of Connaught Square near Marble Arch, not my usual patch but well worth it for the sophisticated get togethers with the 'gilded youth' that I was beginning to get to know. For some time I had been amusing myself by making up limericks, a five line rhyme popularised by Edward Lear.

Here is a limerick I made up for Arabella:

> Arabella von Hoffmannstahl
> Was heard at a party to snahl
> 'That Spurrier boy
> is beginning to cloy,
> Getrunket ist er jedes mahl.' (He's drunk every time)

We remained friends and life went on.

At Christopher's what I enjoyed most was the bottling, which was directly from the cask through a two-spout spigot into bottles which were taken away in a 24 bottle sort of wheelbarrow to be corked. The barrels, containing 61 dozen from Bordeaux and Burgundy up to the 55 dozen 'pipes' of Port, were allowed to rest until they 'fell bright'. Victorian fathers used to 'lay down' a full pipe of Port for their sons, even for godsons. When Nicky had a son named Edward in 1964, I bought for him, bottled at the château, a full barrel of Château Beauséjour-Fagouet, a 1st Growth Saint Emilion, but when Edward's first son was born, all I could come up with was a case of the 2nd Growth Saint Julien Château Ducru-Beaucaillou, a comment as much on the rising price of Bordeaux as on my declining fortune.

'English bottling', as it was known, was of the highest quality, in most cases superior to the Bordeaux châteaux's own efforts. Château Lafite-Rothschild 1953 was bottled over a 9-month period, the workers turning to this when there was no work in the vineyards or it was raining. The corks especially, bought directly from Portugal, were superb, the best being known as 'full long', two and a half inches in length, and we triple-washed them, once in hot water, again in cold and once again in wine. Corking was done by hand and the better, smoother end of the cork was selected to be in touch with the wine. The care and precision of the bottling and corking regime stayed with me a long time.

Christopher's had a good reputation for the claret they bottled, but perhaps not up to that of their Saint James's neighbours Berry Brothers & Rudd or Justerini & Brooks. In the City of London Coates and Corney & Barrow were very highly regarded and a friend of my father's introduced me to Mr Harcourt of the Army & Navy Stores in Victoria from whom, once I began to collect wine seriously from 1966, I bought several cases of 1959s and 1961s. There was also Patens of Peterborough, where Harry Paten had a fine palate and refused to buy wines that were not up to his high standards, and of course Bristol, the original port to which barrels of Bordeaux were shipped from the 1300s, was famous for Averys and Harveys. Then, of course, there was The Wine Society, or to give it is full name The International Exhibition Cooperative Wine Society. This was founded in 1874 to supply wines and spirits to the professional middle classes, Berry Bros, Corneys and J&B having cornered the upper classes. As a cooperative, the members owned the company and any profits were re-invested for their benefit. They published fully annotated wine lists four times a year, regularly sent out special offers and I learnt almost as much from these as from the books I could get my hands on. They are unchanged today, just bigger and better and I have never had a bad bottle from them over more than five decades. In later years people often asked me how they should go about buying wine and my reply was always the same: 'Find a wine merchant you can trust'. Today is a golden age for every kind of wine drinker, but this rule remains valid. The Wine Society remains a beacon.

The summer holidays arrived and for some time I had had a new car, a convertible Triumph Herald that was fun, sporty and quite unthreatening and I set off for the allowed two weeks with Christopher Powell-Brett, a friend from Rugby at whose wedding the following year I would be best man. We toured the wine regions of France – Chablis, the Beaujolais, down to Provence and across into northern to Pamplona and San

Sebastian, then back via Bordeaux. There were no real wine tastings, but I began to pay attention to what we drank along the way. When asked what the difference is between tasting and drinking, my reply is simple: 'Paying attention.' Tommy Layton's *Wine Primers* gave one the information, but it took Michael Broadbent (whose first wine trade job was with Tommy Layton) to describe the whys and wherefores of tasting in his seminal book *Wine Tasting*. Over the years I have taught myself how to look at art, but it was this book that taught me how and why to taste wine. Even with long stints as a merchant, the focus of my life in wine has been education and communication and it is true to say that without Michael Broadbent's *Wine Tasting* there would have been no *Académie du Vin*, France's first private school which I created in late 1972, certainly no Christie's Wine Course which Michael asked me to set up and where we taught from 1982 to 2012, and probably I would not be the current President of the Wine & Spirit Education Trust (WSET) – Michael was of course the first in 2005 – whose 90,000 students world-wide testify to the value of wine education.

Back at the Hollen Street cellars in September, Christopher's had a surprise for me: I was to be sent – at my own expense – to Burgundy for a week and then on to Champagne for another week to work in the cellars there at vintage time. For Burgundy the choice was the *négociant* Liger-Belair in Nuits-Saint-Georges. I booked myself into the Hôtel de la Côte d'Or less than a hundred yards away that had the best restaurant in town where I took my *en demi-pension* dinners. The Liger-Belairs were local aristocrats and two of the *Monsieur le comte's* grandsons have re-blazoned the family name with parcels of inherited vineyards and much more imagination, but in the mid 1960s the company was coasting along as so many were at that time. On my first day in the cellars I heard a succession of muffled booms, which turned out to be cannons firing buckshot into the heavy clouds to break up the potential hail that was forming, turning it into heavy rain. Just as well and Burgundy enjoyed a wonderful 1964 vintage, the better wines still good today. I have little recall of what I actually did, but it was all new and all real. After work I jumped into my Triumph Herald and drove along the *route du vin* passing through villages whose names – Vosne-Romanée, Chambolle-Musigny, Gevrey-Chambertin – I had only previously seen in books.

Then it was off north to Champagne, where I was privileged to be staying at Moët et Chandon's Château de Saran on the hillside vineyards outside their huge headquarters in Epernay. At vintage time the château had a constant flow of visitors, both trade and social, and the social side was managed by Lady Moyra Campbell, a consummate hostess. I was lodged in one of the maid's rooms under the rafters and of course seated 'below the salt' at dinner, but nothing could beat this first experience of the true *vie du château*. Two of the guests were wine-loving members of the House of Lords, who on hearing that I would be spending three months in Bordeaux early the following year, said in unison that I should 'stay at Madame Duret's, bang in the centre.' Madame Duret and her husband Paul accepted trainees from the classic English wine merchants, as did Madame Grès, the Durets being the tops, of which more later. There was so much to learn in Champagne, the vineyards, the Champagne method, the value that the main Houses, who were known as *Les Grandes Marques* put on their individual style of wine and the huge stocks in the kilometres of cellars that they needed to keep it that way, and I was lucky enough to be told to go to Reims to visit Ruinart, a small Champagne company that actually pre-dated Moët et Chandon, so of course they had to buy it. It was run by a charming man named Bunny d'Ayala and after a tour and a tasting he suggested lunch at a place he liked outside the city and seeing my open top car, suggested I drive him there as it was a sunny day. I had been having problems on the way there, no fluidity of movement, which was obvious as soon as we set off. *'Mon cher, vous avez un gicleur bouché'* (a blocked carburettor, news to me as I didn't even know where it was) and Monsieur d'Ayala jumped out, removed it, blowing into it and cleaning it further with his handkerchief and, after giving him time to wash his hands, off we went as smooth as silk. Apparently he liked tinkering with cars and told me that his sister was married to the millionaire Nubar Gulbenkian, owner of many splendid cars and when staying with them in England spent as much time as was polite with the mechanics. I was beginning to learn that the wine people were just as interesting as the product they made. Many years later I came to the conclusion that wine was the 'Three Ps' — the Place, the People and the Product. Vineyards anywhere in the world are nice to look at and to walk through, the People who tend them, own them and make wine from their grapes are generally nice people and if they are not they will not make good wine, which means that the Product at whatever level is generally good. In life this doesn't happen very often.

Bella had gone to Oxford in September to get some A Levels. She had left the girls' school Heathfield at 16 to 'finish' for a year in Paris. Heathfield was at that time fashionable but not academic as girls were supposed to marry well and not work. When Vivien Clore, daughter of the tycoon Sir Charles Clore, got a scholarship to Oxford, the whole school was given a day's holiday. Bella realised she needed some more structured learning and we still saw each other when she was in London. Work at Christopher's went on as usual, leading up to the Christmas rush after which I knew I had only one month to go before leaving for what was to become an eight month odyssey being taken on by their main suppliers across France, Germany, Spain and Portugal, Italy still not being a contender. Bella and I were able to spend a few days together before I set off in early February to cross the channel into France. That evening I spent the night in Normandy at a comfortable hotel with a good restaurant, sending a postcard to Bella the following morning with the menu and wines and signing off 'I miss you, but no doubt I will get over it'. I don't think she appreciated the irony. Three years later, almost to the day, we crossed the channel together in two first class sleeping compartments on the Golden Arrow – 'one to be sick in and one to be in afterwards' advised my father and he was correct – on the day of our marriage for a new life in France.

4. Living the Trade

After a year of indented, if informative, labour under the Taylors in Hollen Street, I had decided to make it plain to each and every one of Christopher's principals, as their major suppliers were called, that I was with them to learn as much as possible and since this would be a privilege, I would not expect to be paid. This proved to be a sensible move, for while working normal hours in the cellars, on the bottling line or whatever, I was often called to set up the room and glasses for their clients' tastings and allowed to taste the wines while clearing up. Sometimes I was asked to lunch at the Bordeaux headquarters or at one of their châteaux, something that my fellow *stagières,* as we trainees were known, were not, as they were toiling away earning their keep.

To support myself over the projected eight months away, I took out a Letter of Credit with Lloyds Bank for £2,000. This was a splendid document of Victorian origin of several pages with which, if taken to a bank with passport identification, I could draw down as much or as little as I needed up to the limit of £2,000. Heaven knows how the tiny banks in Yugoslavia or Greece ever got paid back by Lloyds, but they all went along with it In the 1950s up to the early 1960s there was a limited £50 allowance that a British adult could take abroad on their holiday. If they were accompanied by children, each child could take an additional £25. This was part of the reason why my parents regularly took Nicky and me abroad with them on a sort of 'rent a child' basis. On our first trip to Paris they stayed in the Hôtel George V and we in the Pension George V, usually reserved for servants and chauffeurs, round the corner. The first time I went to Paris on my own was in 1958, when the 'old Francs', at 100:1 to the new Francs, were still the currency. My single room at the Hôtel du Nord, opposite the station, was 900 Francs, about 17 shillings, worth about 70p today. Even in 1965 the set menu at the two Michelin star restaurant Hiély-Lucullus in Avignon was 12 Francs (19 shillings), 3 Francs extra if one took 'Le Gigot des Alpilles'. Certainly £2,000 was a very nice sum; eight marvellous months on the road saw it used up.

Thanks to my grand fellow guests at Château de Saran the previous

October, I had already got myself accepted by Madame Duret for my three months in Bordeaux. The Durets lived in a classic double-fronted town house with a substantial lower ground floor which housed the kitchen, pantry, laundry, cellars and all the necessary spaces that allowed a smooth existence, managed by the charming, yet formidable Madeleine Duret. Her husband Paul was half English and a substantial size, taking up every inch of his armchair to the left of the fireplace in their double drawing room, the latter part being the dining room, very much the centre of daily life. They only rented out two rooms, both large and airy on the top floor, for they ran a small olive oil and vinegar business and I had already recognised the Duret name on such bottles in the Wine Society's list. Paul was also Honorary Consul for Bolivia, and the Bolivian flag was raised from time to time. The house was bang in the centre, just behind the elegant 18th century Allées de Tourny in the Rue Jean-Jacques Rousseau, which ended fifty metres later at an intersection of five streets called La Place des Grandes Hommes, which housed a daily market offering a cornucopia of produce from the Gironde Department and beyond. The Durets' table was recognised across the city for its quality, which probably accounted for Paul Duret's splendid physique, Madeleine Duret knowing every single stall holder at the market by name. Many times I helped her with the shopping, learning as I went along. Unlike the famous cuisines of Normandy, Burgundy and the Loire Valley, which are based on butter, or those of Provence which is based on oil, both with an extraordinary range of local foods from the fields and the farms, the Bordeaux cuisine was relatively plain with few richly-sauced dishes.

Bordeaux is France's finest 18th century city. Known as Burdiglia under the Roman occupation it was already a trading port, the Garonne and Dordogne rivers joining there on their way to the sea 100 kilometres further north to form the wide Gironde Estuary. By the middle of the 16th century wine was being exported to Bristol, London and Edinburgh as well as to Holland and northern Europe. Both commercial and residential life was firmly based on the river's left bank and during the century that followed prosperity allowed the city to be transformed, using the golden colour limestone that for centuries had been excavated below the town and the vineyards of Saint-Emilion, from the magnificent Place de la Bourse, one of the grandest and most harmonious squares in Europe, along the quays to end with Les Quais des Chartrons, whose classical facades housed the offices and vast 'chais' as the barrel cellars were called, the level of the water table preventing the construction of true underground cellars or 'caves', of the wine merchants, who were known as 'Les Chartronnais'. The city is now totally renovated, thanks first to Jacques Chaban-Delmas from the late 1970s and over the past decade to Alain Juppé, two Prime Ministers of France, but in the mid-1960s the glorious golden facades were mostly blackened from soot and general detritus, while commerce went on behind closed doors.

During my time in Bordeaux the doors through which I was privileged to pass were those of the top four merchants: Calvet, Cruse, Cordier and de Luze, all still in family hands then, not a single one remaining now. The *négociants*, from the verb to negotiate, were known collectively and still are as 'La Place de Bordeaux' (a medieval selling system in Bordeaux) and controlled the Bordeaux wine market. The 'châteaux' or producers, even the grandest, had little say in the pricing and marketing of their wines until the watershed 1982 vintage, the balance of power only, and only for the hundred or so best names, turning in their favour from the 2000 vintage. The Bordeaux wine trade has experienced several periods of 'boom and bust', the 1920s being the former, the 1930s with 1934 being the only good vintage, very much the latter and during this decade many estates gave up the expense of producing wine. The run of superb post-war vintages – 1945, 1947, 1948, 1949, even 1950 – gave the region back its reputation, but the money that had begun to find its way back to the châteaux vanished again with the wipe-out vintages of 1954, 1956 and 1958. The 1960s were no better with 1963, 1965 and 1968 suffering the same fate and 1967 (described by Paton's of Peterborough as 'hard, we did not buy') and 1969 not being up to much, so it was only in the 1970s that things improved for the producers. The château I used to visit very often from this first time in Bordeaux was Langoa-Barton in the Médoc's Saint-Julien, a beautiful 1750s 'Chartreuse Style' house that Anglo-Irish merchant Hugh Barton had purchased in 1821, five years before he purchased one third of the historic Léoville estate that was re-named Léoville-Barton. During the 1971 vintage the owner Ronald Barton said that 'thanks to the 1970 vintage we were able to repair the roof on the château and perhaps thanks to 1971 we will be able to repair the roof on the *chai* (an over ground cellar).' Three decades later with many of the surrounding châteaux in full expansion mode, I asked his nephew Anthony, who had taken over in 1982, why so many new cellars were being built if the wines were so easy to sell, to hear the reply 'Perhaps to store the money.' Times had certainly changed.

Back in the mid-1960s the merchants ruled the roost. Wines from the previous year were tasted and assessed in March or April, the merchants setting the price they were prepared to pay, the châteaux meekly accepting since this would give them enough cash to pay the winter bills and to get through to the next harvest. This system was known as selling *en primeur*, since the wines would not be bottled for 12 months or more. The Bordeaux merchants offered the wines once in bottle to their importers up until the early 1980s when they too were offered the opportunity for such purchases, the importers adding a small margin and passing the same opportunity to their customers. Thus began the massive and ultimately greedily speculative *en primeur* Bordeaux market that reached its peak both in prices and volume during the 2011 summer with the very good but over-priced châteaux 2010s. China was one of the largest buyers this time and when six months later they saw prices beginning to go down not up as they had been told, they simply cancelled their orders, causing the merry-go-round to grind to a halt. This and the unexciting 2011, 2012 and 2013 vintages saw prices decline further, to begin a slow but sure rise from the very attractive 2014 and really excellent 2015 and 2016. Everyone hopes that the Bordeaux bubble will not again burst, but knowing the region's commercial history that is not guaranteed.

Such was the tightness of cash flow in the mid 1960s, there was even a *pré-primeur* method of sale before the harvest had even begun, known as *sur souches,* the wines being offered from mid-June at a time when the quantity of the coming vintage could, failing disaster, be seen but not, of course, the quanlity. Back in London the following year with money at my disposal, I looked into this with the merchant Borie-Manoux, wines from good middle of the road châteaux being offered in lots of a single *tonneau* – four barrels or 1200 bottles – at derisory prices. I ended up buying from ten individual châteaux, paying for these potential 120,000 bottles the following month to receive a post-vintage telephone call from Borie-Manoux's Emile Castéja to say 'Steven, you are a lucky gambler.' This system was banned the following year, but not before it forced the sale of Château La Lagune, a well-regarded 4th Growth Médoc, whose vineyard was ravaged by a pre-harvest hailstorm, causing a production of less wine than had been sold three months previously.

This was all in the future, as I was a new boy to everything in Bordeaux that I had not been able to glean from books and while the commercial side of things slowly revealed itself, the well-structured social side was evident from the start. My first two jobs – de Luze and Cruse – were on the Quai des Chartrons, the third with Calvet just around the corner on the Cours du Médoc, and the fourth with Cordier, relative newcomers from the 1900s, up nearer the train station. All four merchants owned wine-producing châteaux, Cordier owning the most, but owning and trading stock was the principal business. The *chais* (cellars) were simply huge, very wide and almost 100 metres long with the standard 225 litre oak barrels stacked three or four high. Only the châteaux classified as First Growths in the 1855 Classification – Haut-Brion in the northern Graves, Margaux, Latour and Lafite-Rothschild in the Médoc, along with top Second Growth Mouton-Rothschild – bottled their entire production at the château, so the volume coming into the merchants' *chais* was immense and cellar work never stopped. The de Luze family owned an estate called Paveil de Luze in the southern Médoc north of Margaux, and their cousins the comtes du Vivier owned the rather larger Château de Malleret nearby. I got to know Geoffroy de Luze a little better in the early 1970s once I had moved to Paris and he had translated Michael Broadbent's seminal book *Wine Tasting*. I had heard that the du Viviers had the only swimming pool in the Médoc but I only got to swim in it a few years later. Despite all the money, swimming pools are still not common on Bordeaux estates, being considered a little 'flash' and for keen swimmers the Atlantic with its marvellous beaches was only 30 minutes away to the west, and just 70 kilometres to the south was the fashionable resort Arcachon and the charmingly less grand Cap Ferret. Alexis Lichine probably had the Médoc's second pool at Lascombes, which I very much enjoyed when taking tour groups to stay there when it was owned by the British Bass Charrington group. In the early 2000s Lascombes was sold to some American investors and the pool disappeared. Meeting one of the new owners shortly after, I said that this was a great pity, as if the water was temperate in September, it boded well for the vintage, and if not, not. He brushed me off by saying that his technicians had more exact means of determining quality.

I have no real memories of my time at de Luze, except that I liked being there. Both families are still very much involved in wine, Geoffroy de Luze's son Frédéric being, until his early death in 2016, President of the

Union des Crus Bourgeois, and Armand du Vivier running the expanded de Malleret. The Cruses, however, definitely made their mark. Of Dutch origin, the Cruse business was the largest of les Chartronnais and, although charmingly-mannered, they knew it and made sure others did as well. They owned two very prestigious châteaux in the Médoc – Château d'Issan, a 15th century moated castle with a fine history, a Third Growth Margaux, still the home to Lionel Cruse, and the Fifth Growth Pontet-Canet in Pauillac, where I met Tommy Layton a few years later. It was here that I helped set up the tastings for clients and I remember a lunch at Pontet-Canet over which the merits of their 1928 and 1929 were discussed before moving onto Margaux 1900. Disaster befell the Cruses in 1972 as a result of what would have been a normal tax inspection. Wine and tax have always been closely linked in France and since it was Bordeaux's biggest employer and biggest earner, the officials from the 'services des fraudes' used to pay regular visits to châteaux and merchants big and small to make sure everything was in order. In those days, since very little wine was bottled at the châteaux and was thus of guaranteed origin, a little blending went on to 'improve' what eventually went into the bottle. The tax inspectors were not venal and usually contended themselves with an overview, if something wrong was found, the wine was destroyed and a fine had to be paid. Their visits were never announced in advance and one day they rang the bell at the Cruse headquarters on the Quai des Chartrons to be told that everyone was too busy to see them, that it was nearly lunchtime and that they should return after lunch and, by the way, use the trademen's, entrance a few doors along. Return after lunch they did, but this time with the police, who imposed a restraining order on the entire management prior to a thorough investigation of their books. What they found was a massive, though in terms of what went into the bottle quite acceptable, fraud.

The base of the Bordeaux quality pyramid was the simple appellation Bordeaux. Bordeaux Superior had to be red, but Bordeaux covered both white and red wines. After the war there was considerable replanting of the vast stretch of vineyards that lay between the Garonne and Dordogne rivers known as 'Entre-deux-Mers' which was mostly with white grapes as that was what had been there in the past. By the early 1960s there was huge over-supply of these nice but light wines and they were sold off in bulk below cost of production, carrying the appellation Bordeaux. At the same time there was vast over-production of sturdy red wine from the Languedoc-Roussillon departments, known as 'Le Midi', and during the next decade over 100,000 hectares would be ripped up. Cruse bought industrial quantities of the unsaleable white, shipping it as 'Vin de Table' to Germany to be made into the cheap sparkling Sekt, while retaining the right to sell the same volume of Bordeaux. Then they bought industrial quantities of honest quality red wine from the Midi, made a pleasant blend with the Bordeaux red wines they held in stock, using the official paper-work to sell it as (red) Bordeaux. In their role as *négociants* or merchant traders, the Cruses took up vast stocks of unsaleable white wine which was then disposed of at a loss, bought vast stocks of unsaleable red, blended it with the real thing and sold it at a profit. This was sensible and beneficial all round, but it was also illegal.

The tax departments in France, as I was to experience myself in the late 1980s were supposed by the French Finance Ministry to make a profit by uncovering such loopholes and the Bordeaux authorities, influenced certainly by their haughty reception and the power of the Cruse family, simply 'threw the book' at them, creating one of the biggest scandals Bordeaux has ever known. In 1974 Classed Growths Pontet-Canet and Château Lafon-Rochet had to be sold to their Tesseron cousins from Cognac; one family member threw himself into the Garonne river from the bridge across the street from their grand offices in shame, and, while the family fought for and regained respect, the company was broken up and sold.

While the Cruses created their own fraud, Cordier who I worked for later, might be said to have had fraud thrust upon them by Christopher's themselves. Christopher's had a small market for Graves Superieur, a semi-sweet white wine made in the southern part of the Graves region, an appellation which most producers by the mid 1960s had abandoned in favour of the dry style. Cordier was the supplier and the annual order had come in but there was no stock available. I was spending a few days in the Cordier laboratory where every single element in wine is tested and the sales team passed the problem to the technicians, who quickly came up with a solution: they had a stock of red Graves so a bottle was ordered up, the wine put through a charcoal filter to remove the colour, filtered again to remove the tannins, white wine flavours were added, sweetening and a little more alcohol to make it richer and finally colour to match the pale gold of the previous year's sample. After this experiment I was offered a glass of each to compare and there wasn't much between them, so off it went.

Cordier owned a fine range of châteaux: Gruaud-Larose and Talbot in Saint-Julien, Meyney in Saint-Estèphe, Clos des Jacobins in Saint-Emilion and Lafaurie-Peyraguey in Sauternes as well as many others in minor appellations, and I was given my first experience of mini 'vertical tastings' of these, a few vintages of each wine tasted young to old, a 'horizontal tasting' being of many wines all from the same vintage. The Cordiers were not members of 'l'Aristocratie du Bouchon – Aristocrats of the Cork' like the de Luzes and the du Viviers, but they were very outward looking and I learnt a lot.

Before my time at Cordier I had moved to Calvet, second in the Bordeaux rankings after Cruse. The Calvets came from the Auvergne in the centre of France, known for the hard-headed approach to money of its mainly farming community. An early Calvet would have introduced the red wine from nearby Hermitage in the northern Rhône to Bordeaux, where it was used during most of the 19th century to 'improve' even the wines of the finest châteaux in weaker years, the Bordeaux merchants outbidding others to obtain the best barrels. In the 1880s it was not uncommon to see on a wine list Margaux-Hermitage selling at a premium to Margaux itself. The Calvets were committed wine merchants and had exclusive rights to many châteaux, especially around Saint-Emilion on the Right Bank, the feather in their cap being Cheval-Blanc. Between the châteaux and the merchants were the 'courtiers' or brokers, who visited all the estates, assessing the vintage, collecting samples and receiving a small commission from both sides if the deal went through for their advice on what price to charge and pay. The brokers had been an integral part of the Bordeaux wine business for centuries and were respected as the essential middlemen. Calvet sent me off for several trips with one of their brokers who took me behind the scenes to very varied estates on the Right Bank or the Libournais as it was known after the city-port of Libourne, never missing a lunch there at his favourite restaurant at the Hotel Robin in front of the train station. The Robin sisters still owned Lafleur in Pomerol and had also part-owned its nearest rival Pétrus until a hard-fought purchase by Jean-Pierre Moueix (another Auvergnat family) in the 1950s, but in those days the restaurant made more money.

Station Hotels, *Hôtels de la Gare*, were mostly a sure bet in those days, for few of the commercial travellers could afford cars, French train links were excellent, so this was where they ate and slept and high standards in the kitchen kept them coming back. I used to seek them out and some were famous for their wine lists as well as the food, the most memorable being the Hotel de la Gare at Montbard in northern Burgundy. The chef had two Michelin stars and he had cooked for many years on the great French liner S.S. *Normandie* and his cellar matched the clientele he had been accustomed to. At the end of our first married year in Provence, Bella and I were driving to England for Christmas and stopped there on the way up. The red wine I chose was Chambolle-Musigny Les Amoureuses 1934 from Domaine comte de Vogüé which was, as expected, magnificent. Towards the end of dinner Bella briefly left the table and, my own glass being long empty, I finished the sip left in hers. This has never been forgotten and Bella has not allowed it to re-occur.

Jacques Calvet, the elderly (to me) doyen of the family invited me to his fine house in the 18th century centre of Bordeaux which was full of the most wonderful furniture and paintings and seeing my admiration told me of a single street near the Musée de Beaux Arts where all the good antique shops were. These were fascinating to visit and while I was not antique-shopping on the first few months of my tour, I did buy a pair of Louis XV silver candle-sticks and showed them to Jacques Calvet who nodded his approval and asked me what I had paid for them. I told him and he put a short note in an envelope to give to the dealer on my next visit. Thinking it was just a word of greeting from a very busy man, I presented it sometime later and the dealer smiled and gave me a few banknotes. It appeared that Monsieur Calvet had told him I had been over-charged, his connoisseur's eye and Auvergnat spirit coming to the fore. The Calvet brand was very strong in Britain and its neck label, with an eagle in the centre, recognisably elegant. One evening on my return a friend and I had reserved a front table for dinner at the Savoy Hotel to watch the performance of the new younger-than-us singing star from Paris, Françoise Hardy. I ordered the wine, Château Batailley 1948 bottled and shipped by Calvet and asked my friend what he thought of it. 'It's a Calvet' he replied 'and very good, too.'

Life at the Durets was wonderful. My co-lodger, Simon Pilkington from the British glass making family, was very nice and the crowd –

James Radcliffe, Richard Raynsford and Julian Tregoning - two dozen blocks away at Madame Grey's, were good fun. James had preceded me as a trainee at Christopher's, Richard was a recent intake and Julian gave up wine fairly quickly to go into the City and we are friends to this day. I was the only one with a car, my convertible Triumph Herald having acquired the nickname 'La Petite' as she often struggled to accommodate the four of us. We had our weekends free and while it was too cold for the beach, Bordeaux had a race track and 'Les Chartronnais' managed to get a cricket team together to play Les Anglais around Easter time. The Durets advised me on the regional restaurants, including one that in season served 'les petits oiseaux', such as thrush and the especially rare ortolan, the favourite dish of President Francois Mitterand, that was served in a bowl and had to be crunched up whole (they were indeed 'petit') in the mouth, bones and all with a large napkin over one's head to capture the incredible aromas and flavours. My favourite place for Sunday lunch was Robinson, on the right bank of the Garonne in a village called Quinsac, known for its dark-coloured rosé. Large, cheerful and family-run as most places seemed to be in those days, Richard Raynsford and I set off one sunny spring day to have lunch on the terrace beside the river, an aperitif, a bottle of white and a bottle of red slipping down with ease, to climb back into 'La Petite' with her top down for a tour of the Entre-deux-Mers. I remember going fast up a hill and turning to say something to Richard to see horror on his face, for I was driving off the road into a churchyard and we ended up smashed into a grave stone. My attempt to hurl myself clear of the windscreen was unsuccessful and the next thing I knew I was on the grass, bleeding profusely from above my left eye, surrounded by small children who had been at Sunday School and their priest, who immediately took control. By unimaginable good fortune there was a nunnery a few kilometres away and I was taken straight to the Sisters of Mercy (Richard had to stay out-side) the wound being cleaned, stitched up and after a little rest I emerged with a fine linen bandage over the left side of my face.

Instructions had been given to tow my car out of the churchyard to a Bordeaux garage and Richard and I took a taxi back to Bordeaux. I recounted, with some embarrassment, the story to Paul and Madeleine Duret who immediately made an appointment for me the following day at their local clinic. Here the bandage was taken off, the examining spe-cialist remarking that he could not have done a better job himself, and

I was wrapped up again for a slow but sure reparation. Today there remains a faint one inch scar just above my left eyebrow. I could have been so, so much worse, but luck was on my side that year.

My next 'stage' as we *stagiaires* described our various traineeships, was at the Cognac house of Delamain in the tiny town of Jarnac in the Charente Département, recently much more famous as the birthplace of President Mitterand. The city of Angoulême was on the way and I remember going down a steep hill and braking slightly to slow down with no effect, immediately crashing the gears into second, grabbing the hand break and ignoring the honking horns behind me. At the bottom I found a garage onto whose forecourt I rolled to present them with the problem. One look under the bonnet showed that the brakes had completely failed, causing the technician to give me a questioning look and ask 'You weren't afraid of dying?' Later than expected I checked into the charmingly simple Hotel de France where I was to spend a quiet week compared to Bordeaux. The following morning I presented myself at the Delamain offices and was taken across the courtyard to the office of the elderly Jean Delamain. As he got up from behind his desk to say hello, I noticed behind him a striking painting by the great Fauvist Belgian artist Maurice de Vlaminck and exclaimed 'Quel beau Vlaminck!' before shaking his outstretched hand. He smiled and said that he hoped I would admire his Cognacs as much as his painting. I had recognised the Vlaminck, since leaving Rugby I was in London looking round the galleries in Cork Street and was struck by two framed Vlaminck lithographs and although I had a cheque book to pay for them, the gallery told me they could not do business with 'minors' and since I was under 18, they made the bill out in my father's name. The holidays before I had attended an auction at Sotheby's and bid for a fine print by George Stubbs of a horse and groom. Thus the first piece of art I ever bought showed respect for the past and the second two pieces perhaps a need for adventure. I have kept both these characteristics as well as the pictures themselves.

Delamain was a small company specialising in purchasing, ageing and blending Cognacs from the two best sub-regions that Grande and Petite Champagne, the other three being Fins Bois, Bons Bois and Borderies, their famous brand called Pale and Dry averaging twenty-five years of age. It is still one of Cognac's finest houses, now with a majority investment by Champagne Bollinger, thanks in part to my suggesting them to François

Sauzet one of the family shareholders who told me in the 1980s that the company was looking for outside investment from like-minded people. I had met François at that time when he was a gangly teenager and his father was Delamain's general manager and we met again when I took over a small wine shop in the centre of Paris in early 1971 along with his striking Czech girlfriend and later wife, Anne, who is a well-known artist on the Paris scene whose work I have managed to buy over the years. The Master Blender working under Monsieur Delamain was Alain Brastaad of Dutch origin whose family had long been in the Cognac business and had married into the family. A few years older than me, Alain had a passion for visiting Romanesque churches for which the Charente is famous as it is on the road from the north for pilgrims walking to Santiago de Compostella in Galicia, which I was beginning to share.

My short time at Delamain, a total contrast to the 'haut commerce' of Bordeaux, was spent carefully labelling the precious bottles, all hand-bottled and slowly polished dry, in the morning, learning to 'nose' the different barrels and blends in progress before lunch and then visiting the small estates who supplied the young spirit from their copper stills in the afternoon. The other, larger Cognac house in Jarnac was Hine, well-known in England as the founder originated from Beaminster in Dorset, a few miles from our own house. Bernard Hine retired only last year. Of course I went to Cognac itself to visit Hennessy, along with Martell and Remy Martin one of the big three, founded in 1765 by James Hennessy, one of the many 'wild geese' like the Bartons and the Lynchs of Bordeaux, who decamped from their native Ireland during the English rule. There were two other trainees there to show me around and a young Hennessy who introduced me to cognac and tonic, the drink they were launching to attract younger drinkers. This was amusing and different from the ubiquitous gin and tonic and for the next two years back in London this was what I ordered in night clubs. Today if I drink spirits as a long drink, apart from one G&T a year to remind me how good this drink is, it is brandy and soda which is both refreshing and can be heavily diluted without completely losing the flavour.

When I was due to leave Jarnac after an inspiring week, taking with me a bottle of their finest blend Vesper, one of the rare Cognacs to carry a vintage, this being the 1920, Monsieur Delamain asked me to lunch. It was just the two of us, his household run by a formidable cook-housekeeper. When she brought the coffee, he asked her to bring the bottle of 1870. She expressed surprise and informed him that his guest was 'far too young for such a treasure.' He insisted and while pouring a little into a small tulip-shaped glass – the large, even small 'balloon' brandy glasses being shunned as vulgar by the classic producers – he told me that the last person he had shared this particular bottle with had been Winston Churchill. Thirty years later I saw a bottle of the 1870 in a Christie's auction and bought it to give to François Sauzet in memory of that moment.

After Cognac I made a brief trip to Anjou in the Loire Valley, visiting Domaine Baumard in the Côteaux-du-Layon region, who were and still are one of the main producers of the sweet Côteaux-du-Layon white wines, made from Chenin Blanc whose natural acidity brought freshness to the finish, and also the richer and much rarer Quarts de Chaume, which in the 18th century had been reserved solely for the Royal Court. My hosts were charming, but it was plain that business was poor, the wines being bottled with high levels of sulphur to stave off oxidation while waiting for a sale. Things are better now though, while the wines of Anjou and neighbouring Touraine are some of the purest 'country wines' of France and very good value, many of the historic estates did not survive.

Then, with the weather getting warmer and La Petite's top down when possible, I set off north to Alsace for a week with Hugel et Fils in the picture postcard wine village of Riquewihr to the east of the river Rhine just north of Colmar. Hugel is still owned and managed by the direct descendants of the founder in 1639 and is perhaps the best known wine name in Alsace, although the Trimbachs in the next door village of Ribeauvillé, were founded in 1626 and are still going strong. Riquewihr with its steep cobbled streets and timber-framed houses rivals Saint-Emilion for France's most popular wine town and its wines, food and people are totally Alsatian, the region having been bounced back and forth between France and Germany over the centuries, while retaining its own characteristics, down to a difficult Germanic dialect. Years later when I was a judge at the Foire de Paris, I often found myself on a table with Alsatians who, when I disagreed with their opinions on a wine, generally finding it less good than they did, broke into 'alsacien' and ignored me completely.

My colleague from Christopher's James Radcliffe had been there the previous year and told me to book into the Hôtel-Restaurant Schmidt half way up the main street, which was good advice all round, with the Hugel offices and cellars just fifty metres further up.

Alsace is a varietal wine in the sense that Vin d'Alsace is the only appellation, the wines labelled with their grape variety and further information according to rising quality. Over time certain villages and sites have singled themselves out and the fifty-one of these have been awarded Grand Cru status and there is now a plan to select a series of Premiers Crus, very much along Burgundian lines. While houses such as Hugel and Trimbach own many vineyards of their own around, as a *négociant* they buy in grapes and unfinished wine from growers, so tend to use words like Réserve and Réserve Personnelle, except where the wine might come from a single vineyard as is the case with Trimbach's Clos Ste Hune. In the mid 1960s, as in Burgundy, it was the *négociants* whose names ruled the market, but now they share this with the individual estates and quality has never been better.

Quality was always at the heart of the great Jean 'Johnny' Hugel, the family's roving ambassador, so well-known and loved in every export market. He oversaw the wines from grape to bottle in the cellars but refused the title of winemaker, saying that such a word did not exist in the French language. Logically it would be *fabricant du vin* or wine fabricator, so he was right and for him œnologue or oenologist hinted at the laboratory. He simply had all the right feelings in his DNA allied to respect for the wine at all moments of its life. Due to the heatwave vintage of 1976 one particular cask was so high in grape sugar that it refused to finish its fermentation. Johnny always wore a hat in the cellar and for 18 months whenever he passed in front of this vat he raised his hat and it eventually complied. Johnny Hugel was almost single-handedly responsible for the 'Selection des Grains Nobles' or SGNs from grapes picked at a concentration far beyond late harvest and by putting the bar higher and higher he ensured that what small quanties of such wines reached the market would be truly great.

The Hugel cellar was lined with tall, narrow vats or 'foudres' of Slavonian oak in which the wines fermented and remained until bottling. This process threw off tartaric acid which solidified itself on the sides of the vats like blocks of sugar, though they were perfectly tasteless. Since the vats could not be moved, this tartaric coating had to be dislodged every few years by sending someone slim enough to ease their way through the very small detachable 'door' and, with a wooden mallet, to bang on the sides which rose to above head height to bring the tartaric crystals down around him. Since the cellars were exclusively male in those days and the Alsatians of impressive size, this usually fell to the trainees, which was sticky work, so thank heavens for the showers in the Hotel Schmidt where I was staying.

I had a marvellous week in Riquewihr, the early May weather was wonderfully sunny – thanks to the Vosges mountains blocking cold and rain from the north east, Colmar is the second driest city in France after Perpignan on the Spanish border – and I managed to get to the local swimming pool most evenings before going on a bar crawl around the 'weinstuben'. The food was pretty solid but the wines made it seem less so. They used to be known as 'wine merchants' wines' as the merchants always bought them, but their customers didn't, so they had to drink them themselves. I became a huge fan of Pinot Blanc d'Alsace and the more complex local variety Pinot Auxerrois or Klevner and when I first thought about planting a vineyard on Bella's farm in Dorset I would have planted this, which would have been another massive financial mistake of the late 1980s, so now I just drink the Alsace version.

Apart from what I had read, Germany and its wines were pretty much unknown to me, so a week with the respected house of Huesgen in the Mosel's charming village of Traben-Trarbach was a revelation. Here again, James Radcliffe had preceded me and lodgings had been arranged for me as for him, with the family of one of the vineyard owners from whom the company bought all the production. Having studied German up to A level standard but with almost no chance to speak it, I was surprised how easy it was, as were my hosts. (In my French oral exam for O level I was asked 'Que fait votre père/what does your father do?' and unable to find the words for the director of transport for a sand and gravel company, I replied 'Hélas, il est mort/alas he's dead.' I was better in French by now.)

Once again, cellar work was much the same, barring the tartrate cleaning, with time on the bottling line, lots of stacking the bottles in huge bins seventy-two across and forty-eight deep, the test of a job well done being if the cellar master could extract a bottle from the middle without the whole bin moving a millimetre, a little time in the laboratory and in the late morning a small tasting. The Huesgen wines were mostly Rieslings, a few Sylvaners and a little sparkling. Dry or 'trocken' wines were not made in the mid 1960s, the entry level being off-dry with no more than 10 degrees of alcohol and 10-15 grams of residual sugar, the alcohol diminishing and the residual sugar rising as the quality rose to Spätlese/late harvest, Auslese/very late harvest, Beerenauslese/very late harvest of individual berries and finally a massively sweet wine of almost treacly textured Trockenbeerenauslese/single raisiny berries. The cellar tastings did not cover the last two, but on the second evening I was taken across to a fine turreted castle to meet Frau Huesgen who welcomed me into a panelled dining room where there was a small table with a white table cloth, a half bottle of wine, a bowl of wild strawberries and a glass. A white-gloved butler poured me a glass and Frau Huesgen said that I should come every evening at 6pm and there would be a different wine and some different berries. So for three more evenings I appeared suitably spruced up to be received by the butler who waited while I tasted and wrote some notes on the very classy wines and went back to my hosts, leaving the rest of the bottle for him.

On the Saturday I was told that Traben-Trarbach was having its early summer wine fair and was packed off with a glass – a small tumbler, not the usual green-stemmed Mosel glass as that would have seemed pretentious – and so attended my first ever wine fair, full of boisterous jollity and friendly cheer and although the road back to my host's house was straight, by late that evening it didn't seem so to me.

My second German 'stage' was in the major city of Worms-am-Rhein at the important company Langenbach, only the historic Deinhard being more important, where one of the trainees I had met at lunch at Pontet-Canet while at Cruse was working and we had agreed to meet up. He had recently got married and was travelling with his wife and tiny baby. He had solved the problem of lodgings by travelling in a very large motorised caravan which he had parked in the well-tended and, being early in the season, fairly empty camping side on the banks of the river Rhein. They invited me over for dinner in the caravan and as I entered I saw the table was laid with the family silver with silver candlesticks and crystal glassware. 'We have so much of this stuff at home' he said 'I just took what I needed.' I think he was going back to work for Justerini & Brooks and would have been quite at home in Saint James's Street.

The wines of the Rheingau are broader and richer than those of the

Mosel and it is even warm enough to make a little red wine, the best coming from Pinot Noir grown around Assmannshausen. Thanks to global warming, careful work in the vineyards and in the cellar, some German Pinot Noirs are now rivalling the finest from Burgundy, both in quality and price, but they were very rare in the mid 1960s. I have few memories of my week at Langenbach apart from the open doors and the learning experience, for I was already looking forward to a quick visit back to England and then up to Stirling for the marriage of my school friend Christopher Powell-Brett to Lorna Dingwall-Main at which I was to be the best man. After Langenbach, La Petite and I went to Orly Airport where I left her, flying to London to spend the first night in my flat for four months and the next but last for another five. Christopher was in training to end up as one of the most respected doctors in London, but still living with his parents in Knightsbridge. He and Lorna were both undecided on where to live post-marriage, so I had offered them free run of my flat until they were settled. From this I was to gain a bonus, for a friend of their's dropped by one evening and on asking how they had found such a nice place, were told it was a friend's flat and he was off touring Europe learning the wine trade. Their guest's mother had recently married Ronald Barton of Château Langoa-Barton, so I was welcomed there on my return to Bordeaux in early October and for many years thereafter.

Back in France driving south from Orly to Beaune I of course stopped off in Chablis, checking into the Hôtel de l'Etoile in the centre of what still felt like a village, old-fashioned, clean and comfortable with polished but creaking floorboards and an unpretentious restaurant which, right up to the late 1970s, had Grands Crus Les Preuses and Le Clos from Domaines Dauvissat and Raveneau at very low prices. Eight years later, having acquired a house in the very north of the Côte d'Or, we always stopped in Chablis to buy provisions for the weekend at a shop in the little square, whose *jambon persillé*, cheese from nearby Epoisses and vine tomatoes I remember to this day. Despite the international recognition of its name, often 'borrowed' by other countries to promote their own wines, Chablis was slow to get back on its feet after the devastating 1956 frost, so severe (as in Saint-Emilion) that the ground was frozen to a depth of many feet, killing the vines stone dead. The following year less than 750 hectares from a possible 6,834 were in production, the post-war recovery having stopped in its tracks. By the mid 1960s things were better, but financially for the *vignerons* not by much. Today prosperity is plain to see – the established Burgundy merchants buying up what they can – but most of the original family names are still there and in my view a Chablis Premier Cru is one of white Burgundy's best values and my cellar is full of it.

My two employers in Beaune were the merchants Joseph Drouhin and Louis Latour, both long-term members of Beaune's elite, which included Albert Bichot, Bouchard Aîné, Bouchard Père et Fils, Chanson and Louis Jadot. Recalling my parents' penchant for stuffing Nicky and me into the top floor 'servants' rooms' in the grand hotels they liked, I booked myself for the time in Beaune at the classic and classy Hôtel de la Poste into a small room tucked under the rafters with the bathroom at the end of the corridor, but with free run of the grand spaces downstairs, as well as being a good address. Early on I met another *stagiaire* and lifelong friend Anthony Hanson, a Master of Wine and early author of the very good *Burgundy*, who was at Bouchard Aîné and living in a small hotel on the way out of town for much the same price. Whereas wine ruled only a part of Bordeaux, it ruled the whole of Beaune. The cellars below the cobbled streets were working cellars and the magnificent 14th century *Hospices de Beaune* or almshouse in the historic centre owned part of its survival to vineyards left to it by benefactors. Now 60 hectares of mostly Grand and Premier Cru vines are sold by auction to great acclaim each year over the third weekend in November that is known as *Les Trois Glorieuses* on the Sunday afternoon.

The *négociants* controlled the market in the same way that *Les Chartonnais* did in Bordeaux, being basically the only clients for the growers' wines in tank or barrel. A handful of top domaines bottled their own wine and Alexis Lichine encouraged this, provided that they sold it to him, but the merchants bought, blended, bottled and sold and for the most part did a very good job. Like Calvet in Bordeaux, it was their name more than that of the *appellation* that the public bought.

Joseph Drouhin had (and still do, much enlarged) 13th century cellars in the oddly named *Rue d'Enfer* (Street of Hell) which contained row after row of 215 litre barrels (the Bordeaux barrel holds 225 litres) of all the Burgundy *appellations* stencilled on their front or head and bin after bin of unlabelled bottles identified by a bin number, which over time acquired a coating of black mushroomy fungus caused by the humidity which was soft and velvety to the touch and generally reckoned to be a good thing.

Managed by the elegantly tall Robert Drouhin, whose father Maurice had been one of the great names in Beaune's history, the company was much admired and remains a beacon for quality in Burgundy. In the 1980s they expanded into Chablis and due to Robert's curiosity were the first French family to plant Pinot Noir in Oregon under the name Domaine Drouhin. For many years now run by his daughter Véronique, this, too, is a quality benchmark. I spent (almost as) much time in the vineyards from the top to bottom of the Côte d'Or, meeting the *vignerons*, pleased in mid June to be looking forward to a good harvest, only to see their hopes dashed by almost constant rain later in the summer. Very few 1965s were good enough for export, 1963 had been just as poor, but 1968 was so bad that annual sale of the *Hospices de Beaune* wines never took place.

Although one of the grand names of Beaune, Louis Latour's working cellars were a little to the south in the village of Pommard and their offices and other cellars at the family-owned Château Corton Grancey, north of the town in Corton, but they, too, had ancient vaulted cellars in the centre of Beaune. Their US importer was Frederick Wildman and Sons and the high spot of my time there was to help set up around a vast round stone table the tasting for the annual visit of Colonel Wildman. I stood in the background listening to the comments and was allowed to taste the wines when he and the directors left for lunch. I also remember Louis Latour Sr (the eldest male of the family is always named Louis) having me to a family lunch and requesting that I help his granddaughter with her English homework. Some free time was spent touring the rich Burgundy countryside and by far the best food to be had was a fifteen minute drive south to Chagny, where the Lameloise family ran a restaurant with one Michelin star, quickly moving to a second and then a third, which they have held for two generations. This was my weekly treat, starting with a *kir* – a dash of *crème de cassis* topped up with Bourgogne Aligote – while reading the menu, half a bottle of white, half a bottle of red and sometimes a *marc de Bourgogne* with the coffee, usually getting change from a 50 (£4) franc note.

Christopher and Lorna Powell-Brett called in on the way back from their honeymoon in Italy, staying in a proper room in the Hôtel de la Poste and we went on the town, not before Christopher had remarked on how much weight I had put on due to the Burgundy cuisine. We made an awful lot of noise in the smart hotel bar on our return and as this was my last night, the hotel was glad to see the back of me.

On the way down to the Rhône Valley, spending time visiting the marvellous churches at Autun, Paray-le-Monial and Tournus, finishing up at the vast Benedictine Abbey of Cluny, I drove through Beaujolais country, but Beaujolais was not highly thought of in England at that time, so I headed south to Lyon, France's second city and a temple of gastronomy. It is said that Lyon is 'watered by three rivers', the Rhône, the Saône and Beaujolais. Certainly there was lots of the latter in the local bistros or *bouchons* as they were called, but I was keen to get on for my final week before a six-week break until starting again in Jerez de la Frontera in southern Spain on 1 September.

My final *stage* was with Jaboulet Aîné in Tain l'Hermitage, then the unquestioned greatest name in the northern Rhône and undergoing a renaissance during the last decade following a purchase by the Frey family who a few years before had bought Château La Lagune in the Médoc. The vineyards of the northern Rhône run 65 kilometres from Vienne to Valance and cover a handful of appellations on both sides of the river as it flows south, of which Hermitage and Côte-Rotie are the most famous, their red wines being made entirely from the Syrah grape. Tain remains pretty much the sleepy town it was then, Tournon across the river being more active, and I had no problem finding the Jaboulet offices and cellars, to be welcomed by Louis Jaboulet. I have always known the patriarchal head of the firm as Oncle Louis, as he was a bachelor and had many nephews one of whom, Gérard, was exactly my age and became a great friend. Bella (who was to join me at the end of the week) referred to him as 'the Elephant' for he was quite broad across the beam and wore baggy grey suits so resembled the back of a pantomime elephant. He was incredibly kind to me, giving me right away a highly-prized set of Larmat maps which showed the entire vineyards of the north and southern Rhône in beautiful detail and telling Gérard to take me up to the steep terraces of the Hermitage Hill before he would introduce me to his wines.

These, when he took me through them vintage by vintage, were a revelation. Hermitage, was bought for high prices during most of the 19th century to bolster up the wines of Bordeaux, but fell completely out of fashion following the devastation of phylloxera in the early 1900s and had not yet recovered. Knowing that I had just been in Burgundy, he told me that his single-vineyard Crozes-Hermitage Domaine de Thalabert sold for the price of a Beaujolais Cru, his Hermitage for a Côtes de Beaune-Village and his iconic Hermitage La Chapelle for that of a Volnay or a Pommard. Today they are justifiably more highly priced, the La Chapelle having become a collector's item. Perhaps there was too much to absorb in Bordeaux and perhaps many of the Burgundies I tasted did not have quite the precision or sense of place that they do today, but I was able to connect immediately with the northern Rhônes (also with Jaboulet's Parallele 45 and Châteauneuf-du-Papes Les Cèdres from the south) and continue connecting ever since.

I told Oncle Louis that my parents had been to a two Michelin star restaurant, the Hôtel du Midi thirty minutes up the hills at Lamastre, and he suggested we go there for lunch. The owner Madame Barratéro was a forceful character and apparently when my father presented himself at the front desk, saying he had parked his car outside, she said that this was not allowed, only to relent when she saw it was a Jensen. Her chef presented a simple menu that didn't change much, as this was a 'destination restaurant' where clients went for the specialities. Our lunch would have been simple, but when I told Oncle Louis that there were two *stagiaire* friends from Bordeaux joining me on Saturday, as well as three charming girls from London, he told Madame Barratéro to reserve us the private room and have the chef prepare his classic menu which was:

Pain d'écrevisses Sauce Cardinale
warm paté of local crayfish with sauce from their pounded shells

Poularde de Bresse en demi-deuil Sauce Albufera
Bresse chicken with slices of black truffle sipped under the skin
and poached in a pig's bladder

Fromages du pays
local cheeses

Vacherin aux fruits rouges
an ice cream cake with raspberrries and strawberries

This was one of the most marvellous meals I had ever had and – because one of the London girls was Bella, with two of her friends from whom she was to separate the following day to spend the rest of the summer with me – so memorable that I asked Michel Roux of London's Le Gavroche to re-create our 40th wedding anniversary in January 2008 for us, our two children and their spouses. Oncle Louis had offered us a bottle of La Chapelle 1961 for the cheese, a wine which has become world-famous which I last saw on the wine list at Hotel Pic in Valence a few years ago at 15,000 euros the bottle. Four decades later I couldn't match this at Le Gavroche, but we did have fine Burgundies from my children's birth years, 1971 and 1973.

The two friends who joined from Bordeaux were Richard Raynsford and Julian Tregoning, who Bella and I were to see later in Venice. In those days, although Bella's parents knew that she and I were seeing a lot of each other, the idea of their daughter travelling across Europe with me would have been unacceptable, so Harriet Pugh and Anne Carey were a front. I had told my father of this, saying that I hoped we would get away with it, but we nearly did not. On our tour we were always in and out of museums and when we arrived in Jerez on September 1st, I collected mail at the Hotel Los Cisnes where we were staying to find a letter from him saying 'the game is up, you were spotted by Bella's cousins in Venice and Madrid, prepare for the worst.' There was nothing to be done and Bella was understandably nervous when she returned later that month, so see her father descending the stairs with a determined look on his face, only to be brushed aside by her beautiful mother who welcomed her saying 'Darling, how sensible to have travelled round Europe with Steven, so much comfortable than with the two girls.'

After that great dinner, we waved goodbye to Tain l'Hermitage and headed south to Avignon where we found a top floor room at the Hôtel de l'Univers with just the minimum facilities but a view, if one stood on a chair, through the skylight over to the Palais des Papes. One evening we dined at Hiély-Lucullus where white and red Châteauneuf-du-Pape *de l'année* was served *en carafe* as it still is in the very good nearby restaurant La Fourcette owned by the same family. We went swimming in the river Gard, diving in from a ledge below the Roman Pont du Gard aqueduct with nobody around; today it is a massive camping groud. Next stop was Aix-en-Provence, passing the beautiful Château Simone, then the sole producer and still the best in the tiny appellation Palette on the right of the N7, and finally on to Nice where we met up with Julian Tregoning and Giles Townsend, who in due course was to be best man at our wedding. Here we stayed in the Old Town near the Flower Market, spending mornings on the pebble beach and discovering the city by night. One evening we passed a noisy bar and walked in only to find it was totally gay. The crowd didn't approve of Bella, but since she had short hair and was very *gamine*, they didn't throw us out and we were considering buying a drink when a powerful looking man with a much younger one in tow brushed past us and, turning to me, said 'Stick around, I'll come back for you later.' We got out fast and in case readers think this story unlikely, Julian reminded me of it only last year.

Bella and I headed off to Italy, spending a few days in Venice and on our last night we were all invited up to the lovely hill town of Asolo where another of the Bordeaux *stagiaire's* family had a villa and the following morning we set off for places virtually unknown.

Passing through Trieste which boasts churches from every religious sect as it was a truly international port, we arrived in Yugoslavia, which was under the firm rule of President Tito. Years later on a visit to taste Slovenian wine, I was to stay in the Presidential Palace, now converted into an hotel called the Villa Bled, sleeping in his personal suite. We drove down the Adriatic coast down to spend a couple of nights in Dubrovnik, passed through Pecs, famous for its inexpensive Riesling, and on down through Skopje and crossing on a car ferry into Greece. From here it was a lovely drive through deserted countryside to Athens and stopping to fill up with petrol we were accosted by a matronly lady with baskets of vegetables and two live chickens who asked to be taken to the city to see her daughter. Most of the way she sang songs in her local dialect and made it plain we should sing her a song. My mind went blank, it was the early days of the Beatles but I couldn't remember a tune, let alone the words, so we ended up singing the hunting song 'D'ye ken John Peel'. Duly satisfied, we carried on in silence, dropping her off in the slightly slummy centre of town. In the 70s we returned to Athens to stay in the Grande Bretagne, the city's grandest hotel, but on this visit it was all a mystery, and we relied, as we had throughout Yugoslavia, on being approached by young men with the proposition 'my friend has good room'. These were always an adventure, generally clean, always charming hosts, but in Athens we ended up in a bunk bed in a room off somebody's kitchen, the advantage being that Mama was a good and generous cook. From Athens we visited Delphi, then Corinth and took the ferry boat from Patras to Bari, Bella was furious with me for taking second class tickets, forcing us to sit up all night with nothing to eat.

Our pattern for the trip was to alternate, where possible, between smart one night and cheap and cheerful the next. Occasionally, in the country side, we slept in the car, which I am not sure Triumph Heralds were designed for. We had pretty adequate things for regular picnics, but no means of keeping the wines cool. I overcame this problem with my next car, upgrading to a convertible Triumph Vitesse, by installing a 'fridge in the boot. In August 1966, driving down from a weekend with my parents to see Bella on her birthday, I had put a bottle of Champagne to cool before setting off. I arrived late afternoon and her father suggested opening a bottle of Champagne to celebrate the birthday before I headed down to London and I said I had had the same idea and had a bottle with me. 'But it won't be cold' – 'it will, sir, as my car's got a 'fridge' – 'Fella's got a *'fridge* in his car!' I was always a touch too modern for Bella's charmingly conservative father.

After freshening up in Bari we drove to Siena and then to Florence, where the time was spent in museums and churches during the day and the trattorias at night, one memorable one being Il Cave in the hills on the way to Fiesole, which we only discovered as we couldn't get into a smarter place we had been told about. A tiny place with a huge terrace above the vineyards, it is now much larger and still going strong.

We were heading to Jerez de la Frontera in the very south of Spain so I could learn something about Sherry and had planned to spend a few days in Saint-Tropez, where a great friend was based during the summer season as he had married the daughter of the owner of Le Papagayo, the hottest night club at the time as well as the entire parking lot on the way into town. They had had a daughter, Véronique, in 1964 and I was her godfather. I had used their address as my first *poste restante* since setting off in February and glancing at the various letters discovered that my stock market dividends had more than kept up with the £2000 letter of credit. Even in August, Saint-Tropez at that time still felt like a village and certainly the locals dominated in *La Place des Lices*, the large open square set back from the port, which was almost entirely given over to the game of *boules* or *pétanques*. I had never seen this game before and was crossing the square to find a ball rolling towards me and several men shouting and waving their hands at me. It crossed my mind that they had lost their ball and wanted it returned, so I picked it up and rolled it back towards them. I was not allowed to walk across the square after that. The fashionable Les Mouscardins at the end of the port was the best place for fish which, if accompanied by Domaine Ott's Blanc de Blancs served in a heavy Burgundy bottle, made for a very good meal.

From Saint-Tropez we drove overnight along the coast to Spain – we often did this to save time as there was so much to see, catching a few hours sleep in La Petite on the way. We crossed the border for a Spanish breakfast of coffee and *churros* which were deep-fried strips of dough with sugar sprinkled on them, much lighter than expected, and headed across country to Madrid for the Prado Museum and a bullfight, before continuing south to Seville where we caught up with friends I had met two years before: John Fulton Short, a fine artist but at that time a professional bullfighter, who had passed his *alternativa* in the Seville ring, moving from *novillero* to *matador* status, and his photographer and writer partner Robert Vavra, both American. We had met in *El Meson*, the busy family restaurant near the bullring and they had recommended a *pensione* in the marvellously rambling Jewish Quarter of whitewashed facades and quiet courtyards, which is where we returned. They lived and had an art gallery nearby and that evening I found myself back in *El Meson*, introducing Bella to *huevos flamencos* and rougher than usual red wine, while they showed me their current project: an illustrated coffee-table size version of the poem written by Federico García Lorca – *A las cinco de la tarde*/At five in the afternoon, the time when all bullfights start and always on time – a lament for the death of the famous matador Ignacio Sánchez Mejías in Seville on 11 August 1934. They were looking for sponsors to make a private printing of just eighty copies and I subscribed for two (one going to our son Christian on his 21st birthday) the other in my bookshelves in London. I brought the dummy of the project to Jerez with me and my employers, the Martinez family, also subscribed. Just last year I showed the book to their great nephew, who remembered seeing it in the family library.

After a marvellous few days in Seville, one of my favourite cities around the world, we arrived in Jerez to spend the first two nights in the Hotel Los Cisnes, the classic and best hotel in town, before having to move to cheaper premises when the Feria Week started on the first Sunday in September. All at once a quite sleepy little town was transformed into a glorious pageant to the history of Andalusia, the horses and the bulls, the handsome boys and pretty girls, the food and sherry. I had already met Beltrán Domecq of the illustrious local family in Bordeaux as we were about the same age — he is now President of the *Regulador de Jerez* and a hugely respected upholder of quality, as was his grandfather José Ignacio Domecq, known as 'The Nose', who was the *Decanter* Man of the Year in 1991 - and seeing him leading the procession on a fine horse wildly impressed me. The Martinez Sherry House was not in the same league as the Domecq or Gonzalez Byass families on the international market, but a fine company with big stocks of old wine in a superb *bodega*, as the sherry above ground cellars were known. Diego Ferguson of Scottish descent who was the director in charge of the blending which is at the heart of sherry's historic and current reputation, introduced me both in the *bodega* and the tasting room to the fabulous range of styles all made from the Palomino grape, from the pale Fino, the darker aged Fino known as Amontillado, the classy Palo Cortado, the richer Olorosos and finally the extra rich Pedro Ximénez, known as PX, from the grape of the same name. He also showed me the Jerezano 'hangover cure', dipping his *venezia* or wine thief deep into a cask of PX in the darkest part of the *bodega*, filling a *copita* and handing it to me with the instructions to hold onto the cask and down it in one. The explosive impact brought stars to my head and tears to my eyes and it worked wonders.

After two days' learning, a visit to the Martinez vineyards was planned and I asked if Bella could come as well. When we got there the vintage was in full swing, the women picking, the men collecting the grapes in large boxes and humping them onto an ox-drawn cart to be taken up to the pressing room. This was too much to resist and I asked the man in charge if he needed a hand and within five minutes I was on the back of the cart, shirt stripped off, down to the vineyards. Bella went back into town and my hosts were visibly surprised, so much so that they telephoned Christopher's to say that it was not expected that one of their trainees should want to join the workers. Christopher's reply was simply that I was unreliable. I did the vintage for three days, Bella dropping me off in the morning and picking me up late afternoon. Throughout our travels, had anyone asked, I always introduced Bella as 'my cousin'. My fellow workers thought she was cute, but were not impressed by how slim she was. The conversation went rather like this: 'She's rather slim, your cousin,' 'Yes.' 'She doesn't have much of a chest.' 'She's only just nineteen.' 'For us,' one said, cupping his hands in front of his own chest, 'we prefer *dos melones!*'

The Martinez family got over their shock of my wish for vineyard work and on the last evening invited Bella and me to join in a magnificent party they were giving for their daughter's 21st birthday, which was a wonderful way to end a magical week.

We had a few days before I had to be in Oporto for the Port harvest and decided to spend them in Lisbon. Reckoning that I had enough funds to see me out, we stayed in a new hotel which had a panoramic restaurant on the 20th floor, not exciting food but a wine list with some very old vintages. Being keen on Spanish Flamenco dance it was natural for us to seek out the best *fado*, the Portuguese national style of song that is beautiful and usually heart-rendingly sad. We had the luck that the great Amalia Rodrigues was appearing in one of the clubs, which was about the equivalent of the Corrida Goyesca (the *matadors* and their equipe all in late 18th century dress) bullfight we had seen earlier in Ronda's Roman arena, a *mano a mano* between Antoñio Bienvenida and Antoñio Ordóñez, where one of the bulls so impressed by its bravery, it was pardoned before the final thrust of the sword, totally and memorably moving. After a final lunch overlooking the city to celebrate that we had had the best time ever, I drove Bella to the airport for her flight back to London and headed up to Oporto.

I had been recommended to stay at the British Club across the river in Vila Nova de Gaia where all the great and small Port Houses or 'Lodges' were. The Port producers' names that are known internationally were and still are mainly of British origin – Cockburn, Croft, Dow, Graham, Taylor – and the splendid 18th century Factory House in Oporto which has a 'double-cube' dining room, one half to dine in and the other side where Port is served (and where I was re-united with Cockburn's 1908) is only open to members from the British family firms. The British Club had a cricket pitch and a wine list that included Château Cheval Blanc 1947, but the streets of Oporto were more fun and two days between the two gave me enough background to take the train up to Pinhão – driving would have taken forever – the little town central to the Douro vineyards, where I was welcomed by Bruce Guimaraens of Fonseca to spend a night before going up to Quinta do Vargellas, owned by Taylor who were the senior partners along with Fonseca. At that time Dick Yeatman – the full name of the company was Taylor, Fladgate and Yeatman and it is now known as The Yeatman Group – was the managing director and his wife Beryl managed the Quinta. While Europe was modernising in the mid 1960s,

Vargellas was not and what electric light there was came from a generator. One took a candle to bed to read by and hot water was brought to me in the mornings to shave. It was like stepping back in time and fitted perfectly with the slowness of the whole process of Port, from the foot-treading of the grapes in the large granite *lagares,* to the slow maturation in oak barrels known as 'pipes' that contained 720 bottles, the selection of a vintage that was bottled in its second year and mature for another fifty, the blending of aged Tawnies and the various other house blends. Dick Yeatman stressed that a great vintage Port should always have 'a touch of green' at the start, the equivalent of tannin in claret. When guests came, vintages were opened but the after dinner Port was usually a 15 year old Tawny OPW, which is still reserved for the Quinta. I was introduced to white Port, Tayor's Chip Dry which they liked to serve iced with a splash of tonic water, and took part in the grape-treading on two evenings to the rhythm of a piano accordion. My days at Vargellas were unforgettable and I have been back often, now under Alistair Robertson and his wife Gillyanne and in full expansion in recent years with their daughter and her husband Adrian Bridge, while Bruce Guimaraens's son David is the head winemaker for both companies. One of the great strengths of the wine world is the families that make up a large part of it and the Douro is a prime example.

By this time it was late September and vintage time in France, though the 1965 vintage is not one to be remembered. Driving north from Oporto I crossed over into Spain and on an introduction from Diego Ferguson called in at López de Heredia in Haro, the historical centre of Rioja. Along with Marqués de Riscal, the company was started by members of the family who had worked in Bordeaux and in the late 19th century Cabernet Sauvignon was planted only making way for Tempranillo after the devastations of phylloxera. López de Heredia are unique in Rioja in their custom of maturing wines for a time in large upright casks, then a longer time in small barrels and finally allowing the wine to settle in bottles before sale. The cobwebs in the reserve cellar get thicker every year and the current management, while modernising under Mariá-José López de Heredia Montoya quite rightly maintains the family tradition and, following some years out of fashion, her wines are now in tremendous demand.

A week in Bordeaux allowed me to see the vintage first hand and revisit my former employers, but by this time I was keen to get back home. A final few days at Moët et Chandon was on the programme, again staying at the Château de Saran and then it was back across the channel to London. La Petite made it to Courtfield Gardens without hardship, but when I took her to the dealership for a service after so many thousand miles, she gave up the ghost. I've never had any interest in cars but I always remember my red Triumph Herald convertible (number plate 201 R) with great affection.

5. Swinging London

Shortly after my return I presented myself at Christopher's Jermyn Street premises to ask if they had a place for me at PM, the answer being unsurprisingly negative. I applied to Dolamore, an established merchant in Baker Street from whom my parents bought wine when they were 'going smart', but got turned down here as well. Years later in the 90s, being part of a dining club called The Cellarmen, one of the fellow members, Freddy Price, a great specialist in German wines was in the Dolamore front office when I appeared spic and span and full of ideas, and told me later that I would never have been a suitable candidate for his very conservative boss. After being refused by two West End merchants, I didn't bother to apply to the few others, but had the luck or so it seemed at the time, to be told about a new company called Murray and Banbury who had premises under a car showroom in Knightsbridge. I went along and as the Christmas period was warming up, they took me on.

Murray and Banbury was David Murray-Threipland a charming but serious gentleman from Wales and Bill Banbury, an expansive and expanded 'bon viveur' who had a true passion for wine and a brilliant palate. They were an oddly matched but surprisingly complimentary couple, only a few years older than me and when the business failed as it inevitably did around four years later, David returned to Wales and Bill joined another wine company until high living and betting on the horses brought him down. I stayed a year and a half and had tremendous fun, swiftly becoming a director and of course investing some money, accompanying Bill to tastings and lunches in London, since as a young company the established shippers were after our business, and on buying trips to France. At this time the established London Wine Trade was in the last stages of a post-war boom before succumbing to hard-nosed and low-priced competition from the supermarkets and start-ups with names like Oddbins and Bottoms Up. Three-piece suits and the public school tie almost vanished from the scene, but today they are right back, rubbing shoulders with the financial worlds of Mayfair and the City of London. Wine has triumphed once again and the French phrase - *plus ça change, plus c'est la même chose/* the more things change, the more they stay the same – seems appropriate.

One of the most successful, and most needed, recent wine ventures is 67 Pall Mall, a members' only club with an amazing wine list that has quickly become the centre of the West End's wine world in a fine Lutyens' building at the end of Saint James's Street.

Murray and Banbury's premises combined both a cellar and a shop, a rather more sophisticated version of the wonderful but more mainstream Peter Dominic. Bill Banbury's upbringing had given him a taste for the best – we even imported the wines from Domaine de la Romanée-Conti – while David Murray was more down to earth but liked to discover new things, both approaches being very appealing to me. While we imported a luxury Champagne from the House of Lenoble in the Vallée de la Marne, whose Champagne was served at my wedding, under the name Prince André de Bourbon-Parme, which we pitched as a rival to Roederer Cristal, we also imported a range of wines from the Loire – Ménétou-Salon, Châteaumeillant, Cheverny and Quincy – quite unknown at that time, which I was only to come across again in the wine bars of Paris some years later. To get these known we gave tastings and I remember hosting one the following year at The Pitt Club in Cambridge, which was attended by Prince Charles who had just gone up. On being introduced to him, I said that these were really just 'French Country Wines' (not knowing that I would write a book under than name two decades later) and unlike what he might be accustomed to, and was put at my ease with his reply 'Yes, we do have some rather good wines at home.' While I was a regular visitor to Cambridge with good friends in Trinity College and had been invited often to The Pitt Club, founded in 1835 named after William Pitt the Younger. One evening stays in the mind from that time, the autumn Bumper Dinner, so called for after dinner, but before the Port, members competed in the time they could drink a 'Bumper Cup' which contained a whole bottle of Claret. My prep school contemporary at Summerfields – Nicho Tollemache who was in the Cambridge Rowing Eight – downed one in eight seconds, a record. While others, me included, haplessly tried to compete, it was discovered that Nicho's cup had contained the dinner Claret, Château Margaux 1934, and he was disqualified. Not deterred, he ordered another Cup of Club Claret, polishing it off in just over double figures and, once declared the winner, went to lie down.

Murray and Banbury were not the only merchants of 'country wines' and indeed the best at the time was Gerald Asher, whose company Asher

Storey went as far afield as the Jura, and whose wines took another half century to become popular in London and New York. He didn't survive the harsh economic climate to come, retiring to France and later splitting his time between Paris and San Francisco as in-house wine writer for *Esquire*. His articles were erudite, poetic and not pretentious, long but certainly not lengthy and in full admiration I one day asked him how he did it. 'I sit down and pretend I'm writing a letter to Mummy' was his reply. My other favourite wine writer in quite a different style, short and to the point, was Frank Prial, American-Irish wine correspondent for years for *The New York Times*, a great friend of Alexis Lichine and a reporter at heart. My question to him was more of a statement 'You must like writing since you write so well' 'No, I like having written'. I'm more a Prial than an Asher. Frank also took a flat in Paris from the 1980s and I have a photograph of us on the terrace of my restaurant Le Moulin du Village just up from my wine shop and wine school, as the sun was fading and the bottles were empty but we were still happily in conversation, on the back of which he had written 'what is the opposite of a Summit Conference?'

I was now back in my top floor flat in Courtfield Gardens and enjoying life in London to the full. By now, Bella had gone to Oxford to study for 'A' Levels, but we got together on her visits to London and she always had a base with a friend in Cadogan Square who provided sufficient cover if needed. I spent Christmas in London, holding a buffet lunch for a cheerful group who had no other commitments over the holidays. I had always gone home to Derbyshire for Christmas and I suppose this was a statement of independence and it certainly felt so at the time. Once we were married, Christmases were always split between my parents and hers, even during the many years we spent living in France. Christmas had always been a family celebration and for us it still very much is.

Working at Murray and Banbury introduced me to a part of the London Wine Trade that I had heard of but not seen while at Christopher's. These were the shippers, importers mostly established in the City of London with warehouses down by the docks. Some were of foreign origin like Deinhard and Sichel from Germany and some were very British with triple-barrel names due to mergers with other companies, notably International Distillers and Vintners (IDV) where I was to meet Martin Bamford, who became one of the youngest Masters of Wine, highly intelligent and highly entertaining and a committed gourmet. For over a decade, until his terribly early death at the age of fourty, he ran the company's base in the Médoc, the beautiful Château Loudenne, built in the Bordelais 'Chartreuse' style over-looking the Gironde Estuary. Visits to Loudenne, several of which will be mentioned later, were memorable for the food and the company, to say nothing of the wine.

The shippers were keen to supply an up and coming wine retailer like M&B, so Bill was invited to their offices for tastings and after a time I was asked as well. A memorable one was at Sichel, where John Salvi (another Master of Wine to be and a previous winner of the Vintners' Scholarship which had sent him to Bordeaux where he still lives and thrives approaching his 80th birthday) had called us in to taste some German wines as well as some Bordeaux, particularly Château d'Angludet owned by Peter Sichel and Château Palmer co-owned by the Bordeaux branch of the Sichels, both in Margaux. During lunch – it was unthinkable that a morning's tasting would not be followed by lunch when older vintages would be shown – John received a telephone call from Bordeaux to tell him that his wife had just been delivered of a son, the future count Salvi, the family being of Italian origin and with a Papal Title, though John never used it. This, he said, calls for a celebration and, knowing what was in the company cellar, immediately asked that a bottle of Château Margaux 1900 be decanted, saying to our slight protests that his bosses probably didn't know it was there and if they did, they wouldn't miss it. He was wrong on both counts.

Once back in London, I was catching up with contemporaries, many of them working in the City, who introduced me to Coates's Wine Bar in Old Broad Street, a long dimly lit establishment that served good plain English food and had a wonderful wine list, being part of the Corney and Barrow stable. Most of the clarets were London-bottled and the 1953s and 1955s were offered by the glass or carafe and at ridiculously low prices to take away. I have pleasant recollections of Château Macarthy Saint-Estèphe and Langoa-Barton 1953 both at 13 shillings and 6 pence (65p) a bottle, Pichon-Comtesse just two shillings more and a whole raft of 1955s classed growths at the same sort of price. What with these, and the wine lists from the Army and Navy Stores, Patens of Peterborough and the Wine Society, really good claret was easy to come by.

Certainly the most important thing for my own wine world was the re-opening of the Christie's Wine Auctions in October 1966, where I first met Michael Broadbent, who I have already acknowledged as my mentor. (A dinner was held in Christie's Great Rooms in Saint James's on 11 October 2016, the exact 50th anniversary, at which wines from the 1966 vintage were served. Michael, a sprightly eighty-nine years old, was on splendid form). There were regular auctions in the King Street premises, just off Saint James's and these were preceded the day before by tastings of many of the wines offered in several case lots. One day a range of post-war Vintage Ports might be offered, another might show Sherries and Madeiras and of course Claret was a staple. As Michael led Christie's to great heights in the 70s and 80s – I was their French representative for a decade from the mid 1970s and packed up many extraordinary cellars, of which more later – some auctions were of historic size and quality, but even in the early days there was a cornucopia of wines on offer. Of the many, many successful bids I placed at that time, perhaps the best was for twenty-four half bottles of Château Gazin Pomerol 1945, bottled by Sichel. The wine was simply marvellous, robust from Pomerol's *crasse de fer* irony soil, with mature concentration. One of these bottles formed part of a lunch that I made up to brighten a Sunday of a good friend who was spending a short stay in London's Brixton Prison. I had gone to Harrods for the food – paté de foie gras, half a cold grouse (it was the autumn) and some fruit and cheese – and the goodies had to be unwrapped for inspection and written down, the officer in charge verbalising the contents as he slowly recorded them: 'Slice of meat paste, one half bird, cheese and fruit' and coming to the wine, which I had uncorked as I didn't imagine Brixton would supply corkscrews, 'shato gazin one nine four five, what's the number for?' 'It's just its number' I replied 'your guest has a number and so does the wine.' Some time later, when my friend was 'out', we shared another half bottle, but he said he had appreciated the Brixton one more.

Being a regular at the Christie's pre-auction tastings Michael Broadbent and I struck up conversation and every now and then he took me through some of the wines with a quick look at the colour, great attention to the nose and then the palate, assessing the finish as he spat it out, all very straightforward, but requiring attention and concentration. His manner of tasting, of 'looking at' a wine was very easy to copy, for it was very simple: colour, nose, palate, aftertaste, conclusion, and this formed the basis of his seminal work *Wine Tasting*. It is absolutely true that had it not been for him, his teaching and friendship in those days, and his book, my Paris wine school *L'Académie du Vin* would never have existed.

As Spring 1966 rolled around, I went to various parties, but London held other attractions. I had become a member of Annabel's, the night club in Berkeley Square opened a few years earlier by Mark Birley. It was a glamourous stop after dinner at one of the new smart restaurants that were springing up for a glass or two of champagne at the bar, where it was good to be on first name terms with the barmen, and a turn on the crowded dance floor. Apart from Annabels, there were two 'theatre clubs', The Establishment and the Ad Lib, which were another part of the London scene to be in, Ronnie Scott's in Soho and Annie's Room (run by the great singer Annie Ross) in Covent Garden for jazz and Antonio's for flamenco.

Around Easter, Bill Banbury and I went on a buying trip to Champagne and Alsace. In Champagne we visited Lenoble whose owner, Joseph Graser, took us to the Reims Grand Prix. Motor racing left me cold, but little did I know that in 1969 Bella and I would have front row seats for the Monaco Grand Prix, to watch her cousin's team's car, piloted by James Hunt, almost win it for Hesketh Racing. I liked the stye of the Lenoble Champagne a lot and it was served at my wedding a couple of years later. In Alsace, I went back to say hello to the Hugels, we visited Trimbach and discovered a grower named Louis Sipp, one of the very rare *vignerons* at that time to farm organically, and took his wines on for the UK. Alsace is the most beautiful wine region, causing Louis XIV to remark on his first visit *'quel beau jardin*/what a beautiful garden', and its wines are varied and delicious, but at that time were difficult to sell. As a result, they became known as 'wine merchants' wines', for the merchants bought them, couldn't sell them and so drank them themselves.

Although not so 'trendy' as it became, wine was actually quite talked about in the 1960s, the most sought-after invitation of the year being to one of three days of the Lebègue Wine Tastings in mid June. These, along with Centre Court tickets at Wimbledon and a 'box' at Ascot were recognised high points of the London Season. Lebègue, with merchant houses both in Bordeaux and Burgundy and offices in London, showed their full range of wines starting with a morning tasting to be followed by a splendid lunch for the several hundred guests at which the finest British products were served – lobsters from the Orkney Islands, barons of Angus Beef, Stilton cheese and of course English strawberries washed down with Château d'Yquem. The Bordeaux range went from the minor wines right up to the First Growths and the Burgundies from 'village' wines through Premiers to Grands Crus, ending with the wines of the Domaine de la Romanée-Conti. Held in the vast Lebègue cellars underneath the arches in Bermondsey in the city near the London Docks, it was wildly impressive to someone so young in the wine trade. Bill Banbury, David Murray and I got invitations and I took the tasting part very seriously, while for others it was a social event. Quentin Crewe, very well-known on the scene at that time and the wine and restaurant reviewer for *Harpers and Queen* was also there and wrote his monthly column describing how he navigated the many dozens of wines on offer: 'I followed the young man in the pink shirt.'

As 1966 drew on, my money, carefully invested in the stock market, began to slip through my fingers. This process can best be described as 'lost, stolen or strayed' for, although I made the decisions, I expected the results to be better than they were. I was an easy target for ventures like backing a night club and making a movie and since these seemed like a good idea at the time and were proposed to me by friends, it was both tempting and flattering to go along with them. The 30 minute documentary movie *Dolly Story*, in which I appear as a fashionable wine merchant, which also featured David Mlinaric as the smart interior decorator (which he still is) and the ultra-fashionable night club Sybilla's that I was involved in, almost sold to a US distributor and then didn't. The branches in the Bahamas and New York of Sybilla's never opened, but the Chelsea restaurant named Rupert's after the cartoon Rupert Bear in the *Daily Express*, did see the light of day for a few months, before closing and taking some of my wine collection and art works with it. Also, fitting in with this pattern of life, I broke up with Bella, but not before selling her my dark blue convertible Triumph Vitesse, which I had bought after La Petite had died, trading up to a pale blue Mercedes.

That autumn Bill Banbury and I went to Burgundy for the *Hospices de Beaune* weekend, always third weekend in November. Before joining in the festivities, staying this time in proper rooms at the Hôtel de la Poste, we had a long tasting with Henri Leroy, co-owner since 1945 of the Domaine de la Romanée-Conti alongside the de Villaine family, and father of the formidable Lalou Bize-Leroy, who has been one of Burgundy's figureheads for many years.

We tasted some of the Leroy range and those from the DRC, me concentrating hard, picking out the various aromas in Broadbent-trained fashion, to hear Monsieur Leroy remark that 'this young man knows how to taste'. Two decades later I was at the *Hospices de Beaune* tasting alongside Lalou Bize and afterwards she asked me which *cuvées* had particularly impressed me. I selected two or three that for me were knockouts, to be told 'My poor Steven, you seem to taste for the present, while I taste for the future.'

This was the first of just a few times when I was able to attend all three manifestations of *Les Trois Glorieuses*, the three day weekend of celebrating the wines of Burgundy. The Saturday evening was the grand dinner at the Château du Clos de Vougeot hosted by the Chevaliers de Tastevin, a six course banquet for at least 500 people (now probably 1000) with wines that had been *tasteviné*, selected on a blind tasting from many samples and able to bear the prestigious Chevaliers de Tastevin label, a percentage on every bottle going to the upkeep of the 12th century château, for centuries a Cistercian monastery, which dominates the 50.22 hectare walled in Clos de Vougeot appellation. While this is a formal dinner – black tie for men, long dresses for women – it is regularly punctured by the singing of a *ban bourguingon,* culminating in everyone waving their large linen napkins above their heads. The dinner on Sunday evening, known as *Le Diner aux Chandelles*, used to be a candlelit banquet for a much smaller number in the nave of Beaune's senior church, but has now transferred to the Hospices de Beaune itself. Here only wines from the Hospices vineyards are served and very good they are, too. The final celebration is a lunch in Meursault known as *La Paulée de Meursault*, an occasion rustically robust compared to the previous evenings, where once again tens of dozens of guests – and this is a very prized invitation – join together for a full afternoon's lunch in the village of Meursault. Here, to match the local white wine, the main course is a local river fish known as *pocheuse*, but the main attraction is that *La Paulée* is a glorified 'bottle party.' Bottles are there, of course, open on the trestle tables, but everyone brings their own, always good and not just one, and these are shared around with increasing appreciation. Lunch never ends until well after dark and then it is time for a 'cellar crawl' from grower to grower. When Bill and I were there, *La Paulée* was held, and had been historically, in the vast cellars of the Château du Meursault, then owned by the comte de Moucheron. This ancient Burgundy family had been substantial vineyard owners, not just in the Côte de Beaune, but also in Musigny and Chambertin in the Côte de Nuits. By the mid 1960s the holdings had been reduced to the best plots of Meursault and Volnay and of course the beautiful 18th century château, but a decade later these, too, were sold.

Back in London I was continuing my Saturday forays to the Portobello Road for antiques and odds and ends, building up a collection of 19th century English glasses known as Rummers and an increasing range of Staffordshire pottery figures. I had also been introduced by my brother Nicky to an art gallery at the King's Road World's End run by a charming old boy named John Denny who occupied a whole house with pictures floor to ceiling with his office and his whisky bottle at the top. He seemed only to have three prices - £500, £1500 and £5000 – and I was in the middle range. His 'attributions' were not wholly convincing – the George Stubbs painting I bought of a horse being frightened by a lion, was unlikely to have come from the hand of England's greatest painter of animals, for the lion resembled a wind-up toy unable to frighten even a pony, but it was 'School of Stubbs' and I sold it in the 1980s at Christie's. However, the paintings were good to look at and, apart from the Stubbs and an Italian landscape by (School of) Gaspard Dughet, I still have them. Further down the King's Road were a range of antique shops where bargains were to be had.

The acquisition of all this art and antiques meant that I had to move somewhere larger and in late 1966 I bought a four storey house in Fernshaw Road, SW10, which is now considered to be part of Chelsea, but was not at the time. This was habitable, but needed total renovation, which I went about with gusto. The tired stretch of lawn in the west facing garden was replaced by slabs of York stone, in the middle of which I had placed a fountain with a basin sufficiently large to chill many bottles of white wine; the basement became a dining room and large kitchen, while in its hallway I installed face to face wine racks to hold 360 bottles each and there was also the 'coal hole' under the pavement which I had cleaned out to store wine in wooden cases. On the ground floor there was a study and a double drawing room with French windows at the end but no access to the garden, which was solved by installing a Victorian cast iron spiral staircase. There was a large and small bedroom on each floor and bathrooms on each landing. Just nearby in the Fulham Road was a good decorator named Alistair Colvin, who did all the paintwork, curtains and carpets, a local architect overseeing the general works. It was finished by the end of the year and while giving celebratory drinks to all concerned, the architect took me aside and said 'It's a lovely house, Mr Spurrier, but you'll never get your money back in this part of London.' I was up to around £20,000.

Life was marvellous: my dining room, decorated in 1820 Regency style, seated eight comfortably, the kitchen was Habitat chic and the whole house buzzed with activity. One of the upstairs bedrooms wase lent to my friend Giles Townsend, so on the evenings when I wasn't going out, we had cheerful dinners together. I had cooked quite a bit in Courtfield Gardens and now took it up in earnest. The books of Elizabeth David were a standby, more so since Mrs David herself was a client of Murray and Banbury and although we had a van driver, I often delivered the wines myself to be able to meet her. There were still very good food shops of all kinds in the area, a superb fishmonger from whom I used to buy wild sea trout and even nearer was Curnicks, an excellent butcher. Nicky then lived around the corner from Curnicks, in a large house with his wife and two children and was a regular there. One day I called in to collect a rib of beef for a dinner party and my name was shouted to the back of the shop where everything was prepared: 'Is that the rich Mr Spurrier or the poor Mr Spurrier?' came back. Nicky's wife would have shopped every day for the family, I only shopped for an indulgent dinner party.

The other bedroom on the top floor was lent to a young Swiss girl from Zurich, Susi Spörri, who had been introduced to me by 'Johnny the Joiner' the carpenter building all my cupboards and even a wooden deck between the V of the roof between 44 and 46 Fernshaw Road, which was perfect for sunbathing, the only possible over-lookers being the aeroplanes on their way to land at Heathrow to the west. Suzi was an 'au pair', cleaning up after Giles and myself. She was very pretty and fun, trying to get into the music world and was a decorative and amusing addition to the house. One evening, coming back from dinner, I found the large sitting room filled with people, plainly music friends of Suzi's. A young black guy with an afro haircut, clutching a guitar, got up and said, 'Hi, I'm Jimmy, who are you?' 'I'm Steven,' I replied, 'have a good time with Suzi,' and went up to bed. The following morning Suzi asked me if I had enjoyed meeting Jimi Hendrix.

In early 1967 I was elected a member of Boodle's, the second young-est member ever. A year or so before, during one of his daily lunches at Marston with Grandpa Spurrier, my father, looking around the dining room and gazing out over the lawns, said 'all this is going to Nicky, what are you going to do for Steven?' After a moment's reflection, the answer came back 'I'll make him a member of Boodle's'. Boodle's is one of the three gentleman's clubs a stone's throw from each other in Saint James's Street, that were founded in the 1760s for gentlemen to meet together, first as coffee houses with gaming rooms – everything was bet on in those days, from horses to which drop of rain would reach the bottom of the window pane first – to evolve into substantial private houses with saloons, dining rooms and bedrooms. A light rivalry exists between them and there is a saying that 'the members of Brooks's *think* they run the country, the members of Boodle's *run* the country and the members of White's *own* the country.'

Despite the poor investments I was making, the capital at my disposal remained substantial and I began to think of a place in the sun, in France of course. I had been told of the European Property Company which happened to be not far from Murray and Banbury, so called in one day and was fascinated by a 30 hectare plot of land outside Bagnols-en-Forêt above the town of Fréjus in the Var department, mid-way geographically between Saint-Tropez and Nice, both of which I knew quite well. The property had a ruined farmhouse on it and I was told it was owned by an Australian architect who was now living in England and had to sell up. This seemed like an interesting adventure, so I got in touch with David Langlands, my friend from Cambridge who had married a French girl from Saint-Tropez and suggested he join me to check it out. The day we chose to leave, the Governor of the Bank of England, Lord Cromer, had announced that the Pound Sterling would undergo devaluation and that times were tough economically and the country should 'tighten its belt for the future.'

David and I flew to Nice, and stopped off for dinner and the night at la Napoule. The following morning went to see the place, known as Bayonne. With views south to the sea and north to the Alps, I fell for it immediately and subsequently met the vendor, Paul Calder, and his Norwegian wife Bente in London and we shook hands on a deal. Paul would sell me the land and the ruin and design me a house which, this being around April, I said I would hope to build the following year. This was a dream of a project and since dreams do not often come true, this did not, but it was approached with optimism and trust (sadly misplaced) and will be covered in the next chapter.

In summer 1967 I left Murray and Banbury and, always on the lookout for a distraction, began to toy with the idea of going into the antique business. In the meantime, it was time for a holiday, first at Langoa-Barton thanks to Victoria Vipan who I had got to know having lent my flat to Christopher for a wedding present, then on to Pamplona (no gaol this time) slowly across the Midi to Saint-Tropez, taking another look at the Bagnols-en-Forêt property, then back to London. Life was seemed pretty good and externally it was, but internally it was a bit of a mess. Fortunately this was soon to change.

Her studies at Oxford satisfactorily over, Bella had gone to the Byam Shaw Art School, much smaller than but almost as prestigious as the Slade. Our paths crossed occasionally and she told me she was going to spend the summer in America visiting the cousins she had never met on the East and West Coasts. Her twenty-first birthday was in the middle of August and I telephoned her parents to ask for an address so I could send a birthday telegramme. Her father was unhelpful, but her mother said it was a nice idea and off the telegram went. On her return in early September Bella called to say hello and I asked her to the second of the two opening nights of Rupert's, the restaurant in Chelsea's Park Walk that the Sybilla's crowd were opening, with me advising on the wine list. The first night, to which I had invited the summer girlfriend, had not gone well as the food took ages to arrive – the place only lasted a few months despite all hype – and she walked out as I was spending more time drinking with my friends than paying attention to her. The service was really no better the second night, but Bella and I talked the evening away and I walked the few blocks back home in a very good state of mind.

Slowly but surely, Bella and I got back together. I kept a notebook of the dinners at home and who was there and what was drunk and Bella re-appears for a dinner for six (Puligny-Montrachet Clos de la Garenne 1961, Gevrey-Chambertin 1955) on 11 October, again on the 13th (Hermitage Chevalier de Sterimberg 1964, Chambertin-Clos de Bèze 1955) and once again, just the two of us (half bottles of Corton-Charlemagne 1957 and Château Figeac 1952) on the 20th and then almost without a break. A few weeks later Nicky took me aside and said that I should ask Bella to marry me. 'Why?', 'Because you lost her last time and you can't afford to lose her again.' I recounted this to Bella when we next met, to be told that this was a suggestion, not a proposal, so I went down on one knee to propose and was accepted.

After this, both sets of parents had to be informed. My parents were thrilled, hers a little less so. It was necessary for both sets to meet and a date was arranged, the place being the Grand Hotel at Rugby, exactly half way between them both. Although they had never met, they were almost the same age and knew so many people in common, my father charming Bella's mother, her father falling for my mother, that it was only when the coffee arrived that they realised why they were there and the date of 31 January was set for the wedding in London.

That didn't leave us much time to plan for the future. The UK was in a poor financial state in the late 1960s and the Government was determined to squeeze the rich 'until the pips squeak'. I was still very much in this bracket and had met, via Nicky, someone who had discovered a loop-hole whereby capital could be whisked out of the country to the Cayman Islands and thence to Switzerland. The risk was that if it didn't work out, the Cayman banks would hold onto it. I took the risk and it worked, so roughly 50% of what I had paid across the Lloyds Bank counter in early 1964 found its way to Geneva. The reason for doing this was that if I were to build the house in Provence, the Bank of England stopped anything more than £5000 leaving the country. I had told Bella of this purchase and we flew down to look at it, my question being: should we go and live in the south of France, to which she replied 'Why not?' Bella didn't have capital to export, but we needed to get the Bank of England's permission to export ourselves, to become non-residents for tax purposes. The fact that we had a place to export ourselves to clinched the deal, which allowed us no more than ninety days a year back in the UK. This, taken almost on a whim, turned out to be the best, and perhaps the only good financial decision I have ever made.

Since we had designated the unbuilt house at Bagnols-en-Forêt as our primary residence, I could keep the house in London, so nothing had to be moved. My plan now was to become an antique dealer, and for this I needed a large station wagon type car, so the Mercedes was sold and I ordered from via Citroën's London agent, a DS Safari, certainly the most interesting car I have ever owned, to be collected on our arrival in Paris the day after our wedding.

The wedding itself had our friends all looking dashingly glam-ourous and/or eccentrically exotic. One of my first flatmate Nicholas Gormanston's friends from school, a wayward artist known as 'Boots'

Wedding reception at the Hyde Park Hotel,
31 January 1968

Bantock arrived with his shaggy black spaniel under his arm and to the Maitre d' announced himself as 'Mr Boots and Lady Hermione Bantock'. Michael Fish, owner with Barry Sainsbury of Mr Fish, London's most fashionable haberdasher refused my suggestion that he shouldn't desert his clients just to come to a wedding by saying 'the shop will be shut, for all the interesting clients will be there.' I had got up at 5am that morning to go to Covent Garden to select the food for lunch for my best man, Giles Townsend, and the four ushers and I had commandeered (in January!) the punnets of *fraises des bois* from Morocco, destined for Annabel's. Getting up that early and preparing lunch for six people on my own wedding day does seem a bit odd now, but it didn't at the time. We then trouped off and they all watched while I had my hair cut, which was a mistake as Bella said she hardly recognised me from the back as she walked down the aisle at The Brompton Oratory.

That evening, I carried Bella over the threshold of Fernshaw Road. We changed out of our wedding gear and collected the marvellous packed supper my mother had prepared for us as well as a bottle of Château Pape-Clement 1953 to sustain us on our voyage from Victoria Station on the Golden Arrow to Paris for a new life in France.

6. Var from the Madding Crowd

On arrival in Paris at the Gare du Nord we sped to the Hôtel Vendôme on Paris's superb Place Vendôme, only to be told their rooms were under renovation and they had put us nearby in their sister Hôtel du Calais. Here renovations had been completed and our room possessed a fine *lit matrimonial* which, with a few francs in the slot, would vibrate for thirty minutes. We saved our money.

It was all a bit new, being married, so we spent the first day casually, wandering around, and writing this reminds me of the dinner we had had at the restaurant Lapérouse on the Quai des Grands Augustins on New Year's Eve the year before when the aged sommelier rescued what was becoming a dismal evening. Lapérouse was one of the oldest restaurants in the city, still holding two of its previous three Michelin stars, with a classically rich menu and a superb wine list. For the main course, *Faisan Subaroff* I think, he advised a Burgundy, but I knew better and ordered claret, Brane-Cantenac 1955. He didn't approve. The wine arrived, beautifully decanted and it was as dry as could be. I began to sulk and conversation stopped, then with the cheese the sommelier said that, since it was *une soirée de fête*, the house would like to offer us a half bottle of red Burgundy with which to end the meal. What had become small screen, black and white and silent exploded into wide screen technicolour and the evening was well and truly saved.

The following morning we went to the Citroën showroom at the top of the Champs-Elysées to collect the car, the most advanced at that time of their ground-breaking range. In repose, the car was down on its haunches, the body almost touching the ground, but once started it rose up hydraulically about a foot. The headlights could swivel either manually or automatically, to lead you around hair-pin bends which were always announced by a sign reading *attention aux lacets*. To describe a tight corner as being 'lacy' seemed very elegant. The brake pedal was not a pedal but a large button which had to be treated with respect. Heading off around the Arc de Triomphe, hazardous in the best of times, I stamped on it to avoid a taxi and the car almost stood on its head. Once I had mastered the controls, the DS Safari provided the smoothest ride I have ever experienced.

We headed south, our destination being the ski station of Méribel, where Lorna Cooper-Key had a floor of a recently built a chalet at 1800 metres, the highest at the time, and she had lent her own private part to us for a week as a wedding present. I hadn't skied since my prep school days, but Bella had and I made the best of it until we decided to take the lift right to the top and ski down to Courcevel on the other side. This was a 'black run', the simple ones being blue (my favourite colour), and I had to be helped down by a guide and kept to the easier runs after that. Méribel was a perfect ski resort, and throughout our time in Paris in the 1970s, Lorna offered us the larger part of the apartment for a week after New Year, so our children learnt to ski from an early age.

After this it was down to Provence. The vendor of the Bagnols-en-Forêt property, who described himself as an architect but, although an excellent draftsman was not qualified as such, had designed me a substantial villa very much along classical lines and had moved himself, wife and young daughter down to Fayence, a nearby village, to oversee the works. My plan was that, once the house was finished, to furnish it with antiques, pictures and objects, all of which would be for sale, an idea based on that of Mallets, one of London's top antique dealers, at Bourdon House off Berkeley Square. This never happened, the servants' house was finished, where we lived for two years, a swimming pool which I had paced out to a nice size that turned out to be 18x10 metres was lined with pale blue ceramic tiles and surrounded with off-cuts of marble from the Cararra quarries in northern Italy, but the main house was never finished. This ended up in court, the only one of three court cases that I won, and the 'architect' Paul Calderari, of Greek origin but a naturalised Australian now Paul Calder, ending up in prison, for Bella and I were not the only people he had defrauded. The previous summer I had given a large house-warming party at Fernshaw Road, to which Paul and his wife, came as did my parents. As our time in the Var department progressed, we began to refer to him as 'the wily Greek' but by that time it was too late. Despite the outcome, the loss of money but more importantly the loss of a probably unrealisable dream, our two and a half years in Provence were pretty magical.

Calder knew of a house to rent in lovely Provencale countryside on the way to Bagnols-en-Forêt from Fayence (already quite fashionable, now completely over-crowded) and we moved in. We had to become bonafide residents of France and so went to the Prefecture at Draguignan to apply for our *cartes de séjour*. A wife resided with her husband, so Bella's papers followed automatically after mine, but mine needed a few justifications: Profession? My passport said I was a wine merchant but I no longer was, so I replied Writer. 'What was I writing?' asked the official. 'A book'. 'What is its title?' Stunned by this, I had an inspiration thanks to Thomas Hardy, not imagining that two decades later we would be living in south Dorset which is famous for this great author, and replied 'Var from the Madding Crowd', pinching his title *Far from the Madding Crowd*. If written, this would have pre-dated Peter Mayle's *A Year in Provence* by quite a bit, but it at least got my papers signed and we left as legal residents of France where we were to spend most of the next fourteen years.

There was a good restaurant in the centre of Fayence and a bustling little café opposite, but nearer to our new home was a roadside bistrot called *Les Quatres Chemins*, run by a husband and wife team who resembled the characters 'Jack Sprat who ate no fat and his wife who ate no lean', he being bent and skinny while his wife, Madame Hélène was simply vast. This became our local and it was also where we made our telephone calls, generally with an hour's delay to get connected outside the country. We had gone home for Easter and travelled through Paris on the way back, checking out the antique shops in the Rue Jacob, where there was quite a vogue for British Victoriana. Here we had witnessed the student riots which are now in the history books, the paving stones on the Boulevard Saint Germain being ripped out and hurled at the advancing ranks for helmeted and shielded police, but down in Provence it was quite quiet. Around early May 1968 the whole of France went on strike and while Bella had been able to get a flight from Nice to London to attend the wedding of one of her friends, she found she couldn't get back as all modes of transport had been cancelled. Her elder half-brother from her mother's first marriage was a member of the famous Red Arrows acrobatic flighing team and, having his own light aircraft, offered to fly Bella down and spend a few days with us.

Off they set, James filing a flight plan, landing in Le Touquet and able to refuel because he knew people there, leaving with shrugs from the shoulders of the officials. They flew on in an eerie silence until the radio burst into life above Lyon with an order to land immediately. James (who was later to move to Saint Rémy-de-Provence and plant a vineyard where Bella and the children spent happy holidays from the early 1970s) responded by turning the radio off and gaining altitude, only to be joined shortly after by a military jet whose pilot gesticulated furiously that he should descend. This he did, but only to read the signs on the Autoroute A7 to make sure he was heading in the right direction, and the jet, imaging it had been obeyed, vanished. Not daring to make radio contact for directions, he and Bella then followed the autoroute south to Aix-en-Provence, took a left and landed at the tiny Fayence airstrip with an inch of petrol in the tank. Their arrival was a welcome surprise to me and we celebrated by a long dinner at Madame Hélène's, whose friendly food suppliers, unable to sell to the shops who were on strike, kept her well-stocked in victuals and alcohol.

It took several days and Madame Hélène's contacts on the black market to get the aircraft re-fueled and in the meantime we went to Saint-Tropez to see David and France Langlands and my now four year old goddaughter Véronique. Walking down to Les Mouscardins we stopped for a drink in one of the quayside cafés, where we were approached by a striking lady of a certain age who offered to read our palms. I had always been fascinated by palmistry and star signs and accepted right away despite a hefty price. Her method was to ink our palms to obtain a printout on a paper that showed the lines with great clarity. After some study she both 'read' the palm out loud but also wrote on the paper what she 'saw' from the various life, head, heart lines and the rest. For me, she made two major predictions: 'change of profession within three years' and 'possibility of lasting fame.' Since I didn't have a profession, the first seemed unlikely and the second ludicrous. Yet, by October 1970 I was working for the wine shop in the middle of Paris that I was later to take over and in 1976 created a wine tasting that became known as The Judgement of Paris thus proving her predictions quite correct.

Apart from the occasional trip to Saint-Tropez, Cannes, Nice or Grasse, most of the time we were on the property getting the building going. For the first eighteen months or so I have to admit that this was very much teamwork alongside Calder and his Tunisian work force. This manual work, lots of heavy lifting, was a welcome change from the previous two years of partying in London to the extent that, returning for a visit to Bella's parents that summer, her father (who had thought my slimness to be bordering on the effete) was heard to remark 'Good heavens, he's got a torso.' The property was spread over 30 hectares, mostly terraces of cork oak trees leading down from where we were to build the house where the ruin was, tucked into the side of the hill. The hill rose steeply to an exposed red volcanic rock peak where we owned another portion of land that had, what looked to us, to be a small sunken chapel, all that was visible above ground was the semi-circular vaulted roof of which only half remained. That summer we had the workers cut us a path up through the long-abandoned tree and scrub covered terraces and dragged a wheelbarrow, picks and shovels up to what we now called the 'Pagan Chapel' and over the next year totally dug it out, tipping the stones and earth onto the overgrown terraces below. A few years later when we had abandoned Provence and were installed in Paris, I received an agonised communication from a geological expert who had known of the 'chapel' and had done some preliminary research to prove that it had in fact been a water cistern from the times of the Roman occupation. He had been away from the region for all the time we were there and returned to find the chapel/cistern totally cleaned out to reveal firm walls and a solid stone floor, with 2000 years of history tipped over the edge.

We were entirely alone on the side of the hill running down to the sea for nobody had lived there due to lack of water – I have to hand it to the 'wily Greek' that he solved this problem at some expense by discovering a natural spring almost a kilometre down from the house, which we tapped into a holding tank, installed a pump to bring it to a much larger holding tank near to a structure we built to house the generator for power and from there to another tank which gave us water for the house on a gravity flow. This water came in more than useful the following March, when some picnicers had unknowingly started a small fire while stopping for lunch near the Chapelle Notre Dame which formed the start of the two kilometre track to us from the local road. I could see flames leaping from tree to tree and told Bella to pack some valuables, a change of clothes and be prepared to camp down by the swimming pool. Within an hour, we were being engulfed by a full-scale fire. The Canadair firefighting planes flew over dumping water taken from a nearby lake and the Fayence fire brigade turned up with two engines and a full team to ask us where the water was! The following day in the local Var Matin newspaper there we were standing by the house surrounded by charred and smoking trees with the caption 'Monsieur and Madame Spurrier, thanks to their swimming pool filled with water, were saved…'. The vegetation grew back surprisingly well and surprisingly quickly.

Wine still played a part in my life at that time, for at a Christie's auction of stocks lying in Bordeaux, I had made successful bids for five cases each of châteaux Pichelèbre and Canon de Brem 1964 from Fronsac (Fronsacs were under-rated then and still are, but in the late 19th century they outsold all but the best Saint-Emilions. I continued to buy from the de Brem family, who also owned Château La Dauphine, for my shop in Paris, Malescot Saint-Exupéry 1960 and Siran 1961 from Margaux and La Lagune 1962 Haut-Médoc and had arranged to have these delivered to our Fayence house. The La Lagune was surprisingly 'Burgundian' and fooled many of my friends who came to stay. At Bagnols-en-Forêt there was *La Bagnolaise Cooperative Vinicole* which provided a range of wines from the surrounding vineyards, none of them being able to support a commercial business on their own. We used to have a 20 litre glass demijohn filled up with the 11 degree red and bottle it to keep us in everyday wine, which I remember with great affection. Some of the local wines were as good as their reputation, important as a few styled themselves *Crus Classés*, notably Château Minuty for whites and roses, and Châteaux de Rouët and Sainte-Rosaline for reds. All three are still leaders in the Var department.

Eventually the great General de Gaulle, having referred to the May 1968 riots as *un chien lit*/a dog's dinner, solved the problem the following month by sending in the army to break the strike of the petrol stations and declared a week-long national holiday, so of course even the students stopped throwing paving stones at the police, jumped into their cars and headed out of Paris. But this was not in time to save the May Cannes Film Festival, which Bella and I attended in some style due to new and then life-long American friends David Fromkin and Richard (Rick) Herland. Not normally on our radar, we had been invited to this thanks to Bobby Ho, a delightful American-nationalised Chinese who happened to be a patient of my doctor friend Christopher who had introduced us a year or so before. Bobby was a true eccentric, highly intelligent, beautifully mannered and an addicted 'chartist' playing the commodity markets with substantial sums based on their historical movements on highly technical charts, not always with great success.

His friends David and Rick had suggested he join them in Cannes, where they had taken a suite at the Hotel Carlton, and Bobby, being temporarily broke and of modest height, accepted on the condition he slept in the bathtub so as not to have them take another room. David was a lawyer and historian – one of his many books *A Peace to End All Peace* on the evolution of the Middle East following the carving up under the Sykes-Picot Agreement of 1918, has never been out of print – had a passion for Burgundy and blondes. Rick was a film producer and was in Cannes to promote his movie *The Mini-Affair* starring the pop star Georgie Fame. All three of them would remain close friends over the next few decades, our escapades always being linked to food and wine. Bobby was a fine cook and gave us the perfect recipe for boiled chicken: place the trussed bird in a large pot and cover with cold water, bring to the boil, turn off the heat and when cooled raise again to boiling point, repeat this a third time and the chicken is deliciously moist yet cooked through. Thanks to David's generosity I drank many of the greatest Burgundies over the years: 1919 and 1921 La Tâche, Côte de Nuits Grands Crus from the best years of the 1940s, 1950s and early 1960s. Rick Herland took a spare room in my London flat in the late 1990s and after many years in Rome was an expert on pasta. On its third day, the Cannes Film Festival shut down in sympathy with the demonstrations in Paris, and we returned to the more bucolic countryside of the Var and Madame Hélène's sustaining cuisine.

The plans that Calder had drawn up were elegant and impressively simple: five bedrooms, with our suite and three others with views down the valley to the sea fifteen kilometres away as the crow flies, descending by an open-tread spiral staircase to the ground floor and out onto a wide terrace that ran the whole length of the façade of seven French windows. To the left there would a reading room, a triple bay *salon* and then my study, to the right would be summer and winter dining rooms, kitchens and store rooms behind and of course a cellar, dug deep into the rock. Although the structure was built with the striking volcanic rocks and stones that littered the hectares on the windswept and inhospitable north-facing hillside opposite, which we just rolled down and pitched onto our flat bed truck all for nothing except physical labour, the interior was never remotely finished. After two years it had become plain that the quote that Calder had given me to complete both the servants' house and the main villa had already been spent and our relationship had come to an unpleasant end which was to finish in a long drawn out court case. Faced with this impasse, we decided to leave our life in Provence. We finally left after the summer of 1970 and although I returned from time to time, Bella never did until the mid 1980s, when we were once again staying with friends in Saint-Tropez, having sold it all to a property developer from Cannes a few years before. He turned what was planned as a self-indulgent dream into a kind of hotel, splitting up the spacious rooms to provide much more accommodation. In August 2015, as we were driving back home from Italy, I decided to pay another visit only to find the access locked and barred, the entire property abandoned. This made me feel very sad, as the views and the purity of the space was amazing and needed to be enjoyed.

But in the meantime, life continued well, with parcels of books arriving from John Sandoe's bookshop in Chelsea – I have never, ever read so much – and friends coming to see us. In February 1969 I turned up uninvited to the first French professional tasting of my life, that of *La Foire d'Orange,* that concentrated on the wines of the southern Rhône. My passport defined me as 'Wine Merchant' so I was admitted to the cellars under Orange's magnificent Roman Amphitheatre and joined a panel of three tasting on an upturned barrel in murky light. My French was just good enough to express my views and I was surprised by how poor many of the wines were and while they didn't get medals, they were not criticised. Compared to my mentor Michael Broadbent's meticulous concentration to analyse every single aspect of what was in the glass, this was just 'yes, maybe, no' which, come to think of it, is what wine, food and even books and films should be about, and my fellow judges were on home ground and I was not. A few years later, judging with Jon Winroth, my then partner in *l'Académie du Vin* on tables at *La Foire de Paris*, it was often difficult to get our criticisms accepted, particularly on a table of wine growers from Alsace, who just broke into their local dialect to shut us up. I was allowed to join in a cheerful lunch and taste again in the afternoon and would go back several years running with the Perrin family from Château de Beaucastel, but this was my first introduction to another world, which I was subsequently to make my own. Spending the night in a nearby country inn – Bella had gone skiing for the weekend with another ex-pat Provence friend – I ordered a Lirac from Château de Saint-Roche, really liked it and visited the property the following day and this wine from the Verda family became a regular on my wine list in Paris. This was how in the future I was to discover a good many wines and the wine part of my life was once again beginning to take form.

At some point we met Bernard Laudon, owner of the Domaine des Férauds near Vidauban, which was quickly to become one of the cutting edge producers and whose wines a few years later I was to use to gain entrance to a *Gault & Millau* tasting at the Hôtel George V in Paris. Bernard was married to a very pretty girl from Kansas named Karen and they lived high up in the hills on an old property on the way to Saint-Tropez, so we called in often. Even with with just 12 volt electricity and only only occasional hot water they seemed to me to have the ideal life, Karen running the house with charming efficiency and Bernard, whose uncle Paul Rival owned the First Growth Sauternes Château Guiraud while showing more interest in aviation, ripping up a stretch or two of vines to create a landing strip, was creating modern wines with fruit to the fore. They had an Australian *stagiaire*, Andrew Pirie from Tasmania, later to create Pipers Brook Winery, in which I later became a small investor, and begin to push the borders of Pinot Noir, now one of the island's greatest strengths.

Once the cellar had been dug out under the bedroom floor of our house in Bagnols-en-Fôret I imported twenty or so cases from London, mostly Burgundies and northern Rhônes alternate with Bordeaux for special occasions. At some point Patrick Fegan, later to become the leading wine columnist in Chicago and creator of the Chicago Wine School, came into our lives and house sat my wonderful sheepdog Digby when we had to be away in England for a month the following year, educating himself with free access to what was quite a good selection. There were few wine shops of interest even in Cannes or Nice, but the supermarket at the new complex Cap Trois Mille near Nice Airport had some nice wines, notably a Bordeaux Primeur from the *négociant* Pierre Coste at Langon. This was a marvellous *Bordeaux de l'année*, which bore out Pierre's philosophy that a fresh young claret was preferable to a tired old one, a revolutionary idea in the late 1960s. Pierre Coste became one of my most regular suppliers to my shop in Paris and he was a mentor to Denis Dubourdieu (*Decanter* Man of the Year 2016), who did for Bordeaux whites what he had done for the reds.

That autumn we were invited to spend a week for the vintage at Château Langoa-Barton, where we had stopped a couple of days on our way to Spain the year before and Ronald Barton had asked us to come back for longer. Driving from the Var, I decided to stay in Cahors, famous for its 'black wine' which was used to bolster up the lesser Bordeaux reds while Hermitage was preferred for the grander ones, but also famous for a two Michelin star restaurant in town with a marvellous wine list. I selected, probably with *confit de canard*, the Haut-Brion 1952. Bella tasted it and said it was 'a bit flat'. I disagreed and told her that the following day we would be in Bordeaux and due to have lunch with Peter Sichel before driving up the Médoc to Langoa and he had got for me the just-released copy of Edmund Penning-Rowsell's seminal work *The Wines of Bordeaux*, and this book would prove her wrong. On arrival I grabbed the book and, hardly thanking Peter for it, turned to the chapter on the Graves to find 'the Rowsing Pencil's' (as he was known) comment on the 1952: 'a good wine, but a bit flat on the finish'. I have long since admitted the superiority of the female palate.

It was on this visit that two dinners stick firmly in my mind, for very different reasons. The first was at Langoa, mid-way through our visit and since it was vintage time, the château was full and visitors frequent. Ronald suggested that for this special evening I help him choose the wine. Bordeaux châteaux had a tradition, which still exists, of exchanging wines with each other, so the cellar was filled with many names from many vintages and it was customary that if a fellow château owner was present, their wine would be served. Ronald himself had recently retired from the merchant house Barton et Guestier, but had retained close contacts with Hugel family in Alsace and the Lupé-Cholet sisters in Burgundy, so exchanged wines with them as well. At dinners like this one, Champagne – always from Paul Bara a fine *récoltant-manipulant* in Bouzy – would be the aperitif, a dry white with the first course, three reds and Sauternes with dessert. Since it was autumn – Bordeaux vintages began in early October in those days, a month later than today due as much to better vineyard management as to global warming – Ronald decided to skip the white and go for four reds, each a decade apart. He selected Cantemerle 1953 as the owner Henri Binaud would be present, then Langoa 1947 and hesitated on a wine from the 1930s, which had been an appalling decade for Bordeaux with only 1934 being respectable (Berry Brothers and Rudd bought the *entire* crop of Beychevelle and substantial volumes of the classed growths as the owners were desperate for money) the other passable year being the lean 1937, which Ronald Barton's nephew Anthony told me 'came round thirty years later for about fifteen minutes'. Looking around his eyes fell on a bin of Pommard 1934 from Lupé-Cholet and he suggested this would go fit well with the meal and be a surprise, the final wine being Léoville-Barton 1928.

It is also a tradition that the wines are served blind, and a guessing game goes around the table for a few minutes before the identity was revealed. (I remember a dinner at Loudenne in the early 1970s, where the great Martin Bamford would tease his guests for a little longer, the hint this time being that it was 'a great wine from a great year'. I was quickly up with 'Margaux 1961' which left Martin non-plussed because I was right. 'It's simple' I said 'a great wine means a First Growth and a great year really means 1961 and I have tasted all the First Growth 1961s except Margaux and don't recognise this, so it must be Margaux.') Henri Binaud recognised his Cantemerle 1953, Edmund Penning-Rowsell was spot on with the Langoa 1947, while the third wine was much admired and brought discussion: certainly Right Bank, but was it Pomerol or Saint-Emilion? The young Peter Sichel said it was so rich it could almost be Burgundy and was told to stop being silly. When Ronald told them what it was, the majority of guests pushed their glasses away, for they hadn't come to Langoa to drink Pommard. Bordeaux and Burgundy were different countries in those days, their wines seldom occupying the same cellar. Another time when at Loudenne, I had spent the day in Saint-Emilion whose wines are dominated by the fleshy Merlot grape, while those of the Médoc were substantially from the more austere Cabernet Sauvignon and because the former opened up earlier, they were sometimes referred to as 'the Burgundies of Bordeaux'. On my return I mentioned this to Martin, adding that I had read somewhere that 'Bordeaux wines appealed to the head, Burgundies to the heart.' 'Yes' he replied 'you don't have to be very bright to drink Burgundy.' One would not be allowed to say this today.

Martin Bamford was one of the six people that week who journeyed to the Restaurant Darroze in Villeneuve-de Marsan in Les Landes on the way to Toulouse. The Darroze family were committed restaurateurs and today Hélène Darroze continues the tradition with Michelin-starred restaurants in Paris and London. The Darroze wine list was famous and we were there as guests of David Fromkin to drink the 1806 Lafite. Bella was with me and the other guests were Rick Herland and his beautiful Persian girlfriend. David had spotted this wine on the list the year before but being on his own decided it needed company. The 1806 had been re-corked at the château in 1953 and on the advice of Raymond Baudoin, founder of *La Revue du Vin de France* and hands-on adviser to the top restaurants in the country, 6 bottles were sent to Le Chapon Fin in Bordeaux, Taillevent in Paris, Le Coq Hardi near Paris at Bougival and Darroze. A decade later, Michael Broadbent and I were to pack up the cellar at Le Coq Hardi for Christie's and a year or so before that I had done the same for at Darroze. While the Lafite was the reason David had convened us, so were the superb Burgundies that he so much enjoyed. We were to have Dom Pérignon as an aperitif, probably the 1955, then Montrachet Marquis de Laguiche 1962 bottled by Drouhin, and compare Domaine Rousseau's Chambertin and Chambertin Clos de Bèze from 1952. The order was left to me and I said that the Lafite should be the first of the reds and that it should not be decanted, but poured directly into the glasses after opening. A seventh glass was poured for Monsieur Darroze, who took it around the room to share with other guests. We approached the wine with reverence: the colour was still a fine, if light, red, the nose showed fragrance and purity of fruit, the palate was delicate yet also firm and for twenty minutes of so it was beautifully, captivatingly alive, before fading into dryness as our glasses emptied. A very moving experience and certainly the most memorable, in the true sense of the word, wine I have ever tasted along with the Cockburn 1908, one hundred and two years its junior, sixteen years earlier. The price on the Darroze list was 1500 French Francs, about £120. (In an auction at Christie's in London in late 2017, one of the bottles from Le Coq Hardi cellar was sold for £38,000.)

Earlier in 1969 we had acquired a Berger Briard puppy, having seen its splendid mother in the smart restaurant in Fayence and told that she would soon delivering a litter. A little smaller than the Old English Sheepdog and much less hairy, Briards come in various colours; the mother and puppy were pale brown, known by the breeders as Champagne coloured. I named him Digby after a South African friend of ours from London, as they had the same very bushy eyebrows. Digby and I were inseparable and he came on all our travels, the Citroën Safari being the largest kennel he could ever have imagined. He moved with us to Paris but was a country not a city dog and we later found him a good home back down in Provence. He lives on in my memory and on the frontispiece of my *French Country Wines* book, which is dedicated to him.

Bella's younger sister Caroline was spending the summer of 1970 at a school in Antibes so we saw her occasionally and Bella's parents came to stay that July, quite admiring my cooking – Bella never really cooked until I started working in Paris, but loved all the food markets – and we took them on a tour of Provence. At the restaurant Hiély-Lucullus in Avignon, I was bringing up the rear of the five of us, Caroline at sixteen being pretty with long slim legs and the shortest skirt imaginable, to see a gentleman diner seated near the door turn his head to follow her progress into the dining room and putting a forkful of food in his ear, which did not amuse his companion.

With the collapse of our house project in Bagnols Bella recommended returning to London, while I said that we hadn't gone to all the trouble of moving to France to go back so soon and anyway the London wine world seemed too 'old boy' for me, so said we would move to Paris and I would find a job in the wine trade, which was basically all I knew. We did indeed move to Paris, but the wine trade that I had imagined to find there did not exist.

7. Bonjour Paris

Although, apart from a few trips, our base had been Bagnols, we had also been exposed to a bit of Paris from meeting people here and there. So we knew we would not be alone when we finally closed up the property, packing the Citroën Safari with everything we thought we would need including Digby, and heading north.

Two other changes were afoot, one immediate, the other not for a few months. The first was that Bella's mother died from cancer in mid September at the early age of fifty-seven. The second was that Bella was pregnant and fortunately her mother had been happy to know this. Both these changes confirmed, along with the other reasons, that our bucolic life in Provence should come to an end and we needed a place to live in Paris. Having had so much space both in London and in the Var, I wasn't keen on moving into a flat, but that seemed all that Paris had to offer until one sunny late September day Bella and I were crossing the exuberant Pont Alexandre III and I was admiring the barges, big and small, moored along the quais on the Right Bank. On one, the largest and smartest, a drinks party was in full swing and we went down and I asked Bella, who was more fluent in French from her days in Paris than me, to ask one of the crowd who the owner was. He appeared, coincidentally we learned later named Monsieur Debarge, plainly not ready for a long conversation, so I asked him directly where I could buy a barge like his. He pointed curtly to the wheelhouse and said 'ask in there'. In there we found someone busy repairing the electrics and posed the same question. He introduced himself as Monsieur Van Den Bosch and he maintained and dealt in canal barges on his private dockyard out at Gennevilliers to the north of Paris, replying that he would soon have one for sale, 'better than this one' and asked us to go and see him. This we duly did, to be shown a 39x5 metre barge from the 1950s built for transporting petrol, that had one more trip left before being retired. The price cleaned up but before installing living quarters into the hold, would be £8,000 and he agreed on a 10% deposit and would be in touch when the boat returned to his workyard.

Thus began what was to be a magical decade in Paris, where everything was so much fun and nothing seemed to go too far wrong. Under a year later we were installed on the *Orion*, moored on the Right Bank near the Pont de la Concorde, a nice stroll to the Caves de la Madeleine my wine shop and within a couple of years I had acquired a house in Burgundy, 49% (the wrong percentage) of a vineyard in Vacqueyras in the southern Rhône, and had opened, France's first wine school and of course still had the property in Provence and the house in London. I was to lose them all, and more, but it didn't look like that at the time.

With our accommodation fixed for the future, we needed something for the present and the Paris *Herald Tribune* provided the answer through its classified ads on the back page. The *Herald Tribune*, or the *Trib* became woven into my life and I still buy it every day in its reincarnation as the international version of the *New York Times*. What I found was a large five roomed flat *entre cour et jardin*/between the entry courtyard and the private gardens, on the second floor of a 1900 block of buildings at 49 Rue des Martyrs in the 9th arrondissement. The rooms were spacious and light, the rent was reasonable and the street was buzzing with shops of all kinds, mostly food. Later that month, lunching at Les Ministères with smart Paris friends, one of whom asked if we had found a flat and I told him where, to see a frown and a slight pause and then 'how chic, my dear Steven, no one has lived there since Proust.' Viewed from his smart 18th century Saint-Germain apartment, this was a fair comment and in fact the nearest hotel was the Hôtel Proust, but it was indeed a 'chic' decision, to be proved by the publication in 2016 of *The Only Street in Paris – Life on the Rue de Martyrs* by Elaine Sciolino, former Paris bureau chief for the *New York Times*, who lived there herself. This book was given to Bella by Pamela de Villaine, Californian born wife of Aubert of the Domaine de la Romanée-Conti. There is always a wine connection somewhere and another one is that my old friends Tim (Juveniles Wine Bar) and Stephanie Johnston have lived for ages right opposite at No 50.

This was to be an ideal introduction to Paris. The street was very long, starting at Eglise Notre Dame de Lorette on the northern edge of the sedate old financial district, it burst into life right away, rising steeply up as it went north towards the Boulevard de Clichy, finally ending in the 18th arrondissement near to Pigalle with the nightclubs and nude shows. On my nightly walks Digby, a well-brought up country dog, always refused to cross the Boulevard. The food shops were amazing and the weekend market one of the best in Paris. Shopping was a continuous joy and once I began to work long hours at Les Caves de la Madeleine I stopped cooking and Bella took over, getting advice from the boulangerie, boucherie, charcutier, fromagier and poissonerie as how dishes should be prepared. Occasionally I made a *sauce Béarnaise or beurre blanc*, but that was it. Paris today has lost many of these vibrant neighbourhood streets to clothing stores, both up and down market. From 1975 for over thirty years we had a flat on the edge of Le Marais, the now totally renovated historical 4th arrondissement, and the Rue Saint-Antoine, running from the Bastille Métro to that of Saint-Paul, while less vibrant than the Rue des Martyrs, was principally a food street. Now there is not a single butcher, nor fishmonger and just one cheese shop. As Elaine Sciolino's jacket cover says 'The Only Street in Paris that will make readers hungry for Paris, for cheese and wine and for the kind of street life that is all too quickly disappearing.'

It was while walking up such an old-fashioned little street, just a *passage* between the broad and aptly named Rue Royale that led from the Place de la Concorde to the Place de la Madeleine, and the Rue Boissy d'Anglas, with my lawyer friend Christopher Mitchell-Heggs on the way to lunch at a popular restaurant that we passed a little wine shop that would become the centre of my life in Paris for the next eighteen years. A couple of weeks' research in early September had made it plain to me that the wine trade I had imagined might resemble that of London with its structured importer/wholesaler and retailers did not exist. The wholesalers were there all right, in the process of being evicted from Les Halles au Vin in the 5th arrondissement and housed in big warehouses at Bercy in the 12th, near the Gare de Lyon, but the wines they dealt in were mostly branded *vins de table*. The retail sector was dominated to great effect by the Nicolas family, whose massive cellars further out of Paris at Charenton housed millions of bottles from *vins ordinaires* to Burgundy Grands Crus and Bordeaux First Growths and supplied over one hundred Nicolas shops in the city, four or five in every *quartier*. Then there were independent shops ranging from those announcing *vins-charbon-bois*/wine-coal-wood, providing domestic fuel as well as internal fuel in the cheaper districts, to well-stocked *cavistes* right up to the luxury establishments for the carriage trade. It was obvious that there was no place in any of these for a young Englishman with only passable French (in which I stammered more than in English, with a much smaller vocabulary to choose from), however much I knew about wine, so setting up on my own was the only answer.

As we entered the mews-like street with an open market in full swing, we passed a small wine shop which looked as though it had seen better days called Caves de la Madeleine. We stopped and I told Christopher that this was *exactly* the kind of shop I would like to buy. 'Let's go in' he said and inside was a huge chest acting as a counter, behind which stood an elegant lady of a certain age, who after a while asked if there was anything we wanted to buy. 'Yes' said Christopher in his very good French, 'my friend would like to buy your shop.' Due to the lunchtime crowd and the market which was there on Tuesdays and Fridays, it was very busy and Madame said that perhaps we could return later, which we did. She told us that the shop had been unofficially for sale for two years and mentioned the price for the *fonds de commerce*/the business and good will, of 300,000 Francs, or £25,000. Further discussions were held at her substantial apartment near the Gare de l'Est on the Boulevard Magenta and it appeared that her husband – *un grand caviste* - had died two years before and she was carrying on with the help of her sturdy little helper Mauricette (who was also her housemaid and cook) and Bernard who did the heavy lifting and the deliveries. (I am very happy to say that, forty seven years on, both Mauricette near Chartres and Bernard in Saint Lô in Normandy are both still going in their 80s, well-looked after by the French pension system.

As discussions continued, me never doubting the outcome, Bella with her supportive 'why not' attitude, Madame Fougères began to have doubts that I could manage the business up to the standards of her late husband. Remembering the wise move I had made during my *stagiaire* days of working without pay, I suggested that I work for her for six months for free and that at the end of that time if I had gained her confidence, we would finalise the deal. Duly on 1 April 1971 (the French version of April Fool's Day is *le poisson d'avril* and anyone fooled has a paper fish pinned to their back, but the fun ends at midday) Madame Fougères handed me the keys to both the shop and the cash desk, retired gracefully but continued to do the accounts for me for several months. The following day I placed a classified ad on the *Herald Tribune*'s back page under the heading 'Your wine merchant speaks English'.

But before then there was an important family event, the birth of our son on 21 February. This took place in London and within a week or so

Bella and the baby were back in Paris. For a first name we wanted something that would be as easy in French as in English so chose Christian. Bella's father thought this was a girl's name but we got our way by adding John before. Nicky then generously suggested that he could have Marston as his third name, as was the habit of every eldest Spurrier, but we kept the M and chose Mark. The christening of John Christian Mark Spurrier was held at the Marston church and was referred to by my grandfather as 'The Gipsy Christening' as we and the godparents were dressed in early 1970s finery.

In those days, much of the Caves de la Madeleine's turnover came from *vins ordinaires* which were bottled from tanks at the back of the shop and a big barrel in the cellar. All these came from a reliable producer called Prefontaines and were sold in the classic six star litre bottles with a plastic stopper. All over the country these wines were the daily drink, out of tumblers in the small kitchens of the workers, served from carafes into crystal glasses on the dining tables of the *bourgeoisie*. Brands were dominant, one of the biggest being Gévéor, billing itself as *le velours de l'estomac*/velvet for the stomach, while it was anything but. Selling wines like this, clients bring in empty bottles to have them filled up directly from the tanks, which might have made sense at *La Bagnolaise Cave Vinicole*, but not in a charming little street whose neighbours were the Embassies and the luxury shops on the Faubourg Saint Honoré, but in those days the social status of a *caviste* was the same as that of a *pompiste* or petrol pump attendant. Henri Gault and Christian Millau had founded their ground-breaking gastronomic magazine *Le Guide Gault & Millau* in 1969, bringing the chefs out of the kitchens onto their pages, to be followed by the *vignerons*, the *sommeliers* and finally the *cavistes*. Within just a few years I was part of Gault & Millau's intimate circle of wine tasters, my palate being described 'as precise as the finest Sheffield steel blade', ending up on one of their covers in the early 1980s, but I was in a hurry to put into practice the ideas that had evolved during the six months as the shop's delivery boy and general dogsbody. Madame Fougères had informed her suppliers of the sale and the suppliers – she had never of course set foot in a vineyard herself – came to be introduced, the Prefontaines salesman greeting with horror the fact that within the week the tanks and barrel would be gone and the bottling a thing of the past, telling me that I would lose 'half my clientele', which was exactly the half I intended to lose.

I had to buy all the stock and while there were some nice wines from the major appellations in France and the usual Champagnes, Monsieur Fougères's influence had been succeeded by safe buying of popular brands. During the previous winter Bella and I had discovered several cafés who specialised in wine and we talked to the owners about their suppliers. I also checked out the three major *cavistes*, whose shops were a revelation: Jean-Baptiste Chaudet and Jean-Baptiste Besse on the Left and Lucien Legrand on the Right Bank. Lucien Legrand and I were to open a substantial wine operation together within a couple of years, but in the mean time I bought bottles from all three and got in touch with the producers, always citing whose shop it came from, if I wanted them for my own selection. Bit by bit the brands, especially those of spirits and aperitifs, were removed despite financial offers to keep them. Wine shops like *Les Caves de la Madeleine* were visited regularly and since I was in the 'golden triangle' between the Place de la Concorde, the Gare Saint Lazare and the Arc de Triomphe, only the best salesmen came by. The man from Black and White whisky with its two border terriers on the label, made a generous offer to fill my small window with his product, only to be told that the 'window was not a kennel.' My aim was to sell wines from producers I knew to people I knew would like them, so it had to be personal. Being very much a 'square peg in a round hole' it didn't take long for the Press to come looking to see what was going on in La Cité Berryer.

It was all so exciting, just me and the ever cheerful Mauricette. Bernard had moved a couple of floors up in the building to deliver hand washed shirts, much less heavy than wine, and to replace him I began to employ a long line of 'junior year abroad' students mostly with parents at the British Embassy nearby. Writing in the *Trib* on 14 October 1991, under the heading 'The Rise and Fall and Rise of a Wine Guru', recording the 50th birthday party that I had given for friends and family at my former restaurant Le Moulin du Village, Mary Blume stated that 'Spurrier's delivery boys looked like the sons of belted earls, and perhaps they were.' Wines came and went with the range always expanding, my major suppliers being Pierre Coste for Bordeaux, Pierre Ferraud for Beaujolais and all the Crus, Burgundies from small domaines and what were to become household names from Alsace, the Loire and the Rhône, but in those days were hardly known. One day that autumn after lunch at *La Cloche des Halles* one of the bistros that had kept going once the great food market had been banished to the outskirts of Paris, thus taking the heart out of a centre of Paris that has never been revived, walking past a bookshop my eyes fell on a copy of *Connaissance du Vin* remaindered at 5 Francs (40p), a book that was to influence my life in wine more than any other.

The author was Constant Bourquin, a Swiss literary editor, publisher and philosopher, who, as I was to discover later, had founded *L'Académie Internationale du Vin* (AIV) in Geneva in 1971 with the purpose of waging a war against poor quality in wine. Today, when 90% of wines are not only good to drink but also true to their origin, it is hard to remember the everyday fraudulent behaviour from producers to merchants. The French rules of *Appellation d'Origine Contrôlée* (AOC) were laid down in 1933 thanks to Baron Leroy de Boismarie, owner of Château Fortia (and co-founder of the AIV) in Châteauneuf-du-Pape, the first AOC going to Châteauneuf itself, the second to Quincy in the Loire and it was not until after the 1953 vintage that AOC ranking was given to the commune of Margaux, previously under Haut-Médoc. The rules were based on *usages francs, loyaux et constants*/practices above-board, true and enduring that had been learnt from the past. These rules could not prevent poor wines being made, but they laid down what was, and was not allowed.

This concept of origin that is now accepted all over the world – basically a 'sense of place' due to soils, climate, exposition, grape varieties, wine making and ageing – did not bother the UK market when I started in the Trade. Around that time the *Sunday Times* exposed a massive fraud in Suffolk – just two vast vats of wine, one white and one red, with dozens of different labels for the merchants to choose from – under the title 'Château Ipswich.' Over in Bristol, the great Ronald Avery, doyen of one of the country's oldest wine merchants, did not hide the fact that many of his red Burgundies were 50% from the village of origin and 50% from 'the south' to give them more body. This perhaps explains my father remarking on the Pommard he had chosen to go with the famous jugged hare at Rules in London's Maiden Lane: 'this is how I like my Pommard, so thick you can stand a spoon in it.' It may also hint as to why I was able to buy two very good 1972 reds from the southern Rhône, a Châteauneuf-du-Pape and a Gigondas, under the Leroy label, who had never offered anything but Burgundy. I asked Lalou Bize-Leroy why she bought them and she said because they were of exceptional quality. My view is that her 1972 red Burgundies from a rainy and cold vintage turned out not to need any 'help' of this sort.

In his preface under the simple word *Argument*, Bourquin states 'What I am writing won't please everybody: it's not because of my opinions, for these, even the most unorthodox, won't stop anybody sleeping, but what will shock them is my attitude, for I have the audacity to bring to light certain practices that I find unworthy and the lack of tact to insist on this again and again.' His over-riding theme was that naturalness was all and that 'improving additions' were the thin end of the fraudulent wedge. This book was quite simply both a revelation and an inspiration and was responsible for additions to the Caves de la Madeleine range, but more particularly for two precise and ground-breaking ideas.

The first concerned Champagne. Bouquin did not approve of *dosage*, the *liqueur d'expedition* added after *dégorgement*, a blend of still Champagne, sugar and a little brandy, which enriched the final blend by much as 12% residual sugar, thus masking the high acidity of this sparkling wine from cool, northern vineyards. I had come across the *Vin Nature de la Champagne*, the still, unsweetened wine now known as AOC Côteaux Champenois, at the Restaurant Drouant in the Place Gaillon where since 1914 it had historically been served to the prestigious judges of the famed literary prize *Le Prix Goncourt*. Not knowing where to start, I called on Lucien Legrand, whose shop on the Rue de la Banque nearby was a wine lovers' mecca and is still, in different hands, today, for I had noticed that he sold a Vouvray Nature, a sparkling wine from the Loire Valley. Legrand, also very much a purist, agreed to help and in January 1972 we set off to see François Legras in the Premier and now Grand Cru Chouilly in the Côte de Blancs. Legras strongly advised against the idea and said he would go along with it only if we guaranteed to buy the whole *cuvée*. After tasting, we settled on a 1966 'dosed' with 1959. Looking for a name, I suggested Brut Intégral, for I had seen the Pigalle Club's advertising their nightly shows as *Nues Intégrales* and presented it to my mostly English clientele as being 'naked in its purity.' Brut Intégral caught on fast and we followed it with a Brut Zéro from Bonnaire-Bouquement in the Grand Cru Cramant. Competitors came up with Brut de Brut and Brut Sauvage, and then, as the fashion for *nouvelle cuisine/cuisine minceur* faded in the later 1970s, the market went back to more classic blends. Today *non-dosé* is back, principally from single growers and recently superb examples such as Pol Roger Pure and Louis Roederer Brut Nature, but, thanks to Constant Bourquin, Lucien Legrand and I got there first.

The second, more important, inspiration from Bourquin's book was his hatred of *chaptalisation,* adding sugar to the fermenting must to bolster up the alcohol content, a practice named after Professor Chaptal and declared legal by the *Institut National des Appellations d'Origine Contrôlée* (INAO) for most French regions except the south. It was particularly evident in the Beaujolais where, in Bourquin's opinion, it countered the freshness of the Gamay grape. Again, Lucien Legrand and I travelled down during vintage time in September 1973 to find what we were going to call *Beaujolais à l'Ancienne.* My supplier Pierre Ferraud introduced us to one of his growers in Brouilly who agreed, like François Legras, provided we purchase the whole cuvée, this time a much larger volume. Barrels were shipped to Legrand for bottling, the wines labelled *Beaujolais Nouveau* being embargoed for sale until the third Thursday in November. The day dawned and I placed two small barrels known as *feuillettes* marked A and B on either end of the bar in my *Académie du Vin* wine school, asking people to mark their preference on a bit of paper. The votes went 60/40 in favour of our 10% abv compared to the 12% 'classic', while consumption was 70/30. The following day I filled my shop window with our bottles, tying two lumps of sugar around their necks under the banner 'if you want sugar in your Beaujolais, add it yourself.' This was short-lived as our adventure was written up in the Press and came to the attention of the Government, who, knowing that the sugar for chaptalisation came from the sugar beet farmers in northern France, who had a lot of votes, insisted I abandon the window display under the threat of a substantial fine. At the time I bumped into the commercial director of Georges Duboeuf, the region's famous and to become more so *négociant* and asked him how his *en primeur* sales were going to be told 'in spite of your efforts, Monsieur Spurrier, very well thank you.' Today, *chaptalisation* is almost a dirty word. Constant Bourquin was a prophet.

Following the launch of Brut Intégral, I wrote to Constant Bourquin to thank him for having introduced me to his world of informed reflection on wines and their production and he gave me the address of his nephew Bernard Furth-Bourquin who lived in Paris. Only a few years older than me, Bernard turned out to be keen on art, wine and jazz and was also a Libra, so we got on fine. His day job was researching into oil extraction which kept him travelling a lot and in his spare time he ran a little wine company called DIVO-France, an offshoot of his uncle's *Défense et Illustration des Vins d'Origine* (DIVO-Suisse) based in Geneva. The small selection, the producers all appearing as examples of 'wine purists' who Bourquin admired in his book, was impeccable, among them were Champagne Leclerc-Briant, Huët in Vouvray, Gouges in Nuits-St-Georges, Marquis d'Angerville in Volnay, Chave in Hermitage, Rougier of Aix-en-Provence's Château Simone, Peyraud from Domaine Tempier in Bandol and Dr Parcé from Banyuls. Bernard gave me introductions and these wines began to make up the ever-expanding list at Caves de la Madeleine. But Constant Bourquin was responsible for more to come, for, sensing that I was on his wavelength, he asked Bernard to bring me to the meeting of *L'Académie Internationale du Vin* that December, where I was to meet such people and many others. Bourquin had founded this organisation based in Geneva in 1971 and in later years I referred to what had by then become an international 'think tank' as 'the conscience of the wine trade.' I had brought my copy of *Connaissance du Vin* with me for him to sign, which he did, adding 'a reader, and already an accomplice.' Before the 1973 meeting, always in Geneva the first week of December, I was informed that I had been elected as a member, the youngest by a long shot and the first from the UK. Even my acknowledged mentor Michael Broadbent had to wait a few years before joining the English contingent, but while I was given *Le Grand Prix de l'AIV* in 2002, only the third time it had been awarded, he beat me to this in being the second recipient.

Since then I have attended almost every December meeting and many of the summer excursions, even hosting a tour of English vineyards in Kent and Sussex in May 2013 which opened with a dinner at Boodle's and closed with a dinner at the Vintners' Hall, and have become truly committed to how Constant Bourquin's quest for *Le Vin Noble, le Vin Nature, le Vin Vrai*/Noble, Natural and True Wine, has grown immensely in stature and influence, which will continue long after I am gone.

In early 1971 Monsieur Van den Bosch had contacted me to say that the barge, named *Orion* after the astral constellation, had been retired from active life and was ready for conversion into a floating apartment. Where the petrol had been transported revealed a volume 30 metres by 5, the largest space we ever owned in Paris, and I roughed out a floor plan: entrance via steep steps a little back from the prow, where the huge anchor which was to come in very useful a year later, was stored, lavatory under the steps, a passageway off which was a bedroom, bathroom, bedroom and

Orion on the Seine opposite the Gare d'Orsay, 1972

kitchen-dining room (complete with 120 bottle wine rack), opening up into a 5×5 metre salon with opening roof, my study-dressing room and our 5×4 bedroom and bathroom at the end. The Van den Bosch team rose to the challenge and the result was simple but splendid. However, they forgot to tell me that boats, even stationary canal barges, are lower in the water at the stern than at the prow, and our lavatory had to be raised by a metre (exiting straight into the Seine, of course) causing me to have to pee sitting down. That summer we left the Rue de Martyrs and Bella, Christian, Digby and I moved in, happily moored upstream from the Pont de la Concorde with *La Gare d'Orsay*, later to become *La Musée d'Orsay*, on the opposite bank.

The two years we spent on *Orion* were simply wonderful. We didn't have a telephone connection and there were no mobiles in those days, so friends just drove or walked by and if we were on board joined us for a glass or wine or a meal. When we came to sell up after Easter 1973 – Bella was expecting another child and Catherine (Kate) arrived on 10 July which confirmed the Spurrier rule of Boy/Girl, except in my case, and we opted for more stable surroundings – I placed a classified ad in the trusty *Herald Tribune* under the heading 'A Penthouse on the Seine', for it really felt like we had the river at our feet. Quite often, while dining on deck, the large tourist *bateaux mouches* that passed up and down the river turned their spotlights on us to show how good life on the water was. My father didn't think much of my running a small wine shop and living on a barge ('you have all that money and you and Bella behave like hippies'), until he was handing in his car at the Hertz desk at Bordeaux airport after a week with my mother at the Hôtel du Palais in Biarritz, to be asked by the clerk noticing the name 'you're not the well-known wine merchant by any chance?' This produced a parental visit which went off very well.

Early in 1972 an imposing gentleman came into the shop introducing himself as Sir Guy Salisbury-Jones to tell me that H.M. The Queen and Prince Philip would be paying their first official visit to Paris around Easter and, as the owner of Hambledon Vineyards in Hampshire he would like very much for me to import his wine to be present on that occasion. Sir Guy was a Major-General and had been attached to the British Embassy after the war and, with his wife, would also be present. The village of Hambledon was the birth-place of the game of cricket and there had been a vineyard around the Manor House in Roman times, which he had replanted with hybrid varieties such as Madeleine Angevine to make a pleasant just off-dry white wine. I agreed to take sixty bottles, the wines were flown into Orly Airport, but when I turned up at the customs office to collect them I was told it was *Pas possible, Monsieur,* for the simple reason that English Wine did not exist in the customs' books, so how could he clear for delivery something which did not exist? (I was to hear *Pas possible, Monsieur* quite often during my life in France and there was always a way round, but this was first time when logic beat reality). The following day I returned, pointing out to the officer that the five cases did exist, being on the floor just behind his desk, only to receive the same answer. Then came the following exchange:

— Does your job exist?
— Of course, *Monsieur*, I am a custom's officer.
— Well, very soon your job will not exist as these wines are due
   to be served to President Pompidou by H.M. The Queen this very
   evening at the British Embassy.
— In that case, *pour mon Président*....and the papers were stamped
   and I took the wine away with me. The wine was of course never
   supposed to be served at the Embassy.

My shop window with Hambledon wine. Me on the left, Digby's head in the centre.

Back in Paris I filled the shop window with Sir Guy's bottles, placing a fine photograph of the Queen alongside them, with the proclamation *Il y a deux bonnes choses qui viennent d'Angleterre, la Reine et le Vin/* There are two good things that come from England, The Queen and Wine. Little did I know then that four decades later this slogan was to prove absolutely true.

It was thanks to Hambledon's white wine that I finally met Jon Winroth, the wine correspondent for the *Herald Tribune* and the future founder with me at the end of the year of *L'Académie du Vin*. Since taking charge of the Caves de la Madeleine I had sent the odd bottle to him at the *Trib*'s offices in the Rue de Berri to tell him of my existence, but had received no reaction. An English wine, I thought, would do the trick and I took it along personally late one morning. Asking where I could find him, I was told on the 3rd floor and emerging from the small, rickety lift almost bumped into someone and asked whether Jon Winroth was around and it turned out to be Winroth himself. I introduced myself to be told 'Oh, you're the guy sending me all these wines, I'm going off to lunch, why don't you leave the bottle here and join me?' We went to one of those noisy *brasseries* that have disappeared from the 8th arrondissement, shared several glasses of Beaujolais with the *plat du jour* and separated as firm friends. Jon was of Swedish descent, his surname appropriately meaning 'wine root', only a few years older than me, from Illinois and had moved to Paris with his wife Doreen, another half-Swedish Illinois resident, and lived with two very young boys in a tiny top floor flat off the Boulevard Saint-Germain. Doreen was the secretary to a doctor who specialised in liver and kidney diseases and was involved in helping female students from the US to learn as much as they could from the few weeks they spent in France on their 'junior year abroad' programme. Of course, one of the things they had to learn about was wine, and Jon gave them afternoon lessons in the back rooms of his favourite *bistrots à vin*, many of which exist to this day.

I had built up a clientele of mostly north American expats from the finance and legal professions which were very strongly represented in the centre of Paris at that time, many of them within walking distance of my shop, especially IBM who were in the next door street. On Friday evenings many of them crammed into the shop to taste and hear me talk them through my new discoveries. One of the regulars said that if ever I could do this on a more structured basis, they would love to take a wine course. Over the summer Jon and Doreen were regular visitors to the barge, Jon introduced me to wine bars in every part of the city and we felt something could be done, but where? Then, as luck would have it (the 70s were a very lucky decade, but the 80s got their own back), the premises separated by only a stairway from the Caves de la Madeleine, a locksmith with a large workshop on the ground floor and a three roomed office above, shut down. The space went up for auction and since nobody seemed keen to continue in the locksmith business I was able to acquire it at a modest price. The request to change the use from that of a locksmith to an organisation communicating to students the history and the qualities of the wines of France did not pose a problem for the authorities. The original name I had in mind was *L'Ambassade du Vin*, but searches disclosed that it had been taken, so I tried for *L'Académie du Vin* and this simple, generic name was not, another piece of good fortune.

As work went on during the autumn, the ground floor to be the tasting room, the upstairs much needed office space and eventually an impressive library from which books could be borrowed, the authorities asked me whether I was going to sell wine that would be consumed on the premises and if I was, I would not be allowed to, as that was the prerogative of cafés and restaurants. Everything around alcohol was licensed in France and for the shop, selling to take away being the equivalent of the UK 'off-trade' I had a License No 1. License No 4 was the ultimate, allowing the premises to offer alcohol of any kind with or without food, while License No 3 was for wines and grape based-products of 20 degrees or under for sale with food, neither of which I could apply for. License No 2 was not mentioned and this appeared to be for special occasions when a normally un-licensed premises – like a church or school – wished to present wines on a commercial basis. This suited me fine, only to be told that I couldn't apply as I would be selling wine on a regular basis. My answer to this was that I was selling education, not wine, wine merely being part of the teaching process, but that I would indeed need a License No 2 for events like the launch of Beaujolais Nouveau, where education was not part of the package. They finally agreed.

Jon, who was the most honest wine critic I ever knew, was well-accepted in Parisian wine circles and told me I should meet Odette Khan, the tall and elegantly stylish editor of *La Revue du Vin de France*, the very good wine magazine. She was holding *Le Concours du Meilleur Sommelier* not too far away near the Opéra and we went along and he introduced me. Madame Khan saying she didn't have time to talk as the written exam was about to start. I asked if I could take it, receiving in reply a surprised *Pouquoi pas?*/Why not? I completed the papers quite quickly, handing them back in saying I needed to get back to my shop and hoped we she would call in at some time. The following day she did just that, congratulating me on a pass rate of 100%, which had never been achieved by any competing sommelier. Thus began a mutually admiring relationship until the day on 24 May 1976 she took part in the tasting I held comparing California wines to their French counterparts which came to be known as The Judgement of Paris, after which she accused me of 'spitting in the soup of my adopted country' and I was never spoken to again.

This was far in the future and in the meantime thanks to Jon's contacts, I was invited to be a judge alongside him at the *Foire Agricole de Paris* and *La Foire de Mâcon*. The former, out at the Porte de Versailles in early April, presented everything that was agricultural in France. One of the halls was reserved for food produce of every shape and size, raw or cooked and the wine stands were part of that. In the vast adjoining halls were the animals, fish, fowl and of course the four-legged beasts of the field, whose bellowing, moo-ing, bleating and baa-ing could be heard as we settled at tables of four on the pre-opening Saturday morning to taste the just-bottled or about-to-be bottled wines. The basic rules for the tasting tables were that there should be two judges from the region concerned, one a producer, the other a merchant, and two from Paris, one a merchant and one from the Press. Jon and I fitted the Paris bill well and the first year we found ourselves tasting Alsace, flanked by two burly *Alsatiens*. Ranking was on the 20 point scale, the whole 20 being used in those days, and the difference between their marks in the high teens and our's hardly in double figures caused heated discussions in their local dialect before some sort of agreement could be reached. In future years we opted for the calmer waters of the Loire Valley.

The week of the Fair was jammed with Parisians keen for a sense of their countryside and here good contacts were made so the producers could sell direct to the public, the same producers coming back year after year. In the early days even established growers like Gaston Huët, Mayor of Vouvray who twenty years later was successful in forcing the Paris-Bordeaux TGV line to be diverted around the Vouvray vineyards rather than through them, was behind his table to make the sales which, with few export markets in those days, took up an important part of his annual production. I was already a Huët client, but my annual visits to the Paris Fair always delivered something new.

The Mâcon Fair in the middle of May was smaller and more focussed on Central France. Both awarded Gold, Silver and Bronze Medals and the international wine competitions today still use the same system, the ranking for most now being on the 100 point scale. The little round stickers that the successful wines have on their bottles was always an indication of quality and it was a no-brainer to propose this system to *Decanter* magazine when I was asked to set the ground rules for the *Decanter* World Wine Awards, for many years the world's largest wine competition with 18,000 wines entered in 2017, back in 2003. While the Porte de Versailles was just a metro ride away, Mâcon before the TGV arrived on its doorstep long after I had left Paris, entailed a three or four day drive south through Chablis and Burgundy, tasting at a few domaines on the way. Jon had been a judge for some years and Pierre Ferraud, my Beaujolais supplier made sure we got onto some good tasting tables. This wouldn't have mattered as the atmosphere was both more professional and more convivial than in Paris and the hard morning's work produced good results. I kept up my attendance here right into the mid 1980s and always enjoyed it.

In the early years Pierre Ferraud always proposed lunch at the excellent restaurant in Chénas owned by the Robin family and with a few others generally six or eight of us made sat down to a cheerful table. On arriving after the tasting in 1974 I saw a photographic session being set up on the tree-line terrace of the hotel-restaurant that overlooked the Chénas vineyards. An enquiry into what was plainly an Englishman told me that it was a shoot for advertising Piat Beaujolais, a leading brand that had recently been taken over by International Distillers and Vintners (IDV) who owned the beautiful Château Loudenne in the Médoc, managed by my old friend Martin Bamford where I used to stay at least once a year. Martin had been given an office in Mâcon to oversee the new direction of Piat, whose quality was good but not great. I told the gentleman from the London advertising agency that if he 'needed some real Beaujolais drinkers, we would be in the restaurant', thinking nothing of it until half way through out first course he rushed in to say that one of the male participants hadn't turned up and could I come take his place right away as they needed to shoot while the sun was right. The faithful Digby had travelled down with me and since he was in the car on a hot day, I said I would, so long as I could bring my dog. He had no choice but to agree and the shot took time to be set up and when the moment came to take the final images, I made sure not to be photographed drinking a wine that I would not have wanted in my shop. The full-page advertisement duly appeared in the UK in *Punch* and other magazines throughout the summer with a text in French to show how *Français* the Piat Beaujolais was. Simply translated it reads:

'To give yourself an idea of summers in France, you should drink Piat de Beaujolais nice and cool. Almost every Sunday in summer friends get together to have lunch outside. While the trees offer an agreeable freshness, we like our drinks to have the same freshness and perhaps you will be surprised to know that we serve Piat de Beaujolais well-chilled. But this is how we find the wine so agreeable and aromatically seductive. You, the English, should try this and perhaps it might make you forget the miseries of your terrible English summers.'

No sooner had this appeared than I received a furious telephone call from my friend Martin: 'What the hell are you doing in my advertisement and with that damned dog of yours!?' Digby had already fallen foul of Martin the year before at Loudenne. The château had a wonderful butler and cook couple, Sylvain and Josette, who had previously worked at Moët et Chandon's Château de Saran outside Epernay. Sylvain was always perfectly turned out, with a stripey waistcoat during the day and a dinner jacket in the evening. Martin and the house guests were comfortably lounging in the large double salon late one Sunday morning, looking forward to the pre-lunch aperitif, usually *Lillet Blanc* on the rocks, known as a 'sharpener'. The telephone rang and since it was Sunday, Martin didn't answer it. Suddenly Sylvain burst through the door leading to the dining room (where he had presumably been setting up for lunch) dashing to get to the telephone, while Digby, comatose by my chair, woke up sharply and his sheep dog genes telling him that here was an intruder from whom the company should be protected, rose to his feet and with one bound caught Sylvain on the shoulders with his front paws, bringing him to the ground. The telephone rang off. After a short silence Martin turned to me and said 'Steven, will you please get your dog off my butler'. The Piat advertising campaign was a great success and Martin never referred to it again.

Richard Bartholomew, a recent acquaintance and also a friend of the Ferraud family, was tasting at Mâcon that May and we headed down south to Vacqueyras in the southern Rhône together as I had recently become his 49% partner in a nine hectare vineyard with an attractive stone farmhouse or *mas* called *Le Clos du Caveau*. This came about since while at Murray and Banbury I had met a charming man Nicholas Barrow with wine trade connections who had left for Bordeaux in the early 1960s to purchase a tiny vineyard near Arcins in the Médoc called Château Courant, along with an equally tiny but charming house. Nicholas was a dreamer and nothing he ever did in wine over the next decade came to anything, but one of his bright ideas was to create a mobile bottling company, which would turn up on the château's demand to do their bottling, which saved them installing a bottling line which was only used once a year. This was not a new idea, as there was a very successful one based in Saint-Emilion, where the average size of the estates was much smaller and an automated bottling line un-economic. In the Médoc the estates were larger, but in the early 1970s there was very little money to invest and so the Barrow Bottling Line served a real purpose. Nicholas needed funds for his business and I could see the potential – even Léoville and Langoa-Barton hired him to bottle their 1972s – and so became his sleeping partner. The company didn't prosper, Château Courant had to be sold and Nicholas ended up briefly the technical director of Château Malescasse which had been bought by an American consortium. Before this, he and Richard Bartholomew had acquired the Clos du Caveau in a run down state, the latter living there with his wife and two small children. Nicholas admitted that the collapse of the bottling company was his fault and being a 'gent' and unable to return even a part of my investment, made over to me his shares in this estate.

I liked Richard Bartholomew. He looked after the vineyard and made the wine, but he wasn't over-industrious and the place was a mess. For a week in that August I helped him bottle the very good 1973s, using a borrowed hand pump as the mechanical one was broken. Patricia Gallagher, who had taken on the running of *L'Académie du Vin* in early 1973, said that the house would make a wonderful 'summer school' (which of course it would have done) but we were both too busy in Paris to take this much further. The Crédit Agricole approached me and said that they were about to foreclose on the property for its debt of around £7,000 and added that if I gave them guarantees to settle this and refinance the company, they would indeed foreclose, evict the Bartholomews and return the company to me. Being well-brought up, I thought that one didn't do that sort of thing to one's friends, but set about raising funds from my well-off clients in Paris. Once again, the *Herald Tribune* carried my classified ad, this time headed 'Invest in the Booming Wine Trade' and I prepared a sales document which led off with the caveat that in France 'there were three ways to lose money: horses were the quickest, women were the most fun and agriculture was the most certain.' I quickly raised around £15,000, which would have paid off the bank, put the *mas* back into shape for the new investors to stay in and planned to rent out the vines to neighbours and shut down the wine operation. Innocently, I repaid the bank and told Richard that I had saved the company from going under and would now run the house on a profitable basis and he and his wife would have to find somewhere else to live. The problem was I still had only 49% and his wife refused consider moving and within a few months the whole place was sold for not much money to one of the Testut brothers from Chablis who had bought a small estate in Lirac, later to a very nice Swiss family called Bungener, who still have it, now farmed bio-dynamically and making very good wine, to this day. My investors were repaid and to make up for their disappointment received some bottles of the 1973, which I had labelled up *Cuvée des Actionnaires*/shareholders' blend. The property was simply lovely, tucked into the spiky ridge of hills known as *Les Dentelles de Montmirail* which ran past Gigondas to Beaumes de Venise, but I had a lot on my plate and it was the one that got away.

Back in Paris my Burgundy-loving friend David Fromkin, who had become a tiny investor in the Caves de la Madeleine, was there during the summer, treating me and a few others to some marvellous wines in restaurants with great cellars, some of which I helped pack up a few years later for auction at Christie's. We made a series of successful forays to Prunier, only a few streets away on the Rue Duphot, where we had the bright idea of ordering meat – generally a superbly prepared *steak tartare* – which allowed us to plough through their red Burgundies from the late 1940s and early 1950s which other customers didn't buy for their oysters and *sole meunière*. Just next door in the Place de la Madeleine was Caviare Kaspia, with a shop downstairs and a discreet restaurant upstairs with caviar of course, but other fine dishes with a Russian twist, the main attraction being their collection of 1928 Champagnes (a full 5 stars in Michael Broadbent's *Great Vintage Wine Book*) at the same price as current vintages and over one week, along with Bobby Ho, we treated ourselves to a horizontal of Bollinger, Mumm, Perrier-Jouet, Pol Roger, Louis Roederer and Veuve Clicquot, three more than even the great Broadbent managed to record.

David not only loved the wines of Burgundy, he decided to buy a house there, as long as it had a vaulted cellar to store what would become his wine collection. He gave me the price of up to $50,000 and I set off with Jean-Pierre Pavillard, an accomplished still life photographer for whom Bella worked part time, who would subsequently become godfather to our daughter Kate and even later take a series of quite superb photographs of wine colours (I used the actual wines, most other books before and since make up the colours) for my *Académie du Vin Wine Course* publication. Transforming David's price into 300,000 French Francs, we looked around, starting south of Chablis, ending up on the first day in Semur-en-Auxois, just on the edge of the *Département* of the Côte d'Or and not far from David's absolute favourite restaurant in France, the Hotel de la Côte d'Or in Saulieu, which had three Michelin stars for ever under its august chef Alexandre Dumaine and then had two under his pupil François Minot.

When friends had come to stay at Bayonne and saw the plans for the villa and the size of the house emerging, I sometimes used to joke that I had thought the plans had been done in feet but they had turned out to be in metres. At a small estate agent just off the main square in what was to become our local country town for many years, I presented the requirements of an old house with a vaulted cellar around 300,000FF, and was told that 'there was simply not even a heap of stones available any more at that price, but he had something interesting at 1,500,000FF'. The agent had assumed, as Jean-Pierre and I had dressed down for house-hunting, that we had been talking in Old Francs (100:1) and had replied in kind, his offer being £1,250 the price of a second hand car. We went to look at the house, a fine 18th century *Maison de Maître* on three floors with a heavy stone roof, two vaulted cellars, a bread oven and a walled in 2000 square metres of ravaged grass in front of it and a roofless *pigeonnier* which had been turned into an outhouse lavatory. There was no running water, a well at the back into which a sheep had fallen and the house, in a tiny village south of Semur-en-Auxois, which had been the agent's house for the surrounding lands owned by a very ancient family in Dijon, had been abandoned for years. My time in the world of antiques told me that the 18th century carved doors alone, with their original handles, were worth more than the asking price, immediately paid 10% down to take it off the market and said I would be back next week with my wife to go ahead or not.

Back in Paris I told David that I had found him a house with cellars and he didn't even have to pay for it, just send his wine down and come and stay whenever he wanted. This suited him fine and we drew up the deeds with the very ancient owner, Madame Degouve des Nuncques, in her grand house in Dijon, who seemed glad to get shot of it. The renovation was put in the hands of an Australian, Peter Ryan, who with his stunning '60s chick' wife Brooke, had become close friends in London after our marriage and had left for Provence, because his great friend and business partner at that time, Peter Clifton, had moved with his wife Elaine into my London house on a short rental agreement. My relationship with Peter and Elaine Clifton was to end in tears, but the introduction to Peter and Brooke was heaven-made and they have remained the closest possible friends despite living since the mid 1970s in Palm Beach, near Sydney. Very sadly Peter died in early 2017.

Peter and Brooke had twin girls – Kashia and Saskia, little blonde angels – and they shared our lives for about nine months, renting a small place in the village next door to ours which was called Marcigny-sous-Thil, the counts of Thil having owned everything as far as the eye could see Peter put together a team of workmen, helped by the estate agent who I thanked with some nice wines for finding me the place, and our house took shape inside to end up with a large three-windowed, high oak-beamed ceiling sitting room with sizeble kitchen dining room off it, two very spacious bedrooms on the first floor with their own bathrooms, and a massive play-room under the oak beams upstairs with a bedroom and bathroom off it for the children. When he saw the house, Jean-Pierre Pavillard said that if I ever sold it, could I offer it to him first? From a buying price of £1,250 to a selling price of £40,000 to him in the mid 1980s, seemed a big jump and naturally the French tax people called on me for a *plus value*/capital gain. We had done a lot of work over the years, a complete re-roofing, putting in heating and so on and I had kept perhaps half the invoices, but even with these the tax people went away empty handed.

We only used the house from April to October, Burgundy winters were very cold indeed and if we forgot to drain the water pipes they burst in the spring causing huge damage, but it was a marvellous weekend break from Paris and for some of the summer holidays, though most of these were spent from 1975 near to Saint-Rémy de Provence, where Bella's half-brother, the airplane pilot James Baring, had bought a charming place called *Le Mas du Cellier*, and was planting a vineyard under the Baux de Provence appellation.

By Easter 1973 we had firmly and sadly decided to move onto dry land, the barge was sold – not into good hands the first time, but we saw it many years later moored on the Right Bank opposite the Eiffel Tower on the Left and dropped in to meet the owners, who were true boat people and had kept it in very good shape and I had no problem selling Fernshaw Road and with the capital bought a second floor flat in the Place des Hospitaliers Saint Gervais, just off the Rue des Francs Bourgeois bang in the middle of the Marais, which was just recovering from a century of neglect to become one of the most sought-after places to live in Paris. The furniture from London looked good in Paris and Burgundy, there was just enough wall space for my pictures. Bernard (Madame Fougère's delivery man) Hopquin's wife Thérèse became the in-house child minder to look after Christian and the newly-born Kate, and life seemed to settle down into a more structured existence.

L'Académie du Vin was finished by the end of 1972, the tasting room with its terracotta tiles on the floor and stripped back oak beams on the high ceiling offering a very sympathetic space with a bare original 16th century stone wall at the end and a horseshoe shaped Napoleon III (1870) marble topped bar, complete with all its ormolu fittings, ready to receive the first students. I hadn't thought of how the wine school was to be set out, presumably just classroom style as there was certainly the space, until the architect builder in charge of the renovation called me to say that there was this bar in a café that was being demolished near to where he lived which he thought would be perfect, but I needed to come and see it, pay for it and take it away that very day before it went onto the tip. The price mentioned was 500FF (£40) quite plainly not a sale price, just something in the pocket for the demolishers to save them the trouble of breaking it up. This was an astounding piece of luck, confirming the 70s as a very lucky decade, and somehow, between my delivery van and a few taxis, this century old work of art arrived in the Cité Berryer to set L'Académie du Vin off on its road to success.

The other thing that arrived in the Cité Berryer in late 1972 and was even more important in the *Académie's* success was a young American lady called Patricia Gallagher. Patricia hailed from Wilmington, Delaware, where her ancestors had landed in the early 1600s. She was an occasional client in the shop, living in the 8th arrondissement writing for newspapers back home and the occasional job for the *Herald Tribune*. We got on very well, both sharing an interest in what might happen next and although we didn't see each other too often, Patricia always seemed to appear at the right moment, this one being the third Thursday of November's launch of 1972's Beaujolais Nouveau. She knew Jon Winroth a little from the *Trib*, so it seemed quite natural when after dismissing the rained off 1972s and starting to talk about the planned wine school, Patricia simply stated that 'what you two need is someone to run this.' A long time later there was some friction between Jon and Patricia concerning the history of *L'Académie du Vin*, with Jon, who became too ill after a few years with a debilitating kidney disease inherited from his mother to continue teaching, fading into the background but never relinquishing his position as co-founder. What he and I had started on a 'let's do this and hope it works'

Steven and Patricia in front of the bar in 1977

idea, Patricia turned into completely structured business which provided something new and finally indispensable in Paris. Of the very many wine ventures I started during my time in Paris, *l'Académie du Vin* is far and away that which I am most proud of.

Another venture of which I am proud, which grew tremendously in size and influence long after I had ceased to be part of it, was Le Chemin des Vignes with Lucien Legrand and Bernard Bourquin. Following the success of the *non-dosé* Champagnes and the Beaujolais à l'Ancienne, Legrand and I were in regular contact and I suggested that both our businesses needed somewhere to expand to, particularly his bottling facilities as it was much cheaper to receive wines from the vineyards in barrel or tank and bottle them (the bottles being re-cycled to save even more money) than to receive wine in bottle. I mentioned that most of the wholesalers in London had warehouses underneath the railway arches in the City of London, with vast space and perfect conditions for wine storage and we should look for this. Legrand came across some abandoned arches, about two square kilometres of them, that supported the Paris-Tours railway lines on the outskirts of the city at Issy-les-Moulineaux. The bus stop outside the entrance was called *Le Chemin des Vignes*, so it seemed pre-ordained. Bernard became a minor partner, dropping out after a year or two

—124—

and selling me his shares, Legrand was the major partner as the bulk of the business for him would be bottling and the interest for me would be storage for my ever-increasing wine purchases. The Paris wine trade was amazed by our ambition and the Press, who were very keen on both Legrand and myself, compared what we planned to the low-quality wholesalers at the Porte de Bercy as *un Bercy intelligent*/Bercy with brains, which was quite correct. Fast forward to 1999 and Vinopolis-City of Wine opened with me as a director and shareholder under similar arches near to Southwark Cathedral which supported the trains from Cannon Street. Both ventures evolved from their original concept and achieved considerable success, alas no longer with me on board to benefit. I have a habit of having wonderful ideas, starting them up and then not paying attention as there was always something else on the horizon. As my daughter Kate reminds me 'Dad, your problem is you're bored with the present', which is too true and has been financially quite disastrous.

But back to the early 1970s, where one of my friends from the London wine trade, Melvyn Master, was to reappear in my life to great advantage and amusement. Melvyn, like me, became rich young and certainly intended to enjoy himself. He got a wine trade scholarship which took him to Jerez and Bordeaux; when back in England he founded The London Wine Company in the late 1960s with three partners that was one of the first to deal in Bordeaux futures. He also loved food and created the Jeroboam Club which met once a month at Wolfe's, owned by the small and spherical David Wolfe and described as 'the long thin restaurant with the short fat proprietor.' I was a regular member and we tried to outdo each other with the bottles we brought to the dinners. The London Wine Company folded in the 1969 recession and he and his wife Janey decided to move to France, Bella and I meeting them by chance at the marvellous 2 Michelin star La Mère Bourgeois restaurant in Priay, near Bourg-en-Bresse. They had driven from England with their Volvo shooting break crammed with everything they would miss from home, like Marmite, oatcakes, and so on, plus sheets and towels for a long stay, enough to start a small shop and showed this off with pride. The following morning the Volvo had been broken into and everything taken. Melvyn's fortitude in front of such a disaster has stayed with him over the years through many, many ventures in the US, where he and Janey still live and have as much fun as ever.

By the time I had taken over the Caves de la Madeleine, the Masters had moved to Aix-en-Provence and Melvyn was forming an export company named Master Wines and Janey was training to be a chef. One of the team was John Livingstone-Learmonth, who wrote (with Melvyn's name on the first edition as he had backed it) the *Wines of the Rhône*, the first ever book on the Rhône valley. John great opus is *Wines of the Northern Rhône*, 670 pages of brilliantly-written, passionate and insightful description of the Place, the People and the Product. John and I got on immediately and he introduced me to Marcel Guigal in late 1971, and the Caves became Marcel's first retail client in Paris. Janey needed an *au pair* girl to look after the house and the babies and hired Stephanie Collins, whose parents ran a very successful pub in Wiltshire. She appeared with her boyfriend and future husband Tim Johnston, who worked for me briefly in 1982 before joining Mark Williamson to become the Rhône Rangers of Paris, both firm members of 'Le Mafia Anglais' as our group used to be called. Finally, they were joined by Robert (Bob) Baker, who became the editor of a little wine magazine that Melvyn had launched for his clients in the US.

Melvyn and I were often in touch and after one of the *Foire de Mâcon* tastings, we agreed to meet at the 3 star Michelin Paul Bocuse just outside Lyon for lunch. In the early 1970s Bocuse was the king of French cuisine, with many disciples of the highest quality. Later he was to become the Emperor. I was with Jon Winroth, who Melvyn hadn't met and we all got stuck into a memorable lunch, which produced one of my limericks:

> With Melvyn and Janey and Jon,
> We're totally, utterly gone.
> We started with Pouilly,
> Then Chénas and Brouilly,
> Fleurie, Morgon, and Moulin-à-Vent.

About forty years later Melvyn (who had exported the Bocuse label wines made by Georges Duboeuf to the US), Janey (who had worked for six months in Bocuse's kitchen), John Livingstone-Learmonth, Tim and Stephanie Johnston, Bob Baker and I all met up for dinner at Bocuse. Bocuse himself was there, looking like a waxwork from Madame Tussaud's, and offered us a bottle of Champagne. While we drank this we chose a good range of wines and then the menu. The meal was a complete disaster, the Maitre d' offering to change our main courses. We stayed for the cheese to finish the red wine and left before the *chariot de desserts* to drive into Lyon for some reviving Beaujolais. The following day I wrote a lengthy and stinging email to the *Michelin Guide* to receive a reply saying that they had never had any criticism of Bocuse and would check it out. The restaurant at Collonges au Mont d'Or still has three stars, but there is not a single other 3 star restaurant in Lyon, the acknowledged gastronomic capital for France, nor in the vicinity, the nearest being Troisgros, 84 kilometres away in Roanne. The *Michelin Guide* did not dare offend Emperor Bocuse, who died in January 2018.

Back in Paris the shop was doing very well as was *L'Académie du Vin*. We held a six session *Tour de France* course, followed by a four session more in depth course on specific regions. Jon taught his junior year abroad students who were delighted to be introduced to wine. He matched them with cheeses from Barthélémy, his favourite *fromagier* near his flat and I overheard him showing the group a Condrieu, the marvellously seductively aromatic yet dry wine make from the Viognier grape in the northern Rhône, and saying that there wasn't really a match to drink it with, when a girl put up her hand and says 'what about a good-looking guy?' The Press soon got wind of *L'Académie du Vin* and we began to give courses in French, Bernard Bourquin introducing his Swiss friend Michel Dovaz, already one of the recognised Parisian wine writers. We began to hold comparative tastings, both vertical and horizontal, often with the proprietors present to talk about their wines. By 1975 we had achieved a reputation that allowed us to break out of the confines of La Cité Berryer and that autumn we held a comparative tasting of the nine First Growths of Bordeaux with all the owners except that of Haut Brion present and Alexandre de Lur-Saluces bringing his own *foie gras* to go with Château d'Yquem. This, choreographed by Patricia, was a great success and by 1983 it had expanded into what was known as *La Baptême du Millésime*, a tasting/dinner (that year barrel samples of the great 1982) which was held at Gaston Lenotre's 3 star Le Pré Catalan restaurant in the Bois du Boulogne attended by 150 people and a precursor to the Union des Grands Crus Tastings that are held all over the world today.

It seems embarrassing to say it, but in terms of wine appreciation, promotion and communication, *L'Académie du Vin* was 'the only game in town'.

8. The Judgement of Paris

When he was about six years old, my elder grandson asked me 'Grandpa, why are you famous?' I took him to my study and showed him the book written by George M. Taber about *The Judgement of Paris, the Historic Tasting that Revolutionized Wine*. It was the account of the tasting in Paris on 24 May 1976 that transformed the wine industry.

The inspiration for *L'Académie du Vin* showing a range of Chardonnays and Cabernet Sauvignons from California to nine of the finest palates in France came from Patricia Gallagher, who had tried without success to find some wines in Paris to show to our students on 4 July, the American Independence Day. Because the shop and the school were in the centre of Paris and more importantly because we spoke English, we began to receive visits from Californian winemakers and US wine writers, but the real starting point was her visit to California in September 1975. As she describes it:

'In saying that 'the British do not celebrate American independence' you credit me with the idea of the 'Bicentennial Tasting', for which I thank you. I am happy to accept paternity of the idea and welcome the opportunity to reminisce and explain why I was so committed to showing California wines to their advantage on the occasion of the American Bicentennial. I had a personal reason and a professional one. Personally, the Declaration of Independence was signed 20 minutes by car (an overnight ride on horseback in 1776) from Wilmington, Delaware, where I was born. Ours is a colonial family, having emigrated from England in 1634, so I was definitely caught up in the excitement of celebrating our 200th Anniversary. Professionally, I had organised two failed 4 July events at *L'Académie du Vin* in 1974 and 1975, disappointing because of the poor quality of California wines available in Paris at that time, even from the luxury shops Fauchon and Hédiard. From passing acquaintance with Robert Mondavi's book *Unfiltered* and Robert Finigan's *Private Guide to Wine*, I knew there were better California wines. The challenge would be selecting the wines and somehow getting them to Paris.

A few days before my 1975 summer vacation in the US, Glenda

Cudaback, a close friend from the *Herald Tribune* days, and her husband David, both natives of Napa, suggested I extend the short trip I had planned to see my sister in southern California and drive north to Napa. For years they had been promoting California wines and encouraging me to visit Napa Valley. This time they offered David's parents' hospitality in Napa and a car to tour the vineyards. As their guest, with Robert Finigan's introductions to Ridge, Heitz, Montelena, Mayacamus and Stag's Leap and his company part of the way, I visited them all. I didn't carry back samples, but I distinctly remember sharing with you my hugely positive impression of the people I met and the quality of their wines.

With exactly two bottles of each wine you selected in April 1976, we honoured an historic event that was important to me by showing some of the finest wines of California. You and I have often said that, as we walked back to *L'Académie du Vin* after the tasting, we were far from imagining the impact it was to have.'

Robert Finigan was a key figure in our selection of the wines. He was also the middle of the 'Three Roberts' of monthly wine guides in the USA. The first, also from California, was Robert Lawrence Balzer, middle-aged and prone to long, floral descriptions of the wines he tasted. By the mid-1970s Harvard-educated Robert Finigan's star was on the rise and his image burnished by having married Marimar Torres, Miguel Torres's younger sister. Finigan also published a restaurant review newsletter and later branched out into reviewing classical music, so perhaps with so much on his plate it was not surprising that he did not pay sufficient attention to the 1982 vintage in Bordeaux, dismissing it as 'untypical', which indeed it was for being both high quality and high volume, only to see himself replaced by Robert Parker, author of *The Wine Advocate*, who had only started in 1978. I remember being shown an early copy of this review at Château Loudenne by Martin Bamford with the remark that 'this is a person to watch.' But at that time, Robert Finigan was the one to be with and he was very good company indeed.

Before meeting Finigan, Alexis Bespaloff, the wine columnist for *New York Magazine*, had come into the Cité Berryer bringing a few bottles of wine from California wineries that were admired in New York. Discussing who else in Paris might be interested in trying them, I had no hesitation in suggesting an ex-New Yorker now Paris resident named Michael Goldman, who I had been introduced to by English artist

Anthony Palliser, whose works I have collected ever since. Michael was the elder son of an important and wealthy Jewish family in Manhattan and had plainly always been something of a rebel. His decision to marry Jackie, a striking looking dancer from the Alvin Ayley Dance Troupe, who happened to be black with Native American blood as well, was too much for his conservative father, who cut him off with a million dollars, banishing him from the family home. Jackie and Michael moved to Paris into a huge top-floor apartment in the Rue du Maître Albert in the 5ème and when we met, Michael was a sculptor working in heavy metal and passionate about food and wine, being on first-name terms with many of the city's top chefs, especially the tyrannical owner of L'Ami Louis, whose cuisine from south-west France is still one of Paris's hottest tickets. His attitude to buying wine was that of a true collector: attending auctions up and down the country and in December studying the special offers from the vast cellars of Nicolas, with their hundred or so shops across every *quartier* in town. On 1 December every year, each of the better-placed shops was allocated a few bottles from the reserves of historical vintages, wines like Château Brane-Cantenac 1928, Château Climens 1947, Musigny Comte Georges de Vogüé 1945 and so on. Realising that just a few bottles would not be enough for his cellar, but visiting every shop which sold them would be not possible, Michael hired four taxis, taking one himself and dispatching three friends in the others armed with a list of wines to buy and sufficient cash to buy them. As the managers of the various shops called head office at the end of the first day to report major sales of the old vintages it became plain to the Nicolas family that that a raid had taken place, but by then it was too late.

Michael was also into music and had bought a rambling basement across the street from his apartment with the intention of opening a jazz club, but planning permission never came through, so he turned it into one of the largest private cellars I have ever seen. This became the venue for many parties with his and Jackie's friends from every aspect of Paris society. But it was not to the cellar, but to the apartment, that I took Alexis Bespaloff for my first introduction to California Cabernets. I remember finding them a bit 'cooked', i.e. from a warm country, as the only other Cabernets I knew were from Bordeaux with its cool Atlantic climate, but they were undoubtedly impressive. A decade after what was to become known as the Judgement of Paris, I re-did the tasting with the very same red wines in

May 1986 and both Bespaloff and Finigan were on the panel of nine judges, the same number as in Paris, as was the young Bartholomew Broadbent.

Before returning to the background to the tasting in Paris, I would like to mention another Michael Goldman evening of almost Gatsby proportions. This was a *mano a mano* in his apartment for two dozen guests between François Minot, two Michelin star chef at the Côte d'Or in northern Burgundy's Saulieu and Alain Chapel, three Michelin star chef at Mionnay further south near Lyon, each taking on one of the six courses. Both Henri Gault and Christian Millau and their wives were there, and as the vintages descended into the 19th century, Henri Gault asked if he could have *un vin primeur.* Michael came back with a bottle of Latour 1964, saying he hoped it was young enough for him. Over the years the cellar parties made inroads into even Michael's collection, he and Jackie separated amicably and, as Michael planned to re-locate to Los Angeles, I packed up some of the remaining great wines for Christie's in London. The memories remain and as I write this in my study in Dorset, I have on my top bookshelf two empty bottles from the Goldman cellar: *Tres Vieux Sherry* from the Private Cellar of Mgr le Prince Napoléon and *Madère Imperial 1835,* both from the Nicolas collection.

By the mid 1970s I was firmly part of the Gault & Millau tasting team, having barged my way into their Côtes de Provence tasting at the Hotel George V with a bottle from Bernard Laundon's Domaine des Férauds a couple of years before. All these tastings were informative, some truly ground-breaking. One, in autumn 1975, covered non-vintage champagne from the *Grandes Marques* or major brands. In those days and up to very recently, wines were marked on the 20 point scale and the full points were used. (In the Judgement of Paris, one taster gave a California Chardonnay 0/20.) The wines were mostly from the rained off and unripe 1972 vintage as a base wine and the quality was very poor, hardly a wine getting into double figures across the board. When the results were reported to the Champenois, they refused to believe them and threatened to withdraw their planned advertising in the Christmas issue unless the tasting was held again, with their own representatives present. One month later Christian Millau convened the same judges, even having a *huissier de justice* present to add weight to the proceedings and the wines were re-judged in front of a group from Epernay and Reims. Christian Millau had asked us all to come early, before they arrived, and told us to 'rank the wines as your feel, but start your marks at 5/20'. Honour was saved and the magazine got its Christmas advertisments.

When Patricia returned from California raving about the quality of the wines she had tasted, I remembered my impressions from Alexis Bespaloff's Cabernet Sauvignons and the following day put a glass of white wine in front of her and asked her opinion. 'Far too high in acid' she said 'I hope you're not buying it.' This was a Bourgogne-Aligoté with its characteristic 'green' acidity, which is why this wine was historically the base for a *vin blanc cassis,* known as *un Kir* after Dijon's Canon Kir who had popularised it. The fact that Patricia's palate was rejecting such a style of wine after two weeks of California's food and wine made me think that if we were to impress our potential panel of tasters with wines from the West Coast, we should take the French palate into account.

As the autumn progressed, Patricia began the groundwork for the tasting. While in California she had met and visited wineries with Joanne Dickenson, the wife of a leading lawyer who had started a company called Wine Tours International, who told her that she was planning a wine tour in France in May to be headed up by the great André Tchelistcheff. Tchelistcheff (1901-1994) from a family of Russian aristocrats, had fled the country with just the shirt on his back in 1919 and had worked as a farmer in France before turning to wine to end up being recommended by his Professor of Œnology in Bordeaux to comte Georges de La Tour, owner of Beaulieu Vineyards in Napa, as the new winemaker to resurrect the famous winery following the ravages of Prohibition. After 30 years at BV, as it was known (his 1946 Pinot Noir is one of the greatest wines I have ever tasted), he retired in the mid 1960s and turned himself into a consultant to the up and coming winemakers, who co-incidentally included both Mike Grgich of Chateau Montelena and Warren Winiarski of Stag's Leap Wine Cellars, whose wines led the field in the tasting that was to come. In February 2017 I attended the prestigious Berlinale, the film festival in Berlin, for the launch of and inspiring and moving film entitled *André – The Voice of Wine* made by his great nephew Mark Tchelistcheff. Joanne Dickenson's tour was for André and his Napa colleagues and friends to return to the regions and people he had known during his time in France. Little did she know then that I was to ask her group of 24 to hand carry the 24 bottles I had finally selected over to Paris. Had they not agreed, the wines, even had they arrived by other means, would have been blocked in customs – I couldn't use my ruse with the Hambledon white for HM The Queen this time – and the tasting would not have taken place.

After the busy Christmas period at the shop, Bella, Christian and Kate spent the holidays in Britain with our respective parents and during the quieter time of January we began to think about who we would invite to taste these New World wines. I think of them now as 'judges' but then they were just 'tasters' as the idea of a comparative France-California tasting had not occurred to me. The idea was simple: this would be just another, but different, tasting event put on by *L'Académie du Vin* and in honour of the 1776-1976 Anniversary, we wished to present wines from California for the first ever time in France, hoping to obtain recognition for their quality. Since we were known, respected and liked, we threw our net wide and high to construct the panel, which needed to be balanced between producers, writers and restaurateurs. The people we invited and who accepted were, in alphabetical order:

Pierre Bréjoux, Inspector Générale of the Appellation d'Origine Controlée (INAO) Board, a noted wine authority.

Michel Dovaz, of Swiss origin and introduced to us by Bernard Bourquin, to become one of the early 'profs' to teach *L'Académie du Vin* courses in French, and subsequently a highly regarded author of many books on wine.

Claude Dubois-Millot, sales director of the *Guide Gault & Millau* and despite the different name, brother to Christian Millau.

Odette Khan, editor of *La Revue du Vin de France* and its sister publication *Cuisine et Vins de France*, very much the ruler of the roost of Parisian wine writers.

Raymond Oliver, Bordeaux-born chef and owner of the 3 Michelin star restaurant Le Grand Véfour (still one of the greatest restaurants in Paris and certainly the most beautiful), which he had owned since 1948 and was then a national figure in France.

Pierre Tari, owner of Château Giscours, the Margaux 3rd Growth and Secretary General of the Association des Grands Crus Classés.

Christian Vannequé, head sommelier at the 3 Michelin star restaurant La Tour d'Argent, at just twenty-five years old the youngest head sommelier in Paris, in charge of the city's most famous cellar.

Aubert de Villaine, co-owner and co-director of the Domaine de la Romanée-Conti, the most famous vineyard in Burgundy.

Jean-Claude Vrinat, owner of the 3 Michelin star restaurant Le Taillevent, having trained under his father as a sommelier before taking over the reins in 1973.

The next step was to find a suitable place to hold the event, as the tasting room at *L'Académie du Vin* was too small. We had already chosen a date – 24 May – and our first approach was to Ernst Van Dam, a friend and client of the shop who was Food and Beverage Manager of the Intercontinental Hotel a few blocks away in the Rue de Castiglione. I was just after a reception room with good natural light, but Ernst came up trumps offering a ground floor room with picture windows leading to an interior courtyard, which we could have from 3pm until just before 6pm, when it would need to be vacated and prepared for a wedding reception.

So almost the final piece in the jigsaw was for me to go to California and make the final selection. Bella, being one quarter American with many cousins in San Francisco would come with me, Christian, Kate and Digby being looked after by Bernard Hopquin's wife Thérèse, who had been their on-call nanny since the days on the barge. We went at the end of March, staying on the advice of the much-travelled Bobby Ho at the Alta Mira, a quite luxurious low-built colonial style hotel in Sausalito just north of the Golden Gate Bridge, about 40 minutes from Napa. As with Patricia, Robert Finigan helped with the itinerary, but the best thing he did was to introduce us to the Washington Square Bar & Grill, in San Francisco's Embarcadero district. The Square, or 'The Washbag' as it became to be called, was a true Saloon and since its opening in 1973 had become *the* place to be seen in the city by like-minded saloon-lovers. Described by the *San Francisco Chronicle*'s Herb Caen as 'a funky neighbourhood place populated by a few broken-down politicos, over-the-hill columnists, hack writers and jazz pianists' it became my home-from-home for several years until majority owner Ed Moose (see next chapter) and Mary Etta his wife who was behind the stoves, sold up and moved to a bigger place nearby on Union Square named Moose's, where the hamburgers (called Mooseburgers) were the best I have ever eaten. I remember an afternoon there in the mid 1980s with Bartholomew Broadbent, Michael's son, whose wine importing company Broadbent Selections was based in town, watching on television the finals of the Amercian Football League between the San Francisco 49ers and the Dallas Cowboys, which was taking place at Candlestick Park south of the city. The Mayor of Dallas was at the game and had announced that morning that his team would 'whip the asses of those flaky faggots'. Moose and Co. had placed bets against this and the explosion of corks when the home team won in the final innings stays in the mind. It was at The Square that I was introduced to Brian Saint-Pierre from the Wines of California Bureau and we immediately became friends, not knowing that 20 years later he would marry Sarah Kemp, director of *Decanter* magazine, move to the UK and become a permanent part of my life.

Through his restaurant review guide Bob Finigan knew everyone and everything that was happening in the Bay Area and one night booked us into Chez Panisse, the famous restaurant in Berkeley that had been created by Alice Waters and still flourishes under her watchful eye. Chez Panisse served only a set menu in the evening and the chef at the time was Jeremiah Tower, soon to become San Francisco's leading culinary light, a tall, strikingly good looking man with a combative temperament. We arrived late enough to cause some concern from the front of house, but wine was immediately ordered and the four course meal began. The main course was roast lamb and Bob's plate arrived with some fatty bits on it. He complained, the three of us offered to swap plates, but no, he was a restaurant critic and this should not happen to him, so he called over a waiter and told him to take the plate back to the kitchen. A few minutes passed and the waiter returned with the same plate, to Bob's great annoyance. 'What did the chef say?' he asked, 'the chef said "tough shit", Mr Finigan.' We had to laugh.

Patricia had visited many wineries and had given me a list to check up on, our aim being to get six Chardonnays and six Cabernets to illustrate what was going on in California. After the event we were often asked why there was no Mondavi, no Beaulieu Vineyards or Buena Vista and the reply was that we were only looking for small, family-run wineries, described in France at the time as *boutiques*. Such wineries – nine of the twelve wines came from Napa, three from the Santa Cruz Mountains south of San Francisco - all being representative of the new age of California wine. They were generally small operations run by the founders, who were for the most part on a second career. On my visits I began to realise that for many France was their model – Paul Draper of Ridge Vineyards had previously worked with Cabernet Sauvignon in Bordeaux and Chile – while for the others the intention was to get the best out of their soil and their grapes, principally Chardonnay and Cabernet Sauvignon.

Thanks to Patricia's groundwork and Bob Finigan's assistance, most of the visits went well, with two exceptions: Heitz in Napa and Ridge in Santa Cruz, where there was almost no visit at all. My call to Joe Heitz, well-known in the Valley as a 'charming curmudgeon', began with a brush-off: 'if you are a journalist, I don't received them, if you are a merchant, I don't export and anyway I don't have time.' I told him that he was so famous that a visit to Napa would not be complete without him and was grudgingly given a time slot to call in at the winery on the Silverado Trail, east of St Helena. After a tour of the cellars, during which I admired the large upright redwood storage tanks – while wondering what on earth a redwood-stored wine would taste like – he said he had just time to show me two wines, the first being his Chardonnay and I was asked to comment on what was probably only the third California Chardonnay in my life. I said it reminded me of a Meursault. Joe Heitz beamed and said that Meursault was his wife's favourite wine and this was what he tried to make. The tasting finally encompassed his full range and I left with two bottles of Heitz Martha's Vineyard 1970.

Ridge Vineyards I knew was a must although it was a two hour drive from Sausalito. I called and was told that they didn't have a tasting room, didn't expect nor receive visitors and anyway, once again, didn't have the time. Bella and I simply turned up late one morning to be met by one of the partners David Bennion, who, seeing an Englishman getting out of the car, shouted over 'you're the fellow I told not to come, but since you're here you'd better taste some wine.' We ended up staying for a scratch lunch and leaving with two bottles of Ridge Monte Bello Cabernet Sauvignon 1971, which, while coming 5th in Paris in May 1976 and 2nd in a re-match of just the red wines in New York in May 1986, finally triumphed in the tastings that were held simultaneously in May 2006 at 10am in Napa and 6pm in London to be placed 1st by both panels.

By the end of a week the final selection had been made, the bottles collected and paid for and as a result of the arrangement first proposed by Patricia to Joanne Dickenson, the wines were delivered to her house in San Francisco. After agreeing to help, Dickenson called a TWA representative with whom she was working on her upcoming tour and asked if it would be okay for the wine to travel with the group. TWA was at the time trying to establish a relationship between the wine-producing areas of the world that it called a 'Wine Bridge' and they were delighted to handle it. This was another great bit of luck, but, as I have said earlier, the 1970s were a lucky decade.

The California wines on their way to Paris, in alphabetical order, were:

CHARDONNAY

Chalone Vineyard 1974
Located 100 miles south of San Francisco, Chalone was deemed to have soils similar to Burgundy and in 1923 was planted with Chardonnay, Chenin Blanc, Pinot Blanc and Pinot Noir. Dick Graff, a young banker, bought into the winery in 1965 and within a few years his wines were receiving high praise from both Julia Child and André Tchelistcheff. (This was my bet for the best Chardonnay.)

Chateau Montelena 1973
Dating back to the glory days of early California wine, the vineyard and winery were created in the late 1880s by Alfred L. Tubbs and it remains today on Tubbs' Lane. More famous for its red wines, Montelena did not survive Prohibition, to be acquired by Los Angeles lawyer James (Jim) Barrett and partners in 1972. Mike Grgich, a disciple of André Tchelistcheff and then at Robert Mondavi, was hired as winemaker.

David Bruce Winery 1973
David Bruce, a student at Stanford University, in 1961 bought a 40 acre plot above the town of Los Gatos at 2,200 feet of elevation and well-drained sandy soil that seemed perfect for Chardonnay and Pinot Noir. Both a technician and an experimenter, Bruce used very little sulphur in his wines, the lack of which led to his 1973 being out of condition when it arrived in Paris. This wine was a recommendation from Robert Finigan, who described the bottle we tasted at the winery as having 'the essence of Chardonnay'.

Freemark Abbey 1972
I had met Jerry Luper, the winemaker at Freemark Abbey, in Aix-en-Provence with Tim Johnston (Luper is now long retired and lives with his wife in southern Burgundy) and was impressed by his French-influenced approach in the cellar. The 1969 Chardonnay had already bested some top white Burgundies in New York at a tasting arranged by Robert Balzer. The 1972 struck me as being very elegant and was my second bet after Chalone.

Spring Mountain 1973

The ebullient Mike Robbins (he had once dated Grace Kelly) was a real estate developer with a passion for wine. In 1962 he purchased a fine Victorian home (after a sale it became known as Chateau St Clement) with a small vineyard and winery north of St Helena. From the early 1970s his Chardonnays were regular Gold Medal winners. This was Robert Finigan's bet for the tasting.

Veedercrest Vineyards 1972

A.W. (Al) Baxter, a home winemaker with serious ambitions, purchased 300 acres of land on Mount Veeder on the western side of the Napa Valley. While the planting was progressing, grapes were bought in, the 1972 coming from Winery Lake Vineyard in the cool Carneros district, soon to become famous for its Chardonnays and Pinot Noirs.

CABERNET SAUVIGNON

Clos du Val Winery 1972

John Goelet and Bernard Porter, the two men behind Clos du Val, were both born into the French wine business: Goelet was a descendant of François Guestier the founder of the merchant Barton et Guestier in which he was still a partner; Bernard Portet's father was the technical director of Château Lafite. While negotiating to buy a property in France, Goelet employed Portet to travel the world to study wine regions for potential investment. He recommended two regions – California's Napa Valley and Victoria in Australia. Goelet took Bernard Portet on as his partner in Clos du Val and made Bernard's brother Dominique a partner in Taltarni in Victoria. Being French owned and made, this was an obvious choice, proving its worth by coming first in the 1986 New York re-run.

Freemark Abbey Winery 1969

Freemark Abbey was the only winery to have two wines in the tasting and this was chosen for its maturity and elegance, a blend of 88% Cabernet and 12% Merlot. Its maturity did it no favours against the younger reds in the tasting.

Heitz Cellar Martha's Vineyard 1970

Joe Heitz had been stationed in California during World War II and decided to stay, joining the wine programme at UC Davis, following which he worked at Gallo, from 1951-58 at Beaulieu Vineyards under André Tchelistcheff, then left to buy a small vineyard and winery south of St Helena. In 1965 he bought Cabernet Sauvignon grapes from Tom May, from a vineyard in Oakville that May had named after his wife, Martha. As these grapes turned out to make the best barrels, Heitz decided to bottle it separately using Martha's Vineyard on the label and another Napa Valley icon was born. The 1970 cost more than double all the other Cabernets.

Mayacamas Vineyards 1971

Bob Travers (still presenting his wine around the world in his 80s) joined Joe Heitz as a cellar worker in 1967 and the following year purchased the Mayacamas (which means 'cry of the mountain lion' in the language of the Wappo Indians who once lived there) as a functioning winery when its owners retired. He quickly reduced the production to just Chardonnay and Cabernet Sauvignon, holding the latter back from selling for longer than his neighbours. I had been really impressed by the 1970 tasted with Finigan at The Square, visited Mayacamas and was told they were out of stock. Bob Travers agreed to sell me the not yet released 1971. It took until the 30th anniversary of the Judgement of Paris in 2006 for it to show its real quality.

Ridge Vineyards Monte Bello 1971

Vines were first planted on the 2,300 elevation Monte Bello Ridge in the 1890s and what were left were just 25 acres by the time David Bennion and three friends from the Stanford Research Institute purchased the 80 acre farm in 1959. The partners slowly expanded the vineyards but needed professional help. Bennion had met Paul Draper earlier, who joined them in 1969 and (although retired) has never left. Draper made the 1971 noting that 'our Cabernet grapes reached their balance in 1971 at slightly lower sugar than usual and produced a wine with more elegance and finesse that we have yet seen.' How right he was.

Stag's Leap Wine Cellars 1973

Warren Winiarski was on the way to becoming a professor at the University of Chicago after his post-graduate studies there before a visit to Italy introduced him to wine in 1953. He started making wine in his college apartment before spending a week during the vintage at the Martin Ray Winery, finally throwing up his future in Chicago and, bundling his wife Barbara and three small children into a station wagon, set out in 1964 to start work with Lee Stewart at Souverain Cellars in Napa. From there he moved as assistant winemaker at Mondavi, buying his first vineyard in the Stag's Leap district and planting his first Cabernet Sauvignon in 1970. The 1973 which was to come first in the Paris tasting was these wines' first vintage.

In early May the group, organised by Joanne Dickenson and headed up by André Tchelitscheff, arrived off their TWA flight at Roissy airport and when I saw the two cases of wine on the carousel I was overjoyed. Joanne was horrified, as one carton was stained red, the breaker turning out to be one of the two bottles of Freemark Abbey 1969. But I needed only one bottle for the tasting and here they were. The following day I gave the group a 'Tour de France' tasting from the major French regions at Le Chemin des Vignes, after which they headed off to Champagne for the start of their own tour of France, which was to culminate fifteen days later at Alexis Lichine's Château Lascombes in Margaux. Now that everything was lined up for 24 May, a thought began to nag at me. The reason for this tasting was altruistic: to gain recognition for California wines via the selection that Patricia and I had made, using the Bicentennial as the reason. Looking through the list of our first choice of tasters, all of whom had accepted except Christian Millau, who had proposed his brother Claude who we knew well, I realised that only two of them – Aubert de Villaine whose wife Pamela came from San Francisco, and Christian Vannequé who had been introduced to California wines in 1971 by the movie director John Frankenheimer who was in Paris to make *The French Connection*, would have ever tasted these wines before. I became worried that the other judges, all great wine experts and top of their individual trees, might view California, being just north of Mexico on America's West Coast, as a 'southern' country like Portugal or Spain and good though the wines were, the tasters' innate Frenchness might result in their being 'damned with faint praise.' With just a week to go, I made the decision to turn it into a 'blind' tasting, with four of the best white Burgundies and four of the best Cabernet Sauvignon-dominated red Bordeaux from my shop. The wines I selected to match the vintages from California were:

WHITE BURGUNDY

Bâtard-Montrachet Domaine Ramonet-Prudhon 1973
From one of the five Grands Crus across the Chassagne- and Puligny-Montrachet vineyards, Bâtard-Montrachet is considered, along with Chevalier-Montrachet from a slightly higher elevation, second only to Le Montrachet itself. I had both the 1972 (a fine but lean vintage) and 1973 (more ripe and open) in the shop and telephoned Monsieur Ramonet to ask which vintage he would recommend. A few years earlier he had been on the cover of the *Gault-Millau* magazine, and had pronounced that he 'had been put on earth by God to make great wine'. My question was met with surprise and the reply that both were excellent, so I went with the 1973 to match four of the California Chardonnays. (The wine turned out to be low in acidity and was not well-received by the judges. The following autumn, on a buying tour of Burgundy, I was physically thrown out of the Ramonet cellars by Monsieur Ramonet's son André for having caused such an insult to the family name.)

Beaune Premier Cru Clos des Mouches Domaine Joseph Drouhin 1973
Joseph Drouhin is one of the oldest and most respected *négociant-éleveurs* in Beaune and the walled-in Clos des Mouches is a flagship in their portfolio. Described by

Clive Coates MW as being 'delicate at first with a lot of intensity underneath and above all great integrity of *terroir*', this was an obvious choice.

Meursault Premier Cru Les Charmes Domaine Roulot 1973
The village of Meursault is to white Burgundy what the little town of Nuits-St-Georges is to red, both being well-known by wine drinkers as the benchmark of each type of wine. Guy Roulot was a pioneer of the elegant style of this sometimes slightly robust Chardonnay until his early death and the domaine has reached spectacular heights under his son Jean-Marc. To add a twist, American Ted Lemon was in the Roulot cellar for the 1973 vintage, and is now the producer of top Chardonnays and Pinot Noir from his Littorai Winery in California's Sonoma County.

Puligny-Montrachet Premier Cru Les Pucelles Domaine Leflaive 1972
The village of Puligny is has the justified reputation of producing some of the world's greatest white wines and the most revered producer is Domaine Leflaive. The gentlemanly Vincent Leflaive said he was looking for 'elegance and harmony' in his wines and in his book George Taber quotes Clive Coates MW as saying that Les Pucelles in Vincent Leflaive's hands should be ranked as a Grand Cru.

RED BORDEAUX

Château Haut-Brion Premier Cru Classé Graves 1970
Founded in the 15th century, Haut-Brion has a history second to none in Bordeaux. The vineyards are now surrounded by the expansion of the city of Bordeaux, but have remained intact since that time. In 1935 the estate was bought by Clarence Dillon, a Francophile American financier (apparently the weather was too foggy for him to visit Château Cheval-Blanc in St Emilion, his other choice), his descendants continuing the very beneficial ownership. 1970 was an excellent year, highly regarded at the start, even more so as it matured.

Château Mouton-Rothschild Premier Cru Classé (1973) Médoc 1970
Purchased by the Rothschilds in 1853 in a comparatively run-down state, Mouton did not attain the ranking of Premier Cru Classé in the 1855 Classification, but was placed top of the Deuxième Crus. From his arrival in 1920, the young Baron Philippe de Rothschild was determined to regain his rightful position and this was the first Bordeaux estate to bottle all the production sold under the château label at the château. In 1973 the classification was changed to raise Mouton to a Premier Cru, a reputation it had enjoyed for five decades. This wine came consistently top of the clarets.

Château Léoville-Las Cases Deuxième Cru Classe St Julien 1971
According to the great historian of the wines of Bordeaux Edmund Penning-Rowsell, the commune of St Julien produces 'quintessential claret' and of the three

Second Growth Léovilles, Las Cases is considered (and considers itself) superior to its neighbours Barton and Poyferre. 1971 was a good year, a little lighter and less tannic than 1970, thus very suitable for the tasting.

Château Montrose Deuxième Cru Classé St Estèphe 1970
St Estèphe is the most northern of the four major communes in the Médoc with Margaux, St Julien, Pauillac to the south, and produces what is recognised as some of the most 'robust' wines from a high percentage of Cabernet Sauvignon grapes. Under the ownership of the Charmolue family, the wines were always totally classic and for them the 1970 was a great vintage.

It is plain from the origins and quality of these wines that I did not expect the California wines to get the result they did. All we were after was recognition that there were some very good wines coming out of California which deserved attention. Patricia and I went to the Intercontinental Hotel with no preconceived hopes other than that the tasting would prove worthwhile for all our efforts and would not have been a waste of time for the judges. In hindsight, I have said that I would have been happy with just a couple of wines in the top half of the ten, and it certainly would not have suited me as a wine merchant in Paris to see 'unknowns' from California beat the benchmarks from France, but this is what happened on the day. To quote from George Taber's book: 'May 24th 1976 was a beautiful sunny day in Paris and Patricia Gallagher was in good spirits as she packed up the French and California wines for the tasting. Organizing the event had been good fun and easy compared with other events that she and Steven had dreamed up. The good thing about working with Spurrier, she told friends, was that he was so supportive of her ideas. Many of their conversations began with her saying 'Wouldn't it be fun…..?' to which he always replied 'Great, let's do it.' The two weren't looking for fame nor money. They were young people doing things strictly for the love of wine, and to have fun.'

Of course, we wanted recognition for *L'Académie du Vin* as well as for California, but we had not invited wine writers from the newspapers *Le Monde*, *Figaro* and *Libération* and the weekly magazines *L'Expres and Le Point*, as our panel of tasters were of sufficient importance on their own. Jon Winroth, now mostly retired from *L'Académie du Vin* due to ill-health, was away. Patricia then remembered that a certain George Taber had recently taken one of our wine courses and called him at the office

Patricia Gallagher, Steven Spurrier, Odette Khan on 24 May 1976

of *Time* magazine located just at the Rond-Point des Champs-Elysées, as since American wines were there, she thought so should he. He accepted, adding that if something came up, he wouldn't be able to make it. On the day, nothing did and he was there, as was my wife Bella to take some photos. Had George Taber not been present to witness the tasting and to report the story in *Time* on 7 June under the title 'Judgment (sic) of Paris' our little adventure would probably have sunk without trace. As it was, it became 'The Historic Tasting that Revolutionized Wine' a description which over the years turned out to be entirely true.

One final thing had to be done before the tasting could start, which was the order in which the wines would be poured. Putting them in alphabetical order was dismissed as it would have put two heavy-hitters first for the whites and grouped the Bordeaux in the middle for the reds, so all I did was to write the names of all the wines on scraps of paper, fold them up and once at the hotel ask our intern at *L'Académie* to draw them out of a hat which set the order, the bottles being marked 'Chardonnay 1-10 and Cabernet 1-10.' I have no record of the actual order of serving.

The room was full of natural light and the tasting was to be seated on a long table with one judge at each end, myself in the middle with Patricia on my right and Odette Khan, very elegant in a summer dress with opera length pearls on my left. Once everyone was seated I said a few words of welcome and announced that I thought it would be interesting, instead of just tasting Chardonnays and Cabernets from California, to match them up against some benchmarks of similar vintages from Burgundy and Bordeaux in a friendly 'glasses across the ocean' blind tasting as part of a celebration of the War of Independence, which the French General Lafayette had himself supported, fighting on the American side. Fortunately they accepted with murmurs of '*bonne idée*', '*pas de problème*'. Tasting sheets were prepared, the wines to be marked out of 20 as was then the norm, but the whole ranking being used whereas in later years the 20 point scale began at 10 and the 100 point scale began at 50. As hosts, neither Patricia's nor my rankings were allowed in the final tally.

George Taber was having a slow day at the *Time* office and was happy to be present and to be given the identity of the wines and the tasting order by Patricia. In Chapter 19 of his book under the title 'A Stunning Upset' with a quote from Robert Louis Stevenson that 'A bottle of good wine, like a good act, shines ever in the retrospect', he describes that he saw and heard.

'The nine judges seemed nervous at the beginning. There was lots of laughing and quick side comments. No one, though, was acting rashly. The judges pondered their wines carefully and made their judgements slowly. As I stood only a few feet from them, I could listen to their commentary and I copied into the brown reporter's notebook that I always carry with me such phrases as: 'This soars out of the ordinary', 'A good nose, but not too much on the mouth' and 'This is nervous and agreeable'. From their comments, though, I soon realized that the judges were becoming totally confused as they tasted the white wines. The panel couldn't tell the difference between the French ones and those from California and they began talking to each other, which is very rare in a tasting. They speculated about a wine's nationality, often disagreeing.

'At one point Raymond Oliver was certain he had sipped a French wine, when it was a California one from Freemark Abbey. Shortly after, Claude Dubois-Millot said he thought a wine was obviously from California because it had no nose, when it was France's famed Bâtard-Montrachet. The judges were brutal when they found a wine wanting. They completely dismissed the David Bruce Chardonnay, Pierre Brejoux giving it 0 and Odette Khan just 1 point out of 20. The David Bruce was rated last by all of the judges. Robert Finigan had warned Spurrier that he'd found David Bruce wines at that time could be erratic and this bottle appeared to be erratically bad.

'After the white wines had been tasted, Spurrier called a break and collected the scorecards. Using normal procedure for wine tastings, he added up the individual scores, divided this by the number of tasters (his and Patricia Gallagher's marks not being noted) and ranked them from highest to lowest. The judges spoke quietly to each other and I talked briefly with Dubois-Millot. Even though he did not yet know the results, he told me a bit sheepishly that 'We thought we were recognising French wines when they were Californian and vice versa. Our confusion showed how good California wines have become.'

'Spurrier's original plan had been to announce all the results at the end of the day, but the waiters were slow clearing the tables and getting the red wines together and the program was getting badly behind schedule, so he decided to announce the results of the white wine tasting. He had been personally stunned and began reading them slowly to the group:

> Chateau Montelena 1973 (132)
> Meursault-Charmes 1973 (126.5)
> Chalone Vineyard 1974 (121)
> Spring Mountain 1973 (104)
> Beaune Clos des Mouches 1973 (101)
> Freemark Abbey 1972 (100)
> Bâtard-Montrachet 1973 (94)
> Puligny-Montrachet les Pucelles 1972 (89)
> Veedercrest 1972 (88)
> David Bruce 1973 (42)

'When he finished, Spurrier looked at the judges, whose reaction ranged from shock to horror. No one had expected this and soon the whole room was abuzz. The scores of the individual judges made the results even more astounding. California Chardonnays had overwhelmed their French counterparts. Every single judge rated a California wine first, Chateau Montelena was given top rating by six judges, Chalone being rated first by the other three. Three of the top four wines were Californian. Claude Dubois-Millot gave Chateau Montelena 18.5 points out of 20, while Aubert de Villaine gave it 18. Chateau Montelena scored a total of 132 points, comfortably ahead of second place Meursault-Charmes which got 126.5.

'As I watched the reaction of the others to the results, I felt a sense of both awe and pride. Who would have thought it? Chauvenism is a word invented by the French, but I felt some chauvinism that a California white wine had won. But how could this be happening? I was tempted to ask for a taste of the winning California Chardonnay, but decided against it. I still had a reporting job to finish and I needed to have a clear head.

'As the waiters poured the reds, Spurrier was certain that the judges would be more careful and would not allow a California wine to come out on top again. One Californian wine winning was bad enough, two would be treason. The French judges, he felt, would be very careful to identify the French wines and score them high, while rating those that seemed American low. The French reds, with their classic, distinctive and familiar tastes would certainly stand out against the California reds.

'There was less chatter during the second wave of wines. The judges seemed both more intense and more circumspect. Their comments about the nationality of the wine in the glass were now usually correct. 'That's a California, or I don't know what I am doing here' said Christian Vannequé of La Tour d'Argent. I looked at my card and he was right, it was the Ridge Monte Bello. Raymond Oliver took one sip of a red and proclaimed 'That's a Mouton, without a doubt'. He too was right. Because of delays in the earlier part of the tasting, the hour was getting late and the group had to be out by 6pm, so Spurrier pushed on quickly after the ballot were collected. He followed the same procedure as he had for the Chardonnay tasting, adding up the individual scores of the judges and dividing the total by nine. The room was hushed as he read out the results.

> Stag's Leap Wine Cellars 1973 (127.5)
> Ch. Mouton Rothschild 1970 (126)
> Ch. Haut-Brion 1970 (125.5)
> Ch. Montrose 1970 (122)
> Ridge Monte Bello 1971 (103.5)
> Ch. Léoville-Las Cases 1971 (97)
> Mayacamas 1971 (89.5)
> Heitz Martha's Vineyard 1970 (84.5)
> Freemark Abbey 1969 (78)

'This time the stir in the room was even more pronounced than before. A California wine had won again! Who would have believed it! The judges sat in disbelief. The results for the Cabernet wines were much closer than for the Chardonnays. Ch. Haut-Brion got the most first place votes of all: three. French wines were rated first, in some cases tied for first, by seven of the nine judges. Stag's Leap was rated highly by most judges, but only Odette Khan put it first and Raymond Oliver had it in a tie for first. The French red wines rated much better overall, taking three of the top four positions, while California wines were relegated to the last four slots. Based on overall scores, the results were very close with only a five and a half point difference between the top four finishers. Stag's Leap won by just a point and a half over second place Mouton-Rothschild. But, as the old saying goes, 'close only counts in horseshoes'. Stag's Leap was the winner that day. It was the judgement of Paris.

'Spurrier's suspicion that the judges would attempt to identify the French wines and score them higher while rating the California ones low appears to have taken place. In the Cabernet tasting the judges had a significantly wider scoring range than with the Chardonnays. The judges may have honestly felt the quality differences were that great, but they also may have been out to make sure a French wine won. Odette Khan, for example, gave two wines (Clos du Val and Heitz Martha's Vineyard) only 2 points out of 20, one (Freemark Abbey) 5 points and one (Ridge) 7 points. All her other Cabernet scores were in double digits, but if she was trying to score California wines low overall, she didn't succeed, for her two highest scores went to Stag's Leap and Mayacamas. Four other judges also had the same pattern of rating several California wines in single digits, which is unusual in a fine wine tasting.

'The California reds did very well on Spurrier's and Gallagher's scoring cards. Spurrier in a moment of indecision had a four-way tie for first: Ch. Montrose, Ch. Mouton-Rothschild, Ridge and Stag's Leap. Gallagher gave first place to Martha's Vineyard.

'After the final results were announced, Odette Khan marched up to Spurrier, gathering together all the force of her strong personality, elegant presence and aristocratic demeanor. As editor of *La Revue du Vin de France* she realized better than probably anyone else in the room the importance of what had just happened and the impact this wine tasting might have. 'Monsieur Spurrier, I demand to have my scorecards', 'I'm sorry, Madame Khan, but you're not going to get them back', 'But they are *my* scores'. 'No, you agreed to take part in this tasting and your scores, like those of the others, belong to *L'Académie du Vin.*'

'The judges lingered for a little while longer, sharing a glass of Champagne and talking freely about the results of the tasting. I spoke with five of the nine. Their immediate reactions were candid. They were generally complimentary about the California wines they had just tasted. Most said they had heard that winemakers in California were doing interesting things, but they had little first hand experience with the wines. Said Aubert de Villaine, 'I tasted my first California wines in 1964 and since then there have been more and more good wine houses there'. Pierre Bréjoux told me, 'I went to California in July 1974 and I learned a lot – to my surprise. They are now certainly among the top wines in the world, but this Stag's Leap has been a secret, I've never heard of it.' Pierre Tari said 'I was really surprised by the California whites, they are certainly the best – after France. They have come a long way but they have a long way to go.' Christian Vannequé told me, 'The white wines approached the best of France, without a doubt. The reds, though were not as good and didn't have the character of a Bordeaux. They are a bit minty, very strong in tannin and lack finesse.'

'There were also a few sour grapes among the judges. Tari complained that 'French wines develop slower than California wines because of the climate, so the test was not completely correct.' Added Aubert de Villaine: 'In general there is still quite a difference, the French wines are still superior.' Snipped Odette Khan: 'It was a false test because California wines are trying to become too much like French wines.'

This observation that the red Bordeaux were too young was heard over and over again and so in 1986 I held a tasting in New York with the same red wines, again with nine tasters, all American with the exception of Georges Lepré head sommelier of the Ritz Hotel in Paris, and Bartholomew Broadbent, the prestigious others being: Michael Aaron of Manhattan wine store Sherry-Lehamnn, Alexis Bespaloff of *New York Magazine*, Barbara Ensrud of the *New York Daily News*, Peter Morrell of Manhattan wine store Morrell, Frank Prial of the *New York Times* and Robert Finigan. At that time the results were:

> Clos du Val 1972
> Ridge Monte Bello 1971
> Ch. Montrose 1970
> Ch. Léoville-Las Cases 1971

Ch. Mouton-Rothschild 1970
Stag's Leap Wine Cellars 1973
Heitz Martha's Vineyard 1970
Mayacamas 1971
Ch. Haut-Brion 1970

(The three other red Bordeaux had come directly from the châteaux at my request. Haut-Brion refused to participate and the bottle was purchased in New York from a top merchant, but had plainly been badly stored. Freemark Abbey admitted that their 1969 had faded and decline to participate.)

The publicity surrounding the unexpected confirmation on the quality of the California Cabernets coincided with the Union des Grands Crus Classé's tour of the USA to promote their 1995 vintage and I was accused by its President Pierre Tari of 'single-handedly sabotaging their campaign'. As a result, I had no intention of holding a re-match 20 years on, but with the encouragement of Jacob, Lord Rothschild (himself a substantial shareholder both in Ch. Lafite-Rothschild and Ch. Mouton-Rothschild) and Robert Mondavi, a re-enactment was held in simultaneously at Copia in Napa at 10am and at Berry Brothers and Rudd in London at 6pm, the wines sourced from the wineries, nine tasters present at each, including from the original tasting Christian Vannequé in Napa as well as Patricia Gallagher and Michel Dovaz in London alongside myself, and the results with both panels' marks added together, the taster's top wine earning one point, their second wine two points and so on, the combined results were:

Ridge Monte Bello 1971 (61)
Stag's Leap Wine Cellars 1973 (79)
Heitz Martha's Vineyard 1970 (86)
Mayacamas 1971 (86)
Clos du Val 1972 (92)
Ch. Mouton-Rothschild 1970 (93)
Ch. Montrose 1970 (106)
Ch. Haut-Brion 1970 (116)
Ch. Léoville-Las Cases 1971 (132)
Freemark Abbey 1969 (139)

That the California Cabernets took all the first five places rather dashed the argument that the red Bordeaux would age well and they would not. But I should mention here that after the blind tasting in London which was only for the nine on the panel and myself, there was a non-blind tasting for about 40 guests of the same or similar wines from the 2000 vintage and here the Bordeaux wines simply wiped the floor with those from California. Aubert de Villaine had described the 1976 event as *'un coup dans la derrière pour les vins Français*/a kick up the bum for French wine', which it indeed was and turned out to be both necessary and beneficial. My view of the 1976/2006 tastings is that is showed that in the early 1970s the benchmark Bordeaux were resting on their laurels and by the late 1990s, so were the classic Californians. The world of wine never stands still.

After closing up at the Hôtel Intercontinental, Patricia and I walked back to *L'Académie du Vin*, toasted each other with a glass of Brut Intégral and said how pleased we were for California and that it had all been a bit of a surprise. I went on home to be asked by Bella, who had had to leave after the Chardonnays to collect Christian and Kate from school, how it went for the reds and replied that I hadn't expected it, but California had come out top there as well. Then I read the children a bedtime story, Bella prepared supper and we talked about something else.

The person who wasn't talking about something else was George Taber. He called Patricia the next day in order to track down the Dickenson-Tchelistcheff group and tell them the news. She had their itinerary and told him that they would be having lunch at Alexis Lichine's 2nd Growth Château Lascombes in Margaux. He called at the moment the group and many château owners, keen to meet them were enjoying an aperitif on the terrace. George Taber once again takes up the story:

'Dickenson spotted Barrett across the room, walked over and told him he had a 'phone call. He was surprised and thought it must be bad news. The two followed the Lascombes' staff member to another building and into a tiny office. All Dickenson heard was Barrett's end of the conversation as he said "No ...Yes ... Okay". Barrett finally flashed Dickenson the okay sign and mouthed the words that everything was all right, so she went back to her hosts and the reception. Once Barrett identified himself I asked him, "Have you heard that your wine came first in the tasting that was held on Monday in Paris?" "No, I haven't. That's great." "Well, you won in the white part of it. And a California red wine also won, so it was a Californian sweep. What's your reaction to beating the French at their own game in Paris?" Barrett's mind started racing, but the careful Los Angeles lawyer came to the fore and after a second's hesitation he said "Not bad for kids from the sticks." With this, I knew I had a quote.

'After our conversation ended, Barrett returned to the pre-luncheon reception which was just ending. He immediately told his wife about the call, so that she wouldn't be thinking the worst as he had originally. Before sitting down, he sidled up to Dickenson and said "That was *Time* magazine, the reporter told me we had won Steven Spurrier's tasting." He then sat down for lunch. Bob Travers, the owner of Mayacamas who also had a wine in the Spurrier tasting was sitting across the table and asked, "is everything OK?" Barrett looked at Travers with a smile as wide as a bottle of Chardonnay and said "Yes, everything's just fine." The results of the Paris tasting began to spread quietly but quickly from Californian to Californian across the room.

'Some ninety people attended the formal lunch, which was done in the best French style. Dickenson was seated to the right of Alexis Lichine, while André Tchelistcheff was on his left. After lunch Lichine made a gracious, though condescending, speech saying how nice it was that Americans had come to learn from the French how to make great wine and how if they worked hard, someday they, too, might be successful. To Dickenson it was hard to take that speech, all the while knowing that California wines had just beaten some of the best of France in Spurrier's tasting. After lunch the Californian delegation politely thanked their hosts and got back onto their bus. Everyone waved goodbye as the vehicle pulled away from Lascombes. As soon as it had passed the last pine tree and was safely out of sight, the group erupted like football fans whose team had just won the Super Bowl. Everyone was screaming with elation. Barrett hugged Tchelistcheff. There were two more tastings that afternoon to bring the number of wines the Californians had tried in three weeks in France to more than 250, but the group walked through those in a dream. They were more excited about what had happened in Paris.

'Once they had arrived at their hotel, Barrett sent a telegram to the staff at Chateau Montelena which read – STUNNING SUCCESS IN PARIS ON MAY TWENTY FOUR STOP TOOK FIRST PLACE OVER NINE OTHERS WITH PREMIER CRU WINE STOP TOP NAMES IN FRANCE WERE BLIND TASTERS STOP. The staff wasn't sure what Barrett was referring to, but they learned it was something important when Miljenko 'Mike' Grgich, Montelena's wine-maker and a pupil of André Tchelistcheff, got a call from the *New York Times* asking to send a photographer to take his picture. After that call, Grgich didn't know what to do so he started dancing around the winery shouting in his native Croatian, "I'm born again!, I'm born again!" No one could understand a word he said, but who cared? Barrett's son Bo watched Grgich from a second story window and thought he had gone bonkers.

'The next day the group flew back to San Francisco. It was near dinner time when André Tchelistcheff and his wife Dorothy reached their home in Napa and Dorothy thought it might be a good moment to call Barbara Winiarski and tell her about the results of the Paris tasting. Barbara and the Winiarski children were already having dinner when the 'phone rang. When she heard that Stag's Leap had won the red wine tasting, Barbara wasn't sure exactly which wine tasting that was, but thanked Dorothy for the message anyway. The children, though, became excited when they heard they had won something and Barbara motioned to them to be quiet. Once Barbara had hung up the phone and told the them the news, Kasia and her younger sister Julia danced around the table with elation. They couldn't remember ever winning a wine contest before. After dinner Barbara talked to Warren, who was at his old family home in Chicago, wrapping up some matters involving the estate of his mother, who had recently died. Barbara casually mentioned that their wine had won 'that wine tasting in Paris.' Warren also had a tough time remembering which tasting it was. Without realizing the profound impact the Paris Tasting would have on his life and on his winery, he said simply, "That's nice".'

It did not take much time, however, for Warren Winiarski to find a way of describing the importance of that day in Paris. 'I called it a Copernican moment – Nicolaus Copernicus (1473-1543) the genius who proclaimed that the Sun, nor the Earth, was at the centre of the universe – nothing was the same after that. We looked at what we could do with different eyes.' From the following year he was involved in tasting after tasting to re-run the triumph of his wine in Paris. I was often at these events, so much so that Warren said that he and I were 'joined at the hip.' I was the first person he called when the sale of Stag's Leap for $185,000,000 had been finalised with Château Ste Michelle. I reminded him of this, but with no effect.

In his autobiography the great Robert Mondavi wrote that 'The Paris tasting was an enormous event in the history of California wine making. It put us squarely on the world map of great wine-producing regions. I saw the impact everywhere I went. Suddenly people had a new respect for what we were doing, for they saw we could make wines as good as the best of France. I think it is no coincidence that the first vintage of Opus One, the joint venture in Napa between Robert Mondavi and Baron Philippe de Rothschild of Château Mouton-Rothschild, was the 1979.

California benefited first, but after the initial shock, intelligent wine producers went to California to see what all the fuss was about. What they found was a vibrant wine region committed to investment in quality and a determination to prove themselves. Outside investors were there to help it happen, in stark contrast to France where such third party financing was rare. Within a year or two, what had been seen as the first chink in the armour of France's dominance of the wine world began to turn into an outward rather than an inward-looking mind set particularly amongst the younger generation.

However, the country's first reaction was to blame the judges. I became 'persona non grata' in certain circles, but since both the shop and *L'Académie* continued to do well, I paid no attention. Claude Terrail owner of La Tour d'Argent chastised Christian Vannequé for having taken part, forbade him to do so again for 'this is very bad for the French wine business'. There were calls for Pierre Bréjoux to resign from the INAO and Lalou Bize-Leroy, Aubert de Villaine's partner in the Domaine de la Romanée-Conti, accused him of treachery. Odette Khan got her side of the story into print in her magazine under the title 'On the subject of a small scandal' attesting that I had falsified the scores. Even in the early 2000s while researching for his book, George Taber told me that the judges found the memory of 24 May 1976 very painful. When the 30th anniversary took place in 2006 I was in touch with all those still living and they confirmed that they had been given a really hard going over and it is to their immense credit that not a single one of them told me at the time, for they knew that the tasting that Patricia and I had created had been honestly handled with only the best intentions.

Twenty years later, in 1996, bottles of Chateau Montelena 1973, Chardonnay and Stag's Leap Wine Cellars 1973 Cabernet Sauvignon were placed in the Smithsonian National Museum of American History and a further twenty years later, in May 2016, Bella and I were guests of the Smithsonian over a three day celebration of 24 May 1976 in Paris, a date that the House of Representatives had recently voted to become An Important Day in American History, in honour of which they gave me a signed and sealed document and an American flag. The second night there was a 'black tie' dinner for 600 people at the Smithsonian in honour of the event and the effect it had had on American wine. I was asked if I would like to say a few words at the end and, taking in the room's anticipation, said: 'It is very just and fitting that we should be here at The Smithsonian to celebrate how a Croat (Grgich) and a Pole (Winiarski) made American history in Paris with a little help from an Englishman.'

9. Here, There and Everywhere

In the Cité Berryer and in the Spurrier family, life was good. Having decided to move onto dry land, I sold the London house quickly and easily and bought a first floor flat on the Place des Hospitaliers St Gervais right in the heart of the historical part of Paris, Le Marais. We were ahead of the trend: what was to become the Musée Picasso was still a vast, boarded up wreck and the magnificent Hôtel de Sully on the Rue Saint Antoine was just beginning to be renovated. We were on the corner of the Rue des Francs Bourgeois which led south to the Place des Vosges, one of the most beautiful squares in the city. The bistrot Ma Bourgogne was busy and cheerful and is now a magnet for tourists but then seemed more for locals. Christian was in a school nearby in the Rue des Archives and I used to take him there on the handle bars of my bike before heading off to the Rue Royale. Kate was in a local *crèche* or baby-minding place which gave Bella a good half day to continue working for Jean-Pierre Pavillard, the photographer and Kate's godfather.

After about 18 months, we moved again to rent a large fifth floor flat off the Boulevard Henri IV on the edge of the Marais near to the Place de la Bastille, famous for the breakout from its prison which supposedly started the French Revolution and which was a little later under President Mitterand to get its own Opera House. This was to be our base for the rest of our time in Paris as a family and indeed we kept it for thirty years, finally giving up the lease in 2006. In the meantime I had sold the previous flat, the funds going into my ever-ambitious plans as a Parisian wine merchant.

The Caves de la Madeleine — although my name had long replaced that of the Caves on the now renovated shop front, I still answered the telephone with '*Bonjour, Caves de la Madeleine…*' — was by the mid 1970s one of the best-stocked wine shops in Paris. Thanks to Constant Bourquin and my membership of *L'Académie Internationale du Vin* I was on first name terms with the owners of some of France's finest vineyards who were happy to sell to me. At least one weekend a month we went to a wine region to visit the established names and discover new ones, never a trip ending without two or more wines added to the shop's small space, which

The Shop

always seemed to expand to accommodate them. My approach was much more 'communication' - 'Try this, you'll like it' – than commercialisation. My aim was that my customers should have two reactions when opening a bottle for friends: 'Gosh, that's good' and 'Where can I buy it?'

A selection of sixty-six of my firm favourites that I served at a street party in June 1981 to celebrate Ten Years in the Cité Berryer appears in the next chapter, but a quick tour of France from north to south would come up with the following names, many little-known at the time, who became suppliers and also friends. From Alsace, Hugel and Trimbach of course, but also Leonard Humbrecht (whose son Olivier was France's first Master of Wine), Colette Faller, Marcel Deiss, Jean Meyer and André Ostertag. From Champagne Etienne Gosset and Jean Vesselle. From Savoie Jean-Pierre Quénard and from the Jura the Rolet family. From Chablis René Dauvissat, whose wife made the best *gougères*, little cheese puffs so good after tasting young wines being readied for bottling before going onto older vintages. From Burgundy, Bella and I had met Becky Wassermann, still the region's finest broker in her early 80s, and she introduced me around, so the list was long and would include Domaines Rousseau, Dujac, Rémy, Roumier, Grivot, Rion and Gouges from the Côte de Nuits, Tollot-Beaut, Chandon de Briailles, de Mérode, Drouhin, de Suremain, Coche-Dury, Lafon, Roulot, Leflaive, Pousse d'Or, de Montille, Matrot,

The School

Blain-Gagnard, d'Angerville, Comte Armand and Thévenin from the Côte de Beaune, and Juillot and Michel from the Côte-Chalonnaise. All of my Beaujolais came from Pierre Ferraud and apart from Beaujolais and Macon I sold all nine of the *Crus,* and the wonderful Pouilly-Fuissés from Château de Fuissé that belonged to his brother-in-law. In the Rhône I renewed my contact with Louis Jaboulet and his nephew Gérard, met Marcel Guigal in 1971, Gérard Chave via the AIV and August Clape via John Livingstone-Learmonth in the north. A tasting with Pierre Perrin of Château de Beaucastel in 1972, who showed me the individual grape varieties – Beaucastel along with Montredon was then the only domaine planted with all 13 (7 red and 6 white) allowed by Baron Le Roy when he created the appellation – still in cask, some young vintages and then put the wine on my list, taking one wine per decade, down to 1919. I became a regular judge at the *Foire d'Orange,* sourcing out the Gold Medal winners for possible purchase. In Provence it was Château Simone and Château de Vignelaure either side of Aix-en-Provence, Clos Sainte Magdeleine in Cassis and Tempier in Bandol and in 1977 I was the first person to stock Domaine de Trevallon, owner Eloi Durrbach being a friend of Bella's half-brother James Baring, who had moved near to Saint-Rémy-de-Provence and created a small vineyard named *Le Mas du Cellier,* but his wines never made it to the Caves de la Madeleine.

Along the River Loire from east to west I visited Gérard Pétillat at Saint-Pourçain, Vincent Delaporte in Sancerre, Landrat et Guyollot in Pouilly-Fumé, Pierre Mardon in Quincy, Lucien Legrand and I bought masses of Sauvignon Blanc from Jean Gueritte in Cheverny and a little of the very rare white grape Romorantin, Henri Marionnet in Touraine, Gaston Huët and Prince Poniatowski in Vouvray, Pierre Couly and Charles Joguet in Chinon, Paul Maître in Bourgueil, Denis Duveau in Saumur-Champigny, Madame Joly at *La Coulée de Serrant* before her son Nicholas created the bio-dynamic movement in France, and Château de la Roulerie in Anjou, M Boivin for his superb Château de Fèsles Bonnezeaux, and from Muscadet Léon Boullault and his family at Domaine de Dorices, who made a marvellous *vin de grande garde* which passed six years on its fine lees in cement tanks below ground before bottling, which he reserved for me and for Jean-Pierre Coffe's restaurant La Ciboulette.

Going south towards Bordeaux, Madame de Saint-Exupéry's Château de Tiregand that led the Pécharmant appellation (and still does), there were some pleasant Bergeracs and my minor Bordeaux all came from Pierre Coste at Langon, who introduced me to Denis Dubourdieu's red and white Graves Château Reynon and especially his now cult Clos Floridéne. (Dubourdieu's accomplishments, both as an inspiring wine maker, world-wide consultant and Professor at the University of Bordeaux were recognised by *Decanter* magazine who made him the 2016 Man of the Year, an award he was able to accept just before his untimely death.) Much of my Bordeaux came from *courtiers* or brokers on *La Place de Bordeaux* and the rest from personal visits to lesser known appellations like Fronsac, Côtes de Castillon, Côtes de Francs and Côtes de Bourg and Blaye. Finally, moving east, I helped launch the Madirans of Alain Brumont, which in Cahors bought from the venerable Clôs du Gamot and the up and coming Château de Cèdre. There were many, many other wines from other regions, notably the emerging *Vins de Pays*, a category created by the INAO in 1973 to illustrate and protect the local regional wines, sold previously as *Vins de Table*. My interest in these helped me to write my first wine book *French Country Wines* a few years later.

When I started in the Cité Berryer I used to ask the salesmen who came to the Caves de la Madeleine whether they had sold their wines to the three top *cavistes* in Paris, Besse, Chaudet or Legrand. If the answer was yes, this was already a reference for me to give it a try. By the mid 1970s my own name was being widely used as a reference, which was a flattering measure of recognition. The shop was always busy, the volumes we sold quite surprising despite the tiny shop and staff. I remember Melvyn Master introducing me to a very rich American wine collector who had heard of me. 'How many shops do you have?' he asked. 'One'. 'And how many employees?' 'Two.' 'Gee, I guess you must be kinda exclusive.' We weren't, but I wanted my customers to feel that we were. Being bang in the centre of Paris was one of the keys – location, location, location – but the other was 'vocation, vocation, vocation.' This was what I had been cut out for and in the first few years of the Caves and *L'Académie* I could not have been happier: the hours were long, but this wasn't work, it was a way of life.

I should have had enough to do with running the Caves and teaching at *L'Académie*, but I always found something to distract me from these two core activities, provided it turned around wine. One of my well-off American clients was 'Stony' Stollenwerk (I have forgotten his first name as I and everyone else knew him as Stony) who was Paris bureau chief for the book department of *Time Life*, one of the US pioneers of sales by mail order. In France this was known as *la vente par correspondence* and it was in its infancy. One such club, The Savour Club, had started in the early 1970s, based in the Beaujolais region and specialising in these wines which were supplied by Georges Duboeuf, who was subsequently to become well-known as *Monsieur Beaujolais*. He supplied all the local restaurants, including Paul Bocuse in Lyon and the Troisgros brothers at Roanne, who put their names and knowledge behind The Savour Club range. Stony's experience of mail order was vast and having seen the 'communication by education' effect on sales in the shop from students at *L'Académie*, suggested that these elements could be wrapped up in a mail order package that would provide wines with a newsletter to match. What it needed, he said, was a name everybody would recognise and by chance I had earlier registered the name of *Les Amis du Vin* for use at some point in the future.

Les Amis du Vin was a hugely successful mail order company in the US, which somehow side-stepped the rigorous 3-tier system of importer/wholesaler/retailer, because they were a club, not a retailer. Just as the name *L'Académie du Vin* had not been registered as nobody before me had had the idea of a wine school open to the public, nobody had thought of registering *Les Amis du Vin,* probably because it was just too vague. A few years later I was able to take advantage of another name that was simply descriptive of what the company did, creating in 1978 with Michael Liekerman, director of Terence Conran's Habitat store in Paris, *Le Bistrot à Vin*, on the Esplanade of La Défense, the new business district on the outskirts of the city. The many cheerful bistrots in Paris that specialised in the wines from one region or another were, of course, *bistrots à vin*, but it took two Englishmen to grab the name for themselves. Similarly, as the 1980s rolled along, such places began to be known as *bars à vin*, notably the wonderful L'Ecluse chain launched by Georges Bardawill, but it fell to my ex-shop manager Mark Willamson to anglicise this to Willi's Wine Bar, to this day the most talked about *bar à vin* in Paris.

Stony Stollenwerk and I began to work on our new venture and for the newsletter he introduced me to François Sauzey and his girlfriend and future wife Anne Duval. By co-incidence I had first met François in 1965 as a gangling teenager in the week I was at Delamain in Cognac, where his father was Managing Director and many years later I was to give him a bottle of the same Delamain 1970 that Jean Delamain had insisted his housekeeper bring at the end of our lunch, purchased at a Christie's auction. Anne, whose mother was Czech, was a budding artist who would do the illustrations and design some of our 'own label' wines, who went on to become a recognised name and I am lucky enough to have some of her works. Our plan was to offer six wines, three whites and three reds, and the mailing went out to about 50,000 addresses, culled from *Time Life* and other mailing lists. Stony would finance this, the replies being handled by a part time girl working from *L'Académie's* offices above our tasting room. He was quite formal: if we did not get a positive response of 2% of above, he would not go ahead. We just missed this target and the idea died a death. Around this time one of my clients was an incredibly clever Englishman named Neville Abraham, who was at the INSEAD business school in Fontainebleue who, seeing the possibilities for wine on the London market at this time, was setting up a company and needed a name. We saw a bit of each other and since the Amis du Vin name was no longer any use to me, I gave it to him, complete with the logo, as he had asked me to be one of his seed suppliers for the wine list. Neville's business did well and in the early 1980s he opened what was to be a hugely successful wine bar in Covent Garden, naming it The Café des Amis and modelling it on Michael Liekerman's and my *Bistrot à Vin*. Michael took 20% of this venture, while I, again not paying attention to the value of a brand, had just 0.5%, but even with this I made a little money when Neville's restaurant empire, having by that time expanded into the Chez Gérard chain of brasseries and the fine Indian restaurant Chutney Mary, was finally sold.

As business in the Cité Berryer expanded in 1977 extra hands were needed. One of the early cellar rat/delivery boys had been Steven Fitzgerald Steede, always shortened to Steve Steede, a strikingly handsome product of an Anglo-Irish marriage who I had met in Mother Earth one of the ethnic American style joints which were slowly replacing the void left by the disappearance of the food market in Les Halles. As I was ordering a glass of wine, he moved over and said 'that sounds like an English accent, perhaps you know Steven Spurrier as I plan to see him and ask for a job in his shop.' With that approach, he was taken on right away and remained with me off and on with varying and increasing responsibility until everything was sold in 1988. Another, who replaced Steve when he went travelling for a year, was an employee who I shall call 'Chuck', an attractively cheerful young Chicagoan in his twenties, who would end up running *Le Moulin du Village*, the restaurant at the other end of the Cité Berryer that I was to buy the following year, where he did not acquit himself with honour and had to leave.

Two people I was to meet in 1977, who were to have a very positive influence on my wine businesses and still are in the forefront of Parisian wine life today, were Mark Williamson and Isabelle Bachelard. Mark, the owner of Willi's Wine Bar since 1981 and the smarter restaurant next door in the Rue des Petits-Champs called Macéo since the mid 1990s, would end up taking over the Moulin du Villages and its adjoining wine bar The Blue Fox when I was unloading everything in Paris in 1988. We had met with Tim Johnston in Aix-en-Provence and he had trained in the Savoy Hotel kitchens in London and was working with way through restaurants in Provence with a plan to return to the hotel business in London. I suggested he stop off in Paris to learn about wine and he has never left.

Isabelle Bachelard was introduced to me by Gregory Usher, a young American who was working under Anne Willan at the recently-opened La Varenne cookery school on the Left Bank, for whom *L'Académie du Vin* did the wine tastings, before moving onto *Le Cordon Bleu* and finally creating the cookery school at the Hôtel Ritz in the Place Vendôme. Gregory lived with Isabelle's elder brother Patrice, who edited one of the city's best art magazines, and their parents ran an hotel with a good restaurant in fashionable Saint-Germain-en-Laye. Isabelle had recently been studying in Portland, Oregon, so spoke good English, which was needed for *L'Académie* even though by this time the French clientele was almost outnumbering the Anglo-Saxons. Patricia welcomed another pair of hands and when, the following year she married her French boyfriend Gérard Gastaud and began a young family, Isabelle was to take over *L'Académie* on a daily basis.

Just a look at the Monday night tastings that we held in autumn 1977 astounds me today, but such was our commitment to offering something nobody had done before. In addition to the regular courses – six evenings on the *Tour de France* course and three on the Advanced Course – these were created to allow our students to follow the evolution of *Appellation Controlée* wines in several vintages and compare wines of the same vintage across the same appellation from different producers. They also provided an opportunity to taste rare and expensive wines no longer available on the market and we did not limit ourselves only to France. We admitted that *L'Académie du Vin* was fortunate to have the cooperation of embassies, *négociants* and the owners of various châteaux and domaines, without whom these tastings would not have been possible. Here is the autumn 1977 programme with the prices – 10 FF equalled a little less than £1 – at that time. The world of wine education was indeed young and it was wonderful to be able to offer such tastings, but at those prices we never made much of a profit.

Monday 12 September – 1973 Saint-Emilion Grand and Premier Grand Cru Classés 40 FF
Monday 19 September – Branded Wines of Bordeaux 30 FF
Monday 26 September – Pommard 1er Cru Les Epeneaux 1964-1975 Comte Armand 50 FF
Monday 3 October – Château Talbot 4th Growth St Julien eight vintages from 1960s and 1970s 50 FF
Monday 10 October – Volnay 1er Cru Clos des Santenots Domaine Jacques Prieur 40 FF
Monday 17 October – 1971 Médoc Grands Crus Classés 40 FF
Monday 24 October - *Bordeaux 1st Growths 1957, Ausone, Haut-Brion, Latour, Margaux, Mouton-Rothschild 60 FF

Monday 7 November – The Best Wines of Austria from the Austrian
   Embassy 40 FF
Monday 14 November – Musigny Comté de Vogüé, six vintages from
   1957-1970 60 FF
Tuesday 15 November – Beaujolais Nouveau with Pain Poilâne
   and Brie 20 FF
Monday 21 November – Château Giscours, 3rd Growth Margaux 50 FF
Monday 28 November – *Romanée-Saint-Vivant Grand Cru
   1962/64/66/69/70, 75 FF
Monday 5 December – The Best Wines of Chile from the Chilean
   Embassy 40 FF
Monday 12 December – Château de Pez St Estèphe, nine vintages
   1945-1971 50 FF
Monday 19 December – *1928s, Brane-Cantenac, Carbonnieux,
   Margaux, Montrose, Palmer 75 FF

The * signified that the wines had come from the vintage reserves of NICOLAS.

Another wonderful meeting in 1977 was with Julian and Sheila More
on the introduction from David Russell, a gentlemanly advertising executive with a beautiful house on the Berkshire/Wiltshire borders whose
large cellars were stocked mostly from the Caves. Buying for himself
and for his advertising company when he found a wine he liked on his
frequent visits to Paris, David's orders were always for 'a dozen dozen'.
Julian More, about ten years older than me, was very well-known in the
UK theatre world for writing the 'book' for musicals, his big hits being
Irma La Douce, Grab me a Gondola, Expresso Bongo and *Songbook*. He and
Sheila were moving to Paris and David said we must meet, so I suggested
a drink in Le Café Les Deux Magots on the Boulevard St Germain. Julian
asked how he would recognise me and I said I would be with Digby, my
Champagne-coloured Berger Briard. We got on superbly from the start,
as did Bella with Sheila, who represented the works from the estate of
Alphonse Mucha, the Hungarian Art Deco artist.
   At one point during our many get-togethers, Julian said he was surprised that nobody had written a TV series or 'soap opera' as they were
known, on wine, as there were so many great stories. I agreed and we put
our heads together, Julian leaving the first plot outline to me. The title
from the very start was 'Corkscrew' and while my first scenario was aban-

doned early on to concentrate on the wine world around Bordeaux, this is how it stayed for a further fifteen years while Julian and I attempted, never losing confidence and having the best fun writing and re-writing.

When Julian and I started Corkscrew back in 1978 it was planned as a ten hour package. This almost sold to BBC 1, but didn't and although I got a good deal of interest during the time Bella and I spent in New York in 1981-2, it was beaten to the post by a soap opera named Falcon's Crest, based of course in California. The last script was from mid 1993, when it was on the verge of being accepted by Britain's Channel 4, with Timothy Burrill, who I had first met in Bandol at Domaine Tempier as he had a summer house in the Var, as Producer, but even this never saw the light of day.

Shortly after moving to Paris, Julian and Sheila bought a small farm-house surrounded by vines in the commune of Visan, well-known for its robust wines from the southern Rhône. Bella and I spent many happy moments there, as well as with a friend Araminta 'Minty' Lalanne, who lived nearby lost in countryside near Vaison-la-Romaine, with marvel-lous views over to Mont Ventoux. She was known as 'Auntie Minty' for her never ceasing hospitality and hardly a summer passed without a visit of several days. Julian turned to writing books which were illustrated with photographs by Carey, one of his twin daughters. All were beautifully published by Pavilion. In the early 2000s the Mores left Visan for a fine modern flat in Marseille, where in one of the local restaurants we shared the best bouillabaisse of my life, washed down with the white Cassis from Clos Ste Magdeleine and then went swimming with Julian at that time aged eighty. He died the following year, a very great loss.

With both Christian and Kate in school during the day, Bella was look-ing around for something to do having learnt as much about photography as she could with Jean-Pierre Pavillard. Through the British Chamber of Commerce we learnt that Bernard and Laura Ashley were planning to open a branch of their Laura Ashley shop on the Rue de Grenelle in the fashionable 6th arrondissement and applied for a job, to be taken on along-side Annie Bingham. Bella and Annie were known as *les petites Anglaises* and proved very adept at selling the very pretty fabrics and wallpaper that had made the brand's name, alongside the dreamy flowing dresses. Rules in French shops were very strict, even at the Caves, that any payment by cheque should be accompanied by a *piece d'identité* or ID card. One busy Saturday afternoon a very elegant Parisienne had made substantial purchases, paying by cheque on the *Banque de France*. *'Piece d'identité, s'il vous plaît, Madame'* said Bella, the request being met with a surprised look. Bella repeated the request, pointing to the card in the shop that stated the rule, adding that the lady should write her address on the back of the cheque, as was also the rule. From the depths of her very smart bag, an ID card was presented, showing that she was Madame Giscard d'Estaing, wife of the then President of France, and slowly on the back of the cheque she wrote *Palais d'Elysée, Paris 8ème*.

Annie Bingham went on to open the Laura Ashley shop in Aix-en-Provence and rising to managerial levels within the company before returning to Paris in the mid 1980s to work as a head-hunter for the international fashion business and moving into our flat in the Rue de la Cérisaie. As as a family we had moved back to London in 1982 and I was commuting to from there to Paris, so slept in the spare room. Her time at Laura Ashley had shown Bella how much demand there was in Paris for *le style Anglais* and in 1978 she opened with friends a shop in the Rue de Verneuil, not quite as fashionable as the Rue de Grenelle, but good for me as it was next door but one to *Le Tan Dinh*, one of the best family-run Vietnamese restaurants in the city, whose young chef Robert Vifian was passionate about wine and was to become a teacher at *L'Académie du Vin*. The restaurant still exists, with Robert behind the stoves and his wife Isabelle front of house, with one of the greatest and best value wine lists imaginable. Searching for a name for Bella's shop, I suggested a simple one The English Trading Company, based on the very successful store The General Trading Company (GTC) in London's Sloane Street, which soon became known as ETC. They sold everything from oatcakes to kilts for women made to measure in Scotland and for a year or two it was quite successful.

Even without a base in London, we went back from time to time, keeping in touch with parents and friends especially in the winter, as the house in Burgundy was too cold to use between November and April. Christian had been put down for Eton at birth as Bella's father had been there, which made me happy, and so we would have to find a Preparatory School for him from 8 years old, and my father, sensing that at some point we would move back to the UK, suggested he buy a house for our future use. In the meantime my close friend David Zambra who had preceded me as a lodger of the baroness, had begun buying wine from me to sell on to friends and, becoming progressively bitten by the wine bug, decided in 1975 to leave his job with W H Smith and open a wine shop. He found an ideal premises in the Chelsea part of the Fulham Road, opposite the cinema, part of what was already known as 'The Beach' as the clothes shops, cafés and restaurants were so appealing that casual strolling up and down was a pleasure. Naturally, it was called Les Caves de la Madeleine and David bought from the same suppliers for many years. We were friends so I didn't consider charging a royalty and anyway it was nice to have an outpost of the Caves in fashionable London. In the mid 1980s the shop was taken over by Graham Chidgey of Laytons – Graham having gone to work for the great Tommy Layton right out of school, subsequently buying the business – and a few years later repurchased by Charles Lea and Patrick Sandeman, both ex-Laytons. Charles Lea had spent a year with me in the early 1980s on his junior year abroad and then gone on to work for Mark Williamson at Willi's Wine Bar. Patrick was of the Sandeman Port and Sherry family whose logo of The Don is still recognised today and his mother was a Valdespino, whose bodegas in Jerez produced a Delicioso Fino and a Tio Diego Amontillado of the highest quality. Lea & Sandeman are still in the Fulham Road and with three other shops in London are one of the city's best retailers where I am always pleased to see remnants from the old days like Vincent Delaporte's Sancerre and Marcel Deiss's Alsace still on their shelves.

Mentioning Patrick Sandeman, whose tragic death in a sky-diving accident in 2012 deprived the wine world of a future Master of the Vintners' Hall as well as a brilliant, always charming taster, reminds me of a massive auction of Sandeman Sherries at Christie's around this time. The company had recently been taken over by Seagram though, who decided to close down the Sherry operation – Patrick's elder brother George Sandeman headed up the Port side until his retirement. No doubt the thousands of butts of Sherry maturing under the Solera system of year-to-year blending found quick takers from the long-established Jerez bodegas and the bottled stock was consigned to Christie's. I had just been appointed Christie's agent for France for wine and was of course in regular touch with Michael Broadbent and well aware of the auctions. Once I saw the catalogue with over two thousand cases of all styles from the driest Fino to the sweetest Amaroso and the estimated prices, I flew to London for the tasting. The Parisians didn't drink Sherry and if they drank Port it was a light Ruby as an aperitif and they bought Madeira only for cooking. My week with Martinez in September 1965 had shown how marvellous some of the older blends could be and the quality of the Sandeman range was extraordinary. I ended up buying around 150 cases across the entire range of Fino, Amontillado, Palo Cortado, Oloroso and Amaroso, to be told when they cleared customs through Bercy that this was more Sherry shipped to Paris than in the past six months. Although I did not have, and still lack, a business bone in my body, I was good at promotion and communication and this investment was a golden opportunity. My Anglo-Saxon clients had heard of Sherry but had not tasted wines of this quality and the French clients were amazed by what was put before them. I made comparisons with the classics, aged Fino being likened to the Jura's Vin Jaune, the extraordinary Amaroso aligned with Château d'Yquem. *Gault & Millau* wrote them all up, my restaurant friends like Alain Dutournier of Le Trou Gascon put them on their list and within a month or so there wasn't a bottle left. It was groundbreaking and exciting.

In June 1977 Lucien Legrand and I were invited to Bordeaux to the *Cité du Vin*, a complex devoted to wine on the famous Quai des Chartrons, as representatives of the Paris retail trade to take part in what was called *Les Premières Journées Mondiales*. Having created Champagne Brut Intégral together in 1972 and the Beaujolais à l'Ancienne in 1973, Legrand and I were accustomed to exchanging opinions and ideas one of which, since both of us were out-growing our city centre space, was find a much larger space as near to Paris as possible to continue the very profitable bottling from bulk shipments (for him) and storage for maturing wines (for me). Briefly referred to in chapter 7, we found just the place in Issy-les-Moulineaux and in 1975, with Constant Bourquin's nephew as a minority partner, we opened *Le Centre Culturel du Vin, Le Chemin des Vignes*, from which I stupidly parted company after a few years, but which thrives along with its own small vineyard and restaurant, under Lucien's son Yves to this day. The meeting on the Quai des Chartrons was a testing 'think tank' with a few dozen potential 'opinion formers' to discuss what in 1979 would emerge as Vinexpo, the great international wine fair held in Bordeaux every odd year and later in Hong Kong and the US in even years. Jacques Chaban-Delmas, Prime Minister under President Pompidou, was the Bordeaux Mayor planning to spend lots of the city's money to drag it into the modern world. He pretty well succeeded and it recently fell to Alain Juppé, Prime Minister under President Chirac, to complete the job, Bordeaux now being in my view the finest and most functional city in France. In the early days Vinexpo was small, but well supported by the châteaux, who began to open their doors to visitors, something that had been pioneered from the early 1960s by Alexis Lichine at Le Prieuré and Lascombes in Margaux, and very much frowned on by his Médoc neighbours. For some time there have been three major wine fairs in Europe: Germany's Prowein in Düsseldorf in mid March, Vinitaly in Verona in early April and Bordeaux's Vinexpo in mid June, as well as the London Wine Trade Fair in late May, but this is tiny compared to the others. The saying is that 'you go to Prowein to do business, the food is better at Vinitaly and the girls are prettier, but the parties are better at Vinexpo.'

After the Judgement of Paris I became a regular visitor to California. On the first anniversary of the Paris Tasting, the Vintners' Club in San Francisco decided to hold a rematch of both the Chardonnays and the Cabernets and invited me to be co-host. Not surprisingly the results were again in favour of California, but I had already done my bit for the Sunshine State and was more interested in meeting the people who made the wine and here I succeeded. Most importantly, Robert Mondavi was at these tastings and invited me up to Napa. After showing me round his famous winery, he had prepared a tasting of his Pinot Noir against a La Tâche from the Domaine de la Romanée-Conti and his Cabernet Sauvignon Reserve against Mouton-Rothschild. The first showed his ambition, but there was no thread that linked the two Pinots, while there was a sense of common identity between the two Cabernets. Robert Mondavi was certainly the most forward-looking wine producer of his, perhaps any generation and when the first vintage of Opus One, his joint-venture with Baron Philippe de Rothschild of Mouton-Rothschild, the 1979 made from Cabernet fruit from 'the Rutherford Bench', was unveiled in 1981, the wine world paid attention. His subsequent collaborations, always on his instigation, with Marchese Lodovico Antinori in Tuscany and Eduardo Chadwick in Chile's Aconcagua Valley, were perhaps even more innovative and today Ornellaia's Masseto and Chadwick's Sena join Opus One at the absolute pinnacle of each region's production.

The following year I was invited to speak at the Monterey Wine Festival. Each speaker had 10 minutes up on the podium, an orange light appearing at the 11th minute and a red light at the 12th. I was to talk about wine consumption in England and had just made a few notes, planning to fill them out as I went along, my slot being the last of the day. The speaker before me was Robert Lawrence Balzer, already deposed in the hierarchy by Robert Finigan who carried on for a full fifteen minutes, leaving me with an easy wrap up.

After Monterey I went south to Los Angeles, my first ever visit, where I was to give two tastings comparing California and French wines, being put up in great state at the Beverley Wiltshire Hotel. Here I saw my first mobile 'phone, brought to the table of a movie mogul, and that evening went to my first and last 'Roller Disco'. This was in a downtown converted warehouse and was called Flipper's, recently opened by a friend from my London days named Nick Cowan. Brooks Firestone, a scion of the Firestone Tire Company, had planted a vineyard on the family estate in Santa Barbara who I had been introduced to by Geoffrey Roberts, had attended the evening tasting and we had gone onto dinner afterwards and I persuaded him to join me. I had enjoyed roller skating as a boy and ice skating later on Monday nights at the Queensway Ice Rink, but was un-prepared for the booming music and the speed and gyrations of the participants that evening. While I was able to duck and dive a little, Brooks, tall and very East Coast looking, buttoned his suit jacket tightly and with arms akimbo and legs wide apart, moved forward at a steady speed. We gave it up after a little while, but it stays in the mind.

At this point I should say that whatever I might have done for California wines in the broad sense, Geoffrey Roberts did far, far more on the retail and restaurant scene in the UK. Very well off, incredibly handsome and the best dressed of my contempories, he formed Geoffrey Roberts Associates in 1977 and within a year had amassed a vast portfolio of the well-known estates and was making the names for many emerging ones. His annual tastings in London were a vinous and social must and it was only ill health in his fifties that caused him to sell his company to the very bright Neville Abraham. The offices moved from Chelsea, where he lived, to White City in west London. By this time I was back in London and he and I used to lunch often at his clients' restaurants in the centre of town and I asked him how he felt about the new premises. 'I don't feel anything' he replied 'as I don't go there.' His memorial service at St Luke's in Chelsea's Sydney Street was overflowing and sufficient funds were left by him and increased by benefactors to create the Geoffrey Roberts Award that offers a substantial travelling bursary every year to a young member of the wine trade who can show particular commitment to the wines of the New World or of emerging regions. Trustees, amongst them his great friend Jancis Robinson, whose husband Nick Lander's Soho restaurant l'Escargot had the best list of California wines in the 1980s, managed the award since 1996 and since 2013 it has been administered by The Vintners' Company.

One great advantage of my trips to California was the time I was able to spend at the Washington Square Bar and Grill, becoming increasingly friendly with its ex-newspaperman owner, Ed Moose. In 1998 the Taylor Company of Dallas published a book by Ron Firmite, a senior writer for *Sports Illustrated* and an habitué at Moose's place, called The Square. I have a copy in front of me signed on 12 June 1990 by Ed, with the laconic note that 'some of this is true.' Chapter 8 is entitled 'Splendid! What's Softball?' and I know that this is true, for I was there. The Square had opened in 1973 and Mary Etta's cooking and Ed's 'table-hopping, celebrity-greasing hostmanship' kept the place buzzing and in the meantime Ed became quite a celebrity himself. I will let Ron Firmite tell the story:

'As his fortunes increased, Moose began to travel more. Rome was one of his regular stops and so was Paris, where he soon developed friendships with vintners and restaurateurs. He grew particularly friendly with a young Englishman named Steve (sic) Spurrier, who was an internationally respected wine connoisseur and the part-owner of a restaurant near Maxim's called Le Moulin du Village. Spurrier had become a frequent visitor to the Napa Valley wine country north of San Francisco and, because of his friendship with Moose, a regular on these visits to The Square, where he and Ed would enjoy long and vinuous lunches together. And when Moose was in Paris, he unfailingly stopped in at Le Moulin. It was at one of these Moulin meetings in October 1978 that Spurrier, growing sentimental, suggested that the two restaurants engage in some sort of forks-across-the-sea exchange. What could they do, he asked Moose, to bring the staff and customers of each place together on common ground? Moose pondered this for a moment and then was seized with inspiration: 'Why don't we play softball?' he blurted out. 'Splendid,' replied Spurrier enthusiastically, 'what's softball?'

'Le Moulin, quite naturally, had no team, but there were some on staff who, unlike Spurrier had at least heard of the game. The Square had had a team of sorts for several years, one hastily assembled by Moose for an annual game with Cookie Picetti's Star Buffet at the North Beach playgound's asphalt diamond.

'Spurrier was unaware of Moose's increasingly meticulous preparations. The Englishman, of course, wouldn't have recognised a good team if he'd seen one. He was content to round up what few persons he knew who could tell a softball from a grapefruit. The preliminary plans were made in secret by Moose and Spurrier. Then in the winter of 1978, Moose began informing his players (one of them the author) that next year they would play Cookie's as usual and then on Mother's Day we would travel to the Bois de Boulogne to play Le Moulin du Village.

'The game itself was, regrettably and unavoidably, a comedy of errors. There was little chance it could have been much else, considering our opponents' unfamiliarity with the sport (several of the players put gloves on their *throwing* hands) and the site of the game, a rutted and rocky soccer field in the Bois. Moose's normally scrupulous attention to detail failed him embarrassingly in this regard, for he must have entertained some romantic notion that every stretch of lawn in the Bois had the texture of a putting green. In reality, there was scarcely five feet square anywhere that did not look like it had been a battlefield. As a result, such elementary skills such as fielding ground balls became adventures in dangerous living. As it was he didn't help much and the final score was 40-22 in favour of The Square's team, a high score for four innings, but Moose was not pleased with our performance.

'He was hardly displeased, however, with the publicity this otherwise forgettable game generated. Four journalists had made the trip from San Francisco, so Moose had every reason to expect some ink afterward. He was staggered by the final outpourings, for both San Francisco newspapers, the *Chronicle* and the *Examiner*, ran lengthy feature stories. And *Sports Illustrated* ran some seven thousand words, complete with illustrations. The Square was just beginning to be known as *the* spot to be in San Francisco; now it was becoming famous nationwide. Moose was receiving challenges from bar owners all over the country and he became a talk-show regular from San Diego to Portland, Maine. Wisely, he rejected all the various challenges as being unworthy. Besides, he had his own agenda for our team, an agenda ordered to take every advantage of this first rush of publicity: Les Lapins Sauvages, the name that Moose had come up with for his team, would only go where the action was.'

It was Ron Fimrite who wrote the *Sports Illustrated* article under the heading 'To Paris with Glove' (based presumably on Ian Fleming's first James Bond book *From Russia with Love*) and it remains one of the most read pieces ever in this national magazine. Ed Moose took his team all over the world, to London in 1981, to Moscow, to Hong Kong and in 1987 George Steinbrenner, owner of the New York Yankees, turned Yankee Stadium over to them for a friendly match with his team. Ed talked to me in 1989 about a re-match ten years on, but by that time I no longer owned Le Moulin and he was moving from The Square to the much larger Moose's a stone's throw away. For those present in Paris it was a day to remember and to treasure – a hard core ended up at the brasserie Bofinger, then owned by Eric de Rothschild of Lafite, rather the worse for wear and even though it was only across the Place de la Bastille from our flat, Bella had to guide me home – but by then I knew what softball was.

The acquisition of Le Moulin du Village, the restaurant in the Cité Berryer where Christopher Mitchell-Heggs and I were booked for lunch when we had first walked past the Caves de la Madeleine, in summer 1978 was certainly logical, since it was just up the street and on the sunny side as well. The owner, Monsieur Albert Bégot, was getting on in years and the menu was old-fashioned and repetitive compared to the *cuisine nouvelle* that had become fashionable. Monsieur Bégot's family was from Tain l'Hermitage in the northern Rhône and much of the list was made up of wines from Chapoutier, which were not well-thought of at the time. On two floors, with a large terrrace that was always packed in summer, it was full at lunch and seemed to tick over in the evening. The price for the business was not excessive and I put up a little over half the money to gain a majority share, joined by my Burgundy-loving friend David Fromkin who was often in Paris in the summer, the owner of a little pseudo-Russian restaurant opposite and raised the rest by offering clients of the Caves and *L'Académie* 30% off their forthcoming meals if they came up with 500FF in cash. The manager was going to be Chuck, whose girlfriend and future wife had worked part-time at *L'Académie* and had dutifully typed out the hand-written scribblings of Julian more and myself for the first drafts of our potential blockbuster *Corkscrew*. We also had a young chef from Maxim's, so all seemed set fair.

Chuck was working for the Caves without residence or work papers, so I turned to my original 'fixer' Félix Branger to get him the necessary permits, explaining that since the *quartier* was the centre for American banks and businesses and we would have a French chef and other French staff, it was logical that the manager should be American. This ruse succeeded, something that I was deeply to regret within two or three years. The wines were all supplied by the Caves and I practised a 300% mark up, low in Paris at that time and certainly low around the Place de la Madeleine, which made them around 60% higher than in the shop. For some people *La Cité Berryer* was becoming *La Cité Spurrier* and my taking over Le Moulin came to the attention of Robert Courtine, France's most feared and revered restaurant critic writing under the penname of *La Reynière* in *Le Monde*, who gave the restaurant a passable review, but described me as *'un monsieur touche-à-tout'* or a jack of all trades and presumably a master of none. With the two pillars of Parisian gastronomy against me – Odette Khan and Robert Courtine – I could have been worried, but I wasn't.

As if I didn't have enough on my plate, the same year I went into another restaurant venture with Michael Liekerman, the Director of Terence Conran's newly opened Habitat store. Both being young(ish) Brits wanting to shake up the scene a little, we got on well, Michael having a more progressive vision of commerce than me. The business centre at *La Défense* on the outskirts of Paris across the Seine from Neuilly, considered far away at the time but now with its own Metro station at the end of *Ligne 1* was being built and he had the brilliant idea that it needed a modern *bistrot* to offer sustenance to the workers in all the modern offices. Helped by the influence of our potential partners in this venture – S I C A R E X, government funded experimental wine producers at Listel near Marseille – we were able to obtain a site on the Esplanade in front of two already complete high rise buildings – the much maligned Tour Maine Montparnasse and the Tour Eiffel which were the only constructions in central Paris with a height above nine storeys – and Michael hired the Habitat team to design and construct a single storey metal and glass building with a large basement. We obtained a lease of nineteen years and Le Bistrot à Vin opened its doors in time for Christmas 1978. The manager was Steve Steede, who had left the Caves the year before and was welcomed back into the fold, not an easy character but a very honest one, who knew all my wine producers from whom he bought directly. We were the wine bar to serve

Beaujolais 'on tap' from kegs in the basement and most of the *charcuterie* came from 'Bobosse' just north of Lyon. Half the basement was arranged as a wine shop where occasional wine courses were held. Le Bistrot à Vin was planned by Michael as a template which, if successful, we would reproduce in other major French cities, but this didn't happen.

I was becoming more in demand as a wine judge and the shop needed another pair of hands to help Mark Williamson and the ever-cheerful Mauricette and this appeared in the form of Drew Harré, a young New Zealander who was a student violin maker and had hitched up with a recently divorced French lady who lived in Neuilly. Despite her comfortable surroundings, Drew was fiercely independent and now rivals Mark Williamson as the most successful ex member of *Le Mafia Anglais* with four restaurants, all cheek by jowl in the smart Rue de Seine in the 6th arrondissement, compared to Mark's rather more upmarket two in the Rue des Petits Champs in the 1st. A little far behind is Tim Johnston, whose much loved *Juvéniles* in the Rue de Richelieu (1er) is now run by his daughter Margaux and her chef husband, while Rhône-Ranger Tim still looks after the wines. I had recently been made the Christie's representative in France for packing up wine cellars, one of the best being that of Darroze in Villeneuve de Marsan, with memories of the Lafite-Rothschild 1806, the elderly but very spry Monsieur Darroze having decided that his clients no longer deserved most of the marvellous bottles that he had so lovingly collected. Drew and I spent three full days cataloguing and packing and each lunchtime we were offered a half bottle of a Médoc First Growth, Burgundies for dinner and after that the marvellous Darroze Armagnac, still a highly regarded brand. On the way to deliver the wines to Hillebrand near Bordeaux, we stopped off at Château Margaux which had been purchased the year before from Bernard Ginestet by André Mentzelopoulos. We also had lunch with Alexis Lichine at Le Prieuré, having been warned in advance by Martin Bamford that the chicken, the usual *plat du jour*, would be overcooked and dry, which it was. Alexis was as generous as ever with his wines and as usual did not let us leave before we had re-stocked up on his books.

The *Foire de Mâcon* in late May remained an annual event and I remember that in 1978 I had planned a short break in Florence with Bella, David Zambra my school friend and now owner of London's Caves de la Madeleine and his wife Jane. Jane had made reservations in a nice hotel on the left bank of the Arno away from the tourists and I set off to Mâcon with the reservations in my pocket as although Bella knew we were going to Florence, I wanted most of it to be a surprise. She would take the train from the Gare de Lyon, just one métro stop from our flat, which stopped at Chambéry at around 11.30pm and I would meet her on that, a sleeping compartment having been booked beforehand. Tim Johnston was at the Macon tasting, driving down afterwards to Aix-en-Provence where he was working with Melvyn Master. There was a two Michelin star restaurant in Chambéry and I arranged with Tim that he would drive me there, he'd be my guest for dinner and then he could head south. We left the car in the station car park and walked to the restaurant, which wasn't up to its Michelin rating and, having left earlier than expected, we had time on our hands before the train arrived. Walking back we passed the local cinema which was showing *Saturday Night Fever* with John Travolta, persuaded the usherette to let us in as it had already started, took our seats and promptly both fell asleep, only to come to about ten minutes before the train was to leave. A very quick dash to the car park to get my bag, we charged through the gates to find the train on the platform opposite ready to leave. I gave Tim my bag, dashed across the tracks and mercifully the train door on that side was not locked. I opened it as the train began to move, Tim a little behind me but close enough to throw the bag into my outstretched hands. Gasping for breath, but safely on board, I turned round to find myself face to face with the conductor, who surveyed me gravely and said '*Madame vous attend*'/'Madam is waiting for you.' There were no mobile phones in those days and my planned surprise for Bella would have backfired, as she would have arrived in Florence with not the first clue where to meet David and Jane. Once she had calmed down we had a very good time.

A better, less frantic, moment with Tim was after the Foire de Mâcon the following year, that Saturday in May being his 30th birthday, so I suggested we make up a small party to have dinner at the restaurant Point in Vienne, well-known in the 1950s for the cuisine of the great Fernand Point gastronomic-godfather to Bocuse, Troisgros and many others, still run by his widow and famous for its cellar. I said that he and his wife Stephanie would be my guests for dinner and I'd host the wines for the table. The other guests were Bob Baker, Robert Finigan and Mark Williamson. I remembered vaguely what the wines were and contacted Tim to get them right and here is his reply:

'I have just dug out my notebook on the 30th birthday dinner you gave me at La Pyramide. We started with a Condrieu 1978 with their house label, but I reckon it would have been either from Vernay or Dumazet. We began dinner with 1976 Nuits-St-Georges Clos de la Perrière Blanc, the Pinot Blanc from Domaine Henri Gouges with very refined, crisp, dry fruit. Then we had Château Haut-Brion 1961 on great form, magical. The centrepiece of the evening was a Marie-Jeanne (three bottles) of Château Lafite 1947 which was magnificent, a little dry with tannic structure, great elegance and a very long finish. What a wine! We finished with the Coulée de Serrant 1949 (50FF on the list!), quite extraordinary, sweet but elegant, not cloying sticky. I have always said that it was the only bottle of Coulée de Serrant that I have ever really enjoyed and Nicolas Joly has certainly NEVER made a wine that gets even close to it. (I should add that Nicolas Joly has never made a sweet wine and that the 1947 that I ordered at Point a year or two later was not as good as the 1949). I remember that your friend Geoffrey Roberts and his friend Christopher Selmes were at a table not far from us and were drinking Château Caillou 1921 (at a COMPLETELY different price level), and you swapped a glass with them and we all agreed that the Caillou was less exciting.'

On the way out, flushed with pride at the success of my selection, I said good night to Geoffrey and Christopher and asked what they had before the Caillou 1921. 'Lafite '58' Geoffrey replied. 'Why on earth such a lousy vintage?' I asked. '1858' came the murmured reply.

In 1979 the *Guide Gault & Millau* held a two day blind tasting on the theme *Les Olympiades du Vin*/The Olympic Games of Wine. *L'Académie du Vin* was very much involved in sourcing the bottles to get the widest spread possible and then helped to arrange the flights in which they would be tasted. As a judge, I couldn't be involved in this, but Patricia told me that they were grouped as far as possible in grape varieties and similar price bands. International tasters were invited and I remember Michael Broadbent, David Peppercorn and Serena Sutcliffe from the UK. The first morning I was on a table with Jacques Seysses of Domaine Dujac in front of a range of Chardonnays. Michael was on a nearby table with the ebullient Jacques Manière of Le Pactole on the Boulevard St Germain, who served his house Champagne from Legras in Chouilly *en carafe*. I loved this idea, as not only did the decanting reduce the bubbles a fraction, the simple carafe was so much more relaxed than a Champagne bottle. At the mid-morning break Michael came over in quite a state to say that Manière wasn't spitting out anything, which unnerved him and could I intervene. Before the next group of wines I said hello to Jacques, who knew me well from his restaurant, and said that Monsieur Broadbent was concerned and that perhaps the spittoon might come in useful. His reply was clear: 'Ecoute, mon petit, si je crâche, je perds mon equilibre.' 'Listen, little one, if I spit I lose my sense of balance.' His place was empty for the afternoon session. That evening I introduced the UK tasters to Alain Dutournier's marvellous restaurant Au Trou Gascon in the 12th arrondissement, a marvellous place for the best food and wines from Alain's native south-west France, which over the last three decades he has shown to deservedly high acclaim at Le Carré des Feuillants in the Rue de Castiglione (1er).

No doubt there were many surprises from these tastings, one single 'upset' making the headlines: the Torres Black Label Cabernet Sauvignon from Penedès in north east Spain was placed first in its group ahead of First Growths Haut-Brion and Latour. After a short time, the tasters on that panel, of which I was one, received a single line from Jean-Paul Gardère, the manager of Latour, asking: '*Vous n'étiez pas victime d'un embuscade?*' 'Were you not victim of an ambush?' No, and Miguel Torres didn't think so, either, and the Black Label went onto justify this year after year.

Certainly the most unexpected thing that happened to me at the end of the 1970s, since I hadn't planned it myself, was to take part in an advertising campaign for Coca Cola's venture into wine, under the brand Taylor's California Cellars. Perhaps seeing the success of California since the Paris Tasting, Coca Cola had been smart enough not to buy a major estate, but to purchase a New York State winemaker's brand – Taylor Cellars – and transfer this to California, hiring Richard 'Dick' Peterson, one of André Tchelistcheff's many brilliant pupils, as overall winemaker. Their plan was to make mainstream wines for the popular market. The genius here was Albert E. Killeen, a very elegant and brilliant businessman who had looked after Coca Cola's interests in Africa for some years and, nearing retirement age, had returned to the States. Al (as he was known) had studied the Judgement of Paris and had come to the conclusion that it provided a base to challenge the rules of advertising of the day that did not allow direct comparisons between products. Thus, 'Persil Washes Whiter' and 'Avis, We Try Harder' could not add... 'than Daz' nor '...than Hertz'.

Killeen's theory was that if an acknowledged authority in the particular field said that in their opinion 'x' was better than 'y and z', this would not be overruled. He and Coca Cola's advertising company Kenyon & Eckard had done a small ad for Taylor California Cellars along these lines with a well-known New York Sommelier with no objection and now he approached me to ask if I would take place in a comparative tasting/advertisement for TV and newspapers along the same lines. I can't remember the name of the NYC sommelier, but knew of him and respected him, so I agreed.

What then took place was extraordinary in its complexity, depth and expense, out of which I made a good fee and continuing residuals for a couple of years. Once the date had been set, sometime in summer 1979, the Kenyon & Eckard executives appeared in force, accompanied by Albert and John Maysles, known as the Maysles Brothers and by far the most respected mostly documentary filmmakers at the time. The tasting room at *L'Académie du Vin*, with its historic Napoleon III horseshoe bar, was commandeered and although the Maysles' crew was from the US, a complementary French crew had to be hired to satisfy the French union system, who kept to themselves during the filming. Killeen had chosen three other brands for me to compare the white red and roses from Taylor California Cellars – Almaden, Paul Masson and one I cannot remember, even he didn't dare take on Gallo – and my brief was simple: to make a comparison and come out in favour of the Coca Cola wines. I had met Dick Peterson on a visit to Napa and admired him, so was positively inclined to like his wines. (Incidentally, his elder daughter Heidi married Bo Barrett of Chateau Montelena and became very famous for making Screaming Eagle.) However, I still had to make my own comparison and actually did find the Taylor California Cellars wines better. So the cameras rolled and I said 'Hello, I'm Steven Spurrier, founder of *L'Académie du Vin* in Paris, and I've tasted Almaden, Paul Masson and Taylor's California Cellars (the bottles were in front of me and I touched each as I spoke) and in my view Taylor's California Cellars is the best.' Al Killeen wanted me to say 'by far the best', but I didn't see the point of going the extra mile.

One of the Maysles noticed me arriving one morning on my bike and so to show that we were actually in Paris, they took endless traffic-stopping shots of me biking past the Café des Deux Magots, Notre Dame, the Eiffel Tower and so on. It was all tremendous fun and then I had to go to New

York to do the voice overs. The ads where shown all across the US to great acclaim and even in Mexico, where I was dubbed into deep Mexican as a contrast to my 'Oxford English' tones. I also was photographed for print ads and generally revelled in it all. When Bella and I got engaged, her cousins in California sent her a cutting from the San Francisco *Chronicle* featuring a photograph of Steve Spurrier, a young and very successful coach for college American Football teams, later to become one of the most famous football coaches in the country. Often, going through passport control in the US, the officers used to say I didn't look much like 'the real Steve Spurrier'.

The bosses at Kenyon & Eckard could not understand why I wasn't taking advantage of the hospitality offers. I did accept a car in from Kennedy airport, but generally stayed with David Fromkin on Beekman Place or in the Knickerbocker Club which took up a whole block on Fifth Avenue and had a 'swapping arrangement' with Boodle's. On one of my last visits, they brought this up and asked what they could do for me. I suggested that they fly me back on Concorde and the following day I was seated in 1A with a glass of Dom Perignon in my hand on the 1pm flight from Kennedy to Paris and arrived in time to meet Bella for dinner at Le Moulin that evening. As Mary Blume quoted me in her piece in the *Trib* 'The Rise and Fall and Rise of a Wine Guru' in October 2001, 'one doesn't think much about the bottom line when flying Concorde.'

As the decade drew to a close, things were still very good for the Spurrier family. Christian had just gone to his preparatory boarding school, Wellesley House on the Kent coast, and had enjoyed his first term. Kate was doing well in the French system, Bella was enjoying the ETC, Digby had gone to the kennels in the sky and I had all these wine-based businesses seemingly going well. It had been a quite amazing ten years since arriving in Paris in September 1970 and I had much to be proud of, but by the end of the next decade everything, absolutely everything, would have slipped through my fingers and I would be deeply in debt.

10. A New Decade

After the incredible decade of the 1970s, the 1980s opened quietly, but trouble was already brewing. The reason was simple: when we set up in Paris, I told Bella that we would stay about ten years and then move back to the UK as Christian and Kate would be at boarding school age by then. Our house near Chelsea's World's End had been sold to buy the flat in Paris, this then sold to invest in the expanding business, but I had no doubt that when it was time to return 'home', something would turn up. In fact, by 1977 this something was already there, as my father, quite aware that we would be returning for the children's further education and knowing we no longer had a London base, suggested that he finance a house for us. London prices were still quite reasonable and he was conscious that Nicky would get the whole caboodle in Derbyshire, so this offer seemed fair all round.

He set a reasonable price, but having sold my house in SW10 in what had become Chelsea, in 1974 prices had risen steeply so this was not on the cards. I had no intention of moving west to SW6, which was and still is Fulham, we didn't want to go 'north of the Park', so the choice looked like 'south of the River', which meant Battersea or Clapham. I began to look around in north Clapham and landed on a large classically Georgian house from 1800 that had been sloppily converted to rent out as a 'rooming house' and was being sold as such with vacant possession. The sister of a good friend and client in Paris had married an English architect who conveniently lived nearby, we had a quick survey done which showed, apart from a sagging back wall, that it was in good shape and could easily be converted back in a single residence. All this was explained to my father, who approved of the house and plans for it, if not its SW4 postcode, and the deal was signed. As Bella and I were non-residents tax purposes, we could not own property available for our use in the UK, so the property remained in his name.

It was situated in at the very quiet end of Rectory Grove, so named because it was opposite a fine church which was the venue for our daughter's christening. Although she was born in July 1973, my grandfather had died the following year and we didn't consider another christening in the family church, so this seemed both a good choice and a good omen. Once re-converted, the house was wonderful, with huge windows, many spacious rooms, a separate flat in the very light basement and even a cellar with stone-built bins that featured widely in *L'Académie du Vin*'s *Wine Cellar Book* one of the many books I wrote under *L'Académie*'s name in the early 1980s. When we eventually moved in as a family in autumn 1982, we could not have been happier, but our occupation any earlier was to be blocked, the cause for the storm clouds on the horizon at the start of the decade, with worse to come. Once finished by mid 1977 the house was of course empty and I had already moved some furniture and wines there from storage to have already suffered one break-in. I told the architect, Peter Cavanagh, who had become a good friend and was to be one of the partners with Bella in The English Trading Company, that we would have to find a tenant, but more of a 'house sitter'. He replied that one of his girl friends from the distant past had recently gone through a divorce and was looking for a place to live while she re-set her life. She was called Anne, we met on one of my quick visits and I asked her to telephone my father to tell him that she would be moving in to look after the house. This she did and was very correctly offered a temporary leasehold arrangement, since my father had also found her suitable after a brief conversation. All seemed set fair, but it was not to be. The Labour Government in power in the UK at that time had recently passed a law protecting tenants. The very presentable divorcée, now living in a five-bedroom Georgian house that had been converted at some expense and paying a peppercorn rent, acquired a boyfriend who happened to be a property lawyer and executing the terms of the lease so correctly offered by my father, they 'squatted' there, legally protected from whatever I tried to throw at them, for the next four years. It is safe to say that out of all those who caused me and my family substantial damage, both financial and otherwise, by abusing situations with which they had been entrusted for their own profit, this person takes the biscuit.

Back to the change of the decade and although Bella and I were as busy as could be in Paris, the children were fine and there were no money worries, the London situation began to have an effect. I was becoming more and more tense and although physically fit began having back problems and early in 1980 completely seized up, able to walk but not bend even an inch. Medical care was so good in Paris – the marvellously named Dr Gentil looked after the children and was a regular client at the Caves – that I was not hospitalized, but placed under the strongest medication, emerging a week later with a neck brace and a lengthy course of physiotherapy. As my friend Bob Baker said at the time 'you should listen to your body, it knows more about you than you do yourself.' I didn't and plunged back into my role as Steven Spurrier *Marchand de Vin* to compensate for the disruption of my plans for the next step of my life.

The summer before, thanks to David Fromkin, I had spent two weeks across France filming for what was planned to be another ground-breaking idea for *L'Académie* and the Steven Spurrier brand. This was to be recorded onto a 'video disc' the brainchild of William 'Bill' Connell, a good friend of his from Washington DC, who was convinced in those early days of 'video tapes' that the 12 inch disc would be far superior in terms of quality of image and sound, so that they, although in their infancy, would be the future. And what better idea to have on disc a complete tour of French vineyards with an acknowledged expert meeting the producers, the 'flip side' planned to be more of a structured tasting course, right up *L'Académie's* street. Setting off from Paris we started in Vouvray with Prince Poniatowski on his Clos Baudoin vineyard, moved to Bordeaux for a few days at Château Loudenne with Martin Bamford, taking in all the grand Médoc châteaux, then a long drive across the Massif Central to Ampuis to meet Marcel Guigal in his steep Côte-Rotie vineyards, up to Pierre Ferraud in the Beaujolais, to Jacques Seysses in Morey-St-Denis, to René Dauvissat in Chablis and finally to Bollinger in Champagne. Later that year I gave a private showing (from a tape, as the software for discs was on-going) to all the participants and many others on the second floor offices of *L'Académie*, which we had recently taken over. Here we could give classes for up to 40, as opposed to a maximum of 12 around the Napoleon III horseshoe bar, and most evening both rooms were filled. Wines from all the growers were served and the 60 minute movie very well received, so this seemed to be time well-spent.

The filming of the more educational part, planned for the following year, was delayed due to technical problems with the productions of the discs and this finally took place in Lavin's Restaurant in New York on W45th Street, where I was beginning to set up the NYC *Académie du Vin*. Being on my own, without the back-up of the other 'profs' in Paris, this was less good than I had hoped, but finally this didn't matter as video discs were beaten out of sight by video tapes and Bill Connell's brilliant idea and the fine work of his team never even went into production.

One of the bright spots in the otherwise forgettable 1980 was *L'Académie Internationale du Vin's* summer visit to Piedmont. Along with our annual meetings in Geneva the first week of December there was always a trip in May to a vineyard region hosted by one or more of the members. This time it was the turn of Barolo's geographer the great Renato Ratti and the recently elected Angelo Gaja. This was my first time in the region, apart from a brief stop with Bella years before, when I had sought out a bottle of Gattinara Spanna, once as well-known as Barolo and described by my father as 'the red infuriator', and I was overwhelmed. The Ratti winery in La Morra had a small museum, now moved to a bigger winery outside the town and much enlarged by Pietro Ratti in honour of his brilliant and charming father. Another recent member was John Salvi from Bordeaux, one of the 'three little pigs' alongside Martin Bamford and John Davies of Château Lascombes, all three MWs and gourmets/gourmands to their fingertips, sadly John being the only survivor today. After the Ratti visit individual plans had been made for dinner as we had had a communal lunch. John had chosen the best local restaurant famous for its angel hair pasta with white truffles from the winter season. There was a group of about eight of us, all reasonably young compared to what Bella referred to as 'the old farts' of which I am of course one by now. John insisted we have a drink on the terrace of La Morra's best restaurant at the top of the town with its superb views and thus slightly delayed we arrived to take up our reservations in this very simple trattoria, just a large room at the back of a food shop, to find a larger party of the older members already installed. John was horrified, turned to me and said 'For God's sake keep them talking, I'm going into the kitchen.' I chatted to the group, discussed the day, preventing them making any move to order a menu, and once I saw John emerging from the kitchen with his thumbs up, wished them all '*bon appetit*'. We got the angel's hair pasta and white truffles and they did not.

John Salvi's obsession with good wine and food knew no bounds. Once Bordeaux's Vinexpo got under way from 1979, Olivier and Anne Bernard began to give dinners for well over 100 guests, at Domaine de Chevalier under the title 'Tour de France'. Their friends from other regions were there, Pol Roger from Champagne, Trimbach from Alsace, Faiveley and Leflaive from Burgundy, Jolivet from the Loire, Chapoutier from the Rhône and many more including Bordelais from the Right Bank and the Médoc. After a lengthy *heure d'apéritif* on the lawns at the back of the château, with marvellous oysters from Archachon, foie gras from Les Landes and the best Bellota ham from Spain, there were a few short speeches and then a rush for a good table in the *chais* (above ground cellars) from which the barrels had been removed for the evening. I suggested that John go in during the speeches and get a table so that our group could all be together. The speeches over, I found him at the back of the room, chairs tilted to show occupation, just near the swinging doors from the main house, sitting at a table which in restaurant terms was known as 'Chicago' – the least desirable table. Asked why he had chosen such an unsociable spot, he replied 'my dear fellow, this is where all the wines come out from and we can get at the bottles before anyone else.' Perhaps his best ruse was at another AIV summer visit, this time to Jerez, where our hosts were the Domecq and the Gonzalez-Gordon families. Apart from the final evening at *El Palacio Domecq*, which ended with a show by their private troupe of flamenco dancers with some of less wise of us joining in, a high spot was lunch at a renown seafood restaurant midway between Jerez and Sanlucar. Except for a few stools at the bar, we had taken over the whole restaurant and the menu had everything one could imagine, or so I thought. Not too long after we had sat down in front of overflowing plates with *crevettes y langostinos*, a waiter came to tell me I was wanted on the telephone. Impossible, but he insisted and there was John at the bar with two bowls of the tiny very rare and very expensive elvers, turning to me with a smile and saying 'these were too good to miss, old boy.' Of course they went on the AIV bill.

My investments since the Paris Tasting had all made some sense, once one accepts the stupidity of expanding away from one's core base of action. Those in 1980 and 1981 did not. One of my regular suppliers told me of a shop that was coming on the market in the 16th arrondissement, due to the ill-health of the owners. This was *Caves Copernic,* in a not very busy street of the same name and there was simply no reason for me to buy it since residents from that rather snobbish residential part of Paris could order from the Caves and we could deliver, but it was a going concern, the price not excessive and I had extra staff to run it, so I went ahead. Compared to

L'Académie du Vin, 18 June 1981. Kneeling in front L-R: Michel Dovaz, Muriel de Potex. Standing L-R: Steven Spurrier, Jon Winroth, Isabelle Bachelard, Patricia Gallagher, Christopher Mitchell-Heggs, Madame Fougères, Mauricette, last figure unknown. Head behind Mauricette is Doreen Winroth.

the Cité Berryer, this was a dreary location and the shop struggled as well as being a time-waster. Consecutively Drew Harre and later, when I had re-juvenated it as a mini wine market, Charles Lea, tried their best, but finally it had to go.

While I could brush off *Caves Copernic* as an error of judgement, the next venture was a blend of folly and fantasy. *Le Chemin des Vignes,* the vast vaulted cellars burrowed into the hillside at Issy-les-Moulineaux which Lucien Legrand and I had opened together was going well, but much more for his needs than mine, except for storage as my stocks had far outgrown every space I could find in the Cité Berryer. Legrand's son Yves was in charge, having taken over from his younger brother who had moved with his wife to a small vineyard in Bordeaux's Côtes de Bourg. Yves had been on the shop floor at Renault and I could sense that he wasn't on the same wine wavelength as his father and while he was a good manager, as was to become evident in the future, I began to look around for other storage cellars that could be run as a wholesale warehouse. Curiosity took me to Bercy, behind the Gare de Lyon, which had replaced *Les Halles aux Vins* on the other side of the Seine in the 5th arrondissement. Here were above ground Victorian warehouses with wide cobbled streets and hundred-year-old plane trees offering an atmosphere of a bygone age. This should have been enough to warn me, but the romantic idea of re-creating a true wine centre here was too strong to resist. I took over the lease on a 40x20 metre warehouse and moved my entire stock from *Le Chemin des Vignes* into what became *Le Chai Steven Spurrier.* Gilbert Winfield, a new recruit to the Caves, was put in charge, the beaten earth floor cemented over to accommodate a fork lift truck and we opened for business in late 1980. The following summer, at the marvellous 10th Anniversary Party I gave in the Cité Berryer, there was a modest Press Release that recounted my endeavours past, present and future. At the end it said:

1981 – Our *Fête* and numerous projects

Bercy – To be closely involved in the renovation of Bercy in order to maintain business there, to make this *Le Centre Parisien du Vin*, with *fêtes*, visits, tastings and wholesale wine warehouses.

New York – to open an *Académie du Vin* in the centre of New York City.

Sadly, both of these were expensive mistakes, but my heart was certainly in the right place for Bercy and the local officials were encouraging until the Mayor of Paris decided to evict everyone in order to build modern blocks of flats. One other merchant - *Fantin Frères*, later nicknamed by us *Les Frères Fantômes*/The Ghost Brothers as their *chais* was always so quiet – and I held out longer than the others, but it was no good. Fortunately a solution for my delivery and storage of stocks of wine was at hand in the form of DIVO-France. This was the small *Défense et Illustration des Vins d'Origine* mail order company run by Bernard Bourquin, whose uncle Constant had created the original branch in Switzerland. Bernard was spending a lot of time in Canada involved in mining pursuits and had passed it over to me and I had passed it on to a French sommelier named Jean-Pierre Civilise, who was using it and his very good palate to supply restaurants in Paris. He was pretty much a one-man band, but had storage space and since I still had shares in the company, he took over that side of things, which was a good solution at the time.

Restaurant-wise, both Le Bistrot à Vin and Le Moulin du Villages were full. Steve Steede was in total charge of the former now buying the wines directly, with the Caves supplying the odd few more expensive bottles.

I kept control of the list at Le Moulin, despite Chuck's attempts to go direct, but in late 1979 I received a visit from the chef, who informed me that '*le patron*', ie Chuck, had his hand in the till and he did not wish to remain there in such circumstances. I said I would look into it, but before doing so called David Fromkin in New York to inform him. David said that Chuck would never do this to us and, not knowing how to confront him, I said that the chef was becoming unhappy and would not stay unless 'things were tightened up a little'. They weren't and the chef left, but was fortunately replaced by a young pastry chef from Maxim's named Nick Gill, who turned out to be a real star with a fresh, modern take. He, too, left in due course to run his own restaurant in London based around a menu of several small plates at once, pre-dating the trend for tapas and dim sum, but after a year or two moved north and vanished from the scene.

I can't remember what came next, but I was worried about Chuck – he had married his girl friend, they had a small child and their lifestyle far exceeded anything he could possibly have been earning. So I had the idea of asking Christian Vannequé from La Tour d'Argent, who had been a judge at the Paris Tasting and was a regular lecturer at *L'Académie du Vin* to join Le Moulin to up its game a bit and at the same time to keep an eye on Chuck. The game was certainly upped, smart shirts with Le Moulin logos were ordered from Cerrutti, just next door on the Rue Royale, the place became more fashionable and when Bella and I left in September

The 10th Anniversary Party: Anthony Palliser, Michael Goldman, Martin Bamford

1981 to go to open *L'Académie du Vin* in New York, I asked Isabelle Bachelard, then in charge of *L'Académie* as Patricia had got married in 1978 to her French boyfried Gérard Gastaud and had started a family, with her parents' background in the restaurant business, to make sure things were being run properly.

When we returned in summer 1982, Isabelle had indeed done a fine job managing the school and keeping a tighter rein on purchases than I had at the Caves (something I was immediately to reverse) but was worried about Le Moulin, which was slow in paying its suppliers, the Caves included. Since I knew it was almost always full, I asked what she thought the problem was, the reply being that she couldn't control what went on there and she thought that things certainly weren't quite right. While I had been too weak to confront Chuck directly, I had totally lost confidence in him and told David Fromkin who agreed that I should do what I thought best. As for Christian, I did confront him with Isabelle's opinion and he admitted that he had taken 'a little off the top as that was what everyone did in the restaurant business.' To my shocked question 'Where is your sense of honour?', he replied *'Je m'assieds dessus'* 'I'm sitting on it'. Very French. Back in London for the weekend – we had finally been able to move into the Rectory Grove house and Bella was looking forward to a less stressful time – I relayed this to her and received the ultimatum that I should have sacked Chuck ages ago and that if I didn't do it now, she wouldn't stick around for much longer.

The following week in Paris, I finally confronted Chuck, with Christian, and told them that I would have a professional accountant from the Restaurant Association go over the books of the two years in detail – Le Moulin's part time accountant was also in the game – and they would have to face the consequences. This didn't happen, for within a week they were all three gone, but not before Chuck had pocketed the takings on the last day and, having a key to the Caves in case the restaurant was short of anything, cleaned out my till as well. The hole in the final accounts was horrendous and the company technically faced with a *dépôt de bilan*, as neither the VAT people nor the rent had been paid for some time. My own accountant advised me to take this route, but I had the crazy idea that debts should be honoured and bought out David Fromkin at a low rate, and carried on with a new team who were honest but the early spark had gone and Le Moulin reverted back to its rather boring former self.

The frustration at not being able to move back to London was causing me a lot of problems, for, although I had never mapped it out exactly, I always had had a ten-year plan in my mind and it wasn't working out. Of course I was still very busy, very well known (perhaps too well-known and this, along with the frustration, was clouding my vision) but needed a change. *L'Académie du Vin* was doing very well, hardly making any money but then the Caves, despite good sales, low rent and a low wage bill never seemed to make a profit, and many people were telling me to open a branch in New York. Spending a few days in late May at a villa in Cap d'Ail that David Fromkin had rented, he told me that a friend of his was planning to spend up to a year in Paris and perhaps we could exchange apartments. The New York apartment was on Central Park West in the 90s, a really smart block of flats where I already knew one owner, James Chace, a political author, who was the editor of *Foreign Affairs*. Finally, it didn't happen for various reasons, but by this time I had mentally left Paris and was planning the next step and just by coincidence had been contacted by someone who was planning to open a wine school in what seemed to be a closed-down brothel on West 52nd Street and had been asked to join them in setting it up and running it. We did in fact move to New York in September and rented a fine triplex on the 9th floor of an early 1900 building on 28th and Broadway. Although down in the not very fashionable 'garment district' the block was noted for having installed the first ever elevator in the city, in which, sometime in the Roaring 20s, 'Diamond Jim' Brady had been gunned down.

Due to a 'prima donna' decision of unbelievable stupidity shortly after settling in, I decided not to accept the offer for gainful employment on 52nd Street, but to set up my own wine school in the basement of Lavin's Restaurant. This would end badly, but in the mean time I had the 10th Anniversary of *Les Caves de la Madeleine* to celebrate, which needed a good deal of planning. This was to take place on 18 June, and of course I had no idea that this was the famous date in 1940 when Général de Gaulle gave his rallying speech to France from London, until Jean-Claude Vrinat of Taillevent replied that he was happy to accept '*L'Appel du 18 juin*'. Long tables were arranged outside the Caves and *L'Académie* to show a range of 63 of my favourite wines and a few bottles of 1981 Gewurztraminer from Nobilo Vintners in New Zealand, sourced by Drew Harre whose elder brother worked there. Thanks to the Paris Tasting, California wines from the New World were slightly known in Paris, but their vintage was in the autumn. To show the Parisians a 1981 wine in June of that year was quite a coup. The bottles on tasting feature in Bella's photograph of me in front of the shop which features on the front cover of this book and the full list was printed under the remark that 'Steven Spurrier would like to thank his friends the vineyard owners who over many years have supplied him with friendly and intelligent wines, a few of which are listed below.' (Anthony Barton was quick to point out that his 1974 Léoville 'might have been light, but it wasn't white.') The *charcutier-traiteur* opposite, Albert Lucas, provided a splendid buffet, the weather was perfect and the evening totally memorable. The photograph taken at the close inside *L'Académie* shows members of the past and present team. June 1981 was certainly the peak of what was my life in the Cité Berryer and in the archives is a photograph of me talking to my concerned-looking bank manager from Barclays, to whom I was to give increasing concern as the decade wore on.

Bella, Kate and I moved flew to New York in September 1981. We had enrolled Kate, then eight years old, in the French Lycée on East 80th Street, to continue her French education. However, soon after arriving, helpful friends, when asked where Kate was going to school, suggested The Fleming School on East 60th, in their view the best (and certainly the most expensive) 'prep' school in the city. Knowing that Kate would be continuing her education at English boarding schools, it seemed, on this advice, a good idea to switch now and so the (free) French Lycée was cancelled and Kate enrolled into an establishment where she was obliged to de-learn French which was her first language and was basically taught nothing of value. The decision to turn down an excellent and tested, if strict, education in favour of an unknown one discombobulated Kate's future schooling, but it was only one of the many horrendous mistakes I was to make. The fact that the Fleming School was expensive didn't bother me, as I had recently sold Bayonne, partially finished thanks to my successful court case against Paul Calder, to a property developer from Cannes who, correctly sensing the damage that the recently elected President Mitterand would do to his business, had contacted me and made quite a good offer, so once again I had money in the bank. The nine months in New York were to run through all that.

While in Paris I had met a charming young Frenchman named Patrick Seré, who had worked for Joseph Drouhin in Beaune and, having married a New Yorker named Melissa, had moved there to be part of Drouhin's importers. Melissa was a founder member of The Society of Wine Educators and we met and got on well. An Italian importer had already introduced me to Richard Lavin, owner of the newly opened restaurant Lavin's, and we hit it off as well. Robert Finigan, divorced from Marimar Torres but now going out with Alexandra Lichine, Alexis's very attractive daughter who lived on New York's Upper East Side, was often in town and knew Patrick and Melissa and suggested that maybe I should 'do my own thing' with them at Lavin's (who had a large basement ready to conversion for an office and room for wine classes), rather than go in with people who weren't in the wine trade and would only need me for my name and ideas. I fell for this flattering scenario and with the funds from the sale of the Provence property behind me, did just that. The potential partners on 52nd Street – I have mentally blocked out so much of the New York experience I can't even remember their names – swiftly asked Alexis Lichine to be their 'name' (he would sell a lot of books) and after a week they had spent with me in Paris they had all *L'Académie du Vin's* ideas already. This was a decision of blinding stupidity in the face of reality and I was to repeat the pattern around the sale of my businesses in Paris, to even worse effect, seven years later.

There is not really much to say about our time in New York as it was a disaster from start to finish. Several of my clients from Paris were now living in New York and I gave a party for my 40th birthday in our stunning (and very expensive) apartment for quite a number of them and the New York wine crowd. In early June the following year we gave a much smaller 'goodbye' party, at which one of the couples who had come to the first and with whom we had been quite friendly in Paris said 'Leaving so soon, we've seen nothing of you.' This was true, for they, and others, had not been in touch. The hard-nosed way of life in the city caused me to write the following doggerel:

> The route to success in New York:
> To be Jewish by birth but eat pork.
> To jog in the morning, drink Sherry on ice,
> And quite without warning be frightfully nice
> To people you think are simply too awful,
> Who are kind, straightforward, well-meaning and lawful.

But the worst thing of all, which only by a miracle was not terminal, concerned Christian. We had spent Christmas in the UK and he had returned with us to New York for New Year and the rest of the holidays. His first visit to New York and he was, at almost eleven years old, very excited. He had had a cold when leaving and after a few days this got much worse and he was complaining of splitting headaches. We had a marvellous old doctor for Kate, very near to the Fleming School, an ancient lady from Eastern Europe, who took one look at him and dispatched him immediately in an ambulance to one of the city hospitals way up north past Columbia University. Apparently the pressure on the flight over had pushed all the mucus from his cold up behind his eyes and into his brain. One day later he would have risked severe brain damage, almost certainly to end fatally. The top specialists set to work and for a week he was on intensive care and remained in hospital for the next two months before he was well enough to be discharged and returned to school, having missed much of the Spring term. As if in sympathy for Christian, the day after he went into hospital Kate got scarlet fever.

While in New York, Bella took up camera work again with Margaret Hunnewell, one of David Fromkin's friends from a grand Boston family, who was making short films for advertising. There were some nice moments, especially a weekend spent with Bob Haas of Vineyard Brands and his wife Barbara at their place in Vermont in October at the peak of the famous Fall colours, Thanksgiving with Digby Bridges (whose very bushy eyebrows had given our Berger Briard his name) and his wife in Key West in Florida, then a short visit to California when we stayed at the newly opened Jordan Winery, where my friend Melvyn Master was in charge of the launch of their iconic Cabernet Sauvignon and one of the gold-plated bath taps came away in Bella's hand. Ed Moose came to lunch at Lavin's and brought with him Tom Wolfe, the author. Then there was a fancy dress party given by Michael Aaron of the Madison Avenue wine merchants Sherry Lehmann, the theme being 'famous couples'. Michael in a gorilla suit and his wife went as King Kong and Fay Wray and the tall and imposing Peter Morrell of Morrell Wines and Spirits and his equally tall and imposing wife went as Tsar Nicholas and Tsarina Alexandra of Russia. I hate dressing up and persuaded Bella to buy a long 1930s dress and a string of fake pearls, while I put on my cream-coloured double-breasted suit, tied a wide knot in my tie and slicked down my hair, to be recognised as Mrs Simpson and the Duke of Windsor.

The New York *Académie du Vin* closed its doors and by the end of June Bella and Kate had returned to London, for our squatter had vacated our house in Rectory Grove at the beginning of January. My last appearance on American soil that year was at a Society of Wine Educators Symposium on Rhode Island, where I was one of the lead speakers on 'How to be successful in Wine Education'. What a joke.

11. Between London and Paris

Finally, fourteen and a half years after we left England for a new life in France, we were back on home turf. The only concession my father's tenants had made in the years they were squatting was, from late 1979, to release the basement flat to our old friend David Langlands. David had a brilliant brain, he had gone on a scholarship to Winchester, passed the exams effortlessly to Trinity College, Cambridge which is where I met him on one of my visits. He became one of my, and my family's closest friends. In fact, between Nicky and us, we pretty well looked after him, for employment and David did not get on together. He passed the time following horse racing about which he knew everything, taking his Stafforshire Bull Terriers – first Fred, then Boswell and finally Montrose – for walks, and drinking. He could quote from memory whole passages from Shakespeare and the classic Scottish authors, was unfailingly charming, but 9pm was about his cut-off point. Anyway, David and Fred moved upstairs into the main part of the house, which was already semi-furnished from furniture in store from the sale of Fernshaw Road, so during the rest of the summer we moved in, my previous experience in the antiques business coming in handy to complete the rest of the house, and by September with Christian at Wellesley House and Kate at The Garden House, a day school off Sloane Square, I was ready for a new challenge.

Happily, this had already been proposed by my mentor Michael Broadbent in a letter he wrote to me on New Year's Day 1982, which I still have:

Dear Steven,
An idea:
I somehow heard that, despite your New York flirtation, the fading charms of Paris were turning your thoughts again to London.

It occurred to me last might that you might just be interested in setting up and running an Academy of Wine in conjunction with the Christie's Fine Arts Course which operates successfully from excellent premises tucked behind Christie's South Kensington in the Old Brompton Road.

For some years I have toyed with the idea of running high grade lectures on wine, but the pace I have set myself is finally coming home to roost and I now intend to reduce my commitments despite the endless temptations. Nevertheless, I am sure my original idea would work.

As The Wine & Spirit Education Trust* does such a comprehensive job I think that whatever *we* do should complement and extend those activities, but with far more emphasis on keen amateurs, company executives – moreover with some courses concentrated in time and of the highest level, to attract overseas students.

I would of course take part and, again for some time, have had the intention of mounting 'Michael Broadbent's Master Classes' (rather pompous, but meaningful and would sell in the right quarters).
Any interest?

Yours,
Michael

How could I not be interested? Of course I jumped at the chance and during my visits to London later that year met with Michael to discuss format and content and with Robert Cumming, director of the Fine Arts Course, to see how we could fit in. It was all so simple: the Arts Course terms were of 10 weeks, during which the premises were fully staffed, there were the occasional evening courses, but Tuesday evenings were always free. The Tour de France course at *L'Académie du Vin* was a six week course, so it was easy to cut this down to five and offer two courses a term, six a year, with the occasional extra evening for Master Classes. The five sessions were to cover Alsace and the Loire Valley, Bordeaux, Burgundy, the Rhône Valley and Provence, Champagne, Sweet and Fortified. The premises were superb, a large, well-lit room that could accommodate 45 students and 3 'student helpers', storage for wine and for the 400 INAO tasting glasses needed each session was more than adequate. On 5 October 1982 – my 41st birthday – Robert Cumming introduced the Christie's Wine Course, the first session to be taught by Michael Broadbent himself with me in attendance. Thirty years later on 25 September 2012, Christie's

(* The WSET was founded in 1969 to give education to the Wine & Spirits Trade. Michael was its first Honorary President elected for a 3 year term in 2005. I became the fifth Honorary President in 2017.)

Education having moved to new premises in Great Titchfield Street, W1, I introduced Michael to take the first session on the 30th Anniversary, over 150 courses and many Master Classes later, Michael then a still very sprightly 85 year old. At the end of that evening, Christie's Education presented each of us with a bunch of flowers.

Whereas in Paris we had a different session most evenings and the students would be taught by the same 'prof' throughout the course, I proposed that each session be taken by somebody different. The roll call of lecturers was impressive from start to finish. From the beginning we were able to take the pick of the Masters of Wine and throughout its history, the Christie's Wine Course was taught almost entirely by MWs, the exceptions being Hugh Johnson and Pamela Vandyke-Price, both prolific authors on wine, and myself. In the early days we had David Peppercorn and his wife Serena Sutcliffe, known as the 'Peppercliffs', who stayed with us until Serena was named Head of Sotheby's Wine Department and decided to launch her own course, which failed to make old bones, and the ebullient Christopher Tatham, main buyer for The Wine Society. Christopher was known as *Monsieur Tat tam* throughout the French vineyards and endeared himself to me by remarking, while wrapping up his positive description of Vincent Delaporte's excellent Sancerre, 'Gosh, I *do* love wine!' For many years we had Clive Coates, another prolific author who had overseen a vast programme of wine buying for British Rail when they decided to invest in wine and art for their pension funds, Remington Norman, author of definitive books on Burgundy and the Rhône Valley, whose private cellar was one of the greatest ever sold at Christie's in the late 1980s, and in more recent years Jasper Morris, Peter McCombie and Nancy Gilchrist, who took over the running of the course from me in 2013.

From the start, the Christie's Wine Course was a great success. The Fine Arts Course took a comfortable fee for rental of the room and staff costs, the lecturers were adequately paid and if they had books to sell had ready takers, the wine merchants realised that it was good to have well-off potential wine lovers actually pay to taste their wines, so offered us a low price and lots of helpful information and 'student helpers' were queuing up to set up the room, serve the wines and clear up afterwards. I was there every Tuesday evening to introduce the lecturer, taking one of the five evenings myself, and then left for Paris on BA's first flight the following morning, returning for the weekend. We were, like *L'Académie du Vin*, for many years the only non-trade course available and had good support from the London merchants, who often enrolled their own staff as our lecturers were so highly regarded. One time, Johnny Goedhuis of Goedhuis & Co. booked in his wife and a couple of her friends. They sat right at the back so could exchange whispered remarks about the wines. I was on the Burgundy session this time and, explaining the system in the Côte d'Or whereby the name of the village adds the name of its most famous wine to bolster its image, the village of Gevrey thus becoming Gevrey-Chambertin, by saying that 'if you were just called Smith and you married a Bingham, you would call yourself Smith-Bingham'. This produced hoots of laughter from the back row, as Mrs Goedhuis was a Smith-Bingham, something of which I was unaware.

Financially, the Fine Arts Course had never made a profit and the Wine Course put it into the black, splitting the surplus after all expenses with me at the end of every year. I have to confess that, when things went so badly wrong at the end of the decade, it was one of my few sources of income. But more to the point, it worked for all the right reasons and was something to be proud of. Time passed and Christie's Education as it had become to be known, published a little book on all its activities and I was asked to write something on the Wine Course. Here it is:

'The purpose of any course is to leave the participant with more knowledge than he or she had before. If this knowledge is enjoyably acquired and can be put to good use, so much the better and better still if there is a financial advantage somewhere as well. When I started *L'Académie du Vin* in 1973 it was as an offshoot to the wine shop I had in the middle of Paris. All we did at the beginning was to give initiation courses on just the basics of French wine, but as soon as my customers had grasped the basics, they wanted to know more about the regions, the grape varieties, vintages, how to store wine, when to drink it and what with. In short, a whole world had opened up for them, where the more they learnt in a relaxed ambience 'glass in hand', the more they enjoyed wine and the better value they got out of their purchases. The Christie's Wine Course is no different. The strengths lie, as in Paris, on top-class lecturers who love their subject and can put it across with verve and skill, good carefully chosen wines, a central location, a large airy tasting room and efficient management. Over the years the wines have evolved to take into account the progress in the

New World, although the base remains firmly European. The quality of the course is high, but we are always looking for ways to improve. The aim is simply to increase our students' enjoyment of wine, answer a few questions, pose a few more.'

Since we are in 1982, the Bordeaux vintage that launched the deserved (and predicted by Martin Bamford right from the first edition in 1978) success of Robert Parker and the Wine Advocate, I would like to address one broad accusation that he made against the majority of people writing about wine in the UK, a stance that he retained for many years, that 'the British Wine Press cannot be independent, since the majority of the writers are in the Trade'. Even in early days, this was true of Charles Walter Berry, Tommy Layton, André Simon, and Michael Broadbent. Later Hugh Johnson and Pamela Vandyke-Price stood almost alone as people who had never bought or sold a bottle of wine commercially, to be joined from the mid-1980s by Jancis Robinson. The simple reason why most of the words written on wine in the UK were by those in the Trade is that such people knew what they were writing about and remuneration from writing was not enough to live on. This is still very true today. Robert Parker (who I have known over the years and like and admire) and others might pride themselves on their lack of commercial attachments, but that alone does not produce independent wine writing.

Back in Paris, things were under control. Mark Williamson had left in 1980 to open Willi's, which he had planned to call 'McCready's' after a wine-loving ancestor, until I told him that this would mean nothing to the Parisians, that Colette's husband Monsieur Willy had lived just next door in the Palais Royale and he should capitalize on that and his own name. In thanks he offered me a half share in the new venture at a modest price and I replied that if I took this up he 'would never escape me' but agreed to supply him with wine on easy terms until he was properly up and running. This was one of my commercial mistakes but for the right reasons. In 1988 Mark had taken over the Moulin du Village and my Blue Fox Bar addition from 1983, for *le franc symbolique*, taking on the debts. These proved so huge that in 1997, when he had arranged to purchase a once fine but fading restaurant next door called *Le Galant Vert*, he bought it with the Moulin du Village company in which I still, for some reason, retained one share. Having finally become Mark's partner by default, I built up my share bit by bit and when funds were needed for my own Bride Valley Vineyards in

Dorset twenty years later, cashed in at a good profit. Mark Williamson is a brilliant all-rounder and Paris is lucky to have him.

Isabelle Bachelard was in charge of the day to day running of *L'Académie du Vin* and had overseen the shop while I was in New York with calm efficiency. Due to the contract with Christie's Wine Department and a small export business I had built up, I had hired a new girl in the office upstairs, but the shop was still staffed by the ever-cheerful Mauricette, a manager, at that time Gilbert Winfield, but from 1983 James Lawther. He was later to become a Master of Wine and move to Bordeaux, the best pair of hands I have ever had, and a delivery boy/van driver. Not over-staffed, one would have thought. After his election as a Left Wing President, François Mitterand began to nationalise the private sector of the financial industry so the bankers, many of them clients of the Caves, left for New York, Frankfurt or London. IBM moved its vast offices from the Rue Boissy d'Anglas to La Défense and while they might have frequented *Le Bistrot à Vin*, they found other places for their wine supplies. I didn't realise, as there seemed to be so much going on, that the peak in real terms of the Caves had passed and would not return. And when a little later I began to realise that the volumes were slipping a little, my reaction was to find another venture to invest in and distract me, showing to myself that the Parisian expansion of *Steven Spurrier, Marchand de Vin* was still going strong.

The Spurrier House of Cards was to collapse in 1988, which will be dealt with in the next chapter, but in the meantime I turned myself into a writer. This I owe thanks to Clare Howell, a perfect example of the English 'bluestocking' at its best: erudite, cultured, charming, lovely to look at and pass the time with. In 1981 she had taken a short course at *L'Académie du Vin*, seen the Caves at work and told me quite directly that what we were doing should be turned into a book. She was not a publisher, but a 'packager', someone who thinks of an idea for a book, finds someone to write it and then finds someone else to publish it. Her partner in the fledgling venture Quintet Publishing was Robert Adkinson and they were both wonderful to work alongside. Only when deadlines loomed did they show a certain strictness and I remember them insisting that, for the final version of *L'Académie du Vin*'s *Guide to French Wines*, which had been accepted by Mitchell Beazley, the UK's top publisher of wine books, they insisted that I spend the last ten days in their offices in Soho to be sure the manuscript would be finished in time. I agreed, so long as they would fund my lunch every day at L'Escargot, recently re-vamped by Nick Lander with Nick Smallwood front of house and Martin Lam, later of the wine trade's favourite restaurant Ransome's Dock, in the kitchen, and they agreed.

The first book, entitled *La Dégustation de L'Académie du Vin* and *Académie du Vin* Wine Course came out simultaneously in French and English in 1983. I was helped by Michael Dovaz, our head lecturer at *L'Académie du Vin* for some years, who covered vinification and many of the regional profiles, and his then partner Muriel de Potex, who wrote the Wine & Food chapters, but wrote the majority myself in six months from autumn 1982. Ian Jamieson MW contributed the profile on Germany, Fenella Pearson on Italy and my friend Geoffrey Roberts on California, Australia and New Zealand. This was the first 'How To' book since Michael Broadbent's *Wine Tasting* which had inspired my wine teaching career in the first place and Michael agreed to write the introduction. It had four sections:

— Foundation Course, covering the vine, vinification, vintages, ageing and storage.
— Intermediate Course, an overview of grape varieties and the wine producing regions of France, Europe and the rest of the world.
— Advanced course, covering twenty one different tastings of 12 wines of all styles and types, with detailed step by step tasting notes. At the end there were 24 photographs of the colour of wines, these being actual wines photographed over two days by Jean-Pierre Pavillard, Bella's tutor, the very first time such exact images with the name, region and vintage of each wine had ever appeared in book form.
— Special studies, covering wine and food, wine and health, fortified and distilled wines, tasting cards and tasting terms and vintages.

This book, of which I am immensely proud, had a huge success and was re-issued many times, translated into several languages including Japanese, sold over 150,000 copies and was the handbook for many future Masters of Wine and Master Sommeliers, including Gerard Bassett OBE, MS, MW.

The next book, the one I most enjoyed writing, was a 175 page handbook entitled *Les Vins Régionnaux de France/French Country Wines*, published in 1984. From my early days in Paris I had seen the sea of *vin ordinaire* slowly replaced by *vins de pays*, the very definition of a 'country wine', and for people wishing to upgrade a little, the *Vins Délimités de Qualité Supérieur*/VDQS onto the highest level of *Appellation d'Origine Controlée*/AOC. Defined as 'one that is drunk by locals and tourists in the place where it is made, which has certain defined regional characteristics and is not too sophisticated nor expensive. A country wine is not always cheap, but at a range of prices and income levels it should be considered someone's everyday wine. In this way, Saint-Emilion is a country wine but the Grand Cru Classé Saint-Emilions are not. Champagne is also drunk by the locals and tourists in massive quantities, but the image which the Champagne producers have given to their wine exclude it from this book. Also excluded are wines with no regional characteristics, branded wines made to match a taste and a price. Thus, Mouton-Cadet can be considered a country wine, since it is a Bordeaux, but Moreau Blanc cannot.'

Throughout the 1970s I had travelled to every wine region in France, sold many of them in the Caves and knew most of the rest by name. To get the facts right, I surrounded myself with all the reference books from *L'Académie du Vin's* extensive library, the descriptions of the wines themselves coming from acquired experience. But in the case of the dozens and dozens of *vins de pays*, the facts were there, but the palate wasn't, so, with all the background information on grape varieties, soil and climate, I simply made it up, with the satisfaction of seeing my opinions confirmed in subsequent publications. I dedicated the book 'In memory of Digby, a French Country Dog' and Hugh Johnson wrote the Foreword, quoting at the end that 'the scene Steven has mastered so thoroughly has not been a static one…over the last ten years the backwaters of French wine have been bootstrapping themselves into official and unofficial notice. Vastly improved technology has been stimulated by foreign competition to raise standards at a rate nobody believed possible. And who was it who orchestrated the foreign competition, bringing France's best names face to face with California's best wines? It was Steven Spurrier and I bet it has postponed his Légion d'Honneur by a good few years.'

The third book was *Les Vins Fins Français/French Fine Wines*, a companion volume to *French Country Wines*, with the dedication 'For Michael Broadbent and the late Martin Bamford, fine wine personified'. The Foreword was by Alexis Lichine, who kindly notes that 'Steven Spurrier has been able to communicate the qualities of the best-known, most venerable of French wines with an honest lack of pretension and, thankfully, he doesn't pull his punches.' In the Introduction I state that 'a fine wine may be described briefly as a wine of quality', but Hugh Johnson later offered a better definition that 'a fine wine is a wine worth talking about.' The aim of this book was to list the better French wines by appellation and by region (adding those in my view of potential quality) describing the tastes and characteristics of the wine and listing the finer producers. This book, like *French Country Wines*, could therefore be used both as a source of information and as a buyer's guide. I ended rather pompously by saying that 'There are three main excuses for not buying fine wines: lack of interest, lack of information and lack of money. I hope that this book may overcome the first two.' It also, thanks to Gregory Usher of La Varenne's Cookery School, had detailed pages on Regional Food and Wine, taking each of the eight major wine regions of France – Champagne, Alsace, Jura and Savoie, Burgundy, Loire Valley, Rhône Valley, Bordeaux and Provence and the Midi – listing a full menu from *apéritif* to *digestif*, with three choices for the starter, fish and meat courses with my choices of local wines and then 'other wines'. This was fun to do and looking at it now makes my mouth water.

These two handbooks were merged in 1985 to become *L'Académie du Vin's Guide to French Wines*, to be translated into French, Italian and the Nordic languages. In 1987 it was republished by Mitchell Beazley and I still refer to it often as a reference, for it was the first complete overview of the wines of France from top to bottom, side to side, written by someone who had lived there and had tasted, bought and sold most of them over fifteen years. While *L'Académie du Vin La Dégustation* was more pioneering, as indeed was *L'Académie*, this was a record of the past, present and hints to the future of what the French vineyards and *vignerons* were producing. The early editions of these two books were such a success that Clare Howell and Robert Adkinson persuaded me to write The Academy du Vin's *Wine Cellar Book*. I never thought much of this one, as it was 'put together and packaged' rather than written from the heart, but looking at it now I rather like it. Described as 'A practical guide to creating and maintaining your own cellar', it is full of sensible information with lots of illustrations and covered all aspects of 'cellarage' across the world. I did not, of course, write it all and the contributors included names well-known in the wine world like Burton Anderson on Italy, Anthony Dias Blue on America, Ian Jamieson on Germany, John Hawes on Spain, Pamela Vandyke-Price on the Southern Hemisphere, Georges Lepré of the Paris Ritz and Jean-Claude Vrinat of Taillevent on their own cellars, Nan Ashcroft on glassware, Conal Gregory on wine investment, Auberon Waugh on The Englishman's Drinking Cellar and my friend and lodger David Langlands on wine and food. What particularly amuses me now are the photographs on Types of Cellar, where The Apartment Cellar, The Kitchen Cellar, and The Family Cellar were all taken in my house in Clapham, moving wine racks around to look impressively like the real thing. Only the last showed photographs from the actual cellar in the basement with brick-built bins and I now look with envy at the bottles of Lafon, La Pousse d'Or and Rousseau, nine bottles of the iconic Sassicaia 1978 and several cases of Pomerol from that same vintage, all well-suited to the classic proportions and size of the house. I couldn't afford such wines today, but then I couldn't afford the house, either.

The final book from this burst of writing – five books in three years - was a joint effort with American Joseph Ward entitled *How to Buy Fine Wine*. Ward was at that time based in London and wrote about fine wines and wine investment for the Wall Street Journal. The Preface was, of course, by Michael Broadbent and here is his advice:

'Buying wine for laying down must not just be a one-off investment but a continuous process, so that a succession of mature wines is planned. And at any one time, one's cellar should contain newly purchased young wine, maturing wine and fully mature wine, some of which can be drunk at its peak of perfection, some sold at full maturity value for re-investment in the new young vintages. (On 2 May 2017 I and fifty-nine other guests attended Michael's 90th Birthday Dinner at Brooks's. The claret from his own cellar was Ch. Cos d'Estournel St Estèphe 2001 in magnums, quite superb, maturing rather than fully mature).

There are additional bonuses. Getting to know wine not only awakens the senses of sight, smell and taste, it quite literally opens doors. Keen wine buffs meet other enthusiasts and all are welcomed warmly by grower and merchant. Wine enthusiasts have a built-in passport not only to earthly delights, to beautiful vineyard areas, but to a variety of delightfully hospitable people.

This book will enable you to become a fine wine passport holder.'

I can't remember which parts we both wrote, but he must have written the introduction to Burgundy as he said 'Buying fine red Burgundy is like playing Dungeons and Dragons' and I had to ask him what this game was. Across the countries, it is not surprisingly that our recommended producers are still, one or two generations later, the same names today.

With Le Moulin in the Cité Berryer running reasonably well on the surface and since I was in London the first half of each week, I accepted an offer from Graham Chidgey of Layton's to oversee the Malmaison Wine Club. Graham had worked for Tommy Layton at his shop/cellar/tasting room right out of school and subsequently bought the business from him in the early 1970s. When we met on my return from New York he had long been installed in vast railway arches in Midland Road below St Pancras Station in north London. I had heard of the Layton's classical yet innovative wine selections based on quality and value for money and was impressed by Graham's creative approach to wine buying which I shared, allied to a hard-headed sense of business which I plainly lacked. He had recently absorbed the huge stocks built up by Clive Coates as a wine investment for the British Rail Pension Fund and had created the Malmaison Wine Club to offer these on a retail/mail order basis. I had only trained in the London Wine Trade during my time in the cellars at Christopher's and found it fascinating to be part of the real thing. James Radcliffe, one of my co-trainees, was Layton's top salesman and he and colleagues engineered a management buyout in 1990 when Graham and his artist wife Angela moved full time to Tuscany.

Many of the people passing through Layton's in the three years I was there are now top of their trees in the wine trade and I learnt a lot in what was very much a changing world. In his chapter (A Cautionary Tale) on me in his 1987 book *Anatomy of the Wine Trade*, Simon Loftus quotes me as saying:

'With wine consumption in England expanding at 10 per cent a year there are bound to be greater opportunities for anyone who's alert in the wine trade. We have to bank on the individual store, offering more than just wine – perhaps books, glasses and so on. You need to offer a range of services and give the customer the feeling that they are buying individually chosen products of impeccable quality. People are going to spend much longer buying wine, treating it as a leisure activity. When you think of the disposable income that is spent on handmade shirts, suits etc, wine seems one of the least expensive items which can enhance life in general. People will discriminate more. We are not selling to the first-time buyer, but to perhaps 5-10 per cent of the wine market because we are asking for much greater effort. If the wines we sell are the best and perceived as such, we will be okay.'

The independent wine sector is in fine health today in the UK and seems to go from strength to strength.

One of the last things Graham Chidgey did before leaving for Tuscany was to found The Bunch, a group of six independent wine merchants of which Simon Loftus's Adnams was a founder member. Current members are Adnams, Berry Brothers and Rudd, Corney & Barrow, Lea & Sandeman (Charles Lea and Patrick Sandeman both ex-Laytons), Tanners and Yapp Brothers. Graham also created the annual Bunch Prize for wine writing, which in my subsequent re-incarnation as a columnist for *Decanter* magazine, I shared with fellow writer Stephen Brook in 1996.

Back in Paris there was always something new to work on. The premises next door to Le Moulin contained a seedy-looking furrier under the sign *Le Renard Bleu*. No business seemed to take place there and we joked that it was a place for 'the white slave trade.' Finally it closed its doors late in 1982 and I thought I would liven up Le Moulin a little by taking it over and turning it into a wine bar, with simpler food, but the same wine list. It was separated from Le Moulin by a stair archway, but had a first floor that went above the arch, so could be joined up to the first floor of the restaurant, adding much needed larger WC facilities. Looking for a name, Mary Blume, whose interviews with people in or passing through Paris took up the back page of the *Trib* on Saturdays (I made it into her column a decade later) sensibly suggested The Blue Fox, the literal translation of its previous existence, and this it became. There were many cafés, expensive big ones and simpler small ones around the Place de la Madeleine, but we opened with a bang and were always popular, '*rendez-vous au Fox*'/'Let's meet in the Fox' being on the smart local's lips. At first it was run by Tim Johnston, up from managing a vineyard in Provence, but he left to join Mark Williamson at Willi's and then opened his own place, Juveniles, round the corner in the Rue de Richelieu, now in its 30th year. Then, the Bistrot à Vin having been sold, Steve Steede took over. At lunch our main clients were the pretty shop girls from Hermès and other *boutiques* on the Faubourg St Honoré, who loved the food but didn't order wine. My solu-

Post lunch at Le Moulin, summer 1987. Frank Prial and Steven Spurrier,
'what is the opposite of a summit conference?'

tion was to impose a glass of wine to match the *plat du jour* at a modest
extra price, which was well-accepted and sometimes a second glass was
ordered. *Le Fox* was fun, but it never made much of a dent into Le Moulin's
pile of debt.

L'Académie du Vin was in good health and despite the failure in New
York, we had associate schools both in Switzerland and Canada. The
Canada branch was in Montreal, where British lawyer Alan Mills and his
French Canadian wife Louise had converted the first floor of their house
in the old part of the city into a tasting room. They were good friends with
Michel Dovaz and his then partner Muriel de Potex who went to conduct
seminars from time to time. I made one visit in the summer of 1982 and
at least one a year thereafter. Young Bartholomew Broadbent moved to
Montreal in late 1982 to represent the Symington Family Ports and in 1983
attended many of Alan and Louise's tastings. He relocated to Toronto at
the end of that year and opened a branch of *L'Académie* the following year,
holding tastings of Lafite-Rothschild, d'Yquem and the first ever vertical (a tasting where several vintages of the same wine are judged against
each other) of Opus One outside the US, the last of which I co-hosted. In
1986 Bartholomew moved to San Francisco to set up his highly regarded
importing company Broadbent Selections. The Toronto branch was taken
over by Marc Nadeau and his younger brother John, who had created The
Wine Establishment, a combination of wine shop, book shop and school.
The most memorable tasting I co-hosted here was on 1982 Bordeaux First

Growths, the first event of a gastronomic weekend for Marc's 40th birthday in June 1997.

I don't recall any franchising arrangement with either Montreal or Toronto, but did become a partner in the Swiss venture that was based in Geneva. In 1981 I had received a visit from Ueli Prager, the founder and major shareholder of Mövenpick, a chain of fast-food restaurants which was becoming a big player in the wine world, especially in Bordeaux. Prager, a wonderfully intelligent and charming man about ten years my senior, had had the inspiration for Mövenpick while walking around the lake in his home town of Lausanne, where his parents had a well-known hotel. Seated on chairs or on the grass on the edge of the lake were the office girls on their lunch break, occasionally throwing a bit of bread into the water, which would be immediately swooped on by *movens* (sparrows), who took off with it in their beaks. He figured that if he opened a café where the girls could dash in, have a quick bite and dash back to the office, it would work. It did, with huge success, attracting every class of consumer such was the quality of the concept which evolved quickly from fast-food to casual and then to sophisticated dining, hence the wine and his interest in holding wine tastings which, if held at all in Geneva, were always behind closed doors.

In Paris, the courses at *L'Académie du Vin* were going well managed by Isabelle Bachelard, but it was Patricia Gallagher, working part-time due to her young family, who created the most extraordinary Tasting-Dinners that we held in December from 1981 to 1984 at Gaston Le Nôtre's splendid Michelin-starred restaurant Le Pré Catalan in the Bois de Boulogne. The inspiration was the idea of *Le Baptême du Millésime/*The Baptism of the Vintage, focussing on the wines from top Bordeaux châteaux one year after the vintage, the final blend being well and truly made, the wines to be bottled the following summer. For many years the Union des Grands Crus de Bordeaux (UGC) has held tasting around the world of the vintage once in bottle – the London tasting of the 2015s was on 17 October 2017 – but in the early 1980s they had not thought to take their show on the road. The dinner was preceded by a tasting of perhaps thirty wines, while at the dinner six or seven wines from much older vintages were served, always with the owners there to present them. These events were 'black tie', fittingly formal for the wines, food and august surroundings, the guest list growing to one hundred and twenty on twelve round tables, a château owner or member of *L'Académie du Vin* team heading each table. At these dinners we were joined by Philippe Cretenend, wine director at Mövenpick.

The menu for each dinner was a finely produced twelve page brochure with full descriptions of the young vintage at the tasting and of the older vintages at the dinner. I have the 1983 brochure in front of me, and for this dinner we welcomed the owners of Champagne Gosset, Châteaux Laville Haut-Brion, Haut-Bailly, Léoville-Barton, Gazin, Figeac, Léoville-Las Cases and d'Yquem, also Domaine de Boingnères from Armagnac. For our first dinner in 1981 to present the 1980 vintage, the rollcall was: Champagne Gosset, Domaine de Chevalier, Châteaux Ausone, La Mission Haut-Brion, Latour, Palmer, Rieussec and Vieux Château Certan. For the 1982 dinner, again with Champagne Gosset, the owners of Châteaux Cheval-Blanc, Cos d'Estournel, Ducru-Beaucaillou, Margaux, Pichon-Longueville Comtesse de Lalande and Suduiraut were present, also Caroline Voisin of Cognac Gourmel. These were very great evenings and of course I could not hold such events in London. However, we did do the Baptism of the Vintage at Christie's for the vintages 1981-84 and had planned to launch the very good 1985s, but a tenth anniversary re-match of the Paris Tasting in New York in summer 1986 saw the California wines do even better against the Bordeaux *Crus Classés*. The publicity that this attracted across the US annoyed the UGC so much that they refused to take part.

I was still travelling to California once a year and September 1983 was invited to be a judge at the Sonoma County Wine Fair, the first of dozens and dozens of 'official' judging positions over the years. Before it started I was invited once again to Jordan Winery, where Melvyn Master was in charge of the marketing and his wife Janie looking after the social side under the glamourous Sally Jordan. On the way I decided to call into Grgich Hills, the winery that Mike Grgich who had made the early vintages of Chateau Montelena, whose 1973 won the Paris Tasting had set up with Austin Hills. The moment I pushed open the large oak door to the barrel cellar, there was Mike, always with his blue beret, telling a group about this tasting and as he mentioned my name he saw me. Mike, one of the great heroes of California wine history, was so surprised to see me, he even took off his beret. Melvyn had told me that, Jordan being near to Healdsburg north of Sonoma, I should drive to the local bar and wait for him there. I found it easily at around the appointed time, pushed open the swinging doors to find myself in a saloon from the early 1950s Westerns, dark and smoky, full of tall, burly men in big boots and stetson hats. I was slim, trim and wearing a suit as usual. I moved to a corner of the bar near the doors and felt I had to order something manly, so went for a Jack Daniels on the rocks. This was served and two of these massive cowmen approached me, standing either side and uncomfortably close, to ask what 'a city fella was doing in their bar.' Without thinking, I replied that 'I've come here to get picked up.' This would have ended badly had not Melvyn and his friends, like the cavalry coming over the hill, burst through the doors.

My first trip out of Europe apart from North America was to Australia in May 1985. I flew to Melbourne where there was a very active wine scene headed up by James Halliday who was increasingly leaving the law profession to become the country's outstanding wine writer and founder of the great Coldstream Hills Winery in the Yarra Valley. I had gone out with the idea of opening a branch of *L'Académie du Vin*, but by the time I got there the two partners in the venture had fallen out, but I still co-hosted the tastings that had been planned and more importantly, along with James Halliday, spent time at Yalumba, owned by the Hill-Smith family. The senior of the two cousins, Robert, I had met before in Paris as he was very much into horses, and was a regular at *Le Prix de l'Arc de Triomphe* at the Longchamp racecourse on the edge of the Bois de Boulogne. This, the final flat race of the season, was held on the first Sunday in October and since my birthday was on the 5th, it was always an excuse to give a cocktail party for friends and visitors the evening before and to take a well-victualled picnic to set up on the grass on the 'common' side of the course, this race day being the equivalent of the Royal Cup at Ascot, but with tickets to access the paddock for a pre-race look at the runners. Robert introduced me to his younger cousin Michael, who the following year was to come to London for the final period of study to emerge as Australia's first Master of Wine, and whom I was to see much more of in the future. Most of the wines I tasted were good, but on the robust and rich side, for in the mid 1980s it was only forward looking merchants like Avery's of Bristol who were importing from specific growers. The Australian Wine Centre in Soho did not do much to show what was going on and nobody was prepared for Australia's bursting on the scene just a few years later and virtually taking it over by the end of the 1990s. The full week I spent there was barely a scratch on the surface.

During the summer I had been introduced to Terry Dunleavy, indefatigable supporter of the nascent New Zealand wine industry, who invited me out to be a judge on the New Zealand Wine Competition of which he was Chairman. Flying into Auckland via Los Angeles in late October (their Spring) was a long haul but worth it to be taken to the Brajkovich family's Kumeu River Estate outside the capital city and taste their Chardonnays which did, and still do, beat many a Premier Cru from Burgundy. We then drove down to the middle of the North Island to The Chateau, a vast pile of an hotel below an extinct volcano, where the tasting was to be held over three days. Apart from the Nobilo 1981 Gewürztraminer that I had presented at the Tenth Anniversary of *Les Caves de la Madeleine*, New Zealand wines were new to me and despite the first vineyards being planted by Scotsman James Busby in the mid 1830s, following his appointment in 1932 as the first British Resident of New Zealand, the industry had suffered very badly during the Depression. Te Mata, the North Island's most renowned vineyard of the Hawke's Bay region, was planted by the Chambers family in 1892, becoming the country's largest vineyard by 1909, collapsed into receivership in the 1930s, only to be revived by Michael Morris and John Buck in 1974. As usual, it was John Avery who was the first merchant to import New Zealand wines to the UK in the mid 1970s.

Terry Dunleavy had amassed a tasting panel of the country's top wine people, including Bob Campbell, who for a few years now has been the Regional Chair for New Zealand at the *Decanter* World Wine Awards. One of the most treasured wine books in my library is *The Wines and Vineyards of New Zealand* by Michael Cooper which the author presented to me as a memento for attending the competition and was signed by all my fellow judges. Its early modern history notes that in 1960 there were only 387 hectares planted but by 1983 this had expanded to nearly 6000 hectares. There is a full-page photograph of legendary wine writer André Simon looking unimpressed by a sample of dessert wine tasted during his tour in 1964, Simon noting later that 'most of the dessert wines lacked any trace of bouquet or breed.'

Things had certainly improved two decades later, for of the 662 wines judged, 31 were awarded Gold, 136 Silver and 231 Bronze Medals despite in a newspaper article I have just found in Michael Cooper's book headlining 'Tougher Judging for Wine Medals'. Apart from the Gault & Millau

Olympiades du Vin in 1979, this was the first 'team judging' I had attended, it was rigorously but relaxedly organised and I could not have learnt more nor had a better time. I had taken up jogging on our return to London, just a three mile run round Clapham Common, and was pretty fit, but needed to be to keep up with my fellow tasters who were keen on sport. The inspiring time at The Chateau produced the following limerick.

> 'After tasting for eight hours a day,
> The Kiwis relax in this way:
> A quick game of footer,
> Golf, tennis or snooker,
> But never a roll in the hay.'

About this time I acquired another wine shop/wine bar on Paris's Left Bank. This was called Le Petit Bacchus right at the start of the Rue du Cherche-Midi in the 6th arrondissement, a very smart residential neighbourhood with many attractive little clothes, shoes and perfume shops, but most importantly right opposite Poilâne, Paris's most talked-about bakery. The only inconvenience of the Rue de Cherche-Midi was that it was a one-way narrow street and if a car halted to collect a loaf of bread, it stopped the traffic. *Le Père Poilâne* as he was known, had created a country loaf known as *une miche/*a wheel of sourdough with a dusting of flour on top called *le pain Poilâne*, which even by then was famous enough to be a registered description in the French language. *Père Poilâne* was smart and he personally delivered his bread to Maxim's in the Rue Royale, making sure photographers were there to see him carrying in the loaves piled on top of each other and emerging with his working apron covered in flour. His younger son Lionel was even smarter and took this to an international level and I am very happy to have been responsible for his opening in Elizabeth Street in Belgravia in the early 2000s. Lionel was a good friend – Jon Winroth who had founded *L'Académie du Vin* with me back in 1983 lived just around the corner and had introduced us, though he stated a preference for the croissants and bread made by Max, the elder brother, who had a bakery in the 15th – and kept on saying that he must, he really must open in London. I heard of a premises coming up for sale and I told Lionel that it was perfect for him, as cars could double park on both sides of the street. After due diligence with the Grosvenor Estate, London's most wealthy landlords, permission was granted for the bread ovens to be built in the basement and I was there with for the official lighting of the fires, which have never gone out since. Very sadly Lionel and his wife died in a helicopter accident over the English Channel a year later, but his elder daughter Apollonia, with a degree from Harvard in her back pocket, took over and the *Poilâne* tradition continues to flourish. When I left Paris, Lionel presented me with a facsimile of the rectangular plaques with white lettering on a dark blue background with a green surround which is on every street or square in the city, stating Passage Steven Spurrier to remind me of the days when I occupied much of the sunny side of La Cité Berryer. I should have given him one with Place Poilâne, but perhaps there will soon be a real one in Paris in his memory.

Jean-Marie Picard was an amusing, artistic type who ran *Le Petit Bacchus* very much as a 'salon' and I used to go there often, slumming it a bit in the Quartier Latin, a contrast to the more serious 'Golden Triangle' where I worked, so named because that was where the money was. In 1983 he and I had founded *Le Guilde des Cavistes-Dégustateurs*/The Guild of Merchant/Tasters, which was based on an association of Britain's still family-run wine merchants known as The Merchant Vintners. About a dozen in all and elected only on universal acceptance, they grouped together for many purchases of wines, Champagne, Sherry, Port and Spirits. Because they were in different parts of the country, this gave them the advantage of bulk purchase while still being able to show an individual selection. Most of the Parisian *cavistes*, usually just with a single shop, joined up and the meetings were held at *L'Académie du Vin*, Jean-Marie being the first President. I suggested to Mark Williamson and Tim Johnston that they join, as they had a retail section called Grapes, but both refused, Mark saying that 'you'll never get that lot to agree on anything.' He was right, and although we did manage to choose a Muscadet and a couple of *petit château* Bordeaux, the collective buying idea failed, while the name remained as they felt it worth belonging to an organisation which had an impressive name but no purpose.

In 1985 Jean-Marie said he was off to open a hotel and restaurant near to Tricastin between the north and southern parts of the Rhône Valley and offered me his shop at a reasonable price based on its turnover and location and in September I moved my wines in – we had many suppliers in common – keeping the name, but adding 'Spurrier Rive Gauche.' I think this was a good investment and I would have got my money back had I not made a great error of judgement three years later. It was always pleasantly busy, particularly as I decided to employ only pretty girls to manage it, the best and prettiest being Kathy Noone, an Irish rose.

Always on the look-out for something new in the wine world, I had met and become friendly with the owner of a château in Bordeaux's Entre-deux-Mers region which had formerly been a property of the Toulouse-Lautrec family, who had invented a system called *Le Cruover*, which kept opened bottles under a system of inert argon gas in a glass-fronted cabinet and, via a method of suction, could deliver a glass that would still be as fresh after a week or so as when first opened. This system has been perfected under the name of Enoteca and no wine shop of wine bar can be without one, though the Coravin system, which is used on single bottles, is better for the private cellar. David Langlands was still our lodger in Rectory Grove, and, remembering that he had been employed as a restaurant assessor for some time by the great gastronomic editor Egon Ronay and knew well the London scene, suggested that if I were to import them, he could pre-sell them to restaurants thereby gaining some useful and not too taxing employment. A small demand soon got us into the Savoy, into David Levin's new bar Le Metro, next door to his Capitol Hotel near to Harrods, and a few other places, but in the end these were not followed up and I relinquished the importing contract.

But it was due to David that I began to write my first series of articles on wine. Simon Courtauld, an old friend of his from Cambridge, had recently been made editor of *The Field*. Courtauld surrounded himself with his Cambridge contempories, one for the Hunting column, one (John McEwan) for Art, David taking over the Restaurant column and suggesting me for Wine. I think the wine columns were bi-monthly, and from February 1985 to December 1987 my diary is full of '*Field* article' to remind me to come up with something, always a full page. They were mostly reporting on trips I had made, the people I had met, and wonderful tastings spread over a weekend – the greatest of which 'A Tasting of Legends in Alsace' hosted by the Hugel family who had been in Alsace's picture-postcard wine village Riquewihr since 1639. I was very happy to write these, but I have to admit that this did cause an increasing lack of attention to the core business of selling wine in the Cité Berryer and in the back of my 1985 diary, on the two Forward Planner pages, I have just come across several notes on financial planning, managing overdrafts and so on and underlined the words 'Essential no more cash goes out of Vins Fins' (my holding company.) This was a pious hope.

In summer 1986 I was asked by *Tatler* to write a piece on the London and Paris Wine Trades at Work. While this was rather 'tongue in cheek' it was absolutely true at that time: the former going more for sociability, the latter for the lunches served, the wines often taking a back place. A year later the editor of the *Tatler*, the charismatic, brilliant cartoonist, Mark Boxer, the Max Beerboom of his day, contacted me and invited me to lunch at Odins, the original restaurant of my friend Peter Langan. As a result I became the wine columnist for *Tatler*, which doubled up with my writing for *The Field*, but the audiences were quite different and never read both magazines. After several months this came to the attention of Simon Courtauld, but by early 1988 a new broom was sweeping through the corridors of his magazine and the Cambridge clique, myself included, lost their jobs.

It was also in summer 1986 that I found myself once again in California at the time of the Napa Valley Wine Auction with Michael Broadbent as the auctioneer, helped by Fritz Hatton. Michael said I should try and attend this prestigious and lavish affair and had left my name with the organisers, so I turned up and asked for an entrance ticket. They asked me my profession, necessary for the badge and I replied 'wine merchant', which would have passed muster had I been a merchant in the US, but not one from France. My second choice was 'wine writer' which went down well and I received a badge with Press on it and was told that members of the Press were offered a limousine and a driver, lunch at a winery, front seats at the auction and a drive home. My driver was a fine, robust gentleman and my lunch was at Phelps Winery. I had already met Joe Phelps, one of the pioneers from the early 1970s, who had just launched his Cabernet Sauvignon 'Insignia' which became an instant success. Arriving at the auction which was held under vast tents, I suggested to my driver that he come to collect me around 6pm. The auction was dramatic, very high prices were paid and it was a splendid experience. At the appointed time, there was my limousine and, about to get into it, I noticed Robert Mondavi and his wife Margrit waiting for a shuttle bus to take them to the parking lot. I of course gave them a lift and returned to base, reflecting on the advantages of being a member of the Press.

Actually, I already was in the UK, thanks to the doyenne of British wine writing Pamela Vandyke-Price, who had proposed me for membership to The Circle of Wine Writers, founded in 1962 by Cyril Ray. In time I was to serve two terms as Chairman and two as President (following on from Hugh Johnson) and to watch it grow from a bunch of cheerful 'scribblers' to an important organisation with members world-wide. Cyril Ray was a splendid character with a brilliant puckish sense of humour, described by Pamela in the obituary she wrote in *The Independent* after his death in 1971 'Cyril Ray was short in stature, but as a personality he was gargantuan.' He was also a committed 'Champagne Socialist' living in The Albany when in London and a large house in Brighton when not, an habitué of many of the best Clubs – he sometimes lunched as my guest at Boodle's – but his Left Wing views remained firmly embedded from his time at Manchester Grammar School. For many years he wrote a wine column for *Punch*, the now-defunct humorous magazine and authored many, many books on wine. The Circle of Wine Writers hosts the annual Cyril Ray Lunch in his memory. An extra attraction for me was his love of limericks, and he produced in 1979 'Lickerish Limericks' which was risqué and highly amusing. Around this time we were on a Press trip together to Moët et Chandon to pretend to be modern day Dom Pérignons, attempting to make a blend from the *vins clairs* of what was to become DP 1985. Jane MacQuitty, one of the three good looking young female wine writers (the others being Jancis Robinson and Alice King) who were known in the Circle as 'The Three Graces' but referred to by Pamela Vandyke-Price as 'The Three Disgraces' for the attention they distracted from the wines at tastings, and after a long lunch we boarded the private 'plane that Moët had put on for us and Cyril leaned towards me to ask who was going to take Jane out to dinner when we got back to London. I scribbled down the following:

> 'To answer your question, dear Ray,
> Jane's getting no takers today:
> Hugh's snoozy,
> I'm woozy
> And the last of our party is gay.'

Hugh was of course Hugh Johnson and the last of the party was Patrick Forbes, the wonderful chronicler of the history of Champagne.

Jane MacQuitty I had met soon after our return to London. She was to replace Pamela Vandyke-Price as wine correspondent for *The Times*, which deepened Pamela's disapproval of her. Jane was already pretty experienced and I still have an article she wrote in 1983 entitled 'Pick of a Birthday Bunch', which began 'Being thoroughly biased towards my profession I have always felt that every wine writer deserves to be born in a good, if not great year' and goes on to reminisce about some superb 1953 First Growths from her own birth year that she had tasted in Bordeaux. (I was born in 1941 and Bella in 1946, two simply terrible vintages, but for consumption purposes we have moved to 1945 and 1953). In her piece Jane also mentioned that she was born in October, as was I. This produced 'An Ode to an Overfortunate Libra', of which I can only remember a few stanzas:

> 'How wonderful to learn, Jane, O writer for *The Times*,
> (I wouldn't dare to speak, except to write in rhymes),
> That we two share a single month, the vintage one October,
> A month when every *vigneron* is almost always sober,
>
> But it isn't just your beauty, Jane, that brings me to my knees,
> It's your many, many years ahead with all those fifty-threes.'

In September 1986 I was in New York, having been persuaded to hold a re-run of the 1976 Paris Tasting with the same wines. This was organized by Dorothy Cann at the French Culinary Institute she ran in the city and the judges were Michael Aaron and Peter Morrell, New York's two top wine merchant, Bartholomew Broadbent, George Lepré (Paris Ritz) and writers Alexis Bespaloff, Barbara Ensrud, Robert Finigan, Frank Prial and myself to make up the same number of judges as in Paris. This time Clos du Val 1972 from Napa came top, and both Stag's Leap Wine Cellars and Ridge were in the top five, which completely routed the argument from the Bordelais that 'California wines showed well young and Bordeaux needed time to show better.' The UGC was crossing the US at that time, promoting the very good 1985 vintage and after this Pierre Tari as their President (and one of the original judges in 1976) accused me of single-handedly wrecking their campaign. I didn't repeat it in 1996.

In Paris *L'Académie du Vin* was asked by David Campbell who was international publishing director at Hachette, to oversee many of the tastings for the first edition of *Le Guide Hachette des Vins*, which is now in its

34th year and a bible for anyone buying French wine. This was flattering, but it amused me to dig out from my files a proposal that I had made a few years before to the editor of the *Hachette Guides Bleus* that they produce a wine guide. The format was much the same for it could hardly have been otherwise, but at that time there was no interest. David said he had never seen my quite lengthy proposal and I believed him, so it's nice that the idea saw the light of day to become a huge success.

At *L'Académie du Vin* we had one or two Japanese students, the Embassy being next door to the British Embassy nearby in the Faubourg St Honoré, and one of them, Mr Yasuhisa Hirose went on the open the very successful Enoteca wine shops in Tokyo. A visitor to the Caves was Mrs Fumiko Arisaka who founded *Vinothèque*, Japan's first specialised wine magazine, who said that she knew some people who would like me to host some tastings for them and maybe this could develop into a branch of *L'Académie*. So on 7 April I boarded an overnight flight to Tokyo for a week of total immersion in a culture of which I knew nothing and which I have appreciated ever since. My hosts owned a fine old building in the historic part of the city named The House of 99 and this was where the very up-market tastings were held, under the supervision of Mr Kimura, a youngish sommelier who is now one of the country's top Master Sommeliers. I was introduced to sake and taken to the best restaurants. At one the speciality was Kobe beef, from animals fed on the finest grass. A young translator was present at all times and I asked how much it cost as there were no prices on the menu. 'About a month's salary' was the reply.

Arrangements were made for a school to be opened and in September 2017 I co-hosted a reception for the 30th Anniversary which featured eight wines selected from my favourite producers at that time. The same wines, mostly from my Dorset cellar, at the re-launch of *L'Académie du Vin* in London that October and in Paris in November. The anniversary celebrated three decades of continuous wine education which had grown to four schools in Japan, two in Tokyo and one in Osaka and one in Nagoya.

Bella's father had died after a short battle with cancer in 1984 and the house and estate put on the market. About a year later Bella announced that if she were to look after a big house with a large garden, she would rather do it in the country. Neither of us wanted to go back 'up north', nor did we want to live in the crowded commuter counties in the south-east, so that meant the south-west and since we could not afford Gloucestershire or Wiltshire, this left Devon, Dorset or Somerset, Cornwall being just too far. Thanks to the Christie's Wine Course I saw Michael Broadbent's wife Daphne regularly, knew she was a great organiser, so put the problem to her. Her reply was very plain: I needed a base in London, so this should be Baron's Court, one Underground stop west of Earl's Court on the Piccadilly Line, so convenient for Heathrow Airport; Bella should call their friend Micky Caruth, who lived in south Dorset and might be selling. We duly contacted him, to be told that he wouldn't be leaving for another two years as a child was still in school, so we spent this time hunting around, but not settling on anything. Two years later, Caruth called and we went to visit. For me it was perfect, a classic early Victorian build with large downstairs rooms, six bedrooms, a proper cellar and a pleasant garden. For Bella it wasn't right as there was no land for the horses she planned to ride, but we were told that there was a farm on the edge of the village for sale and that could provide the land. This turned out to be a 200 acre sheep farm with steep slopes, all in one piece with marvellous views to the sea just four miles away. Negotiations for both were successful and on 6 July 1987 one large removal van set off from Rectory Grove to south Dorset and a smaller one to Queen's Club Gardens in Baron's Court. Daphne Broadbent had been spot on and the Spurrier luck, so helpful in the 1970s, had come up trumps again. It was, however, its last appearance for quite a few years. My expanded business in Paris were not doing very well and I could sense that a chapter in my life was coming to an end, but I had no idea then quite how bad that ending would turn out to be.

12. Au Revoir Paris

In Paris Jean-Pierre Civilise at DIVO-France said he had no room to handle my reserve stocks anymore and advised me to look for an alternative. This appeared in the form of Jean-Pierre Bloud, who had started up in Paris the year before I took over Madame Fougères's little shop, running a warehouse selling direct to the public. I had much admired this and our paths crossed from time to time on the Paris scene and occasionally in the Beaujolais, where his mother owned Le Château du Moulin-à-Vent, a fine estate in the most prestigious of the Beaujolais Crus. That summer he had called me and we met for lunch and he said he was retiring from direct selling. By that time he was working out of a converted apple storage warehouse in Feucherolles, one of the smart leafy suburbs west of Paris, and had heard I was looking for space and offered to sell me the business. The price was not excessive and there was capital over from the sale of Rectory Grove and the purchase of Queen's Club Gardens; so we did the deal and I moved my stocks over before Paris went quiet in August, and moved the reliable Steve Steede over from Le Moulin to run it. When I told the person who had recommended me the Caves Copernic as a good purchase that I had bought Bloud's business she exclaimed '*Mon Dieu, ce panier de crabs*'/'My God, that can of worms.' Apparently he had been hawking it around for some time with no takers. Once installed we realised that Monsieur Bloud had retained his business telephone line and so was plainly carrying on some sort of commerce, but the warehouse was just what I thought we needed and, under Steve Steede's direction 'Spurrier Distribution' as it was called would have proved to be so, had I not made a catastrophic error of judgement two years later.

I had never proposed Bordeaux 'futures' (known as *en primeur*, buying the wine twelve months before bottling) at the Caves and while not being as critical towards the 1982s as Robert Finigan, neither did I see their fantastic future so clearly as did Robert Parker. The 1983s were also good, especially in Margaux, the 1984s were dull and hard, but the 1985s were very good, volumes were high and prices were reasonable. By this time I had understood the *en primeur* system which was quite simply an invitation to the buyer to 'get in early at a good price and if you sell later, make a profit on the way out.' We were very successful with the 1985s, from little-known but very attractive Médocs, Graves and St Emilions, right up to the *Crus Classés*, and by mid-summer 1987 these were all in bottled and needed to be stored in customers' reserves. I had also tasted a wide range of 1986s at Vinexpo in June 1987 – there wasn't such a rush for prices to come out in those days compared to right after the early April *en primeur* tastings today – and had already sold on quite a few of these. Although the volumes of everyday wines were substantially lower than in the 1970s, both Burgundy and even the Rhône wines had to be purchased on release from the estates, so storage was necessary.

On the negative side, Christie's seemed to have run out of grand cellars with wines to be picked up and sold in London, except in and around Bordeaux, so had appointed an agent there and cancelled my contract. This had been a fascinating association and very profitable, for I or my staff could charge a 'per diem' for the work and my office shared in the commission. Apart from superb restaurant cellars from Darroze, Le Coq Hardi and both Pruniers in Paris, the range of cellars was very wide, from converted garages in the suburbs to grand *Hôtels Particuliers* in the centre of Paris where white-gloved butlers would hover, pretending to assist. At one of these, consisting mainly of forgotten bottles from the late 18th and early 19th century, there were a few ancient examples of liqueurs and spirits from which I was asked to take my pick. I chose a bottle of Pernod, which looked exactly the same as the one in Edouard Manet's painting of The Bar at Les Folies Bergère (1882) now in London's Courtauld Institute. In those days Pernod and the other classic brands of *Absinthe,* were made from a series of spices including wormwood, which did untold damage if consumed in any quantity and which were subsequently banned by the health authorities. I was keen to see what the real thing was like and opened it one evening in my Paris flat, pouring it over a lump of sugar on an 'absinthe spoon' from a set a friend had given me, as was the custom at the time and adding water. After a few slow sips, for it was very strong, my head began to spin and the rest of the glass and bottle went down the sink. For a long time on the back wall of *L'Académie du Vin* there was a large framed *fin de siècle* poster (which now hangs in our Dorset kitchen) of a pretty scantily-dressed girl holding glass of a popular tonic wine with the caption 'Vin Mariani, Popular French Tonic Wine, Fortifies and refreshes body and brain, Restores health and vitality', justified no doubt by the presence of cocaine in the blend.

Along with losing the Christie's contract which entailed a good deal of paper work, I had, since the mid 1970s, built up quite a large business sending my mostly American clients back with several cases of wine when returning to the States. The rules from the US side were quite lax, allowing people to move back with a quantity of wine that 'they might have acquired during their time in Paris'. This was often up to twenty cases and was packed up with their household goods and they could even reclaim the TVA/VAT as the wines were not being consumed in France. One client made up a serious collection, but had no cellar in his New York apartment building, so stored the wines in huge closets in his bedroom keeping them at a constant low temperature. His wife later left him and moved to Florida. By the mid-1980s, as the majority of American companies remaining in Paris had moved to La Défense, this business fell off dramatically and I was obliged to let go the very efficient American lady, married to a Parisian, who had run this side of the office. French employees were very well protected in those days, and still are, the employer paying 60% on top of their salaries to the State to pay for all their free health care, insurance and so on, taking an obligatory one month's holiday, often demanding *le treizième mois*/the thirteenth month. With all the religious and national holidays which of course they took, staff were paid fourteen months for working ten. Nice as she was, this lady stood on her (French) rights and took me to the *Prud'homme*, a small court of justice always on the side of the workers, proclaiming 'unfair dismissal' and was awarded another six months' salary. Unsurprisingly, once back in London, I was determined never to have employees and in my life in wine have kept to that.

Attendances were also declining at *L'Académie du Vin*. Patricia Gallagher had proposed an ambitious expansion programme, but the timing wasn't right and she left to create a wine programme for *Le Cordon Bleu*. Aware that many of our usual non-French clients were now working at La Défense and living on the outskirts of Paris or in the smart suburbs, Steve Steede oversaw the creation of a fine tasting room in Feucherolles from Jean-Pierre Bloud's offices at what was now Spurrier Distribution, and we were successful in holding wine courses there. One of the attendees, hearing that I had been a founder of *Le Bistrot à Vin*, told me he lunched there every day and suggested quite correctly that I must be 'sick as a parrot' for not having kept up my interest. The businesses in the Cité Berryer were not in good shape and were more and more reliant on overdrafts at the bank, guaranteed from my bank in London which held my flat as security. In the early 1970s I had been buying so much wine that for a few years I never paid any TVA/VAT. Now, I was selling stock and getting a bill for TVA every quarter which sometimes I couldn't pay, so incurring a fine of 10% with bank interest on top. I was even occasionally behind in the rent. On top of all this, since I was only in Paris two, at the most three days a week, I had ceased to claim even a modest salary. Following a quite good 1987 Christmas period, but nothing like the old days, I decided I had to sell up.

None of this stopped me travelling when I had a chance. September 1987 found me in the Douro for the vintage, staying at Taylor-Fladgate's Quinta do Vargellas where I had spent an instructive week in rather rustic comfort twenty-two years before. Alastair Robertson, Dick and Beryl Yeatman's nephew, was now heading the company and with his wife Gillyanne were wonderful hosts. Gillyanne had poured her skills as a decorator into the house and one of their daughters, Natasha, was working on her first steps to become head winemaker for the family brand. One morning, after a particularly long night ending up with many glasses of Old Partners Wine (OPW) the aged Tawny that was reserved for private consumption, I appeared at breakfast to find the plates and cups of the assembled guests untouched and a questioning, amused look on my hosts' faces. Apparently my last words before going to bed were that 'I'll swim the Douro before breakfast' and they were waiting for this to happen. The Douro river, once a rushing torrent at times, had been dammed a little further downstream to ease navigation and produce electricity, so the stretch in front of Vargellas was relatively calm. I liked swimming in a recreational manner and said that if they thought I was going to swim to the opposite bank and back, they wouldn't be breakfasting until lunch, so Natasha offered to get the boat out and once I had reached the other side, where the vineyard was owned by their rivals Cockburn whose 1908 was responsible for my being in the Douro in the first place, she would take me back. I complied and of course everyone was well into their breakfast when I returned.

In February 1988 I was in Montreal to host some tastings at Alan and

Louise Mills's *Académie du Vin* but also to take part as a taster for the selections of the Societé d'Alcools de Quebec (SAQ), Canada's largest wine and spirits distributer on a monopolistic basis. Wine distribution in Canada at that time was totally controlled by the State Monopolies, the Liqour Control Board of Ontario (LCBO) being second only to the SAQ. They collected a good deal of money in taxes, but also did a very good job in selection, promotion and distribution and were and still are highly regarded by both by their suppliers and their customers. There are similar monopolies in the Nordic countries of Denmark, Finland and Sweden, who of course benefit from the taxes going into their pockets rather than into those of retailers, but whose origin was more to control the supply of alcoholic beverages to a population notoriously keen on its consumption. When I visited the Systembolaget in Sweden in the early 2000s, they were congratulating themselves on how well they had succeeded in reducing deaths per head of population from cirrhosis of the liver, noting that out of 30 countries, the 29th was Sweden. I pointed out that the 30th was Ireland, which had no monopoly but enjoyed a tradition of social drinking.

From Montreal I went to Toronto as a guest of Clayton Ruby, a civil rights lawyer and great wine collector, who bought wines from Lafon, Leflaive, Guigal and Chave from the Caves as they were not available through the LCBO. He had asked me to speak at a couple of wine dinners, a role quite new to me then, but which I was to play more and more in the next decades. It is interesting that collectors, who have wines in their cellars out of the price range of most people in the wine trade, which they know everything about, generally like to have someone independent to talk about them. Such dinners have provided me with many of the best wines imaginable.

In March I went for a quick visit to Tokyo, where *L'Académie* was spreading its wings, and was introduced to Mr Tskamako, a very elegant gentleman, Chairman of Lumière SA one of the major importers of wines into Japan, who wanted to translate the *Académie du Vin* Wine Course into Japanese. It having been the first real 'How To' book in French, English and other European languages, to think of it in Japanese was a great honour.

My father died on 1 April 1988, Easter Friday. After his own father's death in the mid-1970s, he and my mother had moved into the family house, refreshing the rooms a little and adding more comfort. At this time, farming was already into a long decline and whatever decisions my father made towards efficiency was met with 'Captain Jack wouldn't have done this.' On top of this, he had to run the family investments, the Marston-on-Dove Estates company having paid for Nicky's and my education and providing us a small but regular income from rents and other things. This double pressure, not helped by his occasional heavy drinking, began to be too much for him and he had voluntarily checked himself into St Andrew's Hospital in Northampton, a wing of which housed patients suffering from depression or other mental problems. Some years earlier my parents had bought a charming house in a little village called Wick St Lawrence near Weston-super-Mare south of Bristol in the West Country, with its long beaches on which they liked to walk their Boston Terriers. Getting away from Derbyshire was important for them both and finally Nicky had agreed to move into the Marston house, contracting out the farming and taking over the investment company. During his many months in St Andrew's I visited my father regularly, we became close, and I realised that the one thing he should never have done is to have given up the intellectual world of his pre-war London life as a publisher and to work as Transport Director in a sand and gravel company for his over-bearing and non-understanding father. He envied the freedom I had enjoyed, while admiring what I had accomplished. I told him that things were going badly and I was looking for a way out and he was most sympathetic.

That Easter we were all expected for Sunday lunch, Christian was just seventeen and Kate was almost fifteen. My father had checked himself out of St Andrews and was to arrive at Wick on the Friday. When I arrived in Dorset from Paris that evening Bella told me he had called but not to bother to call back as he would be seeing us on the Sunday. I did and he asked how things were going and I had had some positive interest from the Savour Club owned by Edmond de Rothschild, and told him so. He was happy with this and said that I shouldn't expect too much of him as he had lost a few teeth since my last visit (my vanity is a direct inheritance) adding that he was so glad to be back home. The following morning my mother called with the news that she had heard a noise during the night and had gone into his room to find him on the floor, dead from a heart attack. I was so happy to have talked to him and know he had a peaceful last evening and perhaps it was just as well, in case he had become an invalid in his declining years. My mother was a strong woman, but it was a great blow to her and she always insisted that our letters should be addressed not to Pamela Spurrier but to Mrs John Spurrier as before. On one of my visits to him at St Andrews, my father had written down a quotation for me, which read 'When they are young children love their parents; as they get older they begin to judge them, seldom, if ever, do they forgive them.' If he felt some kind of guilt, he should not have, for he and my mother were wrapped up in each other and I had left home mentally and physically after Rugby to grow up in London. What I remember is his social ease, looks and charm: nothing to judge, still less to forgive.

We still went to lunch on Easter Sunday and the funeral was at Marston two weeks later, where there were more Spurriers than I had ever been aware of, my father joining many generations of them in the cemetery of the St Mary's Church where he had been the Church Warden in an unbroken line of our family since 1628. Nicky will be the last, as the house and estates will be sold, neither of his children wishing to live in Derbyshire. They had the choice my father never enjoyed.

Back in Paris, the contacts with the Savour Club came to nothing, as they were interested in *L'Académie du Vin* and not the two shops. Of course I should have pursued this, but I didn't, as Drew Harre, who had run the Caves at the turn of the decade, put me in touch with a director of La Banque de Suez, who were looking to diversify. Bardawill's concept was *'Le luxe en tranches'* or 'sliced luxury', whereby you could have *pâté de foie gras* with a glass of simple Bordeaux, or a *terrine de campagne* with a glass of Château Lafite and so on throughout the menu and wine list. It was a great concept and soon there was a L'Ecluse in every smart *quartier*, Bardawill eventually selling out to Castel, France's biggest wine producer. I was too small for the bankers, but Bardawill put me in touch with a certain Philippe McGarry – French despite the name – who had been director of sales at Nicolas, was now managing the *foie gras* and another product brand *La Comtesse du Barry* and was interested in what might be done with the Spurrier brand.

McGarry was in his early 40s, tall, good-looking to a degree and quite, quite brilliant. The father of Valérie Gans, his beautiful and intelligent girl friend had been big in the beer business and now owned two châteaux in St Emilion – Cadet-Bon and Curé Bon, both on the plateau near all the Premier Grands Cru Classés, both being absorbed later by their grander neighbours at a satisfactory profit. Valérie Gans was to be given this project to manage. Gerard Jongis, the accountant I had inherited from Madame Fougères, who had never really commented on the fact that my businesses had been losing money for the past decade, met with him and was hugely impressed. Behind his charm, McGarry was tough and was known as having *les dents longues*/sharp teeth, who had never lost a business negotiation, so Drew introduced a lawyer to represent me. Coincidentally this very bright lady had come up against McGarry twice and her clients had lost both times, so she was determined to get me a good deal. I just wanted out and should have made this plain. Discussions began on open terms, McGarry meeting and liking Steve Steede and the Spurrier Distribution concept, Valérie Gans meeting Isabelle Bachelard and appreciating what might be done to broaden the appeal of *L'Académie du Vin*. I had already agreed to sell Le Moulin to Mark Williamson for its debts for *le franc symbolique* and despite the heavy financial loss was glad to see the back of it. McGarry's offer was basically that I should retain 25% of the company, he would take over the rest and 75% of the debts and I would receive a good salary for the two or three days a week that I could commit to Paris. His aim was that the Spurrier brand would become *La FNAC du Vin*, FNAC being the benchmark place to buy any and every piece of sound equipment, TV and so on, with stores in all the major French cities. What could be better?

On this basis, discussions continued during May, the deadline being set for the end of the month. My lawyer was pushing hard for to improve the deal, while I had the impression that McGarry was not fully-funded for the project, although he had advanced 100,000 FF to cover some of the Caves pressing debts. The last weekend in May was one of *L'Académie Internationale du Vin's* Summer Symposiums, this time based in Chinon in the Loire Valley's Touraine region. I had a meeting with Valérie Gans at midday on Thursday 26th and felt that a slight effort was needed on my part to ease the deal. That evening I called her in St Emilion to offer to keep my bank guarantees in place for a few months and she said that she would pass this onto Philippe and I was to call him Friday evening around 8pm. The following morning I set off to Chinon, picking up my old friend and fellow member of the AIV Christian Imbert, who after a busy life in Chad 'trading in everything except people', had created the splendid Domaine de Torraccia estate near Porto Vecchio in Corsica. The first day's meetings of the AIV went off well, with a tasting of Chinon at

Couly-Dutheil going back to 1964. I then called McGarry, but no answer. The next day, Saturday, Spurrier Distribution was holding an 'open day' of tastings with discounted prices to bring in clients and I left early to be there, getting back exhausted to Chinon for the dinner that evening. I called McGarry again and still no answer. Sunday morning wrapped up the AIV conference and after lunch I drove back to Paris, this time with Robert Dillon-Corneck. I poured out my problems to him to receive the advice that if the deadline passed, I should cancel the deal. I put this to my lawyer, who agreed, thus getting her revenge on McGarry, so, having heard nothing from either Philippe McGarry or Valérie Gans, I wrote a registered letter calling it all off.

This was a great mistake, but I was in a state of extreme stress and what I did not know was that McGarry had been talking to Steve Steede to plan the takeover, as he had realised that while my name and palate would be what he was buying, Steve would actually run the nuts and bolts of it all. Steve didn't tell me this, although I had been at Spurrier Distribution the Saturday before, but I didn't think to tell him that I was cancelling the deal, thus leaving my trusted lieutenant with a *fait accompli*. McGarry immediately, and quite correctly, removed 100,000 FF of my best stock from Spurrier Distribution and that was that. In hindsight, this deal would have to a great extent valorised my work of over two decades in Paris while providing financial security and hope for the future. Perhaps I should not have listened to Dillon-Corneck's advice, which appealed to my 'prima donna' side, as did Robert Finigan's advice not to take up the offered partnership in New York, but I know that at this time I was pretty much burnt out and had to a large extent lost confidence in what McGarry saw as the Spurrier brand as a benchmark across France.

From that moment it was a rush for the lifeboats. I recall an exchange in the marvellous movie *The Sun Also Rises*, based on Ernest Hemingway's 'paean to the Lost Generation in the wake of the First World War' filmed largely in Pamplona with the running of the bulls. Errol Flynn plays the carefree Scottish playboy Mike Campbell, the former fiancé of Lady Brett Ashley, the beautiful aristocrat played by Ava Gardner. Ashley has a coterie of admirers around her including war hero Jake Barnes (Tyrone Power) and would-be writer Robert Cohn (Mel Ferrer). Around the bar, Errol Flynn's character announces that he has recently been declared bankrupt, to receive the question 'how did that happen?' and replies 'slowly, then quickly.' I made approaches to Jean-Michel Cazes of Château Lynch-Bages, whose *La Compagnie Médocaine* had expressed interest in the Paris market, but their brief researches told them my businesses were too far gone. Then I contacted Corinne Richard, who had taken courses at *L'Académie du Vin* and was second only to her father in *Les Cafés Richard*, a company that owned, or supplied most of the cafés in Paris and had substantial vineyards in Beaujolais. I thought a couple of retail shops and a well-known wine school would add an interesting element to their portfolio, but this, too, came to nothing. By this time it was late June and before descending to Bordeaux for the *Fête de la Fleur*, the black tie celebration dinner for the flowering of the vines which was held that year at Château Coufran for a few hundred. Ewan Fergusson then British Ambassador in Paris and Michael Broadbent were guests of honour, and the hard-sought invitations welcomed well over a thousand. I had met with the owner of two shops in Paris called Le Repaire de Bacchus. These presented a new look: smarter than those of Nicolas, less pompous than Fauchon and Hédiard, my neighbours in the Place de la Madeleine, marketing-driven, reaching out to customers rather than waiting for them to push open the door. We got on fine and he showed great interest in a merger but had no money to invest, but we continued to talk. Corinne Richard got back to me to say that her father was interested in *L'Académie du Vin*, and once again I was stupid enough not to hive this off. I even received an offer for Le Petit Bacchus which would have seen my investment back, but stubbornly stuck to the idea of the Spurrier Brands being kept together. I should have learnt from George Bardawill's *le luxe en tranches* and let them go one by one.

Plainly a decision had to be made before France shut down for August, and the Repaire de Bacchus owners, having estimated my debts at around 3 million FF (which excluded debts to suppliers, but included my high overdraft then running at an impossible 17%) offered to take the whole lot off my hands for the usual *franc symbolique* for each of the three companies, take two years to absorb it all, and pay me 4 million FF from mid-1990. They also said that their fledgling company could not take on the fiscal debts, which they would renegotiate but would have to remain in my name. My accountant Mr Jongis, having seen the McGarry deal disappear, thought this was a bit stiff, but I accepted it. After spending the first week of August assuring the change of ownership, I took the family for a much-needed holiday on Lambay Island, in the Irish Sea a very few miles from Dublin, where Bella's mother lived during her first marriage to Lord Revelstoke.

Returning to Paris in September, I could only admire the energy that Le Repaire de Bacchus was putting into the Caves, but was worried to see them sell Le Petit Bacchus to become a shoe shop, thus keeping the money I should have been bright enough to take from the earlier offer, and close down Spurrier Distribution, moving all my stock and customer reserves into his own warehouse south of Paris. Warning signs increased when my clients asked for delivery of their 2005s only to discover that these had been sold. Fortunately, my lawyer against McGarry had remained in touch and I had given her copies of all the reserves and my clients were compensated. While I was to play an important role in wine selection and my best suppliers remained to take pride of place in Le Repaire de Bacchus shops, which were growing in number, this practice made me most uncomfortable. Early the following year the long-planned renovation of the old-fashioned Cité Berryer got underway to become a luxury little street called La Cité Royale. The Caves de la Madeleine was eventually re-located in a smaller premises and the three floors of *L'Académie du Vin* returned to the real estate developers in exchange for considerable financial compensation.

I can't say that this was an easy period for me, but I was receiving a small salary, the fiscal debts were on hold, renegotiated at a lower rate of interest, and I was still actively involved in the Paris wine scene, while looking forward to the eventual pay out. Earlier that year I had met David Banford, an entrepreneur who asked me to be a wine adviser to his latest idea The Wine Society of America (WSA), a mail order company selling direct to customers into all but the 'dry' States, based in Millbrook, a smart suburb in upstate New York. David had managed to raise substantial funds on the money market and in early October I hosted tastings for a large crowd of members in New York, Chicago, Washington and Boston. These were successful but before too long the old-established sentinels of America's 3 Tier – Importer, Wholesaler, Retailer – wine distribution system, known as The Jewish Mafia, decided that the WSA was in competition with their clients and managed to put it out of business on some legal grounds or another. David Banford and I were to come together again fifteen years later with The Wine Society of India, with much the same concept, which seemed like a very good idea at the time.

1989 opened up with my life on a more even keel: the Christie's Wine Course was doing well, I was enjoying writing for the *Tatler*, there was the occasional speaking commission and the middle of the week was spent in Paris and weekends in Dorset. Early that year Bella and I went on our first visit to South Africa on the instigation of Simon Barlow, whose family owned the superb Rustenberg estate in Stellenbosch. I have just found in that year's diary a ticket from The Table Mountain Cableway, the first visit off the 'plane of a wonderful week. Once again it had been John Avery who had launched wines from the Cape into the UK and while the politics were still uncertain, there was optimism in the air. I was to return the following year as a judge on the South African Airways panel, organised by the ebullient and energetic Peter Devereux, and to become a regular visitor. My fellow judges in Spring 1990 on the International Tasting Panel for SAA were Pamela Vandyke-Price, Piero Antinori from Tuscany, Robert Drouhin from Burgundy, James Halliday, Australia's foremost wine writer, from Melbourne, and local growers Gyles Webb of Thelema and Tony Mossop who made very good Port-style wines. It was a really wonderful introduction to the people in the Cape and the wines they produced, good then, very, very good now.

Around Easter I was contacted by John Chua of Singapore Airlines, who had been a client of the Caves on his visits to Paris and had attended tastings at *L'Académie du Vin*. He told me that SIA was looking to change its wine consultants as the head of Commercial Supplies had been exposed taking large payments from providers and that although the current consultants were not at all suspected, a new Director had been named and a whole new team was to be appointed. He told me that the plan was to hire three consultants, one for Europe, one for the Americas and one for Australia and New Zealand and encouraged me to apply. This I did with alacrity and a few weeks later was summoned to the SIA London offices to be interviewed by Miss Wu, the new Commercial Supplies Director and Miss Chan (later to be known by the consultants as 'the Dragon Lady') Director of Customer Service. I recognised a couple of other applicants, one a Master of Wine, the other a top wine writer and didn't think much of my chances. My CV had already been pored over and I was asked just one question: ' If you were to be taken on as one of the SIA wine consultants, how would you expect to fly?' My reply was that if I was expected to taste the following day (the flights were twelve hours overnight) in Business Class, if not in Economy with a window seat. It appeared that the previous consultants had insisted on the First Class during their tenure, often at the expense of paying customers, so this was a valid question. Apparently no other applicant had suggested Economy and I got the job. Miss Wu, who was to be my boss for ten years, came to Vinexpo in June to be introduced to the châteaux owners and I think was quite impressed by my connections and so began a dream job: two weeks a year in Singapore, with its wonderful food and charming inhabitants and still a bit of culture left at that time, and a more than adequate 'all found' salary. From the start my co-consultants were Anthony Dias Blue from San Francisco and Michael Hill Smith MW from Adelaide, both good friends. We had the most tremendous time together with late nights and quite bad behaviour in the early days, and when I was finally retired in 2014, I had spent a full calendar year in Singapore, my fees increasing as Sterling lost value and I enjoyed every minute. John Chua went on to create the Wine Appreciation Group (WAG) for SIA and if their sommeliers are of the class they are today it is largely due to him.

If the SIA job was the best thing to happen to me in 1989, by far the worst was a demand from the tax authorities of the 8th arrondissement for 1.5 million FF which they deemed I owed for tax evasion! This organisation, *Le Service des Fraudes*, is of course funded by the State, but likes to make a little profit on the side by ambitious attention to anyone possibly getting away with more than they should. New residents in France were given a tax break for three years, nice to have, but also to encourage them to establish an expensive mode of life, and thus be open to tax on their *signes extérieures de richesse*/external signs of wealth. This plainly did not apply to me, but in the late 1970s I began to receive the visits from a Monsieur Le Put of the Fraud Squad who posed me certain questions and received straightforward replies. He would have seen the purchase of Le Moulin, the expansion into the Blue Fox Bar, taking over the third floor for *L'Académie du Vin*, buying Le Petit Bacchus and so on and he would have had access to my company accounts showing their increasing losses during the 1980s. I was always very well-dressed at the Caves and while that seemed normal to me, I probably looked rich to a tax inspector, who plainly could not figure out how I could continue to expand my businesses while losing great chunks of money. In the early summer of 1989 I was presented with an official dossier that took my losses over the past seven years (as far as they could go back) which amounted to 3 million FF and was told that these were in fact false and I had really been making a profit and had quite simply taken 3 million FF out of the country to place it in Bella's account in Geneva (which they were aware of) and therefore had avoided tax on this sum at 50%, so now owed *Le Fisc* the sum of 1.5 million FF.

This was of course rubbish and I set about to prove it. My accountant Mr Jongis declared that his accounts were true and I had made genuine trading losses. I traced every transfer of funds from the UK to France. Bella had had to finance some of my final expansions and funds had transited from Hentsch Bank in Geneva to Coutts in London. My own capital had long since been exhausted and all the previous transfers had come in via Lloyds Bank in Derby, who provided proof. I asked Mr Le Put how he thought I had transferred all this money out of France and he replied that was not his problem, so my final answer was to request Hentsch to open their books over the past seven years to prove that they had received no funds from me. Imagine my surprise when they told me that Private Swiss Banks didn't open their books to anyone! At this point I turned to Mr Jongis for advice, who put me in the hands of Mr Frau, an ex-tax inspector who had been so appalled by the job he was supposed to do, that he had switched sides to defend people in my situation. There then ensued many months of trading backwards and forwards, Mr Le Put upping his demands by charging interest, Mr Frau continuing to maintain that I was an innocent victim of a false claim. All this went on at some expense via a series of *letters recommandées*/registered letters that had to be delivered within fifteen days. Things were not going well for me at Le Repaire de Bacchus and I was gearing up for a confrontation there, so it was with unimaginable relief that I received a call early in February 1990 from Mr Frau to say that Mr Le Put's case had collapsed due to *une vice de forme*. It appeared that he had been so confident of convicting me that he had missed the fifteen day time limit by one day, and in French law that was that. Mr Frau was very pleased as he had believed me and had done an excellent job defending me, but what made him and me more happy was to learn from the 8th arrondissement tax office that Mr Le Put, who had banked a substantial upgrade in salary on the outcome of this case, had been dismissed and sent to a lower grade position somewhere far away from Paris.

I was integrating myself more into wine life in London, thanks partly to having become a member of the Circle of Wine Writers and through this being invited to Trade Tastings. I began to attend the London Wine Fair, always the last week in May at Olympia, a ten minute bike ride from Queen's Club Gardens. Our old friend David Langlands had found another benefactor in Christopher Shaw, a brilliant financier, with whom I had stayed in Los Angeles many years before with the mad, and thank heavens unrealised, idea of opening a wine bar near to Rodeo Drive. Having been the highest paid employee at the Bank of America, Christopher had returned to the UK and rented Hinton Ampner, a small but classic 'stately home' in the most beautiful part of Hampshire, which had been left by its last owner to The National Trust. David was building up a stable of race horses for him and handled the guest list at his lavish weekends, where there were seldom less than twenty at lunch and dinner. I had become an adviser on Christopher's wine cellar and weekends for Bella and I was part of the job.

In mid-July I was invited to attend the Master of Wine conference at Cambridge. The great and the good had come over from all parts of the world, including Len Evans from Australia, who gave a theatrical speech on how to promote his adopted country's wine, where he was a substantial owner in Hunter Valley, ending with a song and dance routine on the theme 'there's no business like show business, like no business I know' which received a standing ovation. Michael Broadbent was the Chairman and while I played only a minor part in the weekend's proceedings, I attended all the tastings and the black tie dinner on the Saturday in Saint John's College, where most of us were staying in recently-vacated students' rooms, and following morning I attended the morning service in the college chapel with its world famous choir.

While I was still very much part of the wine scene in Paris, being a regular taster for Gault & Millau and also, since a few years, for *La Revue du Vin de France*, I was not comfortable at Le Repaire de Bacchus, working now from their offices as my base at *L'Académie du Vin* no longer existed. I was looking forward to the end of my two year contract and to receiving the funds that would pay off the fiscal debts that were still in my name, leaving about £100,000 over. There was a big event to open one of their new shops in early October, during which they honoured several of my old suppliers like Guigal and Château de Beaucastel. The following day I told them that I had enjoyed my two years and felt I had contributed a good deal to the expansion of the business, and would they begin to make arrangements for the payment of the 4 million FF which were in the contract. I was calmly told that they were sorry to see me leave, but I would not receive the money. I replied that there had been a formal agreement between us when they took over my businesses with regard to the debts and future compensation over and above the 'franc symbolique' only to be told that this document had never been signed and legalized. I had, of course, trusted them - so whatever movement I made for payment would be fruitless. The fiscal debts I had agreed to take on when this agreement was made still remained on my shoulders.

It was thus that in October 1990, shortly after my 49th birthday, I returned to London. *Steven Spurrier Marchand de Vin*/Steven Spurrier Wine Merchant, the brand that I had created over two decades, had ceased to exist. My only remaining asset was the London flat and even the value of this didn't meet what I now owed. Meanwhile, life had to go on, broke and bleaker than I could ever have imagined.

13. The Road Back

Once back from Paris – although we kept on the flat in Rue de la Cerisaie sharing the rent with Annie Bingham for another fifteen years – I was quite relieved that it was all over, but faced with an uncertain future. I was not wholly a part of the London wine scene and knew I had to be, as this was all the only way I could earn money over and above the salary from Singapore Air Lines, the fees from the Christie's Wine Course and *Tatler*. It wasn't obvious what the next step would be but it was essential to cut back on expenses, so I sold my dull Peugeot car and rented out the London garage. Christian was now at Edinburgh University and Kate was about to do her A Levels in London. Fees had to be paid and I contacted my solicitors to ask whether there were any funds I didn't know about, only to be told that my father had made a Marriage Settlement for my future children with shares in Marston-on-Dove Estates Ltd, and the income had built up, so they (and this was a pleasant surprise to them as well) took on their own school fees. Nicky advised me very strongly to sell the flat, but remembering how I had so much enjoyed growing up in London, I said I couldn't deprive my children of the same opportunity. My mother stepped in with £100,000 for each of us, so I moved from being in a hopeless situation to a difficult one.

My good friend Georges Lepré, who had been one of the judges on the 1986 Judgement of Paris in New York as he was then working in the US, was shortly after that appointed head sommelier at the Ritz in Paris and was teaching classes at *L'Académie du Vin*. Monsieur Klein, the Manager of the Ritz, and I crossed paths from time to time and in 1987 he had asked me whether I would be interested in running the Harrods Wine Department and I replied that I couldn't do that and also have the businesses in Paris. Things had of course changed since then and around Easter 1991 Georges Lepré asked me to meet him and my brief was simply to write a short report on the Harrods Wine Department, with no prospect of future employment. All I did was visit the shop a few times, check the labels and buy a few Harrods' branded wines and also visit other stores such as Fortnum & Mason, Harvey Nichols and Selfridges, and submitted a fairly damning report along the lines that there was a lot that could be changed for the better.

Time passed, and in early June Mr Klein re-contacted me and said that Mr Al Fayed was considering changing the manager in the wine department and would I be interested in the position of Wine Consultant. Of course I would. This was just before Vinexpo in the middle of June, where I was to talk to the suppliers to SIA, to keep my hand in and also go to the wonderful parties in the evening, confident that the offer would be confirmed later that month. While at Vinexpo the news came from Mr Klein that the then manager of the wine department, a Master of Wine, thinking he might be replaced by me, had handed Mr Al Fayed a copy of Simon Loftus's book *Anatomy of the Wine Trade*, in which the chapter on me is entitled A Cautionary Tale, resulting in the job offer being withdrawn. I fired off a fax (no emails then) to say that this article referred to my sense of business not to my sense of wine, and called Simon Loftus to ask him to put in a good word for me. I have a faded fax copy of his letter dated 26 June in front of me, in which he expresses distress that it had been sent in an apparent effort to discredit me, going on to say that the chapter was a light-hearted contrast to other chapters in his book adding that 'one of his most attractive habits is a modest preference for a good story at his own expense, rather than saying anything in praise of his own very real abilities', ending up by stating that in his view I would be an outstandingly good choice for the future of the Wine Department.

This seemed to do the trick and in late June I was summoned to meet Mr Al Fayed. Mohamed Al Fayed was very much in the news then, had been for years and would become even more so when his son Dodi began a relationship with Diana, Princess of Wales. Mr Fayed Senior was a dramatic character, quite explosive in manner and fond of punctuating his short sentences with a limited range of swear words. He told me to come in for a couple of days a week and 'sort out the wine department'. I started in early July, meeting Hugh Cochrane, the MW department head, in the wine shop on the ground floor, adjacent to the splendid Food Halls, who took me down to the cellar where his office was. Here were racks and racks of wine, bins full of bottles, cases piled high and as we entered he said 'Better take your jacket off, it's warm down here.' 'What about the wine?' I asked. 'That doesn't seem to bother them' was the reply. Having been shown around, the first thing I did was to buy a Polaroid camera and an industrial size thermometer, find an old and prestigious bottle and take a photograph, which showed clearly the temperature of 23 degrees Centigrade/74 degrees Fahrenheit. This I sent up to Mr Al Fayed's office with the note that were it to fall into the hands of any wine journalist, the reputation of the wine department would be destroyed. By the end of the week air-conditioning was being installed.

A couple of weeks later, Hugh Cochrane told me he had found another position in the wine trade and was happy to leave it all to me, noting that Chris Donaldson, a very recent MW had always been an excellent back-up. Harrods confirmed my position and then in September Chris Donaldson also left, leaving the wine department an MW-free zone. Had I wanted a free hand, this was now the case. I set to expanding the French range under the Harrods' brand, previously just Claret and White Burgundy, and soon had red and white Graves, Mâcon-Vinzelles, Meursault, Chablis and red Côtes du Rhône. In my researches a few months earlier, Fortnum & Mason had a superb range of 'own-label' wines and these were just a start. Early in the autumn I was interviewed by Anthony Rose of the now sadly defunct *Independent*, whose long article was headed 'Château Harrods', noting that 'the top people's store is giving its wine department a welcome face-lift thanks to Steven Spurrier. The long-term goal is to 'prepare for the moment when Mo moves us downstairs', describing Mohamed Al Fayed's acceptance of his suggestion to sweep out the basement stables that then housed great iron cages full of wines and to turn that space into 'a purpose-built wine department, the greatest wine department in the world with its own bar'. Glorious vision or grand illusion?' Mr Al Fayed had a right-hand man named Michael Cole, who referred frequently to his previous position in the Royal Household; he was responsible above all for the Al Fayed 'image'. He called me in and reprimanded me strongly for referring to his boss as 'Mo' (which we workers always knew him as) and not bothering to thank me for the very positive article. I apologised but wasn't worried as, once again, I was in my element, buying wines I liked that I was sure people would want to drink, and thinking up ways to promote them.

It was probably the latter which was to cost me my job in late January after the vital Christmas rush and the January sales were over, but that was in the future and with my 50th birthday was coming up, I suggested to Mark Williamson who had bought Le Moulin and The Blue Fox from me a couple of years before, that I take it over for a big dinner on the very day. Nicky and my mother came over, her first visit to Paris since visiting us on the barge in summer 1972 and both floors of the restaurant were filled with friends from all our time in France. Thanks to David Fromkin, I had met Mary Blume, who wrote a weekly column for the back page of the *Trib* about people and places. David suggested that she interview me and the result appeared on 14 October under the heading 'The Rise and Fall and Rise of a Wine Guru'. This covered the ups and downs of my wine career, ending with my jumping onto a table at the end of dinner to thank everyone for coming, ending with the quote 'This party in 1991, I never thought I would have the nerve or the money to give. The whole game starts up again from my point of view.'

Georges Lepré from his base at the Paris Ritz send me a floral note of congratulations for the article, but Michael Cole didn't see it this way. Once again I was called in and told that since 'it was Harrods that meant I could afford to give myself the party (true) I should have talked more about Harrods and less about myself.' I stated that if he looked at how I had changed the wine department in just three months, in another six I would have completed the transformation and then Harrods wouldn't need me anymore, to receive the curt reply that 'It will be quicker than that.' There wasn't much I could do about this attitude and meanwhile there was work to be done on the list, which hadn't even been produced the previous year. I envisaged a magazine-like list with articles on the various regions with particular focus on the major names and suppliers in exchange for sponsorship. This duly appeared in early December and going through the proofs with the advertising department I was told that it looked so good that perhaps I should sign it, so on the first page I wrote a brief introduction and, as head of the wine department, signed my name. This was what Michael Cole had been waiting for. The heads of departments were known to each other as Mr Meat, Mr Game, Mr Fish, Mr Cheese, Mr Fruit and Mr Wine. When we were up in the staff refectory on coffee breaks we didn't use this, but on the shop floor we did. Apparently no head of department had ever drawn attention to themselves in this way, it being against the Harrods 'code', so in the third week of January I was told to clear my desk and leave that evening. My replacement was to be Alun Griffiths MW, the man behind the Fortnum & Mason wine department which I had held up to Harrods as an inspiration only seven months previously. I could have just slammed the door, but I knew and respected Alun and spent the weekend writing a report on everything in the pipeline for the coming few months. He did an excellent job.

The outcome of all this was a full-page article in the *Sunday Telegraph* by Lucy Bailey under the heading 'A man with too much bottle.' In which she asks me the question 'So what now?' and quotes my reply that 'I've decided to turn myself into a consultant and spend my time promoting the *enjoyment* of wine.' My brief six months at Harrods had put me fairly and squarely back in the London wine trade and it was just a matter, being an optimist, of seeing what would turn up. What was to turn up, not right away, was *Decanter* magazine, but in the meantime, while the Al Fayed shilling had brought my debts down a little and Nicky's management of the family investment company was helping as well, I accepted anything that came to hand. Thanks to Peter Devereux, Diner's Club in South Africa was looking for a 'name' to hold wine tastings for their members and in late February I returned to the Cape, this time with Bella, to conduct these and then, again thanks to Peter's advice, spent a wonderful three days in the Kruger National Park.

My regular spring and autumn weeks in Singapore continued and Anthony Dias Blue asked me to be a judge on his San Francisco Wine Competition which took me to the city for four or five days, with time for a catch up visit to Napa Valley. In early 1972 the Prix de Champagne Lanson was created, prizes being awarded for wine writing in various forms and I was asked to be Chairman of the Judges. A dozen years later Lanson gave up on the project, to be replaced by Louis Roederer and I was Chairman of that for the first three years. The few remaining magnums of Vintage Lanson and Louis Roederer Cristal in my cellar are the result. In mid July, thinking where to go on holiday, I was contacted by Arblaster & Clarke, a travel agent specialising in wine tours, who were re-creating the Bordeaux to Bristol sea voyage that over the centuries had transported claret to England. This was to be Weymouth-Bordeaux-Weymouth on a fine three-mast sailing ship named *The Astrid*, co-organised by Bordeaux Direct, the mail order wine club that had been founded by Tony Laithwaite, of which Hugh Johnson was Chairman. There was a double cabin to spare and Bella and I were offered this in exchange for being the resident wine guide and to host a few visits once in Bordeaux, Hugh joining us for a dinner at Château Latour, of which he was a director, then still owned by the brewers Bass Charrington. We also had to help man the ship, running up and down the rigging to unfurl or re-furl the sails, keeping night watch four hours on, four hours off, which was educative and exhausting. After a five-day voyage out of the Channel into the Atlantic, mooring often on the way, we entered the Gironde Estuary and I waved to Château Loudenne as we sailed slowly past. Hugh and Judy Johnson took the return journey to Weymouth, hitting two days of heavy storms, and had to stay with us in Dorset to recuperate.

This first connection with Arblaster & Clarke led to a regular job once or twice a year as a wine guide on their well-organised trips to the wine regions and the day after writing this chapter I will be flying to Lyon to head up a wine tour to the north and southern Rhône. In the north we will visit Georges Vernay, André Perret and Delas Frères on the first day, Marcel Guigal, Jaboulet and Chapoutier on the second, have a tour and tasting at *L'Université du Vin* in Suze-la-Rousse to be followed by lunch at my favourite restaurant La Beaugravière in Mondragon with one of the best and best value wine lists in the world, then taste at Château de Saint Cosme in Gigondas on the third, visit Ogier and Château de Beaucastel in Châteauneuf-du-Pape, then Château de Monfaucon and Domaine de la Mordorée in Lirac on the fourth and travel further south to Domaine de Trevallon and Château de Romanin around Saint-Rémy-de-Provence before flying back from Marseille. Lunches and dinners are at the better local restaurants and I am fed and housed, get to re-visit the *vignerons,* by this time their sons, even grandsons, who I had first met when in Paris and also received a good fee. This has been a very good arrangement for both sides over twenty-five years and when asked why these trips usually go down so well with the clients I always say that all I have to do is to 'get off the bus first.' They will see the owner of the château or domaine welcome me with a smile and know that everything will be all right. It is, of course, all intricately planned and as a result tends to go like clockwork.

On one of our weekend visits to check out (and enjoy drinking) the bottles in his Hinton Ampner cellar, Christopher Shaw introduced me to Jean-Louis Masurel who, after many years high up in the echelons of Moët et Chandon, and having been responsible for the founding and launch of Green Point in Australia with Tony Jordan, had found himself on the wrong side against Bernard Arnault in the creation of the LVMH conglomerate and had left to purchase with colleagues the historic Hédiard,

Epicerie Fine, the great food and wine store on the Place de la Madeleine, a finer rival in my view to Fauchon on the other corner. I had known the store well in the 1970s and 1980s and we began to talk about the possible new directions he might take it, when Masurel calmly suggested that he hire me as a consultant. La Maison Nicolas, the ubiquitous Parisian *caviste*, had recently been purchased by Castel, the largest wine producer in France, and Jean-Loup, the younger of the two Nicolas brothers had already been taken on to run the Hédiard wine selection, but Masurel, later to become a very good friend, thought that another view would be useful. I was back to a couple of days a week in Paris, working with inspiring people on a good salary, so it seemed that the Spurrier luck, so absent in the late 1980s, was about to change.

And change it did even more when I met Sarah Kemp, who had recently joined *Decanter* Magazine as a junior editor only to become Managing Director three years later. Of course I already knew a good deal about *Decanter*, which had been created by Colin Parnell, a bookish and talented musician, and Tony Lord, a young Australian journalist, to fill the gaping hole left by the recent demise of *Wine Magazine*. I had bumped into Colin from time to time, always rather reserved, and Tony, who was anything but, being massively competitive and also a heroic drinker. Early one morning when we still lived in Clapham, I was passing the north side of the Common on my morning run and saw in the mist way ahead of me a figure that looked like Tony Lord, who I knew lived somewhere nearby. I had seen him late the previous evening in a restaurant where he was very much the worse for wear, and couldn't believe how he could now be on his feet at such an hour. Getting nearer, it was indeed him and we seemed on a collision course on the narrow track, so I swerved out of his way, only to hear him growl in passing 'you're in England now, Spurrier, so run on the f***ing left!'. Typical Tony, wine was the link between us, but we were never friends as he had me down as a 'smart Pom' and that was it. While Colin was a rather formal Bordeaux-lover, Tony supported the world outside France and it was this that gave the fledgling magazine its international flavour. The first edition in June 1975 for the modest price of 40p had a cover line 'How to buy Bordeaux and keep your bank manager happy' and an inside story on 'The Confessions of a Lady Wine Bar Proprietress'.

14. Life with *Decanter*

In early 1993 Sarah Kemp, by now publisher of *Decanter*, and I met at a charity dinner for the Benevolent and I was recounting my time at Harrods when she said, 'you're well out of that, come and write for *Decanter*.' I did, my first column entitled 'Wines of the Future?' appearing in October 1993 and I have been there ever since. Alongside my monthly column were regular feature articles and a pretty permanent place on the tasting panels. My other activities still carried on, but after a few years I decided not to order more Steven Spurrier Wine Consultant business cards, but to keep the *Decanter* card with my name on it as it meant much more to everybody.

1993 had seen another trip to the Cape and a pre-Easter week heading up one of many Arblaster & Clarke Wine Tours based at Château Lascombes, which I had known well from Alexis Lichine's days as owner. The AIV had its summer symposium in the northern Rhône that June with an unforgettable tasting in the Chave cellars in Mauves, south of Tournon. We sampled the recent vintage, still in big oak or cement vats and then descended to the cellar to taste a range of white and red Hermitage through five decades. We spat out onto the beaten earth floor, Gérard Chave remarking that in his father's day, nobody invited down to the cellar to taste wine in bottle ever considered spitting. During the Singapore Airlines tasting week in October, I got to know an Indian lady named Usha Lavie, who was married to a fat French airline pilot named Philip Lavie and was in the process, having done the year-long œnology course at Talence near Bordeaux, where I had taken a week's crash course in 1973 under Professor Peynaud, of taking control of an estate in the Entre-deux-Mers called Château Gamage. The 30 hectares of vines provided a nice Semillon-Sauvignon dry white and a pleasant Merlot-based Bordeaux Superieur red but what interested me was the château itself, a fine 18th century *manoir* in need of total renovation. Persuading Nicky that this would be a real-estate not a wine investment, the family company put up a considerable amount of money for this, I personally financed plans from a respected local architect, but it all ended very badly. Dealing with people who are 'difficult' (to put it politely) is time-consuming and costly and Château Gamage became known in the family as 'Château Dommage' and this was to be my final 'partnership investment', causing me to write in *Decanter* that any future vineyard investment would be with someone I could trust, namely my wife.

Looking through my articles in 1994, I come across a January visit to Helsinki in Finland to attend Vinexpo, the State Monopoly's version of Vinexpo. This was my second of many roles as 'understudy' to my mentor Michael Broadbent. The first had been in the mid 1980s when I was at Malmaison, to replace Michael in ITV's television studios in Manchester and take part in something called 'The Sensible Show'. Under the direction of a very well-known Master of Ceremonies, contestants were blindfolded and asked to judge items for texture, weight, smell, taste and so on, often not recognising the item at all or judging it to be either much more expensive or much cheaper than its real price. I was supposed to test them with two wines and, knowing that sweet wines were considered 'up north' as being cheap and dry wines as being expensive, presented them with a top Muscadet and Château d'Yquem, the latter being more than ten times the price. As hoped, they chose the Muscadet as the classier wine. Over the years I received telephone calls along the lines of 'Steven, I've accepted to go to xxx and find I'm too busy, so have recommended you.' Such calls later took me to my first visit to Santiago in Chile, to represent Christie's, to a weekend's wine tasting in Nashville, Tennessee and to an

Sarah Kemp and Eric de Rothschild at a Gala Dinner at
the Royal Opera House

Office Internationale du Vin/OIV tasting in Madrid's Ritz Hotel. At one point, he and I had been contacted to a small luxury cruise line to be the wine guide on a seven-day cruise. The choice was Plymouth to Bordeaux or the South China Seas. Michael took the latter and I resumed my allotted place as Number Two.

My October piece that year had the title Judging the Judges. I open with the comment that 'Golfers play off handicaps, cricketers are judged by their averages, jockeys by their wins per season and even barristers by their record in court. Wine judges are not rated on their average performance and although some are more esteemed than others, it seems that the ability to taste a hundred or so wines in a morning is viewed the same as the ability to judge them.' I went on to note that all blind tastings were to a large extent 'beauty contests' and produce results that are unexpected and often unjustifiable. Such were the results of that year's Business Traveller Awards, which saw an array of eleven retailers, sommeliers and wine writers judge wines from thirty airlines. A 1993 Pouilly-Vinzelles was judged superior to a 1992 Corton-Charlemagne, Château Guerry 1990, Côtes de Bourg beat Château Léoville-Barton 1988, St Julien and Piper-Heidsieck Brut NV topped the Champagnes with Charles Heidsieck 1985 seventh and Bollinger 1985 last. I went on to say that 'For such tastings to be taken seriously, the tasters need to be impeccable on a regular basis. If it were possible, tasters should be tested against a series of wines for recognition of quality, consistency of judgement, palate fatigue and receive a handicap. Tasters like Michael Broadbent, Serena Sutcliffe, Michel Bettane, James Halliday and the like would taste off par, while the opinions of the less experienced tasters would be discounted at x%, depending on their handicap. Then the published results of 'official' tastings could be accompanied by a taster-weighted index, to show relative validity.' Little did I know that ten years later I would be co-founder and Chairman of the first *Decanter* World Wine Awards and in charge of selecting the Regional Chairs to head their tasting tables, many of whom hold the same role today. It is a *Decanter* dictum that the validity of the DWWA results rests on the shoulders of the tasters we invite.

Bizarrely I do not have a single article written in 1995, but in mid-January I was in San Francisco as one of a high level panel of judges to take part in a tasting organised by Robert Finigan, sponsored by Gordon Getty, to compare the top Red Bordeaux from 1990 and 1986. In his book *Corks and Forks* under the title 'Bordeaux Redux', Robert recounts that the 1855 Classification of the châteaux of the Médoc and the Graves into five different 'Growths' from First to Fifth had not totally stood the test of time and that, by getting together an expert panel who would compare two recent vintages in a blind tasting, a modern potential ranking might appear. As a sponsor he approached his friend Gordon Getty, owner of a winery called Plump Jack and a committed fan of opera. It was agreed that Getty would underwrite the event and any profit from the subsequent tasting open to the public and followed by a black tie dinner would go to the San Francisco Symphony Orchestra. The two vintages selected were 1990 and 1986, the former rich and robust and later acknowledged the best vintage of the decade, the latter more classic and perhaps overshadowed by 1982 and 1985. Strong support was given by Sacha Lichine, son of Alexis and then in charge of Prieuré-Lichine, and Bruno Prats of Cos d'Estournel. All the wines were sourced from the châteaux and forwarded in good time to recover before the tasting took place.

Robert Finigan chaired the panel of judges which he had selected as having 'diverse but professional palates', who were, in alphabetical order: Alexis Bespaloff of the *New Yorker*, Michel Bettane of *La Revue Vin de France*, Antony Dias Blue of *Bon Appetit* magazine and also creator of the San Francisco Wine Competition on which I was a regular judge, Mary Ewing Mulligan MW, director of the International Wine Centre in New York and author of the best-selling *Wine for Dummies*, David Peppercorn MW, noted English author specializing in Bordeaux, Frank Prial of the *New York Times*, Serena Sutcliffe MW recently appointed head of Sotheby's wine department and myself. Tasters were allowed to use the 20 or the 100 point scales, the former being multiplied by five to come to an average out of 100. Across the sixty classed growths of the Médoc and the 13 (only Haut-Brion being included in the 1855 classification) from the northern Graves, now known as Pessac-Léognan, here is the ranking of the top 15 wines, 1990 and 1986 vintages taken together.

90.5 – Ch. Pichon-Longueville-Baron, 2nd growth Pauillac
90.2 – Ch. Léoville-Las Cases, 2nd growth St Julien
89.4 – Ch. Haut-Brion, 1st growth Graves
87 – Ch. Pichon-Longueville Comtesse de Lalande,
     2nd growth Pauillac

86.7 – Ch. Margaux, 1st growth Margaux
86.3 – Ch. Cos d'Estournel, 2nd growth St Estèphe
85.8 – Ch. Latour, 1st growth Pauillac
85.1 – Ch. Lynch-Bages, 5th growth Pauillac
85 – Ch. La Mission Haut-Brion, classed growth Graves
84.4 – Ch. Léoville-Barton, 2nd growth St Julien
83.6 – Ch. Mouton-Rothschild, 1st growth Pauillac
83.5 – Ch. Léoville-Poyferre, 2nd growth St Julien
82.4 – Ch. Ducru-Beaucaillou, 2nd growth St Julien
82.2 – Ch. Montrose, 2nd growth St Estèphe
81.6 – Ch. Lafite-Rothschild, 1st growth Pauillac

The 16th wine was Château Palmer, 3rd growth Margaux at 80.5, so I think from this tasting the 1855 classification stood up pretty well, as it still does today. The tasting required two full days of constant attention, tasting at a certain rhythm, the judges giving their marks before moving onto the next wine. Anthony Dias Blue, next to me, was always first to deliver, while Mary Ewing Mulligan was always last, causing Michel Bettane to remark somewhat unkindly 'Poor Maryee, she takes *sooo* long and always gets it wrrrong'.

Then in late February, on the invitation of my old friend Nico Manessis, later to become a member of the AIV and even later Regional Chair for Greece for the DWWA, a position he still holds, I was in Athens for their own Vin Expo. In the mid 1970s and early 1980s, Bella and I had spent a week or so every summer as guests of David Fromkin on crewed sailing boats, known as 'gülets', to tour the Greek and Turkish islands. David maintained that 'the best Greek wine is worse than the worst French wine' and lavish supplies of Dauvissat Chablis, Leflaive Puligny and Pousse d'Or Volnay were shipped out from the Caves to the boats' owners. Nico, whose father was from an old Corfu family, strongly disagreed and would, in 1995, produce the first edition of his *Greek Wine Guide*, a book which, with the help of Steve Daniel then head wine buyer for Oddbins, a popular chain of wine stores owned at the time by Seagram, would launch Greek wine onto the UK market. This visit was eye-opening, but just on the mainland. The following year Nico arranged for a trip to Santorini whose volcanic soils produced superb bone dry white wines from the Assyrtiko grape. In *Decanter*'s November 2015 issue, which celebrated the magazine's 40th Anniversary, I am quoted as saying in my May column 'The next fashionable wine region to capture the imagination and shelf space of the British wine buyers may well not be from the New World, but from one of the oldest wine-producing parts of the Old World: Greece.'

In July I was part of the *Decanter* contingent in Seattle, to attend a wine conference that concentrated on the wines of the West Coast, which included California of course. Pinot Noir from Oregon already much admired where Joseph Drouhin had made the first Burgundian investment, followed by many others, most recently by Louis Jadot, and the wines of Washington State which were totally new to me. It was unimaginable even then how wide and complex the wine world had become compared to the one I entered just thirty years earlier and was to become ever more wide and complex in the best possible sense over the next two decades. The wine consumer is truly living in a 'golden age' and this is certain to continue, for producers know that quality, from the bottom to the top of the price scale, is the only way to go. Vinexpo rolled around for its bi-annual week in June, and I found myself at 'dinner Château Margaux' on the Wednesday evening as though this were a regular occurrence. Then during the vintage there was another Arblaster & Clarke wine tour, this time based at the recently renovated Axa-Millésime owned Château Pichon-Longueville Baron. And to show I wasn't tied to Bordeaux, I attended the *Hospices de Beaune* weekend in mid-November, again packing a black tie for their equally impressive dinners. I had also acquired another consultancy job with a company called Windrush Wines, with shops in London, Hungerford, Northleach, and Oxford, and was very busy and the Paris debts were slowly receding.

My January 1996 column was titled 'Bespoke brokers in Asia' and began 'What do Adam Brett-Smith of Corney & Barrow, Edward Demery of Justerini & Brooks, Alun Griffiths of Berry Brothers (he hadn't lasted too long at Harrods, either) and Lindsay Hamilton of Farr Vintners have in common? Answer: they were all recently in Asia purveying, very successfully, the finest French wines, while in the process confirming London's role as the centre of the wine world and their own role as traditional merchants in an ever-changing market.' I had been in Japan on my way to the autumn SIA week of tasting at the invitation of Ronald Brown, a former executive on the wine side of Jardine's and later at International Distillers and Vintners (IDV) who was in the process of setting up his own business in which I was to become a partner. Brown and I had met at Hédiard and I was to give a series of lectures and tastings in Tokyo. At that time wine represented just 1% of all alcohol sold in Japan, hardly more in Hong Kong or Singapore and next to nothing in China. I ended my piece noting that 'with education, Asia will be the next big market for wine and not just for the best bottles'.

I was beginning to spend more time in Asia, not only for Singapore Airlines and the occasional judging, thanks to John Avery, in Hong Kong, due to my association with Ronald Brown, who had founded a company called La Languedocienne, as he and his wife had a vineyard in the Midi. Ron, as he was known, was a serial entrepreneur which appealed to me, and I quickly became a junior partner in the fledgling business, combining my trips to Tokyo with tastings at L'Académie du Vin. A few years later Ron was to create The Japan Wine Challenge (JWC) and even later the China Wine Challenge (CWC), based on the London-based International Wine Challenge (IWC) that had been founded by Robert Joseph of *Wine Magazine*, the competitor to *Decanter*. I owe to Ron Brown many fascinating trips all over Japan from this time for about fifteen years and I have to confess that many of the building blocks I put in place for the *Decanter* World Wine Awards (DWWA) in 2004 were based on my experience, for a long time with John Avery as my Co-Chair, at the JWC and CWC. As Asia was such an emerging market we were able to invite judges from all over the world and the reputation of both competitions benefited accordingly.

Having helped create the *Decanter* World Wine Awards in 2004, I felt a year or two later that I should only Chair one wine competition and resigned from the JWC and CWC, to be replaced by Lynne Sherriff MW. From 2010, having started Bride Valley Vineyard, I asked Ron Brown to buy me out of La Languedocienne, and a price was agreed but it took me a while to get paid.

Two very different trips highlighted the 1996 summer, the first in May to go to Washington DC to attend a conference on the theme 'Red, White and American' at the Smithsonian Institute of American History which inaugurated an exhibit of assorted wine artifacts, including a bottle each of the Stag's Leap Wine Cellars 1973 Cabernet and the Chateau Montelena 1973 Chardonnay, winners of what had become known as the Judgement of Paris exactly twenty years earlier. The title of the exhibition was 'Doubtless as Good: Jefferson's Dream for American Wine Fulfilled.' Another twenty years were to pass before I was back at The Smithsonian for the 40th Anniversary and to be told that Congress had voted 24 May 1976 an important day in American History and to receive an Amercian Flag in honour of the role I had played.

The second, in August, was to the Tokaji vineyards in Hungary, a country that was just emerging from Communist rule. Hugh Johnson, always ahead of his time, had established The Royal Tokaji Wine Company (RTWC) to revive these great sweet wines that were famous from the early 18th century, the vineyards being classified in 1700, the first official classification of vineyard land in Europe. Under the Communists from 1945 to 1990 the classed vineyards on the higher slopes which could not be farmed mechanically were abandoned for those on the plains. The production of Tokaji Essencia died out, for the concentration – 70% residual sugar with the consistency of glue, a teaspoonful being enough to satisfy the curiosity and lift the spirit – was insufficient and the RTWC produced the first Essencia for fifty years with their 1993. By mid 1996 other investors were in evidence, including AXA-Millésimes Disnoko estate, Vega Sicilia's Bodegas Oremus and a branch of the Habsburg family that had gone back to its Imperial roots by reviving one of their old estates.

My visit was organised by Ben Howkins, a contemporary from Rugby and a great expert on Port, who was commercial director of the RTWC. We were to be joined by three stalwarts from San Francisco: Jack Daniels and Wim Wilson of Wilson Daniels the RWTC importers and Anthony Dias Blue. Before our flight to Budapest the following day, Ben had arranged a lunch for us at Waddesdon Manor, the magnificent home of Jacob, Lord Rothschild, whose wine cellar Ben looked after. Our summer lunch in the converted Dairy came, as Jacob Rothschild told us, 'all from the garden' and since he was a shareholder in both Lafite and Mouton-Rothschild, we had these wines as well. The contrast between Waddesdon and Budapest in 1996 (and to Budapest today) was extraordinary, the latter being grey and poor, but the four-hour drive to the village of Mad in the Tokaji region took us back into a more romantic world of vineyards and timbered farm houses with the odd castle to show previous prosperity. In the past the only Tokaji wine was sweet, made in a unique manner of adding late-picked, super-concentrated 'botrytised' or *Aszu* berries that had been crushed into a paste in small tubs called *puttonyos* and added to the high acid natural white wine from the Furmint grape after fermentation. The sweetness increases according to the amount of *puttonyos* added, the most sweet being a 6-*puttonyos,* above this the wine being labelled Essencia. For Peter Vinding-Diers, co-founder with Hugh Johnson of the RTWC, the 5-puttonyos 'combines sweetness and elegance, a nose of honey and violets with richness supported by chords of acidity: the wine would be like an étude by Chopin – listen to it and you hear the world turn around.' Certainly we tasted enough to hardly keep our feet on the ground as the world turned, and I have a framed photograph of us all, still standing, in the sun outside the RTWC cellars with the caption 'The Tokaji Aszu Experience – It's a Mad, Mad, Mad World'.

Apart from the annual *L'Académie Internationale du Vin* (AIV) symposium in early December, where the members discussed the 1996 vintage which they were generally pleased with, the last word going to Rémi Krug whose brother Henri with thirty-five vintages behind him had never seen as splendid a vintage: 'Perhaps another 1928?', the year ended with three lavish days at Raffles Hotel in Singapore for the Second Wine and Food Experience. My article in the February 1997 *Decanter* carried the title 'Life on the Middle Palate' inspired by Napa Valley's Far Niente Estate owner Larry Maguire's remark about his Chardonnay that 'what we are looking for is life on the middle palate.' Some years before the great wine journalist Frank Prial of *The New York Times* had penned an article entitled 'Death on the Middle Palate' giving advice to people who, when asked to make a comment on wine but being ignorant of the language that wine people use, could say 'a magnificent bouquet but it dies on the middle palate' or 'it dies on the middle palate but comes back strongly on the finish.' A number of top producers from Burgundy – Bonneau de Martray, Drouhin, Dujac, Jadot, Roumier and William Fèvre – alongside Jean-Claude Rouzaud from Louis Roederer, Avignonese from Tuscany and Coldstream Hills from Australia, all agreed that the middle palate was the key. Georg Riedel was also there, showing a new range of glasses and, asked when he thought a wine had reached maturity, replied 'when it tastes better than it smells.' Confirmation came from Dr Ernesto Illy, founder of Illy Café, who gave a tasting of three espressi brewed at different temperatures and times, maintaining that the correct brew will extract only 25-28% of the caffeine but 60% of the coffee bean's flavour. Dr Illy's obsession with flavour rather than extract extended to the perfect coffee cup, which should be in the shape of an egg cut in half and filled to no more than 35%. At first, the flavour is trapped by the foam – as the taste of Champagne is trapped by the bubbles – then the aroma appears and is released onto the palate. Even two decades ago the popularity of good expresso lay in its taste, life and lifted finish, not in the caffeine of which there is much less than in a cup of ordinary coffee. Amateurs of his coffee were looking for increased pleasure from increased yet balanced flavour, just as they were in fine wines. All's well that ends well on the middle palate.

In April 1997 Bella and I spent ten wonderful days in Lebanon and Syria – the latter sadly un-visitable today – where Serge Hochar, owner of Château Musar, and his brother Ronald welcomed us at their winery near Baalbek and we visited almost every historic site that could be reached by car.

Meanwhile evidence that things were improving for me financially – I had paid down over half of the Paris debts – came with the invitation from Mark Williamson to invest in his new restaurant venture. For this he was planning to use the Moulin du Village company in which I was still a nominal shareholder, where there were still substantial fiscal losses to put against any potential profits. Always ready for a new gamble, I showed my bank manager that the London flat had gone up in value and asked to borrow enough to take a 25% share. (When I began to plant Bride Valley Vineyard I told Mark I had to be bought out, which I was at a nice profit.) Maceo, the restaurant that Mark took over, just two doors down from his Willi's Wine Bar in the Rue des Petits-Champs, was in need of complete renovation, which was done with brio and imagination and twenty years later, on 9th June 2017 Bella and I attended a celebration dinner for 60 people. Wines included our Bride Valley Rosé Bella 2014, Champagne Legras & Hass Grand Cru Chouilly 2007 (François Legras who had made the original Brut Intégral for Lucien Legrand and me back in 1972 was a sprightly presence), Savennières 'Clos du Papillon' 2015 Domaine de Closel, and Imperial (8 bottles) of Brouilly 1979 Château des Tours and three marvellous Spanish wines from Telmo Rodriguez, who had just that month succeeded in his quest to have the top single vineyards in Rioja individually classified for their quality. 'Le Mafia Anglais' as my team was known in the 1980s, were out in force and a very good time was had by all.

At Vinexpo that year I took part in a tasting that was a scientific experiment and had never been held since. Under the banner *Les Palais du*

Monde, forty-three tasters from fourteen countries and four continents were gathered together to test the influences of geographic and ethnic orgins, with their acquired memory of tastes and flavours, at the moment of tasting each wine. We were asked to strap a *cardiofréquencemètre* around our chests to monitor our heartbeats and a smaller, watch-like object around our wrists. The difference that morning was that while we were judging the wines, the computer was judging us and it came up with three families of tasters irrespective of ethnic origin:

- 'The permanently unsatisfied.' Negative tasters looking for faults before searching pleasure, most of this group came from countries with an historic culture of wine.
- 'The modest ones'. These tasted with a blend of humility and confidence, leaving the last word to the wine itself.
- 'The enthusiasts'. This group was interested in the wine's personality as though they had never tasted it before, and came from countries where wine growing was rare.

When there were four or more tasters from a specific country, the computer came up with the ethnic profile: the French showed knowledge by reference (all the wines were French), the Belgians were convivial, the Swiss were methodical, the Germans looked for aroma, Scandinavians preferred robustness to delicacy, Canadians looked for balance, the Japanese showing emotional reactions to high acidity, while the British 'were reflective and did not waste words.' At the end of the day we received printouts of our emotional reactions to each wine in the form of a hospital cardiogramme. Robert Joseph's was all over the place, an expression of intensely varying emotion, while mine was flat as a board, perhaps the vinous equivalent of the stiff upper lip.

1997 ended with the first *Decanter* Fine Wine Encounter, the brainchild of Sarah Kemp, which was held over the third weekend in November at The Landmark hotel in London. Two vast rooms were filled with producers from all over the world, each with just a two by one metre table to set out their wares, Sarah's insistence that either the owner or winemaker be present, often both, and never just a salesman. This gave *Decanter* readers the opportunity to meet characters as diverse as Al Brounstein from Napa Valley's Diamond Creek, to Henri Lurton of Ch. Brane-Cantenac and

Simon Barlow of South Africa's historic Rustenberg estate. Master Classes of First Growth Bordeaux or Grand Cru Burgundy were sold out and, spreading much further afield but never descending in quality, still are. It is a sad case that producers seldom meet the public who buy and drink their wines and at the DFWE as it is now known, they do. I was very pleased to be part of this new project.

1998 saw me getting involved in two more ventures, one in Rome and one in London, to spread the word of wine. The Rome venture came from an introduction by Hugh Johnson to Gelasio Gaetani d'Aragano Lovatelli, the most dashing and charismatic member of the Italian wine aristocracy it was possible to imagine, who introduced me to Roberto Wirth the owner of the Hassler Hotel, Rome's grandest establishment at the top of the Spanish Steps. Wirth owned another building, tall and narrow that abutted the Spanish Steps that had been abandoned for years in which he wished to open a wine school. The ground floor and first floor rooms of this five story building were window-less, so classrooms would fit in well with artificial light, a restaurant would be established on the third floor and two suites of rooms on the fourth and fifth floors, which could be accessed from the ground floor of the Hassler right opposite. Thus was formed *L'Académie du Vin di Roma* for which I set a tasting programme, visiting twice a year. In hindsight I don't think it was every supposed to be a long-term venture and it was wound up in 2005, but not before Ian D'Agata, an Italian-Canadian with a brilliant mind, palate and a passion for wine, had become involved. D'Agata is now the Jancis Robinson or Michel Bettane of Italy.

The London venture, Vinopolis-City of Wine, was altogether a different kettle of fish. This was the brainchild of Duncan Vaughan-Arbuckle, who, after retiring from the Army, had gone into the wine trade and had been the first person to bring cheap Bulgarian wines into the UK in vast quantities. Word got to me through Ben Howkins that he had come up with an idea named 'Wineworld' and had recently discovered two and a half acres of unused space under vast brick-built arches to support the railway lines running into Cannon Street Station. In meetings the year before Duncan had outlined his plans for a 'total wine tour experience' and now he had hundreds and hundreds of yards of soaring arches to put it in. This was too good to resist, even with the Paris debts still not totally paid off, and once again my bank manager came through for yet another roll of the

Spurrier wine dice. As the project began to come together, key players were Hugh Johnson, Adrian Webster, once Hugh's publisher and owner of a media company and Tony Hodges, a brilliant advertising man whose vision brought it to reality.

My early contribution, apart from the investment which was a drop in the ocean compared to the £26 million that had been spent by the time the doors first opened late that year, was to suggest a change of name from Wineworld to Vinopolis – City of Wine. There were eighteen different 'rooms', spaces devoted to each wine region or country, beginning with Georgia, where wine had been born in 8000 BC, moving through Greece and into France which had four rooms, including a reproduction of the Roman Arena in Orange for the Rhône Valley, a marvellous space for Italy where four Vespas were set up with a screen in front of the handle bars, on which one could careen through the vineyards and villages. Champagne was on an upper floor, with bubbles on the side of the elevator that took you there, the New World was represented in all its glory and exciting future, the Judgment of Paris receiving pride of place in the California room, South Africa a mass of flowers and fauna, 'pipes' of Port present in the Port room and on and so forth. It was quite, quite extraordinary and sadly a little before its time, if ever its time would have come, for London is well-served for the tourists we hoped to attract. Vinopolis served 150 wines by the glass from Cruover machines and had three restaurants which were themselves very successful, housed the Vinopolis Wine Academy which was my baby and became one of the most sought-after venues for brand launching and publicity parties, as we could cater for hundreds of guests in very special circumstances. We needed 250,000 visitors a year for the tours to make money and never got more than 100,000. It staggered on, with regular injections of capital to keep it going, until 2014, a full fifteen years of life and is now just a memory.

What is not a memory, however, is the Borough Market, which had been a food and produce market since the 12th century, situated near Southwark Cathedral on the banks of the Thames, the City of London being the centre for commerce and habitation right up to the Fire of London in 1666. The market had run down to almost nothing, but the opening of Vinopolis gave it a new lease of life and it is now thriving so strongly that it is one of the most visited attractions in London. A debt is owed to the vision of Duncan Vaughan-Arbuckle and Tony Hodges, to the courage of the investors and while Vinopolis-City of Wine was good while it lasted, it has left a permanent impression with the Borough Market. Another positive influence from Vinopolis's 'before its time' optimism was on the huge *Civilisation du Vin* wine museum that opened in 2016 at the far end of the Bordeaux City docks. Sylvie Cazes, sister to Jean-Michel Cazes of Château Lynch-Bages and many other Bordeaux estates, visited Vinopolis twice as a director of the budding Bordeaux venture to see how the visions compared. When the latter finally opened after long delays and vastly over budget, I bet Véronique Sanders of Château Haut-Bailly a bottle of her wine against a bottle of Bride Valley that it wouldn't work, but would also be seen as 'too big to fail' and would survive un-loved but supported by the city of Bordeaux. My view was that the locals wouldn't visit and that tourists would either wish to be in the beautiful city of Bordeaux itself, or be up in the increasingly tourist-friendly vineyards. I am happy to say that after the first year I had resoundingly lost my bet.

It is interesting to look back after two decades on two articles I wrote in 1998, one on Beaujolais and one on Riesling to see that what I thought was happening then has only really happened now. The Beaujolais came from *L'Académie Internationale du Vin's* Spring Symposium organised by member Claude Geoffroy of Château Thivin in Côte de Brouilly. Over three days we tasted wines across all of the ten *crus* and I noted that 'the producers are ending the century convinced of the uniqueness and pleasure-giving qualities of their product'. Sadly, the wine drinking public was not and the region suffered economic decline until recently when outside investment, particularly from Burgundy and final recognition of the uniqueness of the Gamay grape grown on Beaujolais' granite soil has focussed attention on these under-valued wines. My article on Riesling opened with me saying that 'there appears no doubt that Riesling is finally making a comeback'. Wine merchant Jasper Morris held a tasting dinner with wines from his suppliers Randall Grahm (California), André Ostertag (Alsace) and Johannes Selbach (Mosel), noting that 'Riesling is the grape that has the greatest range of flavours, with the ability to change according to where it is grown, remaining true to itself while reflecting the terroir. It thus makes a wine of identity.' Randall Grahm went further: 'What is Riesling? A lost cause? A challenge? It is the ugly duckling, the Cinderella of grapes: it should be at the ball wearing the crown, but often ends up taking out the garbage.' Britain's greatest supporter of Riesling is

Jancis Robinson and even she admits that only in the last few years has her faith been recognised. The wine trade, always on the lookout for the next new thing, has often ignored what is in front of its very eyes.

A visit in the spring took me to Burgundy, which had rolled through the 1990s with continuing increases in quality and vineyard definition thanks largely to turning their attention from the cellars back to the soil. Some years before the agronomist and later AIV member Claude Bourguignon had shocked the region by remarking that 'there was less active life in the soil of the Côte d'Or than in the Sahara Desert'. Already Domaines Lafon, Leflaive and Leroy were farming according to biodynamic principles, as was Aubert de Villaine of the Domaine de la Romanée-Conti (DRC) who described his winemaking technique as 'picking the grapes when they are fully ripe and then doing as little as possible'. If Burgundy was good then, due to the increasing health of its vineyards, it is a true benchmark today, but the problem, more so today, was already a shortage of stock. I ended my piece saying that 'this century the years ending in '9' have been, with the exception of 1909 and 1939, both successful and plentiful. Why should 1999 break the mould?' It did not and those with 1999s still in their cellars are very lucky.

A first for me in 1999 was to attend the *en primeur* tastings organised the first week in April by *L'Union des Grands Crus* (UGC) around the major Bordeaux appellations. During this time both merchants and journalists descend to taste the wines from the previous vintage, sometimes at the châteaux themselves, more often in the tastings organised by the UGC to show the wines of its members. Representing *Decanter*, I was joined by Michael Broadbent, who asked me to make all the appointments necessary to taste those wines outside those of the UGC and we would be joined by a few fellow journalists and the occasional local such as John Salvi MW and his wife Nellie and later on by Fiona Thienpont MW, wife of Jacques Thienpont of Le Pin. Our little band became known as 'The Broadbent-Spurrier Group' to morph into 'The Robinson-Spurrier Group' when Michael retired and Jancis Robinson MW joined the team. Appointments were made on a half hour basis with geographical calculations to be followed with military precision. Usually one can be a little late for appointments, known in the region as *le quart d'heure Médocain* but we could not be and were not. The UGC tastings were segregated into those who wished to taste 'blind' and those who didn't, Michael and I being amongst the latter, Jancis Robinson, Michel Bettane and Stephen Brook (author of *The Complete Bordeaux*) being amongst the former. While at *Decanter* tastings and all wine competitions I taste blind, in Bordeaux I did not, for the label gives me the information I need about the estate, its style and its track record, while I try to keep an un-influenced judgement. It is often asked how wines at just six months can be judged and the simple answer is that they are judged on that day for potential. While I could not guarantee that my tasting of the eleven *Crus Classés* of Saint-Julien would be identical both blind and open, what I do know is that the labels will have given me enough background to make a more informed judgement than if I just had the glass in front of me, and this makes sense both to me and for readers of *Decanter*. One of my articles around this time was entitled 'Against tasting wine blind' and I stand by my conclusions.

Some of the very greatest non-blind tastings I have taken part in over the years have been organised by Indian-born, Los Angeles-based nuclear physicist Bipin Desai and in early February I spent three days in Los Angeles to taste every single wine ever produced by Paul Draper of Ridge Vineyards in California's Santa Cruz Mountains. Paul Draper, who had trained both in the Old World at Château Latour and in the New World in Chile, was elected *Decanter*'s Man of the Year 2000, an accolade that this tasting showed was richly deserved. (After this news became public I received a telephone call from Warren Winiarski of Stag's Leap Wine Cellars who asked me one simple question: 'Why wasn't it me?'. Well, it wasn't.) I described Bipin as a 'collector' even though the word offended him due to its connotations of possessive hoarding, preferring to define collecting as 'a search for knowledge, a continual pursuit of greatness in wine. The purpose is to experience greatness and my tastings allow many other people to do the same.'

I had first met Bipin Desai in the 1980s in Paris, where he was collecting wines from Domaines Lafon and Leflaive and also the 'La La's' from Guigal, some of which I could supply him with. I became a regular guest at this Paris tastings, always held at Taillevent Restaurant. I have in front of me menus and tasting notes from three of these that featured Classic Clarets, always with the owners present. In September 2006 it was Château Angelus from 1953 to 2004. Then in December 2006 it was the turn of Châteaux Langoa and Léoville-Barton from 1950 to 2003, co-hosted by Anthony and Eva Barton. Anthony Barton noted that 1985, the first wine he made entirely on his own, was his favourite wine and that while the 1986 would probably last longer, it would never be so attractive. Clive Coates MW remarked that the 1986s were 'not cuddly', to be asked by Anthony 'do we make wines to cuddle?' The only wine that had faded was the 1955, but I had enjoyed this vintage forty years previously, having been given a bottle by Anthony's Uncle Ronald to take with me for lunch on the way to Pamplona for the bullfights, chosen by him because it had 'no sediment, a perfect picnic wine'. Then in December 2007 Bipin held a memorable lunch to celebrate Thierry Manoncourt's 90th birthday, with Château Figeac from 1943 to 2005. Here, the 1955 was on splendid form, the 1964 quite extraordinary and the 1982 justifying the reputation of that year. The last of the Desai-Taillevent events I attended was on Château Calon-Segur, featuring the famous 1947 and the one before that was Château Montrose. Back in 1999 I noted that 'if Bipin Desai did not exist, passionate wine lovers would have to invent him'. He has been a beacon in my life in wine.

The AIV's Spring Symposium that year was in Austria, ranging from Schloss Seggau in Styria, an historic bishop's palace on the borders of Slovenia, to the Esterhazy Palace in Eisenstadt, where we were treated to a concert by the Haydn Quartet – Joseph Haydn lived at the palace for thirty years and part of his salary was paid in wine. We went on to Rust where Hugh Johnson has compared their *Ausbruch* sweet white wines to the Hungarian aszu wines from Tokaji and finally to Kamptal in the Wachau region, home to the Bründlmeyer Estate at Langenlois. With 50 hectares and every vintage from 1947 in his cellar, Willi Bründlmeyer blends tradition and innovation to produce wines from his magnificent-ly-sited Grüner Veltliner and Riesling that combine ripeness and finesse, which he referred to as 'the tenderness of wine' to a remarkable degree. In 1996 Brundlmeyer leased the thirty-five hectare estate of Schloss Gobelsburg, a centuries' old monastery and installed the magnificent-ly-named Micky Moosbrugger, a former chef, as winemaker. I returned in 2016 for the 30th Anniversary and recognised the words carved on the portico, which appear on all the wine labels: 'God sees those who drink good wine'. After lunch in the monastery cloisters, I had to leave, but miss-ing the AIV's Gala Dinner was more than made up for by being present at the 50th birthday party of Tim Johnston, owner of Juveniles, the most Rhône Ranger wine bar in Paris. As the 1983s of Chave's Hermitage and

Clape's Cornas gave way to magnums of Château de Mont Redon 1967 from Châteauneuf-du-Pape, the transition from Grüner Veltliner to old Grenache seemed divinely inspired.

The decade ended with *Decanter*'s final request from its columnists of their 'six best wines of the year' before turning to a different format in the new millennium. The pleasure of submitting an 'end of term' report made me realise that at a time when wines that are recognised as great, as opposed to merely fashionable, are harder and harder to come by, the willingness of their owners to pull the corks seems to confirm the fundamental truth that fine wines are best enjoyed in the company of those who appreciate them. This is not elitism, just common sense. This year's six fought to the top through stiff competition: Haut-Brion Blanc 1948, Vouvray Le Haut Lieu 1947 Domaine Huët, Haut-Brion 1966, Hermitage La Chapelle 1961 Paul Jaboulet Aîné, Fonseca 1983 and Yalmuba Old Four Crowns Port 1889. Each wine was extraordinary, with the exception of the Haut-Brion 1966 which was just simply beautiful. Leafing through the dozens of wines that were almost equally fabulous, what is it that made those wines so special? For me, the answer lies in a combination of acknowledged quality, probable rarity and an element of surprise. These wines will have all surpassed my expectations while leaving behind a certainty that I could never again drink the same wine with so much pleasure. How a particular wine can be so good combines total satisfaction, a touch of mystery and an undeniable sense of privilege.

The Spurrier family welcomed the New Year 2000 in Dorset over some very good wines, starting with Champagnes from the 1990 vintage, my favourite being Pol Roger and ending with a 1900 Madeira. Starting the new decade, what was to be one of the best, though far from the most comfortable trips of my life, was in mid March to Georgia, the cradle of wine, where the Tbilisi State Museum shows evidence of grape pips and vessels for wine making dating from 8000BC. The visit was organised by Georgian Wines and Spirits (GWS) a company benefitting from a substantial investment by Pernod-Ricard that is spearheading a crusade for quality in the world's oldest wine producing country. It was thanks to Hugh Johnson's involvement in Vinopolis-City of Wine that a wine pitcher from 6000 BC and a golden drinking cup that had been dated a mere 2000 years younger and many other objects from the museum were reproduced to be shown in the opening room of the Vinopolis tour.

Accompanying me were Nicholas Faith, whose books on Champagne and Cognac were recognised classics and Sophia Gilliatt, both involved in the Vinopolis venture.

Historically famous, the wines of Georgia had almost ceased to exist. Having been a major supplier to Russia's Imperial Court, after a very brief period of independence (1918-21) the Bolsheviks invaded and the wines were lost to the outside world. Production and distribution were centrally planned and quality plummeted. Even the 400 million litres that Georgia produced satisfied only 14% of Soviet demand, so fakes abounded, especially since all the bottling was done in Russia. When the USSR collapsed in 1990, Georgia found itself with ruined vineyards, no conception of the demands from the real world and just two functioning wineries. Only the memory of what the wines had once been like remained. We were in the hands of Levan Gachechiladze of GWS, who was setting up a Wine Institute that would impose regulations from vine to wine and with support from the *Office Internationale du Vin* (OIV) in Paris, the aim was to form the basis of a system of *Appelation Controlée*. I am happy to say that this has been achieved At that time, most of Georgia's vineyards were in the Kakheti Valley, which begins an hour or so's drive northwest of Tbilisi. Of 500 indigenous grape varieties only a dozen were then planted. Rkatsitelli made a fragrant crisp white, while Mtsvane was fuller and fruitier, the best white wine being Tsinandali, a blend of the two. Saperavi virtually monopolised red wine production, its grippiness reminding me of Sangiovese, while the less-planted Matrassa was more plummy with lower tannins. GWS's top brand was 'Tamada' (toastmaster) and at our lengthy lunches and dinners which were served à la Russe, the tables groaning with dishes in no discernible order, many toasts were proposed and enjoyed. After four days I had come to the conclusion that with the Saperavi grape the Georgians had created a 'hangover free wine', for however much I drank, my head was quite clear the next day. So, at a late breakfast on our final morning deep in the countryside, carafes of Saperavi accompanied the usual jugs of fruit juice and I thought, despite the raised eyebrows of my companions, that a glass would do me no harm. This was a mistake, for an hour later I was smitten with the accumulated result of four days of keeping up with the Georgians. I was back in Tbilisi in October 2017 to find both the city and its wines vastly improved, but I did not drink at breakfast again.

My first visit to Slovenia in late May was to taste a very wide range of wines organised by Robert Gorjak, a young wine educator who Bella and I had met in Montalcino a couple of years earlier on one of the *Ante Prima* tasting weeks organised by the Consorzios of Chianti Classico, Vino Nobile de Montepulciano and Brunello di Montalcino. I had not set foot in this country since our 'magical mystery tour' in summer 1965, when it was part of Yugoslavia under the control of President Tito. Erika Schule-Grosso, the UK head of the Relais et Château group was involved and the two days of tasting were to be held in Villa Bled, now Slovenia's grandest hotel on the shores of Lake Bled, then President Tito's personal residence and before that one of the family homes of the Habsburgs. I was offered President Tito's suite which could have housed several families in comfort. To see some of the countryside, I was taken to Movia, a wine estate that crossed the border between Slovenia and Italy run by the charismatic but slightly mad Aleš Kristančič. This was the only estate that had remained in family hands during the Yugoslavia times, since it produced Tito's favourite wines and he quite rightly recognised that they would not remain so in the hands of the State. They were brilliant, if eccentric, while the quality of the less famous wines shown to me by Robert were a revelation of natural fruit and purity of expression. In 2004, the first year of the *Decanter* World Wine Awards, I chose Robert Gorjak as Regional Chair for Slovenia, and over 100 wines were entered, winning several Gold Medals. Robert still tastes for the DWWA, but now being export director for Dveri Pax one of Slovenia's historic estates, he can no longer represent his country as an independent judge.

On 18 June that year, exactly nineteen years after the tenth anniversary for the Caves de la Madeleine, Bella and I threw a big lunch party in Paris, taking over the Lebanese restaurant downstairs, to celebrate twenty-five years at 7 rue de la Cerisaie, the flat I had kept on, with Annie Bingham paying half the modest rent. A year or so later the owner of the building offered us money to leave, as the place could be re-let for double. Annie found a place nearby, and for us on our visits back to the City of Light it would be hotels – actually often The Travellers Club on the Champs-Elysées, the *hôtel particulier* of one of Paris's most famous *grandes horizontales* as such courtesans were known in the years of *La Belle Epoque*, for it has a reciprocal arrangement with Boodle's in London.

In late July Bella and I were in Seattle for the biannual World Vinifera

Conference accompanied by Sarah Kemp, her husband Brian St Pierre, who I had first met in 1976 in San Francisco. Bella and I then hired a car and drove down Route 1 through Oregon down into Napa, ending up staying with Warren Winiarski in one of the guest houses at Stag's Leap Wine Cellars. The Wine Country was hardly recognisable from my first visit in the mid 1970s, Napa being, in Warren's words 'at the stage of the Médoc in the late 19th century – we are turning wine into art and it is now a cultural phenomenon.' In earlier days he said that wine needed 'the 3 'g's – the ground, the grape and the guy/gal' but he had now progressed to requiring the 3 'v's -vineyards, vision and vitality. Thanks to a $20 million endowment from Robert and Margrit Mondavi, Copia – The American Centre for Wine, Food and the Arts, would open in downtown Napa on Thanksgiving Day 2001. This was to be 'a cultural institution, museum and educational centre dedicated to exploring the American contribution of wine and food in close association with the arts and humanities, and to celebrate these as unique expressions of American life, culture and heritage.' It housed, amongst other things, Julia Child's kitchen and the largest collection of tea pots I have ever seen, but it was too good for commercial Napa and very sadly closed its doors. This was in the future and during our visit we attended a dinner given my Al Brounstein of Diamond Creek Vineyards in honour of Jean-Claude Rouzaud of Louis Roederer. Warren was one the many speakers at dinner, expounding on the three 'v's and the cultural phenomenon. In the car on the way back, I asked him about Washington State and Oregon. 'Oh', he replied, 'they're still at the wine stage.'

Undoubtedly the highspot of the year 2000 was a three-day event hosted by Rhône expert John Livingstone-Learmonth in and around Gigondas. For some time John, author of *The Wines of the Rhone* had been planning a dinner at Les Florets in Gigondas to celebrate his 50th birthday. A substantial bet on Sinndar at 16/1 to win the Derby, topped up by un-patriotically backing France to wine Euro 2000, persuaded him that this should be extended over a weekend, to which he asked 60 willing contestants. His personal version of *Les Trois Glorieuses* was timed to begin on the first Friday in November, but Bella and I went down a day early to get into training, staying with Julian and Sheila More above Visan. Arriving at our hotel in Vacqueyras, we found a list of 'The Runners' with John's assessment of our bloodlines, form and chances of survival. My own entry ran:

'A wise old pro of the Rhône, although still dresses more like a Bordeaux man...has a lively running style.' The group split into two the first evening, mine having the advantage of Fiona, John's saxophone-playing wife as hostess. The next day we were further broken up and I led a dozen of the runners to Château de Beaucastel to be welcomed by Jean-Pierre and François Perrin and then lunch on the terrace at La Table du Verger in Châteauneuf-du-Pape, followed by a tasting with Daniel Brunier at Domaine du Vieux Télégraphe. Before leaving our hotel for the birthday dinner at Les Florets, some of us enjoyed an aperitif of Vacqueyras Blanc to prepare us for the avalanche of wines from domaines that John had known since the early 1970s. Well-rested after a late night, Sunday morning found us all welcomed by the Mayor of Châteauneuf-du-Pape, who made John an honorary citizen of this historic little town, followed by an aperitif of four white 1999 Châteauneufs. Lunch at La Mère Germaine presented us with a further three whites, before moving onto three superb reds served in magnums: Clos Mont Olivet 1994, Roger Sabon 1992 and Bosquets des Papes 1989. The meal continued, with jazz from Fiona, until 6pm but, although I was running true to form, Bella had me pulled up at 4pm to catch a train to Paris. Thank you Seagull (as I always call him) and Sinndar for a memorable weekend.

For a few years now I have catalogued my Dorset cellar at the end of every year. I was initially only there at weekends, often due to travel but was much more there now due to Bride Valley Vineyard and less travel. I kept a note of everything we drank when I was there. My brother Nicky, who is brilliant with computers, gave me a 'cellar plan' but I have never been able to figure it out, so I just use last year's printed list, cross off the bottles opened, add those purchased and on 1 January go down to the cellar to check the stock against my list – Bella and the children will have drunk some – and come up with a new list and start all over again. As a wedding present Bella and I received a tome called *The Wine Cellar Book* from Sir Sacheverell Sitwell, a friend of her father. Despite a few years in the wine trade, I couldn't make head or tail of it, and mentioned this to my father-in-law, who passed in onto Georgia, the renowned author's wife, to get the reply: 'the present is not necessarily to be used, for the point is that it has been signed by Sacheverell.' So in March 2001 I entitled a column 'My cellar in the next millennium' noting that the results 'confirmed my preferences and prejudices in a way that makes me feel comfortably old-fashioned (at 59)' At 76, the cellar is still almost entirely European, but it does show a slight shift in focus. At the end of 2000 there were 2,860 bottles and at the end of 2016 this had risen to 3,580 – the great André Simon died with just one bottle in his cellar, a Pommery Champagne but this will not be the case with me – and here are a few comparisons in percentage terms from then to now: Claret 43.8%/36%; Red Burgundy 12.4%/15%; White Burgundy 8.8%/9.6%; Red Rhône 8.9%/16.5%; Italy 4%/8.5%; Iberia 0.1%/3.4%; New World 2%/5.9%; Vintage Port 6.5%/4.6%. A wine collector 'slims down the cellar' rather than selling, and unless I do some slimming down on the Port front, the 180 bottles of which only 3 are opened a year will see out my children. This said, I have 'laid down' 6 bottles each of 2011 Cockburn, Croft, Dow, Fonseca, Graham and Taylor for my grandsons.

Certainly the most interesting trip of 2001 was to New Orleans and later to Nashville in May, recorded in my column as 'Wining and dining in the Deep South'. This happened to be the 25th anniversary of the Judgement of Paris, and I was once again 'joined at the hip' with Warren Winiarski at the 10th New Orleans Wine and Food Experience. The scene was set with an opening dinner at Galatoire's, the French Quarter's most famous restaurant and continued with a surprise lunch with Bartholomew Broadbent at the Acme Oyster House, another New Orleans institution. There were many grand tastings held over two days, the Best of Show Award going to Beaulieu Vineyards Georges de Latour Private Reserve 1997, which harked back to the superb wines made by André Tchelistcheff. Later that year, BV would celebrate the centenary of the birth of California's greatest winemaker, and little did I know that in February 2017 I would be in Berlin for the Berlinale Film Festival for the world premiere of *André, the Voice of Wine,* a film tracing his life from the Russian Revolution to the Napa Valley, made by his great-nephew Marc. The 1976 Judgement of Paris plays a part, for both Mike Grgich and Warren Winiarski, whose wines won on that day, were trained by André Tchelistcheff.

To take a break and see for the first time some of the country, Bella and I drove off on a roundabout route via the cotton town of Natchez with its marvellous antebellum houses, on to Jackson, Oxford home to the University of Mississippi, to Memphis to visit Graceland and eat vast slaps of ribs in the downtown Rendezvous restaurant and finally to Nashville for Un Eté du Vin. Un Eté du Vin, a wine weekend whose purpose is to raise money for the American Cancer Society, was started in July 1980 by local businessman Tom Milam who organised a wine tasting followed by an informal auction that raised $3,000. When I first visited Nashville, in one of my Michael Broadbent's understudy roles, the top lot at auction was a private collection of Château Mouton-Rothschild in magnums spanning 100 years – the 1945 at the gala dinner received a spontaneous standing ovation - and over $600,000 was raised. In 2001, with the auction catalogue bursting with once-in-a-lifetime lots that included fifty vintages of Pétrus from 1924 to 1998 and a bottle of every vintage of Stag's Leap Wine Cellars Cask 23, Fay and SLV vineyards ever made between 1972 and 1995 – Warren himself was of course present – put together by wine collector Tom Black, down to lunch for two couples with me at Vinopolis, to raise $1.2 million. Two things fuel such remarkable events: the passion and generosity of the donors and spenders and the altruism of the US tax system. Donors can write off the cost of their donations at open market value and the buyer can write off every cent above this value. Even guests attending the gala dinner at $5,000 per couple can write off everything except the cost of the food, the wines (of course) being offered by patrons and written off accordingly. One can only imagine how much more fun and successful fundraising events would be in the UK, were Her Majesty's Revenue and Customs (HMRC) quite so generous.

I turned sixty on 5 October 2001 and spent the weekend celebrating. First was a lunch at the Chelsea Arts Club on the day itself. (The Chelsea Arts Club 'founded by artists for artists in 1891' is a splendid example of bohemian life that London has almost entirely lost and a complete contrast to the bespoke Boodle's, my other Club in St James's Street. Fortunately, I am now a Life Member of both, so neither of them can throw me out for bad behaviour.) A suitable number of forty-one people much enjoyed an English meal of scallops with pea purée, rack of Welsh lamb, English cheeses and a fine chocolate birthday cake and consumed the well-balanced quantities of ten bottles of Pierre Gimonnet 1er Cru Blanc de Blancs, 10 bottles of Bernard Morey Chassagne-Montrachet 1er Cru Les Caillerets 1995, twenty bottles of Château d'Angludet 1982 and eight bottles of Vouvray Moelleux 1990 Domaine Foreau, all of which were drinking superbly as I had hoped. Bella had booked us and two of our closest friends on a late afternoon Eurostar, which, after a few glasses of

Champagne and a short sleep, deposited us at the Gare du Nord in Paris from where we crossed the street to the Brasserie du Nord for oysters and Sancerre.

The next event the following day was dinner for my friends in France at Maceo, Mark Williamson's restaurant next door to his Willi's Wine Bar, in the splendidly large, mirror-lined private dining room on the first floor overlooking Paris's most beautiful restaurant, Le Grand Véfour. Thirty of us sat down, after some superb Billecart-Salmon Champagne served from jeroboams, to *gambas grillés, canard sauvage au cassis, brebis fermier* and *raisins en gelée vigneronne*. After the classic wines the day before, Mark had suggested Rhône and Provence, the final selection being Alain Graillot white Crozes-Hermitage 2000, André Perret Saint-Joseph 1999, Château de Pibarnon 1997, my favourite Bandol after Domaine Tempier, in magnums, and Berthet-Blondet Vin de Paille 1996. Despite the calming presence of MWs James Lawther and John Salvi, we continued into the early hours drinking more Billecart-Salmon, this time from magnums.

Le Prix de l'Arc de Triomphe, the final and most prestigious race of the flat season, is held at Longchamp on the first Sunday in October. For years, while we lived in Paris, this gave me an excuse to give a party on the Saturday night, being so close to my birthday, which was always followed by a huge picnic on the racecourse, with food provided by the restaurant I then owned and wines from the Caves. Mark Williamson, Tim Johnston (Juveniles Wine Bar), Drew Harre (Cosi, Fish, and now Semilla and Frenchies) and the various other members of Le Mafia Anglais, as we were known, have carried on the tradition and it was Tim who carved out a square in *le parking* for *un déjeuner sur l'herbe* that included some survivors from the night before. A late dinner at La Fermette Marbeuf, the most perfectly restored Art Nouveau restaurant in Paris, concluded the weekend celebrations.

In November 2001, I spent a magical day at Louis Jadot in Beaune to celebrate thirty years of inspired winemaking by Jacques Lardière, which ended suitably on a ninety year old wine. The morning tasting concentrated on the Jadot holdings in Bonnes-Mares and Corton-Pougets, with Lardière remarking that 'only a great terroir permits a wine to age properly and it is only by ageing properly that a wine can express its terroir.' The guest list was certainly not limited to Burgundians and after asking Michel Rolland, Bordeaux's pre-eminent wine consultant, to name his favourite Corton Pougets (1978 and 1971), the young Pierre-Henry Gagey of Jadot remarked that 'when I was young, we talked about Bordeaux as a colour, but we never drank it; now we go there.' After a light lunch we returned for a range of 29 vintages of Corton-Charlemagne before reuniting for dinner served in Jadot's Couvent des Jacobins. A golden and nutty 1976 Chevalier-Montrachet Les Demoiselles preceded a rich, dense, truffly 1952 Richebourg, ending with a 1911 Corton. In a moving speech, Jacques Lardière said that 'wines should always surprise you and without this capacity they are dead. These wines possessed individuality, generosity, passion and fidelity, transcendent qualities that make them eternal.'

For a change I was not travelling in early 2002 and time was put to good use as Oz Clarke's publisher Adrian Webster had commissioned a book called *The Clarke-Spurrier Guide to Fine Wines*. I was to write all of France and Oz and his team of helpers were to write the rest. It was at least a decade since I had updated *The Académie du Vin Guide to French Wines* and this was a good excuse to bring myself up to speed on facts, while being just as personal in my opinions. It was well-received, won a prize or two, was re-printed and then, like most wine books, faded into history. I had never thought of writing another book until this one.

Two tastings early that year – 1986 clarets and 1977 Vintage Ports – caused me to pen a column entitled 'When to drink fine wine'. I had begun to think that, with all the information available, there were no more mysteries surrounding the optimum date to pull the cork, but these tastings reminded me that there are no rules, only preferences. The only certainty, as Jancis Robinson realised, 'is that one never knows for sure when a wine has reached its peak until that peak is past'. The French, as a whole, avoid this problem by drinking their wines young, enjoying them both for the moment and for their rosy future, while the less sybaritic Anglo-Saxons, having anticipated pleasure for years, sometimes wait too long. Clive Coates MW, who had hosted the Port Tasting that showed most of the houses that had declared a vintage that year, thought that the best had another decade before reaching their absolute peak, while I questioned waiting that long. I seem to have followed my own advice, as I now only have six bottles – 3 Gould Campbell, 2 Taylor and 1 Dow – of this great vintage left in the Dorset cellar.

Most thoughts of wine were suspended by the death of my mother on 13 August. She had been in good health at eighty-six, a little bent from arthritis and on her 85th birthday all the family was present in the Jockey Club at Wincanton Racecourse on 22 October meeting for lunch in her honour. I still have my entry badge, slipped around the neck of an empty bottle of 1900 Madeira, in my Dorset study as I write this. In early July the next year she had had a slight heart attack while driving home, her car going off the road and turning over. Visiting her in hospital a few days later, sitting up in bed wearing discreet make-up and a string of pearls, she complained that the last time she had been in hospital was in Cambridge in 1941 to have me and insisted on being taken home. The doctors agreed and nurses were arranged. At the end of that month she retired to bed, but not before persuading Bella and me to take our usual August holiday and we said goodbye knowing that we would certainly not see her again. Christian and Kate visited in early August to be given a loving and very frail farewell. We called the nurses every day and then it was all over. I had always been somewhat detached from my parents, as they were from me, but we loved and respected each other deeply. It was the end of an era. There was a funeral service at her village Wick St Lawrence near Bristol and then we followed the coffin to Marston, where after a longer service it was lowered into my father's grave. The headstone had all the usual inscriptions, matching those of four centuries of Spurriers nearby, yet all my mother requested to be added above her dates was 'and Pamela, his Wife'.

A long-planned visit to the Douro in early October began as a Symington sandwich. Only a cup of coffee on the early morning flight from Gatwick to Oporto had separated the splendid magnums of Graham 1970, presented by Clare Symington at the Michael Broadbent Tribute Dinner at Spencer House the evening before, from Dow's Midnight, the Symington's newest Port, on arrival with Bella at Vila Nova de Gaia. This and the twenty-eight other Ports and seven table wines that followed, put into motion the British sandwich of Symington and Taylor with a slice of Quinta do Noval in the middle. Lunching and dining in the Douro on plainly cooked local dishes is the moment for older vintages to appear. Of the many superb wines, four stood out for me at that time: the nectar-like Taylor 1966, the amazing Quinta do Noval Nacional 1963 described by Serena Sutcliffe as 'nirvana', the indestructible Dow 1945 and Noval's ethereal wood-aged 1937 Colheita. Nor should I ignore the raisiny sweet Taylor thirty year-old Tawny, two bottles of which were placed in front of me alongside a single candle to celebrate my 61st birthday with Alastair and Gillyanne Robertson at Quinta do Vargellas. Instead of merely asking you to sign the visitors' book and record your thanks for such wonderful hospitality, the Robertsons prefer that their guest write a poem instead. Thus they possess a walk down memory lane ranging from perfect pentametres to downright doggerel. My effort falls into the latter category:

> 'To have one's birthday at Vargellas
> Is not the luck of many fellas,
> Where Gilly's hospitality dims
> Two days of supping with the Syms,
> And Alastair's infectious charm
> Convinces me that there's no harm
> In thinking that the vines *en face* (belonging to Cockburn)
> Produce wine that's only good, alas,
> For putting in a standard blend,
> While all the grapes around us end
> In Vargellas, or the 'Nec
> Plus Ultra' of the Taylor deck.
> And if such thoughts help make me merrier,
> They're further helped by Laurent Perrier.'

One of the guests a few pages before me had been Len Evans, the great Welsh-Australian wine impresario, who had conceived several stanzas in praise of Port, but ending each with the lament 'But Port makes me fart!'

2002 closed and 2003 opened with Bella and me going to Australia in late December, beginning with friends in Perth, on to Margaret River, the first of many visits, then deep-water fish watching off the Gold Coast to join her younger sister Caroline (Baffy) and husband Jamie in time for Christmas in Melbourne. Jamie, a polished player of Real Tennis, was representing his Club in the Over 50s team for a series of matches in Melbourne and Sydney.

Back home, I headed up one of the Gidleigh Park wine weekends that I had been doing off and one for a few years, this time based on Piedmont and Tuscany. American ex-banker and wine lover Paul Henderson with his English wife had taken over this rambling hotel deep in Dartmoor two decades previously and had built it up to be one of the finest of the English Country House Hotels as they were known, with a Michelin-starred cuisine, marvellously comfortable rooms and long treks across the moors designed to work up an appetite. Between two splendid dinners, Paul had raided his cellar for a Saturday morning tasting of eighteen Super Tuscans from 1997 to 1985, focussing mostly on Ornellaia, Sassicaia, Solaia and Tignanello. Ornellaia, a 135 hectare estate near to Bolgheri and part of the Antinori inheritance from the della Gherardesca estates of Piero and Lodovico Antinori's mother, was the brainchild of Lodovico and there is general agreement that it has equalled – even surpassed in some vintages – that of their cousin's Sassicaia estate. Two years earlier I had taken part in a vertical tasting of Ornellaia's Masseto, from the six hectares on the estate that André Tchelistcheff had insisted, against the advice of Bordeaux's Professor Peynaud, that Lodovico plant 100% to Merlot. In the early years Lodovico found that Masseto was behaving more like Cabernet Sauvignon, retaining a certain leanness and grip, so at Vinexpo in June 1991 he approached Michel Rolland , who was to take total overall charge from 1995, reducing yields by 30% and selecting French oak specifically for the blend. The 1995 proved to be the turning point and now, although the ownership of Ornellaia has passed into the hands of the Frescobaldi family, Masseto, thanks to Lodovico's vision and flair, is one of Italy's very greatest wines. But at Gidleigh Park we concentrated on the four other 'Super Tuscans', me rating the first-growth style Ornellaia above Sassicaia, while the 1999 vintages of Tignanello and Solaia were nothing short of sensational.

The major event of early summer 2003 was the wedding of our daughter Kate to Andrew Richards over the weekend of 9-11 May. She was married in the village church, arriving with me in a fine horse drawn carriage and that evening 150 people sat down under a marquee for dinner and dancing. The weather held out and there was a Sunday brunch for as many again. Bella and I took ourselves off to Naples to relax after all the work, then I was off in early June to Tokyo for a week of the Japan Wine Challenge and later that month to Vinexpo, where Sarah Kemp and I were to present our project for the *Decanter* World Wine Awards (DWWA) wine competition, which came to fruition in April 2004 with 4,500 wines entered; in 2017 it received just over 18,000 entries, confirming its position for some years now as the largest and most influential wine competition in the world.

I am often asked what, in my life in wine, I am most proud of and I always reply that it was the creation of *L'Académie du Vin*. The Judgement of Paris of course cemented my reputation, but the DWWA would run *L'Académie* pretty close. For a little time I had been pushing Sarah to create a *Decanter* wine competition and she always pushed back by saying '*Decanter* does events, not competitions.' Then, a month or so before Vinexpo, she said 'Steven, I think the time is right, you set the rules and we'll present it at Vinexpo.' The rules were to be the same as I had imposed on the JWC, when I took it over from Robert Joseph: tasting sitting down on tables of four with a senior judge per table, flights of not more than twelve wines, taste like with like in price brackets with full information except the name of the wine and elect a Regional Chair for each country or major wine region. By the time we unveiled the plans at Vinexpo, the original fourteen regional chairs had been selected, not a few pinched from the IWC, with a contract only to taste for *Decanter*, and several dozen others lined up with a one year's contract. The rules were simple and have been refined but not changed.

Vinexpo 2003 took place in a heatwave that preceded the hottest European summer on record. Temperatures moved above 40 degrees centigrade, the halls of the exhibition had no air conditioning and bottles were literally popping their corks as one walked by. But the heat was nothing to the storm that exploded over Saint Emilion the evening of the *Diner des Millésimes de Collection* held by the Premiers Grands Crus Classés. Here is what I wrote at the time:

'It was a dark and stormy night when I arrived late at Château La Gaffelière, an already threatening sky had turned black, torrential rain was falling and something like a tornado was buffeting the car as we turned into the drive to be met by a scene of destruction: the power of the rain had broken through the middle of the marquee, through which wind had torn, overturning tables set with Limoges china and Riedel glasses. Sarah Kemp had just been saved from a falling strut by David Elswood of Christie's, yet no one, in dinner jackets and female finery, had been hurt. After a few minutes, while owner Léo de Malet-Roquefort consoled his guests, Eric d'Aramon of Château Figeac, President of the Premiers Crus Classés, marshalled his troops. The kitchen tent of a Michelin-starred chef had been flattened, spoiling the entire dinner – from *Crumble de Foie Gras* to *Fraises du Bois Mara* – except for the cheese. With a glass and a napkin in our hands and rolls of bread in our pockets, we filed down into the cellars. Standing up, chatting cheerfully while eating bread and cheese in our fingers and appreciating wines from the 12 different châteaux from 1998 down to 1953, this party will be talked about long after other Vinexpo evenings have faded from memory.'

The true gentleman that he was, Léo de Malet-Roquefort opened his château again at Vinexpo 2005, this time with no disasters.

Certainly the most memorable tasting of 2003 was at a pre-sale black tie dinner at Christie's to experience three centuries of Château Latour. A little under nine years since its purchase by François Pinault from Allied Lyons, thus returning this First Growth Pauillac to French ownership after a hiatus of thirty-one years, Latour had emerged from a period of quiet renovation. Small quantities of 'library stocks' had been made available covering a total of 64 vintages from 1863 to 1996, wines at the dinner ranging from 1961 back to 1881, served from magnums, younger vintages being available at the pre-sale tasting. The nine older wines had all been re-corked at the château between 1990 and 1992. From the oldest trio of 1909, 1890 and 1881, the 1890 stood out being full of life, flavour and grip, quite stunning for a 113-year old wine, while the 1881 had kept a truffly fragrance. The next three were a solid and rich 1952, a rather medicinal 1937 and the revelation of the evening the 1924 with huge warmth and depth of flavour. After this the 1917 failed to shine, but the evening ended with two blockbusters: the 1961, whose intense colour revealed the pure concentration of Cabernet Sauvignon, and the historic 1945 which showed the energy and power from one of the greatest vintages of the 20th century. When the Pearson-Harvey consortium bought control of Latour from the de Beaumont and Contrivon families in 1962, the affair was reported to President General de Gaulle, who merely commented that 'they can hardly take the soil with them.' Whoever owns it, Château Latour belongs to the Médoc.

As if to confirm the rivalry between Bordeaux and Burgundy, another extraordinary wine experience of 2003 took place in Bouchard Père et Fils' 13th century cellars in the centre of Beaune during the November *Hospices de Beaune* weekend. Champagne's Joseph Henriot, who had purchased this grand Burgundy name and its stock of ancient vintages a decade earlier, had taken a lead from the very early vintage in this heatwave year, beginning on 21 August and finishing just one week later – the earliest harvest since 1731, coincidentally the same year that Bouchard Père et Fils was founded – to show early vintages back down to 1846. His premise, that these early vintages rely on fruit rather than acidity to keep them going, was borne out by a Meursault-Charmes 1953 (harvest date 14/9), a Corton-Charlemagne 1952 (18/9), a Meursault-Perrières 1947 (7/9) and a remarkable Meursault-Charmes 1846 (16/9) the oldest wine in the Bouchard cellars, thrice recorked, resembling a dry Amontillado that grew and grew in the glass. The reds were equally extraordinary, beginning with Savigny-les-Beaune Les Lavières 1976 (8/9) another heat-wave year, to be followed by Beaune-Marconnets 1959 (14/9), Beaune-Grèves Vigne de l'Enfant Jesus 1947 (7/9) the nearest vintage in style to 2003, Beaune Clos du Roi 1929 (25/9), a magnificent Romanée-St-Vivant 1906 (22/9) and even the Chassagne-Montrachet Morgeot 1893 (30/8) from pre-phylloxera vines still showed strength and vitality at 110 years old. The final wine of the dinner was Beaune-Grèves Vigne de l'Enfant Jesus 1865, acknowledged to be the greatest Burgundy vintage of the 19th century, still deep in colour, clear and limpid, fresh and sweet, marrying delicacy and power. Eight years previously I had attended a dinner where Joseph Henriot had ended with a Volnay-Santenots from the same year, but the Beaune, drunk on home ground, was even more memorable.

True to form, *L'Académie Internationale du Vin* launched into a bitter attack on what it called 'show off' wines at it annual conference in December. Under the title 'Wine or Jam', Rudolf Trefzer lambasted the interchangeable style – rich, ripe and oaky – of (mostly) French grape varieties made in the New World, which he characterised as 'entry-level drugs made to measure for wine novices.' His hope was for the abandonment of 'cult wines' and a return to the true culture of wine. 'Blockbuster' wines, once a curiosity, had become endemic. Yet this was not new and ten years previously I quoted French critic Michel Bettane as saying 'very soon we won't need to taste wines, we'll just weigh them.' During the meeting, Bruno Prats compared such wines to *vins de parade* or catwalk wines, saying that they were not made to be drunk but to have attention paid to them. Fortunately, the wine world woke up to this threat and a decade later the pendulum had swung firmly back to wines that were made to express, rather than to impress.

15. Free as a Bird

By this time the Paris debts had been paid off and I was back to buying the odd work of art, keeping up the cellar in Dorset and continuing to travel a lot so long as wine was involved and I was getting paid for it. Little did I think, when I accepted an invitation from Eduardo Chadwick to attend a tasting of his top Chilean wines – Don Maximiano, Seña and Viñedo Chadwick – at the recently opened Ritz Carlton in Berlin in late January 2004 that this event would find me travelling around the world with Eduardo, co-hosting events, for the next ten years.

I had never been to Berlin, nor had Bella, so we booked in for a long weekend and only when we arrived the afternoon before the tasting and met up with Eduardo, did I realise that his wines were going to be compared in a blind tasting to similar vintages of the First Growths of Bordeaux and the top Super Tuscans, the common theme being that all the wines were Bordeaux blends. About thirty of the best European palates and wine writers had been asked and that evening Eduardo hosted an overview of the wines of Chile which brought me up to date as I had been there only once, several years ago.

The following morning, René Gabriel, Switzerland's renowned wine expert from Geneva's Mövenpick, and I flanked Eduardo at a table in front of 40 guests. There were sixteen wines and once the results had been annotated, it fell to me to read out the results, going upwards from the tenth wine. I noticed that Eduardo smiled and visibly relaxed when he heard that Seña 2000 had tied for fourth place with Château Margaux 2001. Château Lafite-Rothschild 2000 was third, but, having already received the recognition he was after, Eduardo was hardly paying attention when I announced that Seña 2001 was ranked second and Viñedo Chadwick 2000 was first. Perhaps nobody in the room was more stunned and this event was immediately christened 'The Berlin Tasting' tipping its hat to 'The Paris Tasting' of 1976. The ranking of the wines on 23 January was:

1 – Viñedo Chadwick 2000
2 – Seña 2001

3 – Château Lafite-Rothschild 2000
4 – Château Margaux 2001
4 – Seña 2000
6 – Viñedo Chadwick 2001
6 – Château Margaux 2000
6 – Château Latour 2000
9 – Dom Mazimiano Founder's Reserve 2001
10 – Château Latour 2001
10 – Solaia 2000

What Eduardo Chadwick was looking for in 2004 was recognition that his wines, and by extension the best wines of Chile, could measure up to the benchmarks of the European wine world. This was exactly what I was after in 1976 for the Chardonnays and Cabernet Sauvignons from California and like Eduardo I was not expecting such a startling result with the 'upstarts' beating the benchmarks. Tasting such as these certainly have relevance, but they also bring surprise, even criticism and disbelief. It is therefore important to repeat them with the same wines in different places with different palates, but always blind. During the next decade I accompanied Eduardo to the following cities: San Paulo and Rio de Janeiro, Tokyo, Toronto, Beijing, Seoul, London, New York, Chicago and Los Angeles, Moscow and London between 2006 and 2012, finally ending with the 10th Anniversary Celebrations in Tokyo, Hong Kong and London in 2014.

Steven Spurrier, Eduardo Chadwick, Igor Serdyuk.
Moscow, 25 May 2012

All in all, Eduardo held twenty-two events across fifteen nations and his wines were placed among the top three in 20 out of 22 of these, achieving a remarkable 90% success rate overall. A splendid book entitled *The Berlin Tasting* has been produced and as I leaf through it I'm reminded of how much fun it was and all in a good cause. On our last evening in Berlin in 2014 I took Bella to Borchardt, a *brasserie* that had been famous in the 1930s and had recently been renovated to become once more justifiably popular. To do my bit for German wine, after a carafe of Riesling I ordered a bottle of a red from the Lemberger grape. The young sommelier frowned and said 'Sir, I may be a German patriot, but not for our red wines. I would suggest you take the Chianti'.

The Berlin visit meant that I missed out on the annual Southwold Claret Tasting always held at the end of January. This had begun about a dozen years before, hosted by Simon Loftus of Adnams Brewery and Wine Merchants in the seaside town of Southwold in Suffolk. His family owned all the pubs there and in most of the county and he had completed renovation on their two hotels in the main street, The Crown and The Swan. The guests, made up of the top UK importers from Bordeaux – Berry Brothers, Justerini, Corney & Barrow, The Wine Society and the like – and specialist independents, with at the start one single journalist, Clive Coates. The Press Contingent for a few years was made up of Jancis Robinson, Neal Martin (The Wine Advocate) and myself. The wines tasted were dry and sweet whites and reds from all the Crus Classés and many Crus Bourgeois and 'second wines', from the Bordeaux vintage four years back, the wines having been in bottle about two years, allowing for a 'proper' judgement of the year in question, compared to the *en primeur* tastings from the barrel just six months after the harvest. Two bottles of each wine were sourced directly from the châteaux by Bill Blatch of Bordeaux merchant Vintex and up to a few years ago all complied, even the First Growths. Now, because their reputations and prices are so high and they might be nervous of anything but superlative ratings, some (and even some of the 'Super Seconds) do not take part, but members of the Southwold group have these wines in stock and if not, the tasters club together to buy them in.

The blind tastings, in flights of twelve wines grouped as far as possible by appellations which cover almost two hundred wines over two full days are conducted under the 'Chatham House Rules' which prevents participants from using or referring to any other scores but their own and those of the group, which are 'topped and tailed', the highest and the lowest being eliminated. One of my wine writing colleagues, a prolific and very serious author of books on all aspects of Bordeaux and its wines, ignored this rule on the one occasion he attended and has not been invited back. Apart from giving our rankings – still out of the now old-fashioned 20 point scale – we comment on the wines and all this is transmitted to the châteaux by Bill Blatch. Since all this is handled with the utmost discretion, the majority of the châteaux find it very useful to have the combined, un-biased opinions from such a qualified bunch of tasters and so it continues. In 2017 both the Adnams hotels were under renovation and the group re-located to Farr Vintners, the UK's biggest dealer in Bordeaux, and has been re-named Southwold-on-Thames. That year we looked at the 2013s, a vintage everyone would prefer to forget and from which I didn't buy a single bottle.

An added benefit of being part of the Southwold group is that we are asked to dig deep into our cellars for bottles to share in the evenings. The great, late Bill Baker, whose girth was so impressive that the doors of Wells Cathedral had to be removed to allow his coffin to pass through when he died at just fifty years old, gave us simple advice 'don't bring crap.' It is an opportunity to share one's best in the best company. It is also fun to exchange views on wine styles, which are often very different from those of our American counterparts. Such an example came to a head around Château Pavie from the heatwave vintage of 2003. This fine 1er Grand Cru Classé B estate (now elevated with some controversy to 'A' status along with the slightly less controversial Château Angelus, to join the true First Growths Châteaux Ausone and Cheval Blanc) was purchased by Gérard Perse in 1997, the wines becoming markedly richer and more robust than under the Valette family, until the 2003 split opinions down the middle. The furore was sparked off by Jancis Robinson's tasting note: 'Completely unappetising, overripe aromas. Why? Porty sweet... ridiculous wine more reminiscent of a late-harvest Zinfandel than a red Bordeaux....12/20.' The provoked a reply from Robert Parker of *The Wine Advocate*: 'It is a wine of sublime richness, minerality, delineation and nobleness, representing the essence of one of St-Emilion's greatest terroirs....96/100.' Clive Coates fuelled the flames by stating that 'Perse continues to produce wine that doesn't even taste like Bordeaux and anyone who thinks the 2003 is a wine of merit needs his/her head examined.' But Michel Bettane, France's Robert Parker in terms of influence, described the same wine as 'Monumental in body with enrobing tannins made from grapes of an almost extravagant maturity ...one would have to be devilishly ascetic to resist such a temptation, 18/20.'

Here the question of 'authenticity' doesn't come up, as the wine was made within the AOC rules, but the question of 'typicity' does. The Brits, in this case, found Pavie 2003 profoundly untypical, particularly compared to the classic yet sometimes understated Château Figeac, which was sadly overlooked in the recent promotions from 1er GCC B to A and I wrote that perhaps one could compare these different styles under the direction of each owner to two keyboard musical instruments, an organ and a piano. 'We know what they both look like and sound like and that while an organ is more overwhelming, a piano has more clarity. A piano that sounds like an organ is not a typical piano and if we hear the sounds without seeing the instrument, we will say it is an organ, not a piano. I prefer pianos to sound like pianos and since making pianos that sound like organs costs a lot of money, I prefer to buy piano-St-Emilions like Canon 2000 (£350 a case, RP points 89) to organ-St-Emilions such as Pavie 2000 (£1750 the case, RP points 100). Those who like the louder style have the satisfaction of knowing that it is reassuringly expensive.'

This row went on and on, with Robert Parker going so far as saying that the views of most British commentators could not be trusted as they were part of the wine trade and not scrupulously independent like himself. However, within a few years Pavie had to a large extent abandoned its exaggerated style, perhaps even due to Southwold group criticism, and our differences of views found other topics to latch on to.

A few days before the Berlin trip I had organised a dinner to celebrate forty years in the wine trade. This was held at Ransome's Dock, Chef Martin Lam's restaurant just south of the river in Battersea. Martin, the best chef at L'Escargot when it was owned by Nicholas Lander, had had his own place for about a decade. It was known as 'the wine trade restaurant' for, despite a long, varied and good-value list, he was open to people bringing their own bottles for a moderate corkage fee. Thank heavens it was moderate, for forty-five guests managed to get through fifty-nine bottles, made up from:

12 Champagne Pol Roger 1995
10 Chassagne-Montrachet 1er Cru Les Cailerets 1999
    Jean-Noël Gagnard
16 Ch. Léoville-Barton 1989 Saint-Julien
 9 Château de Beaucastel 1990 Châteauneuf-du-Pape
 7 Brauneberger-Juffer Riesling Auslese 1985 Willi Haag
 5 Fonseca Vintage 1966

This does not mean that my wine trade friends were heavy drinkers and no doubt not every glass was drained to the dregs, but it does show that when the wine is good and the dinner leisurely, one shouldn't skimp on quantity. The most optimistic statement I heard about *consommation à table* came from Georges Thienpont, owner in the 1960s and 1970s of Vieux Château Certan in Pomerol that 'a magnum of claret is suitable for two gentlemen dining together, provided they have had a bottle of Champagne beforehand.' Bella had worked with Martin on the menu and we started with Dorset crab, followed by her own lamb, cooked three ways, then of course cheese and I can't remember what dessert. Clive Coates MW, a proclaimed vegetarian with the exception of *foie gras*, had requested something different to replace the lamb and Martin complied with a plate of fish and chips. It was a very jolly evening.

Of course the big event, even bigger in hindsight, of 2004 was the launch of the *Decanter* World Wine Awards in late April. Taking place in The Worx, a fine series of photogapher's studios with wonderful natural light in Parson's Green, the first year saw us receive 4,500 samples to be judged on the 20 point scale for Commended (14.5-15.4), Bronze (15.5-16.9), Silver (17-18.4) and Gold (18.5 and above) Medals. In the early days the percentages were Commended 25%, Bronze 25%, Silver 12%, Gold under 2%. Entries rose steadily from this first year to over 6,000 in 2006 when Jancis Robinson wrote in the *Financial Times* that 'Sarah Kemp has created a 'salon' with the world's best palates' and quote me as saying that 'I think we will top out at around 7,500 entries, God knows where the International Wine Challenge (then around 13,000 entries) get all those wines.' Well, we continued to grow, chipping away at the IWC, moving ahead of them in 2011 with 12.254 and in 2017, when after thirteen years as Chairman I was 'kicked upstairs' to become Chairman Emeritus to be replaced by three Chairs, Gérard Basset, Sarah Jane Evans and Michael

Hill Smith, to see the numbers reach 18,000. For some time the DWWA had been the largest and most influential wine competition on the planet and not in our wildest dreams did Sarah and I ever expect this volume, now from forty-two different countries, some not even producing wine when we started. The judges themselves, including sixty-eight Masters of Wine and twenty Master Sommeliers, came from twenty-one different countries and the last week in April has truly become a 'salon' as perceived by Jancis, of international importance.

In the last three years the judging has moved to the international 100 point scale, to work out at Commended 83-85, Bronze 86-89, Silver 90-94 and Gold 95 and above. Quality all over the world is getting better and, under constant supervision as the judges are just as strict; in 2017 there were 40.8% Bronze Medals, 19.39% Silver and 2.64% Gold. On the last day, all the Golds within each category are re-tasted and a Platinum Medal is awarded to the best wine in each category. Then a week later the three Chairs are joined by two other judges and all these are pitted against each other in defined categories to arrive at the Platinum Best of Show, of which there were thirty-four such awards in 2017.

Wine competitions can be described simply as 'the meat in the sandwich between the producer and the consumer'. My instruction to the judges was also simple: to recognise and award quality. Any competition is only as good as the validity of the results, the results are only as good as the judges and the judges, for a large part, only as good as the organisation that surrounds them. The place and role of wine competitions, particularly for emerging markets, comes down to just two words: information and trust. An award represents an accolade for the producer and if it helps the consumer to make a sensible, pleasure-giving purchase, this is a win-win situation.

Beginning with Berlin, 2004 was full of travel, and I very nearly didn't make it to the 2004 South African Wine Selection judging in late August, as immigration at Cape Town airport refused to let me into the country, since I did not have a completely clean page in my passport onto which they could affix the temporary entry visa. They were not impressed when I showed them my official invitation and when I helpfully peeled off a defunct visa to the USA, showing them a nice blank page, the official informed me that not only was I an illegal immigrant, but I could be charged with degrading an official document. At this point Owen Jullies,

SAA Food & Beverage Manager, seeing one of his official judges condemned to deportation on the next plane, began to call in some favours. At the British Consulate, Colin, the deputy officer, declined to help, saying that a wine tasting was not a matter of life and death. Reached at her home, Lisa, head of Chancery, agreed to call the official and authorise him to issue the visa, but having mulled it over for a while the official said he required authorisation in writing, by which time Lisa had gone out and Colin hadn't changed his mind. John Platter, whose wine guide is the bible of South African wines, called the Minister of Agriculture, but it was a Saturday and he was on the golf course. Meanwhile, Lynne Sherriff MW, who had organised the international judges, was pulling strings from London. Finally, she made contact with the personal wine adviser to President Mbeki and, after five hours of incarceration the official returned my passport complete with the visa, grumpily stating that powers more important than his has authorised my illegal entry. From that moment, things improved mightily and Bella came to collect me and we spent the evening with friends from London celebrating my release.

SAA is a flag carrier in the true sense of the word. What Air France, Alitalia and Iberia could do for their countries' wines, SAA does with pride. Lynne Sherriff joined the judges the following day to team up with Annegret Reh-Gartner and Egon Müller, both top producers from Germany's Mosel region, and Geoff Merrill from Australia, local judges were Cape Wine Masters Dave Hughes, Allan Mullins and Tony Mossop. On the last morning we visited the historic Rustenberg estate outside Stellenbosch, where owner Simon Barlow remarked that the Cape was becoming 'a vinous Eldorado', his newest neighbour on the slopes of the Simonsberg Mountain being May-Eliane de Lencquesaing of Château Pichon-Longueville, Comtesse de Lalande.

2005 opened with a conference in Paris on the theme 'The Future for Emerging Wine Markets', the concentration being on Asia. I had been to China a few times and of course often to Japan and Singapore and my March *Decanter* column under the heading 'Export eyes on China' gave hints that consumption was beginning to flow down to the middle classes, so I was surprised when Canadian Don Saint-Pierre Jr, head of the largest importer/distributor in the country, announced that 'given everything we have to deal with, the traffic lights for wine are still on amber.' He was followed by Rajeev Samant, a strikingly bright young Indian, who had recently moved from Silicon Valley to Nashik, four hours by train outside Bombay, where he was planting vineyards to create in his home country a vision of Napa Valley. By the next decade his brand Sula, had 50% of the local market and it is still the dominant local brand, so his optimism was well-placed when his opening words were: 'For India, the traffic lights are on green!'. I wish I had never heard that, for later that year I received a call from David Banford, a serial entrepreneur who had created a mail-order company call The Wine Society of America for which I consulted for a while before it inevitably collapsed due to fierce opposition from the rigid three-tier US importation system. He and I had become friends and when he said he was thinking of setting up a similar venture in India, knowing a bit about the country as he had been brought up there, and would I be interested, I immediately replied 'of course I would, I've never been there and in any case the traffic lights are on green.' This proved to be a great mistake and took a considerable chunk of the money that I was beginning to build back up due to the sweat of my brow, but more of that later.

I visited Chile and Argentina in January that year, and there I tasted my first of many Brazilian wines, drank my first and last Caipirinha – a deadly cocktail made from fermented sugar cane and crushed limes – and witnessed first-hand what I thought was a wine market in the process of explosion. Except that it wasn't, just growing year by year from a low base, but everyone seemed very excited. Bella and I returned over New Year five years later to stay with Nicky's daughter Jane, who, with her husband Mark, was living in Rio de Janeiro. We spent a few days in the Vallée dos Vinedos to the south, to discover a true wine culture of mostly direct descendants from northern Italy in the late 19th century. Even today the well-off Brazilians don't take their own wine seriously, preferring to drink imports from Europe of Argentina and Chile.

Over the years Bella and I have spent a week at Fattoria Nittardi near Castellina in Chianti. This is one of the most beautiful of many such small estates, with a present to match its past. Dating from the 12th century and in the early 16th owned by Michelangelo Buonarroti, who assigned the management of it to his brother Leonardo while he was busy in Rome painting the ceiling of the Sistine Chapel. A few *fiaschi* were requested for the pleasure of Pope Julius II, who proclaimed it *nectar dei*, hence the name of the estate. In 1983 the property was acquired in a run-down state by Frankfurt art dealer Peter Femfert and his Venetian wife Stefania and since that vintage Peter has asked his artist friends to not only design a label for the wine, but wrapping paper as well, the buyers getting two bites of the cherry. Both are expressively *joie de vivre* and when Philippine de Rothschild chose Britain's Prince Charles for her 2005 vintage, Peter's choice fell on Yoko Ono.

I had met Peter at various wine tastings in London and we had got on, so when he offered us a week in one of the apartments he had created in the original house, I immediately accepted. While we were there, I asked him why he spoke such good English and he said that for two years in his teens he had gone to live with his aunt in a little town named Belper and had continued his studies there. His school had been that founded by my great-grandfather George Herbert Strutt. There cannot be many of my ancestor's pupils who own an internationally famous art gallery and surely only a single one who has created such a beautiful estate in Tuscany. Fattoria Nittardi is now part of my life, the family connection giving me a covert connection to Peter, that adds something private and personal to our joint passion for wine and art.

It is also the most magical place to visit for over the years Peter has installed a series of large sculptures in the grounds surrounding the house and in the vineyards and every year there is a new apparition. After one visit we were driving back with friends and stayed in Lucca, where there was a huge antiques fair. When I was young I collected lions, mostly ceramic, but then I married a Leo and stopped. However, in the main square one of the dealers had a pair of vast bronze lions, taken from a palazzo in Naples. I knew that Peter liked lions (I don't know if Stefania is a Leo) and had the dealer email him a photo. Peter took the bait, bargained the price down and now these splendid animals guard the entrance to the Nittardi cellar and are known as 'the Spurlions'. Despite owning a few hundred hectares such, thankfully, is the zoning in and around Chianti that he has only a dozen hectares of vines and, not being able to expand at home, some years ago bought thirty hectares of unplanted land in the Maremma, south-west near the coast in the hills around Scansano overlooking Monte Argentario. His first vintage produced two red wines, Ad Astra and Nectar Dei to which he has recently added a white Vermentino named Ben, after Benjamin, usually the name of the youngest son of an Italian family. The grapes are trucked over to Nittardi as so far there is no winery in the Maremma, but plans are afoot and I am pursuing another Spurrier dream to become part of this adventure with the Femfert family.

That March, Bella joined me in Singapore for my week's tasting for SIA as we were to spend two full weeks in New Zealand, both North and South Islands. There was a bit of work involved, not that I really consider tasting wines work, but attention has to be paid and notes taken, but mostly we were free to see as much as we could of the still pristine countryside. One of the many high points was being lent their beach house by the Seifried wine family of Nelson along from Marlborough in the South Island, which over-looked Split Apple Rock, a local landmark, which was a daily target for my pre-breakfast swim. On the way back up north, I visited New Zealand's grand old man of wine, John Buck of Te Mata, and we stopped in Napier, a town destroyed by an earthquake in the early 1920s and rebuilt in colourful Art Deco style. Here, again, there was an antiques fair and I fell for a splendid and sizable bronze lamp from this period, of a slim naked lady whose stretched out hands held two globes for the lightbulbs. Bella was predictably furious when I had it double and triple wrapped and thanks to our free tickets in the front of the 'plane on SIA, it arrived safely in London and sits provocatively on my desk in Dorset providing a perfect light for writing.

On 24 May, thirty years to the day after the original Paris Tasting in 1976, a re-run with exactly the same red wines was held simultaneously at Copia in Napa at 10am and at Berry Brothers in St James's Street at 6pm. This has been referred to in chapter 8, but suffice it to say that this time the Californian Cabernets took the first five of ten places, Château Mouton-Rothschild 1970, as it had done in 1976, heading the Clarets. This result came to the notice of the BBC and at 8am the following morning I was interviewed on the news programme 'Today'. Jancis Robinson, one of the nine judges in London that evening, tuned in and recorded my comments in her article that appeared in the weekend's *Financial Times* on what the Bordelais might have thought of the result: ' 'Rather miffed', was his reply. Miffed indeed. Pure Spurrier.'

That autumn we took a short break in southern Portugal, flying to Lisbon (perhaps my favourite European city, along with Seville) and spending a few days in the Alentejo as guests at Mouchao, founded by the Reynolds family of Scottish descent. In the early 19th century the family was one of the largest owners of cork forests in Portugal, with holding stretching from the Douro to the Algarve and still 900 hectares remain at Mouchao of which 38 are under vines planted 70% to Alicante Bouschet, a grape with red juice as well as black skins which produces a surprisingly elegant wine if left to mature. Then in October it was back to Alsace for a five day tour with what was now called 'The McCormick Group' a spin-off from previous Arblaster & Clarke wine tours, Peter and Kathryn McCormick being wine-loving solicitors from Yorkshire with a few like-minded couples. Starting at Josmeyer in Winztenheim, with Jean Meyer stating that 'Riesling is not a grape, it is a planet', we moved on to the Faller family's Domaine Weinbach housed in an ancient Capucin monastery in Kaysersberg and then of course to Hugel in Riquewihr and Trimbach in Ribeauville, the latter's single vineyard Clos Sainte Hune being the great-est of all Alsace Riesings. Our last visit, before a superb dinner at the three star Auberge de L'Ill was to Jean-Michel Deiss at Bergheim. Deiss consid-ers that the grape variety represents the wine's race or origin, and that the vineyard represents its regional accent, thus Rieslings from two different vineyards will 'speak' differently. Yet he also considers that one voice is not enough for the vineyard to truly express itself and for some years has practised mixed plantings in his mostly *Grand Cru* vineyards. Such has been his persistence and the quality of his wines that from 2005 the INAO has accepted mixed plantings, allowing the name of the vineyard to be used without that of the grape. Jean-Michel, who I knew well from my Paris days, is an eccentric and when we appeared, his young wife gave us a tasting, saying that he would be ready for us later. This was mid-vintage time and after some time a shout came from the winery and in we went to find Jean-Michel stark naked in an open vat of Pinot Noir, punching down the grapes with his feet as was the habit in Burgundy. Peter McCormick remarked laconically that 'this puts a new spin on *coq au vin*'.

Two dinners stood out in the first half of 2007, the first being for Michael Broadbent's 80th birthday at his Club, Brookes's on the day itself. I have the classic English menu – Spiced Brown Potted Shrimps, Roast Rack of Lamb with Mange-Tout Peas and New Potatoes, Poached Pear *en Cage* with Sauce Anglaise, Colston Bassett Stilton and Farmhouse Cheddar – and the wines – Pol Roger 1998, Chassagne-Montrachet Les Champs-Gains 2000, Château Haut-Batailley 2000, Château Lafite-Rothschild 1996, Moscato d'Asti Nivole 2006 Michele Chiarlo, Cockburn's 1967 and Cockburn's 1927. I remember we were about twenty-four guests as well as his wife Daphne and children Emma and Bartholomew. Time passes and on 2nd May 2017 a much larger number of guests, though sadly without Daphne who had died two years previously, convened at Brooks's for Michael's 90th. Once again, the menu was classic – Quenelle of Sole with Lobster Sauce, Fillet of Beef Wellington with Madeira Sauce, Panaché of Vegetables, Blackberry and Pear Fool with Lavender Shortbread, Colston Bassett Stilton and Driftwood Cheese – but the wines were a little more adventurous – Gusborne 2013 Brut Réserve (one of the best English Sparkling Wines), Furmint 2014 Royal Tokaji Wine Company, Château Cos d'Estournel 2001, Michele Chiarlo Nivole Moscato d'Asti 2017 and Graham's 1967. Michael telephoned me recently to say he was saving his last bottle of Cockburn's 1967 for the next Bordeaux Club Dinner of which I am one of the six members, so he won't be serving that at his 100th birthday dinner on 2 May 2027, but I bet there will be Michele Chiarlo's Nivele Moscato d'Asti.

The second was a grand affair at Chatsworth in Derbyshire, where forty-five guests had paid £800 a head to enjoy white Burgundies presented by Anne-Claude Leflaive and Right Bank Clarets by Christian Moueix, preceded by Champagne Salon 1996 and rounded off with a splendid Lot 53 (1953, but at that time Cognacs could not carry a vintage) Cognac from Tesseron. The beautiful surroundings was matched by the simple grandeur of the wines, which stood out for me as benchmarks in their appellations, the ultimate reference point. Perhaps 'the Rolls-Royce of wines' means more than 'the Pétrus of automobiles' simply because more people have heard of the former than the latter, but the litmus test in both is their power to remain at the top. Christian Moueix remarked modestly that 'Our only talent is to be respectful of terroir', but went up a gear in commenting 'here is elegance that goes beyond appreciation, that takes one to another level, that shows we are part of history' on his Château Magdelaine 1961. Such wines do not happen by chance, however unique the terroir. They need dedicated perfectionists to practice good husbandry and avoid the temptation of exaggeration and such people are by definition risk takers. This was summed up by host Adam Brett-Smith on Anne-Claude Leflaive: 'her greatness lies in being courageous… transforming the estate's viticulture, philosophy, yield, quality and perception, when the instinct might have been to do nothing.' The same could be said of the custodians of Chatsworth, each generation taking their inheritance into the future with intelligence and vigour. Benchmarks are essential in all walks of life.

Vinexpo rolled around again in the third week of June in the odd-numbered years and as *Decanter*'s consultant editor and a Vinexpo visitor since 1979, I received invitations. The first party was at Haut-Bailly, the superb *cru classé de Graves,* with nine Michelin stars – Pierre Troisgros, Alain Passard (the chef of the evening) and the Pourcel Brothers from Montpelier – in attendance, the other star of the evening being imperiales (6 litres or 8 bottles) of Haut-Bailly 1985. The following evening was Olivier and Anne Bernard's *Tour de France des Appellations*, with help from their friends Anne-Claude and Olivier Leflaive, Château de Fuissé, the Jaboulet family, Zind-Humbrecht, Faiveley, Sassicaia and Pol Roger. This is Bordeaux's best bottle party, except that the hosts not the guests provide the bottles, mostly in magnums from old vintages. The Monday evening, delayed from Sunday due to the French election, saw Philippine de Rothschild receiving the international Press at Mouton-Rothschild, capping a series of *crus classés du Médoc* from 1999 to 1970 with her 1961. Eight years previously she had served the 1945. Tuesday evening was *Le Diner des Millésimes de Collection* at Château Beau-Séjour Bécot in Saint-Emilion, with six courses prepared by Michel Guerard and great vintages provided by all the *1ers grands crus classés* (including the newly elected – but then still disputed – Troplong-Mondot and Pavie-Macquin, ending up with marvellous magnums of Château Canon 1971. (It should be noted that with the accession of Angelus and Pavie to the *1er grands crus classés 'A'* group, Alain Vautier, the honourable owner of Château Ausone, refused to participate in these dinners and from 2013 they were abandoned.) Finally, *La Fête de la Fleur,* was held at Château Smith-Haut-Lafitte to celebrate the 20th anniversary of the Pessac-Léognan appellation with Haut-Brion 1998 and d'Yquem 1998 crowning the evening, while SHL Rosé 2006 was served on the dance floor to show that pleasure does not always have to be expensive.

Such evenings apart, the most important thing I did during Vinexpo week was to present a dossier on the potential of Bride Valley Vineyard, the sparkling wine venture that Bella and I were to undertake on her farm in Dorset, to Jean-Claude and Jean-Charles Boisset, the father and son owners of the hugely successful company based in Burgundy and also in Napa. The birth (and birthing pains) of Bride Valley are to be found in the next chapter, but suffice it to say that the Boissets were most excited by the idea and as early as September sent Georges Legrand, their top sparkling wine man, down to see us for the first of three visits. The idea was to do a joint-venture if sufficient land could be planted, but after much research and analysis only about twenty-five acres of the 200 acre farm were deemed to be exceptional and, with the Boisset advice and encouragement, we set off on our own.

In September 2007 I had a very bad bicycling accident. I have always ridden a bike wherever I have lived, with the single exception of New York, had had the odd minor accident, but never bothered to wear a helmet as I considered myself both careful and alert. That year *Decanter* had taken the Victorian and Albert Museum as a venue for the DWWA party and I had had much pleasure in presenting one of the top awards to John and Janet Trefethen of Napa Valley for their Cabernet Sauvignon. We arranged to have lunch the following day with Michael Broadbent and I invited them to Boodle's. To get there first, I set off a little after noon on a nice sunny day, knowing the route by heart, going through South Kensington, crossing the very busy Cromwell Road from Thurloe Square to the south to the V&A and kicking off from there up Knightsbridge into Piccadilly and down to St James's Street. I would have reached the pavement outside the V&A around 12.30 and the next thing I knew I was in an ambulance 45 mintues later, having been knocked off my bike by a speeding motorcyclist, apparently gone head over heels across the handlebars, the crown of my head smacking the pavement as I fell on my back. Police were around when I came to and once I was conscious I was asked if I remembered anything about the accident and I replied that I did not, but that I needed to make an urgent telephone call. This was to Boodle's to say that I would not be there for lunch (which Michael had already realised and had taken charge) and then I was whisked off to the Charing Cross Hospital to have my head stitched up. The motorcyclist remained there and drove off when the ambulance set off, the police having told me they had all his particulars.

I was knocked out for well over half an hour and during that time, one of the girls from the V&A who had helped out at the *Decanter* evening had apparently walked out of the museum, seen me face up on the ground, recognised me from the evening before and had called the office. Thus it was that evening that I received a visit from Sarah Kemp with a brand new cycling helmet adorned with *Decanter* stickers. Also a visit from a panicked Bella who had rushed up from the country. This was Wednesday and by Sunday I was going stir-crazy in the hospital and was sent home, but making little sense and my doctor friend from Rugby, Christopher Powell-Brett, had me checked into the London Clinic, where I was to spend a week recovering. (I had one of the Arblaster & Clarke Wine Tours to Bordeaux planned the following week, all visits pre-arranged, and fortunately James Lawther, who had moved to Bordeaux was able to step into my shoes). The specialist in charge of me at the Clinic said he was a wine buff and that he had looked after Harry Waugh, who had smashed his nose and head up in a car accident several years before in Burgundy. He said that I had been very lucky ('one millimetre more and the bone would have gone into the brain') but that the damage done might affect my sense of smell, therefore my sense of taste and hence much of my livelihood. He, rather against my own wishes, introduced me to a legal company who dealt on a 'pro bono' basis for insurance claims of this kind. Of course, by this time I had remembered quite clearly the accident: I had reached the V&A pavement, had swung out into the road to be knocked off the bike, both me and the bike landing on the pavement, with a small tear in the back of my jacket and my shirt and no damage to the bike at all, which had been taken away by the police.

I relayed this in written form to the lawyers and after a week or so received a reply with the statement from the motorcyclist that *I had run into him!* Now, the Cromwell Road is probably the busiest dual carriageway in central London, three lanes each way, and had I run into him and so knocked myself off – vastly unlikely itself as bicyclists do not generally run into motorcyclists – I would have been knocked into the middle lane and probably crushed by the oncoming traffic and of course my bike as well, instead of the clean, but head-damaging fall I had suffered. This I relayed in great detail and to back myself up asked the police for their records when I went to collect my bike. Here, the reply was that the records had been lost. I got in touch with the ambulance services, quoting time, date and place, to be told that they had no record of it, either. I had the number of the motorcyclist, called it to be told that the number had been changed and was now ex-directory.

It was very plain that had I suffered palate-impairing damages, as the specialist said was possible, an insurance claim would have been substantial, so the motorcyclist's insurance company, once alerted to my case, got to work to make sure it did not happen. The legal people said that the police had confirmed to the insurance company my statement that I had no recollection of the accident at the time it happened and that my circumstantial evidence would not stand up against the written, but false, evidence that the motorcyclist via his insurance company had presented. I have respect for the police and ambulance services, but I am not alone to have found that when money changes hands, truth may go out of the window. I did actually lose some of my sense of smell for a while, slowly getting it back to about 90%, and while since then I pay much more attention to the taste and texture of wines when I taste, I can no longer detect the smell of TCA, or a 'corked' wine. Perhaps that is a blessing in disguise?

My physical recovery was much quicker and I was up and about for the 25th anniversary of the Christie's Wine Course. Little did Michael Broadbent think, when he gave the first 'introduction to Wine Tasting' lecture on the 5 October 1982 at age 55, that he would be opening the batting again on 2 October 2007 teaching 'Classic Grapes, Classic Styles'. The only change was that at the first lecture all eight wines were French, while this time only one of them was. In 1982 New World wines were sold by just a handful of specialist merchants, but by 2007 just 10 countries were responsible for 98% of all wine drunk in the UK. Sixty per cent came from six countries in the New World and just 38% from the four main wine producing countries of the Old World. The October 1982 edition of *Decanter* concentrated on Port and Madeira, with only one of its 100 pages featuring a wine from outside Europe. The same edition twenty-five years later was devoted to the *Decanter* World Wine Awards, with 7,500 entries from around the globe. Such a sea change was echoed at the December meeting of the AIV, the think-tank styled by me as 'the conscience of the wine trade', with the *Chancelier* Jean-Pierre Perrin reflecting that 'such is the speed of mutation of wine production around the world, that our original aims to set out guidelines for quality risk appearing too traditional.' Even New World vineyards were until recently situated firmly between the 30th and 50th parallels, but now with China, India and Brazil there is a New World emerging to which the old-fashioned tenets of viticulture might no longer apply. While Perrin acknowledged that the AIV should remain a bastion of the terroir authenticity school, he proposed that it act against excesses in wine production and envisage a global contract that demands total transparency concerning viticulture, vinification and maturation with the aim of producing wines of origin and originality. A decade later, the AIV is still carrying this banner.

Early February 2008, after the Southwold Claret Tastings, found Bella and me escaping the Dorset winter for two weeks in Argentina, beginning with the luxury of the Alvares Palacio. One evening we went to one of the city's well known restaurants for steak, the Argentine staple diet, where the prime cut ordered 'rare' turned out to be 'medium'. I learned later from Dany Rolland that I should have requested 'mucho crudo/very raw' or 'vuelta-vuelta/flip-flop' to have it the way I liked. Several days in Mendoza were spent in visiting vineyards, centred around a tasting that had been commissioned by *Decanter*, requesting not more than one wine from each estate, all red and at that time mostly Malbecs. My co-taster was Chile's Patricio Tapia, for some years now the Regional Chair for Argentina for the *Decanter* World Wine Awards, and as we neared the last of fifty wines, I remarked on one that 'if this is the way wine is going here it will be a disaster.' The wine appeared to be the most expensive in the tasting, a 15 degree monster made by a renowned Californian vineyard, the weight of the bottle being as exaggerated as the wine. A decade later this fashion has passed and Malbecs are being rivalled by very expressive Cabernet Francs.

Of the many bodegas we visited, the finest was that of José Manuel Ortega-Fournier, where his wife Nadia had created an award-winning restaurant. José Manuel, whose family comes from Burgos in northern Spain and who was a banker with Goldman Sachs before being bitten by the wine bug, now makes a large range of wines from what he refers to as 'Cult Grapes' in Maule in Chile and also in Spain's Ribera del Duero, has become a great friend and has over the past few years involved me in his DOSS Foundation project, just 100 cases selected from the best barrels in each of his wineries by Dany Rolland, Ortega himself, his winemaker Jose Spisso and myself, hence DOSS. The wines are sold at $100 a bottle and all the proceeds go towards higher education for under-privileged students. Like his hero Robert Mondavi, José Manuel likes to give something back.

After a two-day turnaround, I was off to India to promote my newest venture, The Wine Society of India. From early beginnings in 2006, David Banford and I had been involved in launching this mail order wine business into a market that was growing at 30% a year, albeit from a minuscule base. Under the banner 'Four Seasons Wine Discoveries' we supplied our members with six bottles of wine four times a year. Banford, who had been brought up in Mumbai, had returned there to run the business and I looked after the wine selections. Over the next two years we had spent a lot of time and money launching our new baby, including giving the largest wine tasting – 900 thirsty guests – ever held in India (a record that is unlikely to be broken by anyone with any sense) without actually getting very far. Following discussions at Vinexpo in 2007, we teamed up with United Spirits Ltd (USL), the largest beer and spirits distributor in the country, based in Bangalore, who were launching a wine division. Even with this weight behind us, the endemic corruption in India's distribution channels made the cost of doing business exorbitant and two years later David Banford was to arrange a further merger with Direct Wines, the world's largest mail order wine company. While they were stabilizing the company and expanding the membership, I continued to visit the major cities to host wine tastings, watching the membership grow to over 12,000 until in 2013 Direct Wines announced that India was a step too far even for them, and the Wine Society of India ceased to exist. I still visit India, now as a consultant for Fratelli Wines, the number 2 in the country after Sula, where I help their Italian viticulturist and wine maker Piero Masi blend a white, rose and red under the M/S (Masi/Spurrier) label, which has a good success. If ever the laws are changed to create even a half level playing field for imported wines, India will become a huge market, but no one thinks this will happen any time soon.

One of my early *Decanter* columns in 2009 was headed 'Late-bottled vintage Port – back from the dead'. This once again justifiably popular style of Port known as LBV was launched by Taylor, Fladgate and Yeatman's Alastair Robertson with a Taylor 1965, bottled in 1970. True Vintage Port is bottled after less than two years in cask and is meant to mature for decades, throwing a heavy sediment which requires careful decanting. Announcing their new brand, Robertson said that 'we have been working on the idea of offering a Port which could be considered vintage, yet could be poured bright and clear, straight from the bottle. The secret is to mature the vintage in wood and then 'late bottle'. Having been a great supporter of LBVs, which sold well in my Paris shop in the 1970s and 1980s, I began to lose patience with them in the 1990s. Finally, in the early 2000s, I confronted David Guimarains, who had succeeded his larg-er-than-life father Bruce as wine maker for Fonseca and now the whole of the Taylor group, of colluding with the total degradation of the category, which by then more resembled a rough Ruby. No doubt this was partially caused by the supermarkets' determination to keep the price in single fig-ures and the competition for market share. This was widely reported and must have struck a nerve, as a late 2008 tasting of a range of 2003 and 2001 LBVs at the Portuguese Embassy showed a complete turnaround. Today the quality of Port has never been higher, while the UK consumption is in slight, but steady decline. The LBVs, preferably unfiltered, and 10 Year Old Tawnies, the two styles that have made Port so famous over the years, are once again a sure bet.

Another hint for the future was my question in a later column 'Is Champagne's bubble bursting?' The financial crisis that had begun in 2008 was in full swing and the *Independent on Sunday* had carried a head-line 'Bye-bye, Bolly' stating that 'Champagne has lost its sparkle for Britons thirsty for cut-price Cava or Prosecco'. The Champenois were not happy, and Andrew Hawes, Bollinger's importer and chair of the UK Champagne Agents Association, said the drop in sales was simply a blip, adding that 'the British have a deep love affair with Champagne and if the past is any way of predicting the future, when things get bet-ter, the market will bounce back.' But in the past, Champagne didn't have Prosecco to contend with and thanks to the Italian government's relaxed attitude to the rules around production, under a decade later Prosecco, at 400 million bottles a year, was producing more than Champagne. At a 2017 conference in Barolo some top Prosecco producers admitted that the fashion might move to some other style of sparkling wine, so they were all fine-tuning their range to attract the quality market, which is what the major Champagne brands have been doing for years. When Bella and I moved to Dorset in the late 1980s, Champagne, unless you were broke or knew some obscure producer from some other region, was pretty much *de rigueur* for parties. Now it is considered almost showing off to serve it.

April 2009 witnessed the planting of the first two hectares of what were to become just over ten on Bella's farm, to created Bride Valley Vineyard. More on this in the next chapter and while Champagne might still remain the benchmark, the extraordinary increase in planting in southern England, with substantial investments from at least two major

Champagne Houses, and the quality being produced, has exceeded even the most optimistic expectations.

The high spot at the end of the year was Pierre-Henry Gagey's celebration of 150 years of Louis Jadot, the Burgundian House that he took over on his father Andre's retirement in 1992. Just twenty-four of us were there to begin the tasting with red wines, as is customary in Burgundy rather than to start with whites, to hear Pierre-Henry announce that he had chosen one wine from each of fifteen decades of the company's existence, 'not necessarily the best wine from the best vintage, but wines that Jacques Lardière (head winemaker since 1970) and I really like'. In descending order they were: Bonnes-Mares 2003, Gevrey-Chambertin Clos St-Jacques 1997, Beaune Clos des Ursules 1985, Musigny 1978, Gevrey-Chambertin Clos St-Jacques 1966, Chambertin Clos de Bèze 1953, Beaune-Boucherottes 1949, Chambertin 1937 (with 1934 one of the only two good vintages of the 1930s), Beaune Clos des Ursules 1929, Corton-Pougets 1915, Beaune Clos des Couchereaux 1904, Clos de Vougeot 1898 (the first 100% pre-phylloxera wine), Clos de Tart 1887, Pommard 1878 and finally Corton 1865. Noted French wine critic Michel Bettane remarked that it was 'a great Corton', to which Gagey replied 'I'm glad you liked it, as these were our last two bottles'. Experiences like these go far beyond privilege.

The Burgundy theme was alive and well that April, at a dinner to celebrate Aubert de Villaine, co-owner of the Domaine de la Romanée-Conti, being named *Decanter* Man of the Year 2010. I first met Aubert and Pamela de Villaine in the early 1970s and immediately bought their Aligoté de Bouzeron, Bourgogne Blanc Les Clous, Bourgogne Rouge La Digoine and the lovely pale *rosé de saignée* that Aubert made in the years of high yield for Pinot Noir for my shop in Paris. One autumn shortly after we met, Bella and I drove down from the weekend house we had in Burgundy for lunch, bringing Digby, our rather rustic Briard sheepdog, in whose memory I dedicated my book *French Country Wines*. The de Villaines had a splendid black Labrador bitch and after lunch the two dogs were nowhere to be seen. Aubert suggested that they had gone hunting and we wait for their return. This stretched through dinner, during which the Lady and the Tramp reappeared, exhausted. On many subsequent visits, Digby stayed in the car.

At the Awards dinner, Sarah Kemp made a fine speech, echoing Adam Brett-Smith's opinion that 'Aubert has that supremely rare gift: a profound humility allied to absolute self-belief' and asked me to present the decanter to Aubert, only to hear him murmur 'Thank you, Steven, but you know we don't decant in Burgundy.' He and I were recently reminiscing about the old days and he remarked that 'things were more simple then, money was less mentioned and we did just the best we could with the grapes we picked', thus stepping lightly over the enormous dedication and responsibility that he devoted and continues to devote to his own vineyards and to the great past, present and future of the Domaine. He is and remains a strong force for good in the world of wine, particularly in Burgundy.

My first trip of the year was to Puglia, where I had not been since late August 1965, when Bella and I disembarked at Bari off an overnight ferry from Greece. Over four days I was introduced to aromatic dry whites from Malvasia Bianco, Fiano and Vermentino, spending more time on the robust reds from Negromaro, Primitivo and the recently revived Susumaniello. Primitivo, named for its early ripening arrived in Puglia unannounced in the 1870s, some saying that it was a degenerative Pinot Noir, others that it was a cousin of the Piedmontese Dolcetto. Research by Professor Carole Meredith at the University of California Davis confirmed in 1998 that along with Zinfandel and Plavac Mali from Croatia, it shared the same parents. Primitivo di Manduria – in those days wines often took the name from the train station from which the barrels were exported - was made a DOC in 1974, but risked being rescinded for 'non use'. By 2010 it was back, with Silvio Berlusconi serving it at presidential dinners and has continued, as has Puglia itself, to conquer more markets.

A wine that has little problem conquering markets is Claret and the 2009 vintage, revealed over the first week of April, showed that the hype that had been building up since the actual harvest was justified. *Decanter* was quoted as saying it was 'The Best Ever' and I was happy to state that 'the top châteaux's second wines are of a quality of the *grands vins* 20 years ago, while many of the *grands vins* have themselves reached a quality winemakers only dream of.' Prices were very high, only to be surpassed by the 2010 vintage, which cynically held back releasing the wines until Vinexpo in June 2011. This was proved to be a mistake and once the euphoria died down, prices declined considerably. Buying wine *en primeur* suffered a crisis of confidence and while this is still the way that Bordeaux merchants place the wines of the sixty or so top brands into markets around the world, the shine has definitely gone. At the Southwold tastings we rank the Bordeaux vintages since 2000 and in 2017 the 2005 was placed top, followed by 2010, 2009, 2000 and 2001. 2015 and 2016, both excellent vintages which has seen the spotlight once again on Bordeaux, are too early to judge, but our recent assessment of 2013 deemed it 'the worst ever'.

Perhaps the most interesting wine trip that year, and certainly the one with the longest-lasting influence, was to the Domaine de la Verrière (whose wines sell under the *Chène Bleu* brand) near Vaison-la-Romaine in the southern Rhône, for a conference on Grenache, described as 'the Cinderella of the wine world.' Personally, I would give this description to Cabernet Franc, but was happy to have been one of people behind this three-day event for a much-planted but underrated grape that Mark Savage MW described as 'both a workhorse and wonder horse'. Currently the fourth most-planted grape in the world with 200,000 hectares, but down from 240,000 in 1998 due to the French government's ideas that the northern Rhone Syrah would be better for the south, Grenache is long-lived and is perfect for blending as well as on its own. True to form, the 'mad prophet' Randall Grahm of California's Boony Doon Vineyards, summed it up as 'a chameleon, for its many colours, a supporting actor rather than a superstar, often seeming on the fringes of wine culture while actually being central to it.' He also described Old World Grenache as *vins de terroir* and New World Grenache as *vins d'effort*. This symposium saw the launch of a Global Grenache Association (*Les Grenadiers du Grenache*) and the creation of an International Grenache Day to be held annually on 24 September around the world.

If the Grenache Symposium required some intellectual effort, our last trip of the year just needed a good appetite. We were guests of Christian Seely, MD of AXA-Millésimes, for a weekend at Quinta do Noval, one of the most famous Port estates in the Douro. Two of the Noval pigs, which had grown in their third year to 300kg each, were to be slaughtered and we were to watch the preparation for what Fergus Henderson of London's St John restaurant calls 'nose to tail eating', savour a few delicacies and drink a little Port. Christian had also invited *Decanter* columnist and DWWA Regional Chair for Asia Ch'ng Poh Tiong, who had promised to bring his own cooks – on a previous visit he had said that to prepare a pig properly needed 3,000 years of history – but they were not available, so Christian had commandeered the two brothers from Au Bonheur du

Palais, Bordeaux's best Asian restaurant. Also staying was Daniel Llose, head winemaker at all the French AXA estates and also those of the Cazes family, who arrived with dozens of bottles.

Under blue skies which made the pre-lunch aperitif over-looking the terraced vineyards all the more delicious, meals were for all eighteen of us, the Bordelais pig-preparers on one long table, the guests on another. The first night brought a cascade of northern Rhônes, the best being Chapoutier's Ermitage 1999, the second day's lunch saw a large range of Languedocs, while at dinner white Burgundies and second-growth 1998 Médocs were served including of course AXA's Château Pichon-Longueville Baron. A mid-morning tasting of Quinta do Noval Vintage Ports – 1994, 1967, 1966, 1966 Nacional, 1963 – and their remarkable single-vintage 1995, 1968 and a memorable 1937 'Colheitas', was followed by lunch which concentrated on the 2000 vintage, beginning with Roederer Cristal, continuing with another range of Médocs.

Early 2011 found Oz Clarke and me in a freezing Zagreb on the invitation of Agrokor, Croatia's largest wine producer, who had hired Tony Hodges, one of the driving forces behind Vinopolis and owner of a company named Brand Story (for Brands have Stories) to help put their wines on the map. Croatia has three main wine regions: the continental region in the north on the Danube (robust wines); the coastal region of Istria on the Adriatic coast south of Slovenia (lively freshness); and the Dalmatian coast (natural richness). Whites are based on Malvazija (Malvasia/Malvoisie) and Grasevina (Welsch Riesling) which showed potential from lemony dry to richly sweet, the reds from the refreshingly aggressive Teran (Veneto's Refosco) and the more chunky Plavac Mili, a brother to Puglia's Primitivo. Oz and I were to return for three subsequent visits tasting everything and offering our advice and I am happy to say that Croatia is catching up on its neighbour Slovenia in proportion of medals awarded.

In the spring I was invited to attend a round-table discussion on cork by the Portuguese Cork Association, at which Antonio Amorin, owner of Amorin, the country's biggest and most innovative cork producer was present. He admitted that the image of cork as a wine closure had been demonised in the 1980s due to obvious and excessive problems, but that producers had reacted with massive investment in research and technology in the 1990s and that it should now once again be admired as a natural closure. While the Stelvin closure, commonly known as screw-caps, continue to gain market share and dominate production in Australia and New Zealand, at that time 60% of the world's wines were still under cork, which had reaffirmed its value for ecological sustainability, while moving closer to 100% security on cork taint, or TCA as it is known. Cork has such a long history, the trees can age more than 200 years, being stripped of their bark every decade or so, that I am totally in favour of it for wines, both red and white, that need to be cellared. I suggested to the group that I hardly thought that Hugh Johnson would have renamed *A Life Uncorked*, his splendidly evocative autobiography, *A Life Unscrewed*, but the meeting actually taking place at Chatham House, this went un-recorded.

Alongside the damage that poor corks had done to wine as a product in the past, continuing damage is being done to the French wine industry by *La Loi Evin*, created by a teetotal member of the French government in the late 1980s. This forbids any advertising that even hints at the pleasures of wine. Nobody believed in the 'Guinness is Good for You' ads in the 1960s that construction workers could actually carry iron girders on their shoulders with a pint in the other hand, but they were cheerful and good for the brand. A meeting of *L'Académie du Vin de France* noted recently that a country that considered its Belon oysters, Bresse chickens and Brie worthy of recognition by Unesco, while vilifying its own viticulture was dangerously myopic and that the damage already done would only get worse. I was reminded of this on a visit to Paris, dining with Bella at La Fontaine de Mars, one of the classic bistros in the city that has remained unchanged, to see behind the bar a lovely print from the 1930s of a glamourous couple in white flannels against a vineyard map of France under the title '*Buvez du vin, vivez joyeux*/Drink wine, live joyously'. The country that invented *joie de vivre* has not been doing its wine producers any favours, but President Macron has appointed a wine adviser and I would bet that *La Loi Evin* will soon be rescinded.

While this is in the future, there was a welcome return to sanity in Tuscany that summer where a gathering storm was averted by a 69% vote by producers of Brunello di Montalcino againt their Rosso di Montalcino being allowed to be produced with up to 20% of 'foreign' grapes. There had already been a big scandal when evidence of Cabernet Sauvignon, Merlot and Syrah had been found in some Brunellos themselves, heavy fines had been imposed and questions were asked. Plainly the producers who had planted grapes other than the accepted Sangiovese were of the opinion that Rosso was just a second label of Montalcino and volume could grow to satisfy a larger market. I am a big fan of Rosso di Montalcino and while I can still just about afford Brunello, it is one third the price and more approachable and the whole point of it is Sangiovese. Permitting other grapes would be the thin end of the wedge and it is interesting to note that while the rules for Chianti Classico do allow 20% of 'other' grapes, there is a trend back to 100% Sangiovese for the DOCGs.

In October 2011 I turned seventy and this milestone was the subject of celebration, which provided great compensation for having been born in such a poor year for wine. The first was organised by Michael Hill Smith during our week in September in Singapore as wine consultants for SIA. The food was spectacular and everyone had brought a bottle, the aperitif being Krug 1988, still very fresh. Three white Burgundies followed: a smoothly textured Corton-Charlemagne 2002 Louis Latour, a fascinatingly youthful magnum of Vougeot Blanc 1er Cru 1998 Domaine Bertagna and Coche-Dury's superb Meursault-Perrières 1999. The two Pinot Noirs: DRC's 1999 Cuvée Duvault-Blochet 1er Cru Vosne-Romanée (my own last bottle) being slightly corked was outclassed by a magnum of Mount Harlan's 1994 Calera Reed Vineyard with a decade in front of it. As an *entr'acte*, Yalmuba's 1941 Galway Claret from the Barossa, sent over by Michael's cousin Robert Hill Smith, was amazing and much younger than me. Three magnums of red came next: Fontodi's elegantly powerful 2001 Flaccianello della Pieve from Panzano-in-Chinati, a beguiling 1997 Hermitage from Chave and a 1990 Mas de Daumas Gassac. The evening finished with two stars: a richly concentrated Château d'Yquem 1989 and a warm yet grippy Yalumba's 1940 Special Reserve Tawny made from Dolcetto, Shiraz, Grenache and Muscadelle, a stunning surprise.

Over the weekend of 8/9 October, Bella and I hosted a large lunch at the nearby Seaside Hotel and the next day gave a vineyard picnic for many more. Michael Broadbent and Napa's Warren Winiarski headed the 65-year age span and producers' wines I had enjoyed over the years were served in pairs. Bollinger Special Cuvée and A&F Boudin's 2009 Chablis 1er Cru Fourchaume as aperitifs; then a citrusy 2010 Shaw + Smith M3 Adelaide Hills Chardonnay contrasted well with a mature, minerally Arcadia Napa Chardonnay Stag's Leap Wine Cellars with salmon. With lamb came O. Fournier's dense, fruity Centauri Red from Chile and Nittardi's earthy, elegant 2008 Chianti Classico. Châteaux Léoville-Barton 2002 and Beaucastel 200 were grand classics with the cheese, while speeches were made over Roberto Bava's Bassotuba Moscato d'Asti and a pear and almond tart. For October the weather was wonderful and as lunch ended around 5pm, Jasper Morris decided to go for a swim, the hotel being on the cliffs above and with direct access to the beach at Burton-Bradstock and surprised our guests staying in the hotel by repeating the performance before breakfast the following morning.

With a full house to manage and our guests expected for coffee around midday before the vineyard picnic, Bella remonstrated with me as I was leaving for the Sunday service in our local church just up the street in our village, saying that I should help her with all the preparations, to which I replied simply that I had a lot to thank God for and went on my way. After the service I thanked our splendid Welsh vicar, Bob Thorne, who said 'Aren't I supposed to come up and bless your vines some day soon?', to which I replied, 'yes, today at 2.30'. He duly appeared in his robes, raised his arms and blessed them as 'little children of God' and lo and behold they delivered just under 500 bottles from vines in their 'third leaf' which had been planted in April two years before. This was a great birthday gift, as was a special cover of *Decanter* created for me by Sarah Kemp. Walking up to the vineyard, Sarah noticed that the farm formed a large bowl, an amphitheatre with the vineyards on the lower slopes, and announced 'what a perfect setting, Steven, you should hold an opera!'

In November, after a brief trip to Moscow to hold two tastings in front of a packed house in what is plainly an exciting, but very problematic emerging market, I was in Hong Kong to attend Wine Future 2011, masterminded by Spain's first MW, Pancho Campo (who subsequently resigned from the Institute of Masters of Wine, as a result of, to my mind, unjustified accusations of using his title for overt commercial purposes). Twelve panels were organised on every aspect of the wine business. Mine was entitled 'Looking Ahead – regions, varities and styles'. Chaired by UK wine writer Tim Atkin MW, my fellow panelists were critic Michel Bettane and consultant Michel Rolland from France, who spoke more of their country's past than its future and winemaker Randall Grahm from California, who gave the future to Mediterranean varieties. My choices were Vermentino for white that I predicted would become the new

Viognier, and Cabernet Franc for red, finally emerging from the shadow of its Sauvignon brother, and, of course, English Sparkling Wine. I have been proved correct on all three.

The Christmas party of the Circle of Wine Writers, of which I was midway through a six year term as President, was that year sponsored by the Virginia Wine Board and held in the august surroundings of The Old Hall in Lincoln Inns Fields. Just four years before the first tasting of Virginian wines had taken place at Vinopolis and the scattering of wine writers who attended immediately spread the word about the elegance and freshness of the wines: lemony Chardonnay, floral Viognier, fragant Cabernet Franc, vibrant Cabernet Sauvignon/Merlot/Petit Verdot blends and even a little of Piedmont's Nebbiolo, all benefitting from the cool climate and surviving the humidity. The contrast in style to wines from the much warmer West Coast is marked, not least for their balanced alcohol that sees 13.5% as a maximum. If 'preppy' is a positive description for wines, Virginia produces the preppiest in America.

In January 2012 the Southwold set met to taste the 2008 Clarets and dry and sweet white Bordeaux, concluding that while it was not the greatest vintage of the decade, it was good overall with no great surprises. Nearing the end of their first decade, I am just opening the first bottles of the mostly *Crus Classés* (the last year I could afford them before everything changed with the 2009s and 2010s) in my cellar and they will give a lot of pleasure over the next few years. Then Oz Clarke and I were off to Croatia again to see improvement and to discover the potential of a grape called Frankova, similar to Austria's Blaufrankisch and Germany's Lemberger, which showed good country-style Gamay fruit and character.

My last visit to Sicily had been with the AIV in 1982 and Bella had never been, so we snapped up an invitation from Andrea Franchetti to attend the Contrada d'Etna that he organises on his Passopisciaro estate where there were still traces of snow among the vines planted at up to 1,300 metres on the volanco's blackened earth slopes. Etna's local grapes are Nerello Mascalese (which shares characteristics with Nebbiolo and is mistakenly thought to be related to Pinot Noir) and the softer Nerello Cappuccino for the reds, and Carricante, which Peter McCombie MW describes as like 'drinking liquid oyster shells' for the whites. The dry summers and long ripening time have encouraged Franchetti to plant Chardonnay and Petit Verdot, while his neighbour Marco di Grazia of Tenuta delle Terre Nere stays with the local varieties, making a totally stunning Calderara Don Pepino from 140-year-old pre-phylloxera vines which he openly admits has been influenced by Chave's Hermitage.

A summer visit to Budapest to host a blind tasting of twelve Cabernet-based wines from around the world attended by 200 people found two local wines in the top six, the results being (with my own ranking in brackets) Stag's Leap Wine Cellars (2), Torres (1), Tenuta Belguardo (6), Sauska (10), Malatinszky (3) and Nicolás Catena (5), the Sauska and Malatinszky Cabernet blends placed within such company showing how far the wineries from Villány in the south of the country and particularly knownfor Cabernet Franc, have moved towards quality. Cabernet Francs also showed stunningly well in a mid-summer tour of the Loire Valley with a group of wine lovers from Hong Kong, the wines of Chinon, Bourgueil, St-Nicolas de Bourgueil and Saumur Champigny never having been better.

The biggest event for me in 2012 was the Symposium of the AIV in London in early June. Having proposed the UK visit at the previous December meeting and found it strongly accepted, I had to come up with a programme for the forty attendees. The welcoming dinner on the Saturday evening was at Boodle's in St James's, which had opened especially for this and had admitted ladies very rarely to the main rooms. The chef prepared a menu of the best of British produce and the wines, except for the Graham's 1980 Port, came from my cellar. Two evenings later, thanks to fellow member John Salvi MW. The dinner was at The Vintners' Hall, the cradle of the country's wine trade since the 14th century, where members' wines were poured and the guests shared in the traditional Loving Cup. On the intervening two days, visits were made to English vineyards and gardens, to Nyetimber and Ridgeview on the first day, to Great Dixter Gardens (thanks to Michael Schuster, another member) and to Hush Heath Estate on the second, both in pouring English summer rain. (The 2012 vintage was so affected that many English vineyards, including Nyetimber and my own Bride Valley, didn't bother to pick a single grape.) To say that the AIV's first visit to the UK was an eye-opener would be a serious understatement.

The trade-off came on Tuesday morning, when the AIV hosted a debate on the question 'Is noble wine a valid concept?'. *Le Vin Noble* has been the *raison d'être* of the AIV since its foundation in 1971, the criteria being quality, authenticity and loyalty to origin. At our annual meetings each December, the AIV speaks only to itself and, thanks in part to *Decanter* Magazine, three dozen writers, critics, merchants, sommeliers and restaurateurs turned up at Jermyn Street's Cavendish Hotel to hear what we had to say. Bruno Prats, who had made 30 vintages at Château Cos d'Estournel and was now involved in the Douro, South Africa and Chile, presented a paper on the theme 'Nobility and History', concluding that while centuries before the vineyards had been owned by the nobility and the Church, today noble wines granted nobility to those who made them. Michel Bettane came next, stating that the soil itself is not noble, but human intervention may render it so. His theme — that diversity leads to greatness and that wines are a succession of different expressions while the terroir remains the same — can be applied to vineyards the world over.

Victor de la Serna from Spain followed by saying that the key to nobility in wine is the ability to age, citing the 19th century vintages still in the cellars of López de Heredia and Marqués de Riscal in Rioja. At this point the room seemed to agree that nobility is the coming together of terroir and human skills. The California perspective was presented by Paul Draper (Ridge Vineyards) and Josh Jensen (Calera Estate), bemoaning the elevated status of California winemakers, who consider themselves 'wine creators', while all a noble wine needs is a sense of place and to be made as naturally as possible. Many other interventions followed and the debate was closed by Angelo Gaja with an impassioned support for 'wine artisans' who transfer knowledge and experience across generations and are driven more by the personality of the product than its possible perfection. A vote was taken, with two thirds of the guests agreeing that the concept of nobility was valid.

My personal conclusion is that 'noble' defined in the Oxford English Dictionary as 'having qualities of a very high or admirable kind' is a too elitist and too restricting an aim for wine. After the debate, some members suggested 'real' a descriptive whose market has been recently cornered by the producers of 'natural' wine. My preference is 'true', defined in the OED as 'faithful, loyal, constant, trusty.' We have all been brought up with the concept of truth, which is more basic than noble and more real than real. At the AIV conference at the end of the year I proposed that we adopt *Les Vins Vrais* — Wines of Truth.

We can now fast-forward five years to June 2017, when Domaine de la Verrerie held a two day symposium under the banner Fine Minds 4 Fine

Wines. The many debating tables all came to the conclusion that 'fine' was too elitist and the description that should be adopted would be 'authentic'. It was good to know that the AIV got there first.

After our usual month of August – all the years in Paris had left me with the conviction that one didn't work in August - driving through one part of France down to Tuscany for a week at Nittardi followed by a week at Castello di Argiano in the southern part of the Brunello di Montalcino DOCG and back again through another part of France to Cherbourg and thence to Dorset, I was off with Sarah Kemp and her crew for the inaugural *Decanter* Asia Wine Awards in Hong Kong. This had been planned since April, in long exchanges with Jeannie Cho Lee, a Hong Kong resident and Korea's first Master of Wine, who had been one of the Vice-Chairs that year. The incredibly glamorous Jeannie, who could well carry the title of 'Miss Wine Asia', helped Sarah convince Time Inc, *Decanter*'s owners, that Hong Kong was the next logical step for the competition and agreed with me that the same rules as in London would apply. She also agreed that the DAWA should be a Asian competition judged by Asian palates for Asian consumers, so apart from the *Decanter* 'home team' of Gerard Basset, Andrew Jefford, Australia's Michael Hill-Smith and Singapore's Ch'ng Poh Tiong under the charming but firm management of *Decanter*'s tastings' director Christelle Guibert, all the judges were Asian, or had worked in Asia for ten years or more. I had met many of them on my travels and six years later over half of them were still on the panels, the Vice-Chairs increased by Li Demei, China's top winemaker-consultant and Shinya Tasaki, the most revered taster in Japan.

Compared to the volume of entries in London, where the DWWA had already broken the 12,000 entry mark and forced the much older-established International Wine Challenge (IWC) to stop advertising itself as 'the world's largest wine competition', our first event garnered just under 2,000 entries, but it gained recognition slowly and surely to reach 2,800 entries in 2016 and a really satisfying 3,200 in 2017, my final year as Chairman and the first year that Sarah Kemp, who had run *Decanter* so creatively for twenty-seven years, was not with us, as she had resigned from the company, leaving her entire staff shell-shocked and tearful, two months before. Many glasses were raised to her at our dinner the Monday evening before the kick-off and her colleague John Stimpfig summed up Sarah's departure well in his column that month as being 'the end of an era'. The DWWA started back in 2004 as a joint crusade by Sarah and me to create the world's best wine competition, and we did so with both this and the DAWA, so the two 2017 events were for me great ones to go out on.

16. Poacher Turned Gamekeeper

When, in January 2014, I participated in the presentation of non-Champagne Sparkling Wines at Liberty's Annual Trade Tasting at the Kennington Oval, pouring glasses of Bride Valley Cuvée Reserve 2011, it was the first time in my whole life in the wine trade that I had been on the selling side of the table as a producer. In my early days as just a trainee, later as a buyer, even later as a critic, I would write notes on each wine tasted, occasionally commenting on and discussing it with the producer on the other side. This was a brand new experience. Having first discussed my ideas for the forthcoming vineyard on Bella's farm in south Dorset with Georges Legrand, the top sparkling wine maker from Jean-Claude Boisset, I told him that I intended to make only one wine, a single vintage Brut. No Blanc de Blancs, no Rosé and certainly not a Non-Vintage built up from stocks of reserve wine as they do in Champagne. I was told bluntly that this was stupid and I had to make at least two wines, if not more. 'Why?' I asked, assuming that my model was simplicity itself. 'Because with just one, the only question you can ask is "do you like my wine?", whereas with two or more, the question can be "which of my wines to you prefer?".'

Of course the tiny, vicar-blessed 2011 vintage only produced the Cuvée Réserve, and I was so thrilled that, tasting it pre-release after a purposefully low *dosage* of 8 grams of sugar per litre – the average then was 10 g/l or more – it represented so clearly the light chalky soil of the vineyard, that I was as proud as any father could be to present it at a tasting. In 2012 there was so much rain during the late summer we didn't bother to harvest, but then neither did Nyetimber, the benchmark producer in the south-east, who said that the cost of sorting the healthy grapes from the rotten ones was not worth the expense and trouble. This washout affected the very young vines and despite a normal growing season in 2013 we only made 2700 bottles from 20000 vines, the Chardonnay and Pinot Noir performing quite well, but very little from Pinot Meunier. My instructions to Ian Edwards, owner of the nearby award-winning Furleigh Estate, to whom we take the grapes for Rosé Bella, were to macerate our best Pinot Noir

The family at Bride Valley Vineyard, September 2015

for 24 hours to bleed off a little colour from the skins. Then to press very slowly to obtain more colour, the resulting pink juice being darker than desired, to be blended with enough white juice before bottling to lighten it. Thus in 2013 we made 900 bottles of Rosé and 1800 Blanc de Blancs, both well-received.

2014 turned out to be a bumper year for English wine and especially for Bride Valley, where the grapes were plentiful and ripe, ending up with 21500 bottles from 30000 vines, split between about 50% Brut Réserve and 25% Blanc de Blancs and 25% Rosé Bella. The Brut was released in January 2017 with an 8 g/l *dosage*, the Rosé in June with just 7 g/l *dosage* to preserve the precision and wild-strawberry Pinot Noir fruit, and the Blanc de Blancs, back up to 8 g/l due to the high acidity from our Kimmerigian chalk soils, in September. Writing this, I can say that the wines are all tasting beautifully, are winning awards and are selling well all over the world. This is the good news; the less good news is that the cold 2015 summer only gave us 7000 bottles of very light wine, the 2016 even less but of better quality and the 2017 from 30000 bottles predicted after 'flowering' in early July, due to an excessive attack of mildew during a rainy August, dropped to just 9000 bottles from 42000 vines. Over the past six years we are looking at an average of under one fifth of a bottle per vine and not even the

Domaine de la Romanée-Conti could survive on that. During the 2009 Vinexpo in Bordeaux I found myself chatting to Eric de Rothschild before a dinner at Lafite and, responding to his asking if I was up to anything new, told him of the inaugural planting in Dorset. Immediately he put his arm around my shoulders, saying 'Welcome to the Club'. At the time I thought of it as congratulation, now it seems more like commiseration. Looking on the brighter side, as I always have, Ian Edwards told me that it takes ten years for a totally new vineyard to establish itself, and that once established one could look for an average of a kilo of grapes per vine. Even though this is much, much less than in Champagne, even less than in the drier and slightly earlier-ripening south-east of England where the majority of vineyards are, it would show me 33500 bottles a year and suit me just fine.

There used to be a saying amongst Bordeaux châteaux owners that 'you only make money on the way out', presumably by finding someone with deep pockets to buy your estate. Prices being paid now for vineyards of recognised quality are becoming stratospheric, even from recent high levels, but while the classed growths of Bordeaux have been in profit since the 1982 vintage, life in the Médoc had been very tough, even for the top names. From 1969 to 1972 Bella and I spent several days in early October at Langoa-Barton, usually during the vintage which was much later in those days. Fast-forward to the mid 1990s, when new vinification and barrel cellars were opening up in the prestigious *appellations* of Bordeaux, I remember asking Ronald's nephew Anthony who had taken over Langoa and Leoville in the early 1980s, what some of them needed all the space for, to get the reply 'perhaps to keep the money'.

English wine has been around for some time. One of the pioneers was Sir Guy Salisbury-Jones, whose Hambledon white wine I imported from Hampshire to Paris in 1972 for the visit of The Queen. The Wingfield-Digbys near Sherborne, north of us in Dorset are celebrating their 44th vintage, but it has only come to prominence due to sparkling wines and this only in the past two decades. When Bella bought the farm in 1987, I noticed that the soil was full of chalk and, still running *L'Académie du Vin* in Paris at the time, put a couple of blocks in my pocket and showing them to Michel Bettane, France's great wine guru and then our top *professeur*, asked where he thought they came from. 'Champagne, of course'. 'No, Dorset.' 'In that case you should plant a vineyard.' A little later I asked

Chablis producer Michel Laroche, who was in England for a sales tour, to come down and take a look at the site, which impressed him enough to take some soil samples back with him, the analysis stating that it was good for Chardonnay and the Pinot family. At that time, I might have planted Pinot Blanc and its humidity-resistant cousin Pinot Auxerrois, but 1987's rainy summer thankfully stopped that idea and I didn't think about it again until the early 1990s, when at the International Wine and Spirit Competition Awards I was handed a glass of something sparkling and asked what it was: 'Easy,' I said, 'Grand Cru Blanc de Blancs, probably Cramant.' It never occurred to me that it might not be Champagne but it was in fact Nyetimber Blanc de Blancs from West Sussex. Several years later, Ridgeview from East Sussex, whose slightly crisper style I had admired at tastings, won the 2010 *Decanter* World Wine Awards Trophy, beating Champagne and sparkling wines from all over the world.

By this time, English Sparkling Wines were well and truly launched, with 1500 hectares under vine across southern England, and a few pockets further north, growing to 2500 hectares by 2017, and all but a few of these new plantings going for sparkling wines. Ten years earlier I wrote an article that appeared under the title 'Le Fizz Anglais'. At that time I was still an observer, and the Boisset team had not yet been out to do their researches and give their encouragement to start planting. I wrote that 'given suitable soil and climate, planting grapes seems to be more profitable than any other legal form of agriculture. You don't need planning permission and you may even get a grant for diversification, but few people have the skills and investment available to make a really fine wine. This is what made Nyetimber stand out: the then owner, Chicagoan Stuart Moss, was a perfectionist and did everything by the Champagne book, buying the best equipment and employing the best people. For the nascent English wine industry to grow, profit has to be the driving factor and profit usually only comes after investment in quality. Sparkling wine is one of the most capital-intensive , technology-driven in the world. Small is not beautiful, for sparkling wines are not made in the vineyard, but in the cellar. You need expert advice and money – and then more money.' This turned out to be only too true.

The Boisset family showed keen interest in my presentation at Vinexpo in June 2007, especially the dashingly handsome and irrepressible Jean-Charles, who had moved to Napa a few years before. He is younger brother of Nathalie who oversees the French side of the business from the family base in Nuits-St-Georges. He bought the old Robert Mondavi home in Oakville, and is continually acquiring new vineyards, is always up for something new. That autumn we received the first visit from Georges Legrand and their head viticulturalist to see what could be done as a joint venture. The original hopes were to find 30 hectares or so to plant and build a winery with a potential production of 100,000 bottles. After two more visits, the last with Pépinières Guillaume their vine supplier, analysis of deeply-dug soil samples from all over the farm, studies of the sloping ground – better for sheep than for vines – exposure and wind factors, visits to other vineyards across the south, Boisset's advice was plain: 'There are really only 10-12 hectares that tick all the boxes, you and Bella plant these, buy the vines from Pépinières Guillaume, take the grapes to Ian Edwards at Furleigh Estate nearby and if all goes well, we will buy all you make.' With that, off we went.

Everyone agrees that great wines are made in the vineyard, but few ask where the vines come from. Pépinières Guillaume at Charcenne in Burgundy's Haute-Saône region north east of Dijon, is recognised as the world's finest *pépinièriste*. All the top Champagne houses and the great and the good of Burgundy are his clients. Pierre-Marie Guillaume's 20-year study of Sangiovese clones in Chianti caused a sea-change in what was planted where current quality from this historic region has never been better. He has a vine nursery in California that supplies the West Coast of America and sends vines east to Virginia. On my travels, I find his name cropping up all the time, to the extent that I send him regular emails saying, '*Pierre-Marie, je ne peux pas vous échapper/*Pierre-Marie, I can't escape you'. On a recent visit, I asked him his secret and he replied: 'to do our job well, you put your boots on, walk the existing vineyards or examine closely those to be planted to get a real sense of the soil and the climate, then propose vines that will show a balanced vigour adapted to their environment and have a long life producing healthy grapes'. Simple. Pierre-Marie Guillaume is the unsung hero of many, many great wines.

So, during the winter of 2008-9, a little more than two hectares were prepared, 'Ernst' from Germany personally overseeing the planting by his mechanised team and Bride Valley Vineyard – so named because the Bride River meanders close to our house and the region of half a dozen villages is recognised as an 'area of natural beauty' – began to exist.

In December I was in Paris for *Le Palais des Grands Crus*, the greatest wine tasting I have ever attended, held at the Petit Palais, followed by dinner at the three-rosette restaurant Ledoyen, which the invited guests accessed via a passage under the street. Served mostly from magnums and double magnums, there were 62 Bordeaux, including all eight First Growths from both Left and Right Banks plus d'Yquem; 33 Burgundies from Domaine Leflaive's Bâtard-Montrachet 2006 to an *Imperial* (8 bottles) of Domaine de la Romanée-Conti's 1989 La Tâche; 10 Rhônes that included top wines from Beaucastel, Chapoutier and Jaboulet as well as all Marcel Guigal's grand cru 'La Las'; 16 Champagnes with Cristal, Dom Pérignon and Krug to the fore. Germany was represented by Egon Muller, Italy by Ornellaia, Sassicaia and Solaia, Australia by Yarra Yering and California by Harlan Estate. Most of the owners were there to present their wines and taste everyone else's while most of the guests were members of Le Club FICOFI. FICOFI is the brainchild of Bordeaux-born Philippe Capdouze, who realised that the world's greatest wine producers might actually want to meet those people who appreciate their wines, while these same people would like to have privileged access to them. For an entry fee and an annual subscription, FICOFI members have access to stocks built up due to Capdouze's close relationship with the producers. In 2012 FICOFI delivered 35 million euros worth of wine to its 150 members, the list now being closed at 200, with the guarantee of perfect sourcing, and a range of concierge services to allow the wines to be drunk in the best possible condition, something appreciated as much by the producers as by the members. In recent years I have hosted tastings for FICOFI in London, Hong Kong, Delhi and Mumbai and have more in the pipe line.

Bella and I spent the New Year in Rio de Janeiro, where my niece and family had moved into a handsome residence on the hill above the city next to the church where the local racing driver Ayrton Senna had been married. We saw in 2013 with a stunning firework display (and Bollinger 2002) on Copocabana Beach before flying south to Porto Alegre for a three-day visit to the vineyards. Brazil is the fifth largest wine producer in the southern hemisphere, behind Argentina, Australia, South Africa and Chile, with five vineyard regions, the most important being Serra Gaucha, north of Porte Alegre. The vineyards include the country's only DO Vale dos Vinhedos, which is known as 'Little Italy' since the estates are mostly still owned by third and fourth generation Italians following an exodus from the Veneto at the end of the 19th century. Our visits were only to wineries that export, the UK being one of their target markets and currently knowing great success. The high spot was an eight course wine pairing exercise at Pizzato, a 42 hectare estate run by œnologist Flavio Pizzato and his brother, with his two sisters on the commercial side and his wife in the kitchen. Further visits to Lidio Carraro, whose wines I had come across on my first visit to San Paulo a few years before, and tasting the sparkling wines from Casa Valduga, Miolo and especially Cave Geisse, whose Brut 1998 was the only sparkling wine presented by Jancis Robinson in her Top 20 in Hong Kong's Wine Future 2011 event, convinced me that Brazil is a wine country to watch.

Late January I was back in Southwold with the usual crowd to taste the highly rated and very highly-priced (until the 2010s went even higher, leading to the inevitable collapse) 2009 Bordeaux in the worst weather imaginable. But not even the deepest snow could keep more than 100 guests away from the memorial banquet held by Bristol's Commanderie de Bordeaux for its founder, wine merchant John Avery MW, who had died in late 2012, an empty chair stating his absence on our first day in Southwold. Aidan Bell, who had worked many years with John, and I battled sleet and fog across deserted roads after the final morning's tasting to arrive in time to change into dinner jackets to enjoy Avery's Champagne Rosé before sitting down to a series of wines that showed Bordeaux at its best: Domaine de Chevalier 2003 white from the Graves, Château d'Angludet 1995 and Château d'Issan 1985 both from Margaux, Château Canon 2000 Saint-Emilion from the Right Bank before returning to the Médoc with a superbly fragrant Château Margaux 1988, then a gloriously rich Château d'Yquem 1989 to finish on 1983 Graham's, allowing us to raise another glass in John's memory. A month later the wine trade filled St James Garlickythe, the 'wine trade church' opposite the Vintners' Hall, for his memorial service.

A mid-March visit to the Rhône Valley with Arblaster & Clarke Wine Tours began at Domaine Georges Vernay in Condrieu and ended at the Clos de l'Oratoire in Châteauneuf-du-Pape, each visit confirming that this region is the best in France for wine drinkers of shallow or deep pockets. As I write the London merchants are preparing their 'pre-release' tastings of the 2016 vintage. The Rhône's great expert, John Livingstone-Learmonth, says that he has never seen such energy and optimism and that even in 'old-fashioned' *appellations* like Châteauneuf-du-Pape, the younger generation is bursting with ideas. Georges Vernay, who sadly died in 2017 at a very great age, is revered as 'the Pope of Condrieu' for, as Mayor in the late 1960s when the total acreage under vine in this *appellation* had fallen from the pre-war 200 hectares to just seven, he refused to give up to the easier money from fruit-growing, or even house-building. By the early 1970s this had crept into double figures and my 1984 handbook *French Fine Wines* states it was only in the low twenties, but more important than saving this historic wine, Vernay saved the Viognier grape for the entire world, as this very capricious grape was known only in Condrieu and nowhere else. Wine occasionally needs heroes like this.

April found me in Russia, my third visit in as many years, but this time in the southern city Krasnodar on the Black Sea, one of the favourite summer watering holes of Catherine the Great. The invitation was to judge the Southern Russia Wine Competition and to attend the trade exhibition Vinorus Vinotech. The other guests were John Salvi MW from Bordeaux, the much-travelled Brett Crittenden from Australia, and editor of *Wine Business Monthly* Lisa Shara Hall MW from the USA. The Russian co-chairs were aided by nine local judges headed by Igor Serdyuk the country's leading wine critic who was, thankfully, fluent in English. The dry white and dry red winners were both from local grapes, the five white Golds included a Chardonnay and a Sauvignon Blanc and the four red Golds showed two Cabernet Sauvignons, the other two being from Saperavi, more famous in Georgia. In discussions at Vinorus Vinotech the international guests praised the overall quality, to be told that an increase in indigenous varieties was not assured, since there is not a single vine nursery in Russia, wine having a low priority for Moscow. Nevertheless, the producers we met, large and small, were all passionate about their wines and open to every kind of advice. Several of them, appropriately named 'Les Garagistes', ignore State rulings entirely, working below the radar to produce wines for a local clientele. With people like these, the future for Russian wines is positive.

Early summer tastings featured 2011 Vintage Port, the last vintage to be generally 'declared' since 2003, causing David Guimaraens of Croft, Fonseca and Taylor to say that 'the 2011s stand out for the purity of the fruit and the quality of the tannins, which are silky and well integrated but provide plenty of structure.' Charles Taylor MW of UK merchant

Montrachet was more precise: 'the best vintage since 1994, possibly since 1963'. I have bought all the recently declared vintages – 1994, 1997, 2000, 2003 – on release and have wines from the 1980s and 1970s in the cellar, but with a consumption in Dorset of three bottles a year, these will see both me and the next generation out, so my two grandsons can now look forward to six bottles each of Cockburn, Croft, Dow, Fonseca, Graham and Taylor, which will be reaching the magic twenty-year mark when they both come of age.

After the biannual mid June week at Bordeaux's Vinexpo, with the usual round of great dinners, the most memorable being at the Conseil des Grands Crus Classés 1855 black-tie event, this time at Mouton-Rothschild, where Philippine de Rothschild, already in fading health, gave a very moving welcoming speech to her 500 guests. Château owners and their representatives were at each table to serve their own wines and I was on a Mouton table to enjoy the robust yet velvety 2005 and the magnificent 1986, the best Médoc from that rather tough vintage. Tuesday evening is usually reserved for dinner in Saint-Emilion hosted by the Premiers Grands Crus Classés B, but following the controversial elevation of Angélus and Pavie to the 'A' group, this association was in complete disarray and no dinner was held. I made up for it and more by attending a lunch the following day at La Fleur-Pétrus in honour of the 100th anniversary of the birth of Jean-Pierre Moueix, hosted by his sons Jean-François and Christian. A small vertical of 2012–2005 (the youngest vintage is generally tasted first) was presented beforehand with 2010 and 2005 standing out for me and magnums of the 1970 – one of the best 1970 Pomerols I have ever drunk and still full of vigour – and the stunning 1998 were served with a wonderful menu created by Michel Guérard of the 3-rosette Les Prés d'Eugénie.

Before my summer August break, I attended the International Cool Climate Chardonnay Conference in Niagara, Ontario, which is based on the highly regarded International Pinot Noir Conference in McMinnville, Oregon and was sold out for the full three days. My first visit to Niagara had been in the mid 1980s, when the grapes planted were mostly hybrid and it was hard to be encouraged by the wines. Now, with hybrids a thing of the past, it is hard not to be encouraged by what Ontario produces. The wine country is situated between the 41st and 44th parallels, on the same latitude as Oregon and central Burgundy, being a little warmer than both during the growing season with cooler nights during the harvest.

Viticulture is on a 'green' basis, many vineyards being organic and a few bio-dynamic. I was the keynote speaker and moderator the second morning over an extensive Chardonnay tasting, aided by an impressive panel of Chardonnay producers from France and California as well as Niagara. My top vote went to winemakers in Oregon and Burgundy as well as Niagara Thomas Bachelder's Saunder's Vineyard 2011, second place to Louis Jadot's Puligny-Montrachet Les Folatières 2010 and third place to François Morissette's (ex Chambolle-Musigny, Meursault and Sonoma) Twenty Mile Bench 2011. Niagara's cool climate Chardonnays are very good, especially if they benefit from outside experience.

Another cool climate is Tasmania, indeed so cool that Jean-Claude Rouzaud of Louis Roederer gave up trying to make sparkling wine there 'losing a hand before losing an arm'. His son, Frédéric, has dismissed planting in England as being 'too windy' and he has a point. Yet, superb sparkling wines like Heemskerk, Janz and Pirie apart, Tasmania is just right for cool climate grapes. At the DWWA dinner at the Royal Opera House in September, the International Chardonnay Trophy went to Joseph Chromy's 2001 from Launceston and with less than 1% of Australia's vineyard area, Tasmania picked up Regional Trophys for Sparkling and Pinot Noir, plus additional Golds for Chardonnay, Pinot Noir and Riesling. Australia's most famous Chardonnay, in my view 'the white Grange', is Eileen Hardy from Hardy's, the historic dynasty established in 1853 by Thomas Hardy, a young émigré from Devon. Later that month his great-great-grandson Bill Hardy presented a vertical tasting of the Eileen Hardy Chardonnay, named after his grandmother who travelled to London at 84 years old to receive an OBE from the Queen. Since the 2008 vintage, fruit from Tasmania has dominated that from the Yarra Valley, the 2012 being quite superb.

Looking through the 2013 *Decanters*, I came across my mentor Michael Broadbent's final column, under the goodbye line 'However arbitrary, 433 consecutive monthly articles is enough.' This is thirty-six years and one month without a break. I am at 292 and hope to make it to my 300th in October 2018, but nobody can ever rival Michael's figure. His first columns appeared under the title 'Michael Broadbent's Tasting Notes' and he remarks that 'it was so much easier in those days. I used to sit up in bed on a Sunday morning, open my current tasting book, find a theme and write. Sometimes it took me as little as two hours.' (After which Michael and his wife Daphne would have their traditional Sunday morning Buck's Fizz.) It was his first employer in 1952, the 'irascible but innovative' Tommy Layton, who told him to take a note whenever he tasted a wine. Michael goes on: 'My first tasting note, a modest Graacher Riesling was made on 17 September and, being a creature of habit, I now (July 2013) have roughly 100,000 tasting notes in 150 identical red books.' Those in possession of his *Great Vintage Wine Book 1 and 2*, with notes beginning from the mid-18th century, know the debt that wine lovers owe to him. He has certainly had a greater influence on me than anyone else inside or outside the wine trade.

The final column had to be celebrated and it was with style in *Decanter*'s dining room for the Michael Broadbent Tribute Lunch, where he was presented with a 60-page book containing his first and last columns, photographs across the years and dozens of memories from *Decanter* readers that included a limerick each from Simon Berry and Hugh Johnson:

> Simon Berry:
>
> The one thing you know about Michael:
> Any wine that he says you will like'll
> Be complex and complete,
> Taste just like Lafite,
> And make you go fast on your cycle.

> Hugh Johnson:
>
> The great thing about Michael B
> Is his utter disdain for PC
> How come all the girls
> Prick their ears for his pearls?
> (I wish it could happen to me.)

> To which I could add:
>
> The aura of Michael, my mentor,
> Transforms rooms he happens to enter,
> His erudite charm
> Does nobody harm,
> While attention 'round him seems to centre.

Of the many memorable quotes from the tribute book, two stand out. First, Michael's own on the frontispiece: 'Wines are like people. Some are perfect but boring, some are precocious but fail to live up to their promise and some may be flawed, but the way they develop is endlessly fascinating.' And Christian Moueix's recollection of Michael describing one of his wines as 'a marvel, like making love in a hammock', something that 20 years later Moueix admitted was still on his to-do list. The lunch showed some of Michael's favourite wines. As an aperitif the Pol Roger 1996 was described as 'Churchillian', while with Loch Duart salmon came magnums of Felseneck Riesling Grosses Gewächs 2010 (steely freshness with two decades in front of it) from Prinz Michael zu Salm-Salm who was on Michael's left at lunch. Château Lafite-Rothschild 1990 ('all the elements in place together') accompanied the roast partridge to perfection and Michael's favourite dessert wine Michele Chiarlo's Nivole Moscato d'Asti 2012 lifted the bread and butter pudding to new heights. Graham's 1970, served from a 2.1 litre bottle known as a tappit-hen, ended the meal with richness and warmth and further toasts to the Broadbents.

My last big trip in 2013 was back to India to hold tastings and dinners for the Wine Society of India in Mumbai, Delhi and Bangalore. David Banford and I had founded the WSI seven years before with too much blue sky thinking - an experienced entrepreneur has been quoted as saying that India stands for 'I'm never doing it again' – to find that selling wine in India might be described politely as 'complicated' and the following year our partners United Spirits and subsequently Direct Wines gave up the struggle with total losses all round. Although there are Wine and Food Societies in each major city in India, there is not yet a wine culture to speak of. Across its vast 1.2 billion population wine consumption is under 20ml a head, the percentage of the population that does drink alcohol consuming 100 times more spirits than wine. Even local wines are taxed at around 40% and imported wines between 200% and 350% depending on the state where it is sold. Alcohol represents the second largest revenue for the government and these taxes, despite strenuous lobbying by the World Trade Organisation, are unlikely to be lowered any time soon. If they were, the sky is the limit for wine sales, for the lingua franca is English, the accepted language of wine, the Indians are social and if their religion allows it, like drinking, and their interest in food would easily spread to wine. Sadly, depite still visiting the subcontinent regularly and even blending some wines at Fratelli Winery that carry my name and sell well, this is unlikely to happen in my lifetime.

A much smaller but much more encouraging country is Croatia. In 2010 Oz Clarke and I visited Zagreb to taste a massive range of wines produced by Agrokor, the country's largest agricultural business, alongside those of many other producers. This was on the invitation of Tony Hodges, one of the leading lights in Vinopolis-City of Wine, whose consultancy BrandStory was working with the Croatian Government to create a recognisable image for their diverse and hardly known wines. We were not impressed by the high alcohols and lack of freshness on the whites and the roughness of the reds and we gave our opinions quite bluntly. We returned in a freezing January the next year to find a lot of changes and a January 2014 visit confirmed the progress. The international grapes varieties are there, but with the exception of Merlot from Istria's Adriatic Coast, these are not the ones to look for. What Croatia is best at is it indigenous grapes, cousins or brothers to other middle European varieties, such as Malvasia Istriana (France's Rolle, Italy's Vermentino), Pinot Sivi (Pinot Gris) and Moslavac (Hungary's Furmint) for whites and Teran (Fruili's Refosco), Frankovka (Austria's Blaufrankisch) and down on the Dalmatian Coast Crljenak, discovered to be Zinfandel by Professor Carole Meredith of the University of California Davis in 2002.

In February I spent a week in Mendoza as one of the 12 international judges for the 2014 Wines of Argentina Awards. On the morning of the last day we re-judged all the Golds, retaining most, downgrading some to Silver and keeping many for the final round for a Trophy. From just 660 wines there were 70 Golds, 12 Trophies and 4 Regional Trophies. The idea of Argentina as a two-varietal country with Torrontés for white and Malbec for red still seemed to hold true in volume and branding, but blends and other single varieties were increasingly to the fore. The welcome surprise was the emergence of Cabernet Franc, a grape which won one Regional Trophy (Bodega Fin del Mundo, Patagonia 2010), two further Trophies and two Golds. Cabernet Sauvignon also showed well with one Trophy and five Golds. Fast forward to October 2017 where, at the Argentina Annual Tasting, I tasted anything but Torrontés and Malbec and still took three hours to complete the circuit, including an incredible Trousseau, the historic red Jura grape, from 100 year old vines. Once again, the wine world is like a kaleidoscope, every time you look at it, it has changed.

March saw my last of twice-yearly weeks spent in Singapore since 1989 as one of the three wine consultants for Singapore Airlines. Since I was a decade older than the country's official retirement age of sixty-two, I had had a good innings, spending more than a calender year in the city-state where, if one wanted to drink wine with the huge variety of Asian cuisines, one had to bring glasses as well as bottles. Now the island must be one of Eurocave's and Riedel's best clients. While I knew that my co-consultants Michael Hill-Smith and Jeannie Cho Lee, respectively Australia's and Asia's first Masters of Wine, had planned a final dinner for me, I had no idea of the array of wines I would come to enjoy in wonderful company over five evenings. To list them here would take too long, suffice it to say that Ausone, Canon and Cheval Blanc, all superb Saint Emilion 1964s, rubbed shoulders with DRC's Richebourg 1996, Hermitage La Chapelle 1982, while Roederer Cristal 2004 and Dom Pérignon 2002 represented Champagne, 2008 and 1998 Chevalier-Montrachet Bouchard Père et Fils and 2006 Le Montrachet Remoissenet represented white Burgundy, Barolo 1964 Giacomo Conterno and my own 2008 Ornellaia Italy and Australia showed brilliantly with Tyrells Vat 1 Hunter Semillon 1998 and Penfolds 1990 Grange. What a send-off. My younger friend Oz Clarke has replaced me, but I bet he won't have such great wines when he is retired.

In May it was Macedonia and I have to confess that before then I had never knowingly drunk a Macedonian wine. After just three very busy days organised by Wines of Macedonia, I was once again reminded why I still so excited by wine for even after fifty years in the trade, you never, ever, stop learning. Vineyards in the landlocked Republic of Macedonia in the heart of the Balkans, bordered by Serbia, Kosovo, Albania, Bulgaria and Greece, cover only 4% of cultivated land, yet wine has been one of Macedonia's symbols for over 4,000 years. As part of Yugoslavia in the second half of the 20th century, the country produced bulk wine from 39,000 hectares and while today this has shrunk to 25,000, in all the wineries I visited quality, even for the lowest priced wines, is the top consideration. The grapes are mostly local varieties that have been grown for centuries, but since the vineyards are on the 41st parallel, just south of Bordeaux and Tuscany, international grapes are being increasingly planted. Along with Croatia (and of course Slovenia) this is a country worth watching.

Macedonia was not at the Vinexpo Asia-Pacific trade fair in Hong Kong at the end of May, where the most surprising exhibitor was Hattingley

Valley Estate from Hampshire. Owner Simon Robinson was overwhelmed by the interest his English sparkling wines attracted, receiving more visitors on the first day than during the whole three days of Germany's Prowein Trade Fair. The Gold Medal he won at the *Decanter* World Wine Awards just a month before for his 2011 Rosé must have helped. The high spot at this very buzzy event was a 'Masseto Retrospective', a tasting of 14 vintages from 1987 to 2010 in the presence of current winemaker Axel Heinz, and consultant from the start Michel Rolland. Masseto is a single vineyard on the Orneillaia estate by Lodovico Antinori, who finally, after two years of telling the brilliant André Tchelischeff, his vineyard consultant, that he wanted Cabernet Sauvignon, finally agreed to André's insistence that it was a vineyard for Merlot. Masseto is now recognised as the greatest Merlot outside of Pomerol.

Long before the film *Sideways* brought Santa Barbara County and its Pinot Noir to wine drinkers' attention, the windswept coastal region of Santa Maria Valley – 210 kilometres north of Los Angeles – became California's third American Viticultural Area (AVA) in 1981. Firestone Vineyards was established in the mid 1970s by Harvard-educated Brooks Firestone, married to Kate, Cambridge graduate and dancer with the Royal Ballet, whose wines I had sold through my Paris shop. Bella and I stayed with them over a weekend in June to be part of the Cellar Classic Auction held at St Mark's-in-the-Valley Espicopal Church in Los Olivos. The auction, kicked off with my offering of a bottle each of Dow, Gould Campbell and Taylor 1977 going for $7,000, raised $321,000 for the church and other charities. The Firestone's son Adam and their British son-in-law David Walker teamed up in the early 2000s to form the Firestone Walker Brewing Company, for many years a regular recipient of America's top awards for craft beer. Our last lunch in Santa Barbara was preceded by a beer tasting, my favourite being Bretta Weisse 2014, based on the traditional Berlin beverage known in the 19th century as 'the Champagne of the North', refreshingly good at just 4.9% abv. The Parabola Russian Imperial Stout 2014, aged in Four Roses Bourbon barrels and weighing in at 14% abc, would be a great nightcap.

Our usual August holiday this time took us across France starting with a visit to Pol Roger in Epernay whose cellars are under the recently named Rue Sir Winston Churchill, down through Burgundy to Fattoria Nittardi in Chianti and the Sesti's Castello di Argiano south of Montalcino, back through Provence to Cahors, my first visit for thirty years, where a renaissance in under way. Home to Malbec, now far more famous in Argentina than south-west France, from a total of 22,000 hectares in the original appellation, only 4,500 remained under vines in 2002 when a charter of quality was proposed to classify the best vineyards into grands and premiers crus as in Burgundy. France's appellation body saw fit to turn this down and a dozen years later only 3,300 hectares remained. But help was at hand from soil experts Claude and Lydia Bourguignon, Claude being a fellow member of *L'Académie Internationale du Vin* (AIV) for many years, who have opened a local office and are replanting a long-abandoned terrace vineyard on a limestone base. While everyone agrees that good wines are made in the vineyard, people like the Bourguignons, Italy's Alberto Antonini and Chile's Pedro Parra work all over the world analysing soils and subsoils in the greatest depth, advising specifically what should be planted where to produce wines of quality and character. The Cru project has been reactivated, a growing number of *vignerons* are practising *pigéage* (pumping down the cap during early fermentation) to soften the Malbec's austerity, and Cahors looks like becoming Burgundian.

The *Decanter* 2014 Men (not Man) of the Year were Jean-Pierre and François Perrin, brothers in charge, now aided by their many children, of Châteauneuf-du-Pape's largest estate Château de Beaucastel. These wines have been a part of my life since the early days in Paris and inspired a visit to the estate to meet Jacques, their renowned father, who took us through a tasting going back to 1919. The brothers hosted a dinner for 80, many previous Men of the Year being present, at the château in early September under perfect Provençale weather. The jazz band that welcomed the guests set the tone for an explosively uplifting range of wines. As an aperitif, Pol Roger's Sir Winston Churchill 2002 showed an elegant grandeur, while the florality and freshness of the white Beaucastel 2012 called for another glass. Dinner opened with the white Beaucastel 2011, richer and starting to develop complexity that prepared one for the stunning white Beaucastel Roussanne Vieilles Vignes 1986, the Perrin's first vintage of this wine that had the freshness, breadth and depth of a Montrachet. Two Beaucastel Hommage à Jacques Perrin reds followed, the 2009 rich with fine clarity of expression, the magnums of 1995 showing both youth and vigour, a great wine. With local roast lamb came magnums of Beaucastel 1970 with a lovely lissom, almost Burgundian texture, to be followed by

Max, Steven, Bella and Maud at the Court House

a white Beaucastel Roussanne Vieilles Vignes 2009, whose dry richness perfectly matched the cheese. (Michael Broadbent has always maintained that white wine is better with cheese than red.) Etienne Hugel, whose family company in Riquewihr dates from 1639, provided the dessert wine, his Gewurztraminer Vendanges Tardives 2007, rich but not too sweet, a joyful way to conclude a magnificent evening.

Back in Dorset, things at Bride Valley were looking good. By early September the vines were full of bunches, the Pinots just beginning their *véraison*, when they begin to turn red, and the Chardonnays looking positively French. As I said earlier, this was a bumper harvest and Dacotah Renneau, an old friend who had once been the photographer at New York's notorious night club Studio 54, came for the weekend to take some lovely photos of the grandchildren in the vines. There will be days like this again.

The wine year ended in splendour in China, with Decanter's inaugural Fine Wine Encounter in Shanghai taking place at the recently opened Ritz Carlton. Concerned that some local wine lovers might get too 'stuck in', tickets were timed 9am to 1.30pm and 2.30pm to 6pm, the hour in between giving the staff time to clean up and the producers time for lunch. In the morning I had co-hosted a Master Class on Chinese Cabernet Sauvignon and Merlot, alongside Professor Li Demei, a wine consultant whose wine had stunned the world by winning the Best Bordeaux Blend over £15 at the DWWA earlier that year. Thanks to Sarah Kemp and her team, the top producers from the Old and New Worlds were there, happy to be showing their wines to such keen tasters. During the lunch break I found myself on a table with Jean-Philippe Delmas of Haut Brion, Alexandre von Beek of Giscours, Peter Femfert of Nittardi and a few others. The menu was enticing but only water was to be served. The producers took only a few moments to rise from the table, go to the next room where their stands were and to return with bottles. Thus the day continued, tasting after tasting, to conclude with a dinner in honour of Jeannie Cho Lee, whose almost rock star reputation ensured that wines suitable to the occasion were served.

Christmas was as usual at home in Dorset. I keep a record of what gets drunk and we opened with Bride Valley Brut 2011, the vintage of my 70th birthday, then a very good white Chassagne-Montrachet Les Grandes Ruchottes 2003 F&L Pillot, creamy and rich, but none of the oxidation from that heatwave vintage. With the turkey came magnums of Château d'Angludet 1996, the fine Margaux of the Sichel family and one of my favourite clarets, which I noted as 'still young and vigorous, top class', to end on Taylor 1977 Port, one of the best post-war vintages, maturing superbly in its fourth decade.

At the usual Southwold Bordeaux three-day marathon, this year for the 2011s, apart from the quality of the very best, we were not impressed by the reds, quite impressed by the dry whites and more so by the Sauternes. Stephen Browett of Farr Vintners, the country's leading wine broker, asked us all to rank the vintages of the century so far in descending order for red wines, the overall result being: 2005, 2010, 2009, 2001, 2008, 2006, 2003, 2004, 2007, 2002 and 2011. Two years later, the top four were unchanged, 2012 was placed next and 2013 last, a position from which I don't think it will ever move.

Shortly after Southwold, I was in Richmond, Virginia, to join a dozen importers, merchants and writers to select the twelve best wines from the State that make up the annual Governor's Cup. I have described Virginian wines as being 'preppy' and this they certainly are compared to California and the even hotter Washington State, and while Bordeaux varieties dominate the reds, there is a little Tannat from southwest France and even some Nebbiolo from Piedmont. For the whites, Chardonnay and Sauvignon Blanc are joined by Viognier, Petit Manseng and Vidal. My third visit was at the end of January 2018, after which Bella and I flew to Charleston, South Carolina, on the 31st to celebrate our 50th wedding anniversary with our old friend Bob Baker, who winters in Charleston and summers in Burgundy, with a generous cellar in both places.

One of the many advantages of my years with Singapore Airlines was that, to make up for the modest (but very useful) consultancy fees, we were offered four round trip tickets a year. While this suited my Australian, American and Asian colleagues down to the ground, I had less use for them and persuaded SIA that if Bella and I could not take them up, perhaps my family could. They agreed, and tickets to far flung places were passed onto my family to use. However, after my retirement the year before, we flew into Perth and then to the Margaret River, probably Australia's most beautiful vineyard region, clocking in with the Petersens at Piero Vineyards, Vanya Cullen and David Hohnen ex-Cape Mentelle now managing partner at McHenry-Hohnen and continuing to make elegantly ground-breaking wines. From there we flew to Melbourne where we stayed at the Melbourne Club, one of Boodle's reciprocal clubs, which it completely dwarfed having been built as a copy of the vastly imposing Reform Club on London's Pall Mall; as we arrived a wedding reception was in progress, all the ladies wearing white gloves and hats. Despite being in the middle of what has become the business district, Melbourne's Chinatown is close by and a visit to the famous Flower Drum restaurant was well worth it. From here we drove along the coast then heading inland to stay at The Royal Mail in Dunkeld which possesses Australia's finest wine list, with three entire pages devoted to their collection of wines from the Domaine de la Romanée-Conti. We chose the tasting menu with local wines by the glass. Then it was across country through the Coonawarra, a stunning drive, to arrive at Michael and Stacey Hill-Smith's modern and airy house in downtown Adelaide in time for tea.

Shaw & Smith, Michael's winery and vineyards, was founded with his cousin Martin Shaw, moving to Brian Croser's Petaluma for eight years prior to setting up the 'flying winemakers' network in France, Spain, Chile, and New Zealand, with a vision to make refined and exciting wines exclusively from the Adelaide Hills that would rank amongst the finest in the country. It is safe to say that they have succeeded and in 2012 they set their sights further away, with the purchase of the exceptional 20 hectare Tolpuddle Vineyard near Hobart in cool-climate Tasmania, to produce Australia's leading Chardonnay and Pinot Noir. The Chardonnay had previously gone to the Eileen Hardy blend, which now had to look elsewhere. After a day of tasting, Brian Croser and his wife came to dinner. Croser, who had put Petaluma on the Australian fine wine map thirty years before, only to see it taken over by local brewers Lion Nathan to end up in the hands of Japanese brewer Kirin, had recently regained possession of his original winery buildings from which he makes the Tapanappa wines, in partnership with Champagne Bollinger. Reflecting on the past, he said that the worst period for Australian wines had been the 1990s, due to the domination of big companies and the over-use of oak. For him, both were a thing of the past, the younger generation going for cooler sites, small lots and total individuality. He also pointed out that the vision of Australia as a hot country was misplaced, since as many as 24 of the officially designated vineyard regions were cooler than Bordeaux.

After two marvellous days at the Hill-Smith beach house at Victor Harbour, we flew to Sydney to stay with Peter and Brooke Ryan, our friends from the 1960s, (Peter very sadly died in 2017) at Palm Beach to talk about old times. Then it was into the city, based at the Australian Club on Macquarie Street with easy access to the museums and the stupendous Opera House. After a morning's tour of the latter, noticing that the following evening's performance was Puccini's *Madame Butterfly* I asked if there were by any chance any tickets, to be told that they had just had two front circle returns and since we had done the tour, it would be 30% off. It was magical and to continue the theme we found a Japanese restaurant nearby.

Our final evening in Sydney was dinner with Andrew Caillard MW, at his home in the quieter residential part of the city. Andrew (British by birth, Australian by adoption) is head buyer for Woolworths, the country's largest wine retailer, as well as having created the Langton's Classification, whose annual edition ranks Australian wines in a convincing manner. He is also owner of a small vineyard in the Barossa Valley and, being a talented artist, designs his own labels. After two fresh and lemony 2012 and 2011 Chardonnays from Portsea Estate on Mornington Pennisula and a beautifully balanced Bonneau du Martray 2008 Corton-Charlemagne, Caillard presented his own spicy and grippy 2012 Mataro

(Mourvèdre) before moving to a really fine Mount Mary Quintet 2001 Bordeaux blend from Victoria. Then came a richly textured Penfolds 1995 Cabernet-Shiraz and a Penfolds 1986 St Henri (which I prefer to the more concentrated and more famous Penfolds Grange) ending on a magnum of Lindeman's St George Coonawarra Cabernet 1980, rich, spicy with a long time to go. Kopke's Colheita 1938 wrapped things up. Wines like these, most wines in fact, are meant to be shared, long after the cost of purchase has faded.

At the end of March it was back to Bordeaux for the *en primeur* tastings, this year the 2014s, an overall good vintage and a great relief after the dire 2013s. I had been attending this crammed week of tastings, along with several hundred wine writers, critics and merchants from around the globe since the late 1990s and a small group had centred around Jancis Robinson and myself called *Le Groupe Robinson-Spurrier*. A good number of the châteaux whose wines we had to taste for our various magazines were part of the Union des Grands Crus (UGC), but many, particularly all the First Growths and an increasing number of 'Super Seconds' were not and to get to taste everywhere required planning of almost military precision. Appointments had to be made at least two months in advance, planned geographically with no more than 30 minutes at each château. Here is a typical day, beginning in Margaux and ending in Pauillac: 8.30 d'Issan, 9.00 Palmer, 9.30 Margaux, 10.15 Rauzan-Segla (more time at Margaux, as Paul Pontallier, the much-missed winemaker and director of 30 years always talked a lot), 10.45 UGC tasting and lunch, 2.00 Saint-Pierre, 2.30 Ducru-Beaucaillou, 3.00 Léoville-Las Cases, 3.30 Latour, 4.00 Pichon-Comtesse, 4.30 Pichon-Baron, 5.15 Batailley, 5.45 Grand-Puy-Lacoste. Then, of course back to whichever château who was putting us up for dinner. For years I had Robert Gorjak from Slovenia as my map reader, for from my school days in the Corps at Rugby this has been never been my strong point, and there was always another passenger or two. My last 'en primeur' marathon was in 2016 for the 2015s, a really lovely vintage which I likened to 1985, a year from which I have never had a bad bottle. In 2017 *Decanter* had decided on a policy of 'one region, one voice' so Bordeaux went to Jane Anson who lives there. It was a pity to step away, particularly since 2016 was another wonderful vintage, but I didn't miss the planning and the fatigue at all.

During a marvellous five days heading up an Arblaster & Clarke trip to Piedmont tasting with Angelo Gaja, Pietro Ratti, Aldo Vajra, Giacomo Conterno, Elio Altare and Pio Boffa of Pio Cesare, I realised once again that for me to really understand these Barolos and Barbarescos, I had to be on the spot. The front cover of April *Decanter* advised 'Piedmont, buy, buy, buy!' and I couldn't agree more, but few of these bottles find their way to my Dorset cellar, the Italian part being mostly Chiantis and Brunellos from Tuscany. And while from Montalcino I am moving more towards the Rossos, for price as much as early drinking, from Piedmont I do buy the more accessible Barberas and Dolcettos.

The following month I was in Paarl in the Cape as one of the three international judges of South Africa's 14th Old Mutual Trophy Wine Show, which I had judged alongside Jancis Robinson a few years before. This tasting was conceived and chaired by the country's leading wine authority Michael Fridjhon and such is the rigour of judging and the reputation of the results, the show attracts the best wines from the top producers. I greatly admire Fridjhon's philosophy, which he sums up in a simple mnemonic: PAPERCLIPS. This stands for Purity, Aesthetic Integrity, Potential, Equilibrium, Refinement, Complexity, Luminosity, Intricacy, Persistence, Savouriness. And he states: 'Wines which manifest these features are hardly ever the result of pure chance. Like other 'created' works of art, they are artifacts of intention. Winemakers talk of how they are merely the midwives of terroir, but every decision they take moves inexorably towards the end result.' 'Judging wine', he adds, 'is more an approval rating that quantifies how successfully the winemaker achieved what he set out to do.' When introducing the 2017 *Decanter* Asia Wine Awards, I told the seven Vice-Chairs that 'they were here to judge the wines, but should let the wines judge them'. This caused a 'that's very Zen, Spurrier' comment from Michael Hill Smith, but it is indeed the case that only by listening very carefully to what the wine is saying, can it be judged correctly.

The bi-annual Bordeaux Vinexpo Fair duly rolled around in mid June and on a gloriously sunny evening after the second day 480 guests including 275 journalists from 37 different countries were welcomed to Château Margaux by owner Corinne Mentzelopoulos and her family for a tour of the new cellar and winery buildings created by the architect Norman Foster to celebrate the 200th anniversary of the château itself, certainly Bordeaux's most impressive and memorable private residence. The new buildings are in total harmony (the key element in a great wine) with the past. As Lord Foster explained in his evocative yet modest speech at the opening of the dinner, his original idea was to create something new – one can think of Frank Gehry at Rioja's Marqués de Riscal or Christian de Portzamparc at Cheval Blanc – but the more he visited the estate and regarded the historical records, the more he was drawn back 200 years. The menu was conceived by the 3 star Parisian chef Guy Savoy and for the first two courses wines from the 1855 Classification were served *au hazard des tables*, depending on who were hosts at each table. I had the great good fortune to be on the table of Martin and Melissa Bouygues, owners of Château Montrose who three nights later concluded Vinexpo with an unforgettable Fête de la Fleur Dinner for 1,500 guests, and Frédéric Engerer of Château Latour, so we were served these two wines from the 2006 and 1995 vintages. Although such wines were hard to improve on, the Margaux 1985 served in magnums (Paul Pontallier's first vintage) did just that, a truly great, supremely elegant wine, the epitome of the château itself. The meal ended in grandeur with Château d'Yquem 1988 and the guests mingled long after the dinner was over. At Mouton-Rothschild two years before there had been a firework display. It was not needed that evening.

July was dashed by the death from cancer of the pancreas of my greatest friend Giles Townsend. Asked by his widow Victoria to give one of the addresses at his memorial service a few months later at Chelsea Old Church, I recalled that he and I had shared a mutual passion for Spain and had spent the July San Fermin Festival together in 1962. At the end of this exhaustingly exhilarating experience we went down to Madrid for a few days and then set off in different directions to the south, me to Valencia for another week of bullfights, Giles to Andalusia which he had already fallen in love with, agreeing that we would meet back in London. Giles was an organised traveller and had one 'must not forget' code – TMPK- standing for Ticket, Money, Passport, Keys. Ten days after we had said our good-byes in Madrid, I stepped onto the platform at Barcelona off a night train from the south to see, a dozen yards in front of me, Giles's back view, but hardly recognisable due to the slumped shoulders. I caught up with him – his train from Malaga had connected through Valencia – to be told that during the night his wallet had been stolen, so T, M and P had all gone. He was planning to find the British Consulate to see how he could get home.

Since we had both been travelling third class on wooden bench seats with chickens and other animals, we were not in a Consultate state, so I suggested we go to a barber shop for a shave and brush up. Giles then went off to report his loss and get a temporary passport and after an early, but lengthy lunch I put him on a train to Paris, where he had planned to meet his father Peter Townsend before going on to London. I told this story for one single reason: that moment on the Barcelona platform was the only time, in over fifty years of friendship, that I had ever seen the Townsend shoulders slumped, not even in the last few months of his life. Giles, more than anyone I have ever known, took life as it came, the rough with the smooth, the more important things being friends and family.

Another great loss to his wife and wine trade friends two years later was Tim Stanley-Clarke, also, along with Giles, one of the Christopher's trainees in the late 1960s, and Tim even made it to head office in Jermyn Street. Known to us all as 'Tim Standing-Joke', his wit and pranks were unsurpassed as were his skills in organising vinous get-togethers. One of these, named 'The Shortest Day Lunch', was held at his Club the Garrick on 21 December (except if it was a Saturday or a Sunday) with us all bringing bottles, generally magnums and not supposed to leave the table until it was dark outside. Hearing of his death, I noted that this was the darkest day.

After our usual summer holidays in late July and August, I was back in Dorset to check on the progress of the vintage, which had suffered from a cold summer and ended up being very small and not very ripe, with the result that only a little Rosé Bella was made, three-quarters of the juice being kept back to blend with the 2016s to make a non-vintage, something I had never expected to be part of the Bride Valley range. Since I always intended the Brut Réserve to carry a vintage date, my decision following the 2016 crop, better quality but also small volume, was to make a Rosé Bella and a Blanc de Blancs, but blend the rest with most of the 2015s but to make a Crémant NV, a wine with 4.5 bars of pressure compared to 6 bars for the Brut Réserve. This, I think, will be the first Crémant English Sparkling Wine and I have high hopes for it.

Soon it was off to British Columbia, the only Canadian wine region I had not yet visited, at the invitation of Maggie Anderson, Marketing Director of the BC Wine Institute and DJ Kearney, Vancouver's well-known wine writer, consultant and expert taster.

While some European, even New World countries might have a much longer history and grander wines, I had seldom encountered such beautiful scenery, such passionate viticulturists and winemakers and tasted wines of such encouraging quality that really showed a 'sense of place'. One of the many people I met was Anthony von Mandl, already known as 'the Robert Mondavi of the Okangan' for his formidable aesthetic vision alongside his vinous one. His two landmark wineries, Cedar Creek and Mission Hill as well as two smaller ones Martin's Lane and CheckMate (which specialises in Chardonnay) are finding their way onto the world's markets where they deserve a place alongside the well-known names. Another surprise came at the BC Pinot Noir Celebration organised by Jak Meyer of Meyer Family Vineyards. Although Merlot at 30% is BC's most planted red grape, Pinot Noir (21%) carries more reputation, the style being more Old than New World and often distinctly Burgundian. To conclude my visit, DJ Kearney had organised a 'Judgement of Vancouver' comparing twelve Chardonnnays and twelve Syrahs to benchmark varietals from around the world. Sadly the best-ranked Chardonnay, Blue Mountain Reserve 2013, only found 6th place, but C.C. Jentsch 2013 Syrah came first in its flight. British Columbia is a region to watch.

My final trip of the year, and perhaps the most memorable, was in mid-November to Marqués de Riscal's cellars in Rioja to taste a full century of their wines, from Don Guillermo Hurtado de Amézaga's first bottling in 1862 down to his direct descendant's splendid 1964. From these years, only eleven vintages were missing, the remaining ninety-two having slept undisturbed in the cellars known as The Cathedral since their birth. Very few of the wines had been recorked, as is the practice in Bordeaux once the wines enter their 5th decade, and none recorked before 1926. Every bottle was opened with Port tongs, clamped red hot around the neck of the bottle below the cork, breaking it off clean with no disturbance to the sediment. The wines were served in nine flights each covering a decade or so. Just a few brief notes can only hint at how moved we were by this 'Travel through Time', all those present sharing a profound sense of exhilaration that the wines could so genuinely represent the vintages as experienced by those who had created them.

1862-1873
The 1862 set the scene with its red-brown colour and naturally
ripe fruit that tasted barely 50 years old, the 1870 tasting like
a 1970 claret.

1874-1884
With vines (all brought from Bordeaux) maturing, this was an
exceptional flight, most wines showing a deep mahogany red colour.
1874 was elegantly robust, full of natural sweetness.

1886-1896
A wonderful flight, the wines showing purity, warmth and harmony.

1897-1909
Phylloxera struck in this decade, the 'golden age' ending in 1900, 1906
being the first vintage from grafted vines.

1910-1920
A much better flight as the vines aged, the 1920 dividing the room
due to American oak being used for the first time.

1921-1931
A superb decade, the wines having totally regained their natural
warmth, depth and vigour.

1931-1945
World depression and war turned this into a variable 14 years, the 1934
(Bordeaux's only good vintage of the '30s) being fine and harmonious,
the 1945 showing superb depth.

1946-1955
As in Bordeaux, marvellous wines from the late '40s, with the 1953
really lovely with caressing texture.

1956-1964
Quite an even flight, ending in glory, the youngest of all finding oak,
richness and tannins blended together, explosive yet controlled.

We were asked by our hosts to name our five finest wines.
Mine were 1874, 1897, 1922, 1945 and 1964.

In early December the AIV annual symposium was held in Berlin, since our retiring President, Mariano Fernández Amunátegui, was at that time Chile's ambassador to Germany. As ambassador to Britain a decade earlier, he had been a firm supporter of his country's wines, perhaps only exceeded in ambassadorial promotions by his counterpart from Portugal. Bella came with me as Berlin is such an exciting city for art and we had last been there for what became known as The Berlin Tasting in January 2004. After the chancellor Raymond Paccot, whose Swiss wines from Domaine La Colombe are superb and in whose honour the AIV moved to Lausanne the following year, stressed that in wine, as in all walks of life, it was individualism that mattered and that the AIV's mantra of '*le vin vrai, le vin naturel, le vin noble*' must, especially today, be supported and maintained. The presentations began with Raoul Salama of *La Revue des Vins de France* and one of the regular lecturers at *L'Académie du Vin* in the 1980, analysing international wine criticism. He stated that our small world 'acts on an intellectual level and to keep its independence, has the right to make errors of judgement', quoting Jean Cocteau's opinion that 'the critic is always comparing the incomparable and it generally escapes him.' Salama was followed by œnologist and chemist David Lefebvre on the ability of humans to analyse wines. He said that the human brain is not set for explaining the smells and tastes it receives, while a dog's sense and memory of smells is 100 times better than ours, but that their sense of colour is less good… and they cannot express themselves very well. My suggestion that at least human tasters could be dogmatic passed without comment.

Looking back, 2015 was a pretty good year.

In late January 2016 I attended the Naples (Florida) Winter Wine Festival, a lavish three-day event that ends with an auction for the Naples Children & Education Foundation, which is dedicated to improving the lives of at-risk and underprivileged children. Over the years this has raised $146,000,000 and I was there to promote a lot that the committee had asked me to create which would offer two couples the chance to spend 48 hours with me in Napa Valley to celebrate the 40th anniversary of the Judgement of Paris. The festival opened with a presentation tasting based around the Paris Tasting, at which Bo Barrett of Chateau Montelena and Ted Baseler of Stag's Leap Wine Cellars, the two winners on 24 May 1976, presented their wines, while George Taber, the journalist from

Time Magazine, whose presence on that day – along with that of Bella as photographer – ensured that the event would go down in history, and I managed to link the past to the present. Montelena showed their great Chardonnay in magnums from vintages 1992, 1998, 2001, 2004 (the best for me) and 2008, while Stag's Leap presented the S.L.V. Estate Cabernet Sauvignon from 1983, 1993, 1998, 2008 and 2012, this last getting my top vote.

The dinners on the Thursday and Friday evenings put even those of Bordeaux's Vinexpo to shame. No fewer than seventeen of America's Master Sommeliers were on hand to advise and pour and more than thirty winery owners, from boutique to big names, were opening their own bottles, with me offering the US its first taste of Bride Valley 2013 Blanc de Blancs. On the Saturday, after a walk-around tasting of top quality donated bottles accompanied by delicious bites, a few hundred people sat down under a vast tent for the auction. To help the bids flow, and flow they did, the Master Sommeliers circulated with great bottles. Among those offered to my table were: White – Poggio al Tesoro Vermentino 2014, Louis Latour Montrachet 2010, Marquis de Laguiche Chassagne-Montrachet 2010 and Kistler Hyde Vineyard Chardonnay 2008; Red – Kamen Vineyards Sonoma 2010, Chateau Montelena 1997 Cabernet Sauvignon, Tablas Creek Esprit de Beaucastel 2013, Château de Beaucastel 2010, Château La Conseillante 1998, Beaune Clos des Mouches 2005 Drouhin, Nuits-Saint-Georges Les Saints Georges 2008 Thibault Liger-Belair, Fontodi Flaccianello della Pieve 2006, Sassicaia 2008 and Ornellaia 2006. The sixty-four lots, all donated, were hedonistic in the extreme. The one I put together with sponsorship from the Napa Valley Reserve, Meadowood Country Club, Chateau Montelena, Grgich Hills, Stag's Leap Wine Cellars and 'Jean-Charles Boisset's Raymond Cellars fetched $220,000. When I went over to congratulate and thank the successful bidder, he said he would have been happy to have paid more.

In late February Bella and I took off for a three week visit to Cambodia, Laos and Vietnam, travelling via Singapore, this time on my own dollar. The whole itinerary from start to finish had been mapped out for us by a Dorset friend who specialised in Asia and as we flew into Cambodia, I looked at the cost of it all, over £3,000 a head, and said I hoped it would be worth it. From the splendours of Angkor Wat, to elephant riding in Laos, the sailing round the lakes in a private yacht in Vietnam, it was, and more. While being utterly Asian, the European colonial influence lingered in the restaurants, whose wine lists offered an attractive range at no more than London prices.

Once back on dry land, so to speak, it wasn't long before I was off again, this time heading up an Arblaster & Clarke tour on the theme Biodynamic Burgundy. Biodynamism is a holistic system of agriculture based on a series of lectures given by Austrian polymath Rudolf Steiner in 1924 and is being practised more and more by producers seeking to find chemical-free methods of producing foodstuffs and wine without damaging the environment. In fact, it is scarcely different from the methods used centuries ago by the monks whose monasteries owned most of the Burgundian vineyards, and it is in Burgundy that is most practised. On our first morning Frédéric Magnien, fifth generation vineyard owner in Morey-Saint-Denis, explained that biodynamism aims to 'revitalise and intensify organic life in the soil and to allow the vines to strengthen and energise themselves through the natural powers of the cosmic bio-lunar phases of viticulture.' The following morning at Château de Monthelie, the historic estate abutting Meursault and Volnay, we saw in the courtyard two dozen people either side of a long table very cheerfully knocking the manure out of hundreds of cow's horns, in which it had solidified during six months over the winter buried deep in the Burgundian soil. It is this substance that will be 'dynamised' via a 500-to-1 addition of rainwater, spun both clockwise and anticlockwise to create a perfect vortex and then sprayed on the vineyards, much better for them than the artificial fertilisers of the 1970s and 1980s. There are many detractors of such methods, notably the producer of sublime Sherry and member of the AIV Jesús Barquín who says 'What we see looking over the biodynamic landscape is a vista of starry eyes and good intentions mixed with quasi-religious hocus-pocus, good salesmanship and plain scientific illiteracy.' Fellow AIV Burgundians such as Guillaume d'Angerville, Dominique Lafon and Jacques Seysses would disagree, while my own view is that Burgundy is already kaleidoscopic and biodymanics allow it to shine brighter than ever.

The buyer of the Naples auction lot had agreed to the visit with his wife and another couple to Napa in mid-May and the first evening was at the Napa Valley Reserve, the brainchild of William (Bill) Harlan of Harlan Estate, as was the Meadowood Country Club where we were staying. Robin Lail, daughter of John Daniel Jr who inherited the Inglenook Estate (now owned by Francis Ford Coppola) which produced excellent wines in the 1940s and 1950s, had the brilliant idea of presenting wines that pre-dated 1976 to show the history of Napa Valley. Lunch the following day was at Montelena and in the early evening we visited Grgich Hills, where Milenko (Mike) Grgich, who had made Montelena's winning 1973 Chardonnay, was still wearing his French beret and flirting with the ladies in his 91st year, before a long dinner at Stag's Leap. The following morning, a Sunday, I had arranged with Jean-Charles Boisset to hold a 'Judgment of Napa' at his Raymond Vineyards, his JCB Blanc de Blancs 2012 against my Bride Valley Blanc de Blancs 2013. Earlier that morning, reflecting on how to describe the event, I had come up with the phrase *Rencontre à Raymond*/Encounter at Raymond' and on arrival had told Jean-Charles that it was not quite a 'Rumble in the Jungle' as the famous Cassius Clay-Joe Frazier fight in Zaire was called. Jean-Charles immediately produced a pair of boxing gloves which we donned for the photos. Over 100 guests blind tasted the two sparkling wines and his won, but not by a landslide.

The following morning very early I left for Washington DC, where Bella was to meet me for some anniversary celebrations at the Smithsonian National Museum of American History, where the original bottles of Montelena and Stag's Leap had been lodged two decades earlier and indeed had been cited in their compendium as one of the 101 Objects that Made America. Once again Bo Barret, Ted Baseler and George Taber were there to tell the story and we were joined by Stag's Leap Wine Cellars' founder Warren Winiarski (who remembered fondly that we had been 'joined at the hip' all those years thanks to the Paris Tasting, something he had forgotten about when he sold out to Ted Baseler's Château Ste Michelle a few years previously for $165 million) and Violet Grgich representing her father. Tastings were held and on the second evening a gala dinner took place at the Smithsonian, which I have referred to earlier.

The next day Bella and I visited the museums and before our late evening flight back home attended another tasting celebration in the Halls of Congress. Several Senators and Governors were present and at one point I was called to the podium to receive from the hands of Nancy Pelosi, Senator for California, a signed and sealed document that stated the Second Session of the 114th Congress had approved Resolution

Wine & Spirit Education Trust, The Guildhall, 23 January 2017.
left to right: Hon. Presidents Michael Broadbent, Hugh Johnson,
Jancis Robinson, Gérard Basset, Steven Spurrier, Executive
Director of the WSET Ian Harris.

734 'Recognising and Honoring the historical significance of the 40th Anniversary of the Judgment of Paris and the impact of the California victory at the 1976 Paris Tasting on the world of wine and the United States wine industry as a whole.' I was also given an American flag, neatly folded and boxed up, which I was told had been flying above the capital dome of Congress for two days in my honour! The palm reader in Saint Tropez back in May 1968 who had predicted a 'possibility of lasting fame' had turned out to be quite correct.

Early June found the great and the good together at the Cistercian monastery at Schloss Gobelsburg in Kamptal, Austria, founded in 1137, which I had first visited with the *Académie Internationale du Vin* twenty years before. This two-day symposium focussed on the winemaking styles in the 19th century at the monastery, in Georgia, Madeira and the Rioja and their impact today. A smaller group, dominated by members of the AIV, were to be found the month later at a 'Tribute to Terroir' weekend at the historic Abadia Reuerta estate (another vast monastery, now a superb hotel) on the edge of Spain's Ribera del Duero region. Bordeaux-born Pascal Delbeck, head winemaker since the start twenty-five years before, opened the event by saying, 'Terroir is like music, it can't play itself, it can't even discover itself, it needs the hand of man.' The theme for the day was 'How can man influence Terroir?', which was summed up by Carlos Falcó, Marqués de Griñón: 'By knowledge and desire.' Later, I kept thinking that while terroir obliges us to speak of it, in the end it will speak of us.

My last trip abroad in 2016 was to return to India, nothing to do with the defunct Wine Society of India, but to blend up some wines with Tuscan viticulturist/œnologue Piero Masi at the Fratelli Winery in Akluj in the state of Maharashtra two hours north of Pune. This is a partnership between the Sekhri brothers from Delhi, the Mohite-Patil brothers from Maharashtra and the Secci brothers from Tuscany. Since 2006 they have planted over 150 hectares on sparse, elevated and rolling land and had become Number 2 in the Indian wine market after Rajeev Samant's Sula and only produce wine from their own grapes. I had done some tasting and consulting for them before, but the idea now was that Piero and I would create a new label with wines made for the mid-to-high consumers. I came up with the name P+S (Piero + Steven) only to be told by Bruno Prats that P+S stood for Prats + Symington, the blends they make together in the Douro. So we settled on M/S, hoping that Marks & Spencer wouldn't complain. Piero and I are very different, he tall, angular, wedded to the soil, me a city boy. He didn't speak English and I don't speak Italian, so we communicated in French, generally starting our tastings of tank samples on different ends of the spectrum, but slowly coming together in agreement. From the 2015 vintage we agreed on an 80% Chardonnay/20% Sauvignon White, a 93% Sangiovese Bianco/7% Sangiovese Rosso Rosé and a 60% Sangiovese/20% Cabernet Franc/20% Syrah Red. All three have been very well received and I was back out at the end of November 2017 to make a similar blend for the 2016 red, to drop the Sangiovese down to 5% in the 2017 Rosé and to add a little Chenin Blanc and Müller Thurgau to the 2017 white.

In December I received two bits of news, both of which were great surprises and while recognising my past, gave me a certain direction for what is left of the future. The first was to be offered the honerary Presidency for the statutory three years from 2017 of the Wine & Spirit Education Trust (WSET). My predecessors in this role were Michael Broadbent, Hugh Johnson, Jancis Robinson and Gérard Basset and I was so proud to be standing alongside them at London's Guildhall on 23 January for the Diploma presentations. The WSET now teaches over 90,000 students across the world and for someone whose wine trade life has centred around education, the Presidency is indeed an honour.

A few days later I opened a letter from *Decanter*'s Sarah Kemp to realise that I was to be the 2017 Decanter Man of the Year. This was such an amazingly pleasant surprise that, knowing there would have to be an Awards Lunch, I immediately called Sarah to say that I reckoned I could get the Ladies' side at Boodle's which could seat around fifty. 'Don't worry, Steven,' came the reply, 'we got Le Gavroche and they can go to seventy!' I had been on the Man of the Year panel for a long time, the awards going to those whom the whole panel agrees have 'made an outstanding contribution to the world of wine' and there is a full list of these from the original award to Château Musar's Serge Hochar in 1984 below. I had seen many of my candidates go through and for 2017 had pushed strongly for Eduardo Chadwick. It turned out to be me, but I am glad to say that Eduardo will take the honour in 2018. The lunch on 28 March at Le Gavroche was truly spectacular, with Michel Roux Jnr creating dishes that matched the eight wines, the producers of which were all present or represented. Bella was there of course, so was Bride Valley Rosé Bella 2014 as the last wine, as were Christian, Kate and their spouses and many, many friends, including no fewer than ten previous Men of the Year in person and a further three represented by family members, indicated by asterisks in the list below. Angelo Gaja (1998) made a speech and presented me with a pair of spurs, rather more modern than those on the Spurrier coat of arms.

Decanter Men of the Year from 1984 in ascending order

Serge Hochar*, Laura & Corinne Mentzelopulous, Marchese Piero Antinori*, Alexis Lichine, Max Schubert, Robert Mondavi, Professeur Emile Peynaud, Jose Ignacio Domecq, André Tchelistcheff, Michael Broadbent*, May-Eliane de Lencquesaing, Hugh Johnson*, Georg Riedel, Len Evans, Angelo Gaja*, Jancis Robinson*, Paul Draper, Jean-Claude Rouzaud, Miguel Torres*, Jean-Michel Cazes, Brian Croser, Ernst Loosen, Marcel Guigal, Anthony Barton*, Christian Moueix*, Nicolas Catena*, Aubert de Villaine*, Giacomo Tachis, Paul Symington, Gérard Basset*, Jean-Pierre* et François Perrin, Alvaro Palacios*, Denis Dubourdieu, Steven Spurrier, 2018 Eduardo Chadwick*.

The *Decanter* April issue carried a flattering survey of my career by John Stimpfig with quotes from colleagues. I would like to quote just one from Patricia Gastaud-Gallagher, director of *L'Académie du Vin* from 1973 to 1989 when I sold it: '...every wine lover in Paris at that time remembers L'Académie du Vin and Les Caves de la Madeleine.'

This was appropriate, for Patricia attended the lunch and recognised so many people from the past in Paris that she took it into her head to see what had happened to *L'Académie du Vin*, as it had ceased to exist, apart from the school I founded in Tokyo in 1987 which now has four branches in Japan. Her searches showed that the name and the logo had not been registered for over five years, meaning that they were free to be re-registered. This she and I put into motion in July, asking Canadian Marc Nadeau, who had run a branch of *L'Académie* so successfully in Toronto, and later bringing Mark Williamson on board. On 2 September 2017 in Tokyo I celebrated the Tokyo Academy's 30th anniversary by hosting a Master Class which featured wines I had loved over fifty years in wine. Here they are:

2015　Domaine Weinbach Riesling Schlossberg, Alsace Grand Cru
2012　Domaine de Chevalier Pessac-Léognan,
　　　　Grand Cru Classé de Graves
2006　Domaine Bonneau du Martray Corton-Charlemagne Grand Cru
2016　Domaine Tempier Bandol Rosé
2009　Domaine Chanson Beaune Clos des Feves Premier Cru
2005　Château Langoa-Barton 3ème Cru Classé Saint Julien
　　　　(1995 in Paris)
2005　Château de Beaucastel Châteauneuf-du-Pape (2001 in Paris)
2008　Domaine Huët Vouvray Le Mont demi-sec, Loire

Of course, the Tokyo school already existed, but thanks to Patricia we are now registered across the world and the Académie du Vin was launched with the same wines, five of which came from my Dorset cellar, with me hosting a Master Class at the recently-opened wine club 67 Pall Mall on 24 October 2017 and saw its renaissance in Paris at Mark Williamson's Maceo Restaurant over lunch on 16 November, where Patricia and Marc (over especially from Toronto) were co-hosts. We were joined by Isabelle Bachelard who had managed *L'Académie* day to day in the 1980s and many colleagues from the past. Master Classes are already planned for Paris and the Christie's Wine Course will be revived at 67 Pall Mall, both under *L'Académie du Vin* name. In October 1991 I gave a fiftieth birthday party at Le Moulin du Village, the restaurant in the Cité Berryer that Mark Williamson had taken over when everything went pear-shaped in 1989. In the *Trib* on 14 October, the back page carried Mary Blume's charming article 'The Rise and Fall and Rise of a Wine Guru', which mentioned my what was to be a short-lived stint running the Harrods Wine Department after the disasters in Paris. She ends by my saying, 'Now, the whole game starts up again from my point of view.' It never, ever, really stopped.

December 2017